WEBSTER'S
SPELLER

Printed in USA

WEBSTER'S SPELLER

This WEBSTER'S SPELLER is designed for use in the school, in the office, and in the home, as a Quick Reference Guide to spelling and proper word hyphenation.

Words that contain double dashes (--) between letters indicates a hyphenated word. Single dashes (-) show syllabic division.

© TEXT COPYRIGHT 1990, K. NICHOLS

Distributed by: Nickel Press

aard-vark
a-back
ab-a-cus
  ab-a-cus-es
  ab-a-ci
a-baft
  abaft-ment
  abaft-ed
ab-a-lo-ne
a-ban-don
  aban-doned
  aban-don-er
  aban-don-ment
a-base
  a-based
  a-bas-ing
  a-base-ment
a-bash
  a-bash-ment
a-bate
  a-bat-ed
  a-bat-ing
  a-bat-a-ble
  a-bate-ment
aba-tis
ab-at-oir
ab-ba-cy
  ab-ba-tial
ab-bess
ab-bey
  ab-beys
ab-bot
ab-bre-vi-a-tion
  ab-bre-vi-ate
  ab-bre-vi-at-ed
  ab-bre-vi-at-ing
  ab-bre-vi-a-tor
ab-di-cate
  ab-di-cat-ed
  ab-di-cat-ing
  ab-di-ca-tion
ab-do-men
  ab-dom-i-nal
  ab-dom-i-nal-ly
ab-duce
ab-duct
  ab-duc-tion
  ab-duc-tor

ab-duct-ing
a-beam
a-bed
ab-er-rance
  ab-er-ran-cy
ab-er-rant
  ab-er-rant-ly
  ab-er-ra-tion
  ab-er-ra-tion-al
a-bet
  a-bet-ted
  a-bet-ting
  a-bet-ment
  a-bet-tor
  a-bet-ter
a-bey-ance
ab-hor
  ab-horred
  ab-hor-ring
  ab-hor-rence
  ab-hor-er
ab-hor-rence
ab-hor-rent
  ab-hor-rent-ly
a-bide
  a-bid-er
  a-bi-ded
  a-bid-ing
  a-bid-ance
a-bid-ing
  a-bid-ing-ly
a-bil-i-ty
  a-bil-i-ties
ab-ject
  ab-ject-ly
  ab-ject-ness
  ab-jec-tion
ab-jure
  ab-jured
  ab-jur-ing
  ab-ju-ra-tion
  ab-jur-er
ab-late
  ab-lat-ed
  ab-lat-ing
  ab-la-tion
  ab-la-tive
  ab-la-tive-ly

ab-laut
a-blaze
a-ble
  a-bler
  a-blest
  a-bly
a-ble-bod-ied
a-bloom
ab-lu-tion
  ab-lu-tion-ar-y
ab-ne-gate
  ab-ne-gat-ed
  ab-ne-gat-ing
  ab-ne-ga-tor
  ab-ne-ga-tion
ab-nor-mal
  ab-nor-mal-ly
  ab-nor-mal-i-ty
  ab-nor-mal-i-ties
a-board
a-bode
a-boil
a-bol-ish
  a-bol-ish-a-ble
  a-bol-ish-er
  a-bol-ish-ment
ab-o-li-tion
  ab-o-li-tion-ary
  ab-o-li-tion-ism
  ab-o-li-tion-ist
a-b-oma-sum
  a-b-oma-sal
a-bom-i-na-ble
  a-bom-i-na-bly
a-bom-i-nate
  a-bom-i-nat-ed
  a-bom-i-nat-ing
  a-bom-i-na-tion
  a-bom-i-na-tor
ab-o-rig-i-ne
  ab-o-rig-i-nal
  ab-o-rig-i-nal-ly
a-born-ing
a-bort
  a-bort-er
a-bor-ti-fa-cient
a-bor-tion
  a-bor-tion-ist

a-bor-tive
 a-bor-tive-ness
 a-bor-tive-ly
a-bout-face
a-bove-board
ab-ra-ca-dab-ra
abrad-ant
a-brade
 a-brad-ed
 a-brad-ing
 a-brad-a-ble
 a-brad-er
a-bra-sion
a-bra-sive
 a-bra-sive-ness
 a-bra-sive-ly
ab-re-act
a-breast
a-bridge
 a-bridged
 a-bridg-ing
 a-bridg-er
 a-bridg-a-ble
 a-bridg-ment
 a-bridge-ment
a-broach
a-broad
ab-ro-gate
 ab-ro-gat-ed
 ab-ro-gat-ing
 ab-ro-ga-tion
ab-rupt
 abrupt-ness
 abrupt-ly
ab-scess
 ab-scessed
ab-scis-sa
 ab-scis-sas
 ab-scis-sae
ab-scis-sion
ab-scond
 ab-scond-er
ab-sence
ab-sent
 ab-sent-ly
ab-sen-tee
 ab-sen-tee-ism
ab-sent-mind-ed

ab-sent-mind-ed-ly
ab-sent-mind-ed-ness
ab-sinthe
ab-so-lute
 ab-so-lute-ness
 ab-so-lute-ly
 ab-so-lu-tion
 ab-so-lut-ism
 ab-so-lut-ist
ab-solve
 ab-solved
 ab-solv-ing
 ab-solv-a-ble
 ab-solv-er
ab-sorb
 ab-sorb-er
 ab-sorb-a-bil-i-ty
 ab-sorb-a-ble
 ab-sorb-en-cy
 ab-sorb-ent
 ab-sorb-tion
 ab-sorb-tive
 ab-sorp-tiv-i-ty
ab-sorb-ing
 ab-sorb-ing-ly
ab-stain
 ab-stain-er
 ab-sten-tion
 ab-sti-nence
 ab-sti-nent
ab-ste-mi-ous
 ab-ste-mi-ous-ly
ab-stract
 ab-stract-ly
 ab-strac-tion
 ab-strac-tive
ab-stract-ed
 ab-stract-ed-ly
 ab-stract-ed-ness
ab-strac-tion-ism
 ab-strac-tion-ist
ab-struse
 ab-struse-ness
 ab-struse-ly
 ab-stru-si-ty
ab-surd
 ab-surd-ness
 ab-surd-i-ty

ab-surd-i-ties
ab-surd-ly
a-bub-ble
a-build-ing
a-bud-dance
a-bun-dant
 a-bun-dant-ly
a-buse
 a-bused
 a-bus-ing
 a-bus-er
 a-bus-a-ble
a-bu-sive
 a-bu-sive-ly
 a-bu-sive-ness
a-but
 a-but-ter
 a-but-ted
 a-but-ting
a-but-ment
a-but-tals
a-but-ting
a-buzz
a-bye
a-bysm
a-bys-mal
 a-bys-mal-ly
a-byss
 a-bys-sal
a-ca-cia
ac-a-deme
ac-a-dem-ic
 ac-a-dem-i-cal-ly
 ac-a-dem-i-cal
acad-e-mi-cian
a-cad-e-my
 a-cad-e-mies
a-can-thus
 a-can-thus-es
 a-can-thi
a cap-pel-la
ac-cede
 ac-ced-ed
 ac-ced-ing
ac-ce-le-ran-do
ac-cel-er-ate
 ac-cel-er-at-ed
 ac-cel-er-at-ing

ac-cel-er-a-tive
ac-cel-er-at-ing-ly
ac-cel-er-a-tion
ac-cel-er-a-tor
ac-cel-er-om-e-ter
ac-cent
ac-cent-less
ac-cen-tu-al
ac-cen-tu-al-ly
ac-cen-tu-ate
ac-cen-tu-at-ed
ac-cen-tu-at-ing
ac-cen-tu-a-tion
ac-cept
ac-cept-ing-ly
ac-cept-ing-ness
ac-cept-ance
ac-cept-er
ac-cept-or
ac-cept-a-ble
ac-cept-a-bil-i-ty
ac-cept-a-bly
ac-cept-a-ble-ness
ac-cept-ed
ac-cept-ed-ly
ac-cess
ac-ces-si-ble
ac-ces-si-bil-i-ty
ac-ces-si-ble-ness
ac-ces-si-bly
ac-ces-sion
ac-ces-sion-al
ac-ces-so-ry
ac-ces-so-ri-ly
ac-ces-so-ri-ness
ac-ci-dent
ac-ci-dent-ly
ac-ci-den-tal
ac-ci-den-tal-ness
ac-ci-den-tal-ly
ac-ci-dent--prone
ac-cip-i-ter
ac-cip-i-trine
ac-claim
ac-claim-er
ac-cla-ma-tion
ac-clam-a-to-ry
ac-cli-mate

ac-cli-mat-ed
ac-cli-mat-ing
ac-cli-ma-tion
ac-cli-ma-ti-za-tion
ac-cli-ma-tize
ac-cli-ma-tized
ac-cli-ma-tiz-er
ac-cli-ma-tiz-ing
ac-cli-ma-ti-za-tion
ac-cliv-i-ty
ac-cliv-i-ties
ac-co-lade
ac-com-mo-date
ac-com-mo-dat-ed
ac-com-mo-dat-ing
ac-com-mo-da-tive
ac-com-mo-dat-er
ac-com-mo-da-tion
ac-com-pa-ni-ment
ac-com-pa-nist
ac-com-pa-ny
ac-com-pa-nied
ac-com-pa-ny-ing
ac-com-pa-nies
ac-com-plice
ac-com-plish
ac-com-plish-a-ble
ac-com-plish-ment
ac-com-plish-er
ac-com-plished
ac-cord
ac-cord-ance
ac-cord-ing
ac-cord-ing-ly
ac-cor-dant
ac-cor-dant-ly
ac-cor-di-on
ac-cor-di-on-ist
ac-cost
ac-couche-ment
ac-cou-cheur
ac-count
ac-count-a-ble
ac-count-a-bil-i-ty
ac-count-a-bly
ac-count-a-ble-ness
ac-count-an-cy
ac-count-ant

ac-coun-tant-ship
ac-count-ing
ac-cou-tre-ment
ac-cred-it
ac-cred-i-table
ac-cred-i-ta-tion
ac-crete
ac-creting
ac-creted
ac-cre-tion
ac-cre-tive
ac-cre-tion-ary
ac-cru-al
ac-crue
ac-crued
ac-cru-ing
ac-cru-a-ble
ac-crue-ment
ac-cul-tur-ate
ac-cul-tur-ating
ac-cul-tur-ated
ac-cul-tur-a-tion
ac-cul-tur-a-tion-al
ac-cul-tur-a-tive
ac-cum-u-late
ac-cum-u-lat-ed
ac-cum-u-lat-ing
ac-cum-u-la-tion
ac-cu-mu-la-tive
ac-cu-mu-la-tive-ness
ac-cu-mu-la-tive-ly
ac-cum-u-la-tor
ac-cu-ra-cy
ac-cu-ra-cies
ac-cu-rate
ac-cu-rate-ly
ac-cu-rate-ness
ac-curs-ed
ac-curst
ac-curs-ed-ness
ac-curs-ed-ly
ac-cus-al
ac-cu-sa-tion
ac-cu-sa-tive
ac-cuse
ac-cus-er
ac-cus-ed
ac-cus-ing

ac-cu-sa-tion
ac-cu-sa-to-ry
ac-cus-ing-ly
ac-cus-tom
ac-cus-tom-a-ticn
ac-cus-tomed
ac-cus-tomed-ness
ace-dia
a-cel-da-ma
a-cel-lu-lar
a-cen-tric
a-ceph-a-lous
a-ce-quia
a-cerb
a-cer-bi-ty
ac-er-o-la
ac-er-vate
ac-er-vate-ly
ac-er-va-tion
ac-e-tab-u-lar-ia
ac-e-tab-u-lum
ac-e-tab-u-lar
ac-et-al-de-hyde
ac-et-amide
ac-et-amin-o-phen
ac-et-an-i-lide
ac-e-tate
a-ce-tic
a-cet-i-fy
a-cet-i-fied
a-cet-i-fy-ing
a-ce-ti-fi-ca-tion
a-ce-ti-fi-er
ac-e-tone
ac-e-ton-ic
ac-e-to-phe-net-i-din
a-ce-tous
a-cet-y-late
a-cet-y-lat-ing
a-cet-y-lat-ed
a-cet-y-la-tion
a-cet-y-la-tive
a-ce-tyl-cho-line
.a-ce-tyl-cho-lin-ic
a-cet-y-lene
a-cet-y-le-nic
ache
ached

ach-ing
ach-ing-ly
a-chene
a-chieve
a-chiev-ed
a-chiev-ing
a-chiev-a-ble
a-chiev-er
a-chieve-ment
a-chla-myd-e-ous
a-chlor-hy-dric
a-chon-drite
a-chon-drit-ic
a-chon-dro-pla-sia
a-chon-dro-plas-tic
ach-ro-mat-ic
ach-ro-ma-tic-i-ty
ach-ro-mat-i-cal-ly
ach-ro-ma-tize
a-cic-u-la
a-cic-u-late
a-cic-u-lar
ac-id
ac-id-ness
ac-id-ly
ac-id-ic
a-cid-i-fy
a-cid-i-fied
a-cid-i-fy-ing
a-cid-i-fi-ca-tion
a-cid-i-fi-er
a-cid-i-ty
ac-i-do-phile
ac-i-do-phil-ic
ac-i-do-sis
ac-i-dot-ic
a-cid-u-late
a-cid-u-lat-ed
a-cid-u-lat-ing
a-cid-u-la-tion
a-cid-u-lent
a-cid-u-lous
ac-i-nar
ac-i-nus
ac-i-nous
ac-knowl-edge
ac-knowl-edged
ac-knowl-edg-ing

ac-knowl-edge-a-ble
ac-knowl-edg-er
ac-knowl-edg-ment
ac-knowl-edge-ment
ac-me
ac-ne
ac-ned
ac-o-lyte
ac-o-nite
a-corn
a-cous-tic
a-cous-ti-cal
a-cous-ti-cal-ly
a-cous-tics
ac-quaint
ac-quaint-ance
ac-quaint-ance-ship
ac-qui-esce
ac-qui-esc-ed
ac-qui-esc-ing
ac-qui-es-cence
ac-qui-es-cent
ac-qui-es-cent-ly
ac-quire
ac-quired
ac-quir-ing
ac-quir-er
ac-quir-a-ble
ac-quire-ment
ac-qui-si-tion
ac-quit
ac-quit-ted
ac-quit-ting
ac-quit-tal
a-cre
a-cre-age
ac-rid
acrid-i-ty
ac-ri-mo-ni-ous
ac-ri-mo-ni-ous-ness
ac-ri-mo-ni-ous-ly
ac-ri-mo-ny
ac-ro-bat
ac-ro-bat-ic
ac-ro-nym
ac-ro-pho-bi-a
a-crop-o-lis
a-cros-tic

a-cros-ti-cal-ly
a-cryl-ic
ac-ry-lo-ni-trile
act-ing
ac-tin-ia
ac-tin-i-an
ac-tin-ic
ac-tin-i-cal-ly
ac-tin-ism
ac-tin-i-um
ac-ti-nom-e-ter
ac-ti-nom-e-try
ac-ti-no-mor-phic
ac-ti-no-mor-phy
ac-ti-no-my-ces
ac-ti-no-my-ce-tal
ac-ti-no-my-co-sis
ac-ti-no-my-cot-ic
ac-ti-non
ac-ti-no-zo-an
ac-tion
ac-tion-a-ble
ac-tion-a-bly
ac-ti-vate
ac-ti-vat-ed
ac-ti-vat-ing
ac-ti-va-tion
ac-ti-va-tor
ac-tive
ac-tive-ly
ac-tive-ness
ac-tiv-ism
ac-tiv-ist
ac-tiv-i-ty
ac-tiv-i-ties
ac-tor
ac-tress
ac-tu-al
ac-tu-al-ly
ac-tu-al-i-ty
ac-tu-al-i-ties
ac-tu-al-ize
ac-tu-al-ized
ac-tu-al-iz-ing
ac-tu-al-i-za-tion
ac-tu-ar-y
ac-tu-ar-ies
ac-tu-ar-i-al

ac-tu-ate
ac-tu-at-ed
ac-tu-at-ing
ac-tu-a-tion
ac-tu-a-tor
a-cu-i-ty
a-cu-i-ties
a-cu-men
a-cu-mi-nate
ac-u-punc-ture
a-cute
a-cute-ly
a-cute-ness
a-cut-est
a-cut-er
a-cy-clic
ac-yl
ad-age
a-da-gio
ad-a-mant
ad-a-mant-ly
ad-a-man-tine
a-dapt
a-dapt-er
a-dapt-ed-ness
a-dapt-a-ble
a-dapt-a-bil-i-ty
ad-ap-ta-tion
ad-ap-ta-tion-al
ad-ap-ta-tion-al-ly
a-dap-tive
a-dap-tive-ly
a-d-ap-tiv-i-ty
add
add-a-ble
add-i-ble
ad-dax
ad-dax-es
ad-dend
ad-den-dum
ad-den-da
ad-der
ad-dict
ad-dic-tion
ad-dict-ed
ad-dic-tive
Ad-dis Ab-a-ba
Ad-di-son's dis-ease

ad-di-tion
ad-di-tion-al
ad-di-tion-al-ly
ad-di-tive
ad-di-tive-ly
ad-di-tiv-i-ty
ad-dle
ad-dress
ad-dress-er
ad-dress-ee
ad-dress-a-ble
ad-duce
ad-duc-ing
ad-duced
ad-duc-er
ad-duct
ad-duc-tion
ad-duc-tive
a-de-lan-ta-do
a-demp-tion
ad-e-nine
ad-e-ni-tis
ad-e-no-car-ci-no-ma
ad-e-no-hy-poph-y-sis
ad-e-noid
ad-e-noi-dal
ad-e-no-ma
aden-o-sine
a-dept
a-dept-ly
a-dept-ness
ad-e-qua-cy
ad-e-quate
ad-e-quate-ly
ad-e-quate-ness
ad-here
ad-hered
ad-her-ing
ad-her-ence
ad-her-ent
ad-her-ent-ly
ad-he-sion
ad-he-sion-al
ad-he-sive
ad-he-sive-ly
ad-he-sive-ness
ad hoc
ad ho-mi-nem

ad-i-a-bat-ic
a-dieu
ad in-fi-ni-tum
a-di-os
ad-i-pose
ad-i-pos-i-ty
ad-ja-cen-cy
ad-ja-cen-cies
ad-ja-cent
ad-ja-cent-ly
ad-jec-tive
ad-jec-ti-val
ad-join
ad-join-ing
ad-journ
ad-journ-ment
ad-judge
ad-judged
ad-judg-ing
ad-ju-di-cate
ad-ju-di-cat-ed
ad-ju-di-cat-ing
ad-ju-di-ca-tion
ad-ju-di-ca-tor
ad-junct
ad-junc-tive
ad-jure
ad-jured
ad-jur-ing
ad-ju-ra-tion
ad-ju-ra-to-ry
ad-jur-er
ad-just
ad-just-a-ble
ad-just-er
ad-jus-tor
ad-just-ment
ad-ju-tan-cy
ad-ju-tant
ad lib
ad libbed
ad lib-bing
ad-man
ad-men
ad-min-is-ter
ad-min-is-ter-ing
ad-min-is-tered
ad-min-is-trate

ad-min-is-trat-ing
ad-min-is-trated
ad-min-is-tra-tion
ad-min-is-tra-tive
ad-min-is-tra-tor
ad-min-is-tra-tive-ly
ad-min-is-tra-tion-al
ad-mi-ral
ad-mi-ral-ty
ad-mire
ad-mired
ad-mir-ing
ad-mi-ra-ble
ad-mi-ra-bly
ad-mi-ra-tion
ad-mi-rer
ad-mir-ing-ly
ad-mis-si-ble
ad-mis-si-bil-i-ty
ad-mis-sion
ad-mis-sive
ad-mit
ad-mit-ted
ad-mit-ting
ad-mit-ted-ly
ad-mit-tance
ad-mix
ad-mix-ture
ad-mon-ish
ad-mon-ish-er
ad-mo-ni-tion
ad-mon-i-to-ry
ad-mon-ish-ing-ly
ad-mon-ish-ment
a-do
a-do-be
ad-o-les-cence
ad-o-les-cent
ad-o-les-cent-ly
a-dopt
a-dopt-a-ble
a-dopt-er
a-dop-tion
a-dop-tive
a-dopt-a-bil-i-ty
a-dore
a-dored
a-dor-ing

a-dor-a-ble
ador-ing-ly
ad-o-ra-tion
a-dorn
a-dorn-ment
a-doze
ad-re-nal
ad-re-nal-ly
a-dren-a-line
a-drift
a-droit
a-droit-ly
a-droit-ness
ad-sorb
ad-sor-bent
ad-sorp-tion
ad-u-late
ad-u-lat-ed
ad-u-lat-ing
ad-u-la-tor
ad-u-la-to-ry
a-dult
a-dult-hood
a-dul-ter-ate
a-dul-ter-at-ed
a-dul-ter-at-ing
a-dul-ter-ant
a-dul-ter-a-tion
a-dul-ter-y
a-dul-ter-ies
a-dul-ter-er
a-dul-ter-ess
a-dul-ter-ous
ad-um-brate
ad-um-brat-ed
ad-um-brat-ing
ad va-lo-rem
ad-vance
ad-vanced
ad-vanc-ing
ad-vance-ment
ad-van-tage
ad-van-taged
ad-van-tag-ing
ad-van-ta-geous
ad-van-ta-geous-ly
ad-vent
ad-ven-ti-tious

ad-ven-tive
ad-ven-ture
  ad-ven-tured
  ad-ven-tur-ing
  ad-ven-tur-er
  ad-ven-tur-ess
  ad-ven-tur-ous
ad-ven-ture-some
ad-verb
  ad-ver-bi-al
ad-ver-sar-y
  ad-ver-sar-ies
ad-verse
  ad-verse-ly
  ad-verse-ness
ad-ver-si-ty
  ad-ver-si-ties
ad-vert
  ad-vert-ence
  ad-vert-ent
ad-ver-tise
  ad-ver-tised
  ad-ver-tis-ing
  ad-ver-tis-er
ad-ver-tise-ment
ad-vice
ad-vise
  ad-vised
  ad-vis-ing
  ad-vis-a-bil-i-ty
  ad-vis-a-ble
  ad-vis-a-bly
  ad-vis-er
  ad-vi-sor
ad-vis-ed-ly
ad-vise-ment
ad-vi-so-ry
ad-vo-ca-cy
  ad-vo-ca-cies
  ad-vo-cate
  ad-vo-cat-ed
  ad-vo-cat-ing
  ad-vo-ca-tion
ae-gis
ae-on
aer-ate
  aer-at-ed
  aer-at-ing

aer-a-tion
aer-a-tor
aer-en-chy-ma
aer-i-al
  aer-i-al-ly
  aer-i-al-ist
aer-ie
aer-i-fy
  aer-i-fi-ca-tion
aer-obe
aero-me-chan-ics
aero-naut-ics
  aero-nau-ti-cal
  aero-nau-tic
aero-pause
aer-o-plane
aer-o-sol
  aero-sol-ize
  aero-sol-iza-tion
  aero-sol-iz-ing
  aero-sol-ized
aer-o-space
aero-sphere
aero-stat
aero-stat-ics
aes-thete
aes-thet-ic
  aes-thet-i-cal-ly
  aes-thet-i-cal
afar
afeard
af-fa-ble
  af-fa-bil-i-ty
  af-fa-bly
af-fair
af-fect
  af-fect-ing
  af-fect-ing-ly
af-fect-ive
af-fec-ta-tion
af-fect-ed
  af-fect-ed-ly
  af-fect-ed-ness
af-fec-tion
  af-fec-tion-ate
  af-fec-tion-ate-ly
  af-fec-tion-ate-ness
af-fer-ent

af-fer-ent-ly
af-fi-ance
  af-fi-anced
  af-fi-anc-ing
af-fi-da-vit
af-fil-i-ate
  af-fil-i-at-ed
  af-fil-i-at-ing
af-fin-i-ty
  af-fin-i-ties
af-firm
  af-firm-a-ble
  af-firm-a-bly
  af-fir-ma-tion
  af-firm-a-tive
af-fix
  af-fix-a-ble
  af-fix-ment
  af-fix-a-tion
af-fla-tus
af-flict
  af-flic-tion
af-flu-ence
  af-flu-ent
  af-flu-ent-ly
af-fray
af-fri-cate
  af-fric-a-tive
  af-fri-ca-tion
af-front
af-ghan
afield
afire
aflame
af-la-tox-in
afloat
aflut-ter
afoot
afore
afore-men-tioned
afore-said
afore-thought
a for-ti-o-ri
afoul
afraid
afreet
afresh
af-ter

af-ter-ef-fect
af-ter-glow
af-ter--hours
af-ter-life
af-ter-most
af-ter-noon
af-ter-taste
af-ter-thought
af-ter-time
af-ter-ward
af-ter-wards
again
against
agape
aga-pe-ic
agar
ag-ate
ag-ate-ware
aga-ve
agaze
age
aged
ag-ing
age-ing
aged
age-less
age-long
agen-cy
agen-cies
agen-da
agen-da-less
agent
agen-tial
ag-glom-er-ate
ag-glom-er-at-ed
ag-glom-er-at-ing
ag-glom-er-a-tion
ag-glom-er-a-tive
ag-glu-ti-nate
ag-glu-ti-nat-ed
ag-glu-tin-at-ing
ag-glu-ti-na-tion
ag-glu-ti-na-tive
ag-gran-dize
ag-gran-dized
ag-gran-diz-ing
ag-gran-dize-ment
ag-gran-diz-er

ag-gra-vate
ag-gra-vat-ed
ag-gra-vat-ing
ag-gra-va-tion
ag-gre-gate
ag-gre-gat-ed
ag-gre-gat-ing
ag-gre-ga-tion
ag-gre-ga-tive
ag-gress
ag-gress-ive
ag-gress-ive-ly
ag-gress-ive-ness
ag-gres-sor
ag-gres-sion
ag-grieve
ag-grieved
ag-griev-ing
aghast
ag-ile
ag-ile-ly
agil-i-ty
agin-ner
agio
ag-i-tate
ag-i-tat-ed
ag-i-tat-ing
ag-i-tat-ed-ly
ag-i-ta-tion
ag-i-ta-tor
ag-i-ta-tion-al
agleam
aglow
agly-con
ag-nail
ag-nate
ag-na-tion
ag-nat-i-cal-ly
ag-nat-ic
ag-nize
ag-niz-ing
ag-nized
ag-no-men
ag-nom-i-na
ag-nos-tic
ag-nos-ti-cism
agog
ag-o-nal

agon-ic
ag-o-nist
ag-o-nis-tic
ag-o-nis-ti-cal-ly
ag-o-nis-ti-cal
ag-o-nize
ag-o-nized
ag-o-niz-ing
ag-o-niz-ing-ly
ag-o-ny
ag-o-nies
ag-o-ra-pho-bia
ag-o-ra-pho-bic
ag-o-ra-pho-bi-ac
agrar-i-an
agrar-i-an-ism
agree
agreed
agree-ing
agree-a-bil-i-ty
agree-a-ble
agree-a-ble-ness
agree-a-bly
agree-ment
ag-ri-busi-ness
ag-ri-cul-ture
ag-ri-cul-tur-al
ag-ri-cul-tur-ist
agron-o-my
ag-ro-nom-ic
ag-ro-nom-i-cal
agron-o-mist
ag-ro-nom-i-cal-ly
aground
ague
agu-ish-ly
agu-ish
aha
ahead
ahem
ahoy
aide-de-camp
ai-grette
ai-guille
ai-guil-lette
ai-ki-do
ail
ail-ing

ail-ment
ai-lan-thus
ai-ler-on
aim-less
air-less
air-less-ness
air-borne
air-brush
air-con-di-tion
air-con-di-tioned
air con-di-tion-er
air con-di-tion-ing
air-craft
air-field
air-mail
air-man
air-men
air-plane
air-port
air pres-sure
air-sick-ness
air-space
air-wave
airy
air-i-er
air-i-est
air-i-ness
air-i-ly
aisle
ajar
akim-bo
akin
al-a-bas-ter
al-a-bas-trine
a la carte
alack
alac-ri-ty
alac-ri-tous
alarm
alarm-ing
alarm-ing-ly
alarm-ist
alarm-ism
alas
alate
alat-ed
al-ba-core
al-ba-cores

al-ba-tross
al-ba-tross-es
al-be-do
al-be-it
al-bi-no
al-bi-nos
al-bi-nism
al-bum
al-bu-men
al-bu-min
al-bu-mi-nous
al-che-my
al-che-mist
al-che-mize
al-che-miz-ing
al-che-mized
al-co-hol
al-co-hòl-ic
al-co-hol-ism
al-co-hol-i-cal-ly
al-cove
al-de-hyde
al-de-hy-dic
al-der
al-der-man
al-der-man-ic
ale-a-to-ry
alee
alert
alert-ness
alert-ly
ale-wife
ale-wives
al-ex-an-drine
al-ex-an-drite
alex-ia
al-fal-fa
al-fil-a-ria
al-for-ja
al-fres-co
al-ga
al-gae
al-gal
al-goid
al-ge-bra
al-ge-bra-ic
al-ge-bra-ic-al
al-ge-bra-ic-al-ly

al-ge-bra-ist
al-go-rithm
al-go-rith-mic
ali-as
ali-as-es
al-i-bi
al-i-bi-ing
al-i-bied
alien
alien-a-ble
alien-a-bil-i-ty
alien-ate
alien-at-ed
alien-at-ing
alien-ator
alien-ist
alien-ism
ali-form
alight
alight-ed
alit
alight-ing
alight-ment
align
align-ment
alike
al-i-ment
al-i-men-tal
al-i-men-tal-ly
al-i-men-ta-tion
al-i-men-ta-ry
al-i-men-ta-ry ca-nal
al-i-mo-ny
al-i-mo-nies
aline-ment
al-i-quant
al-i-quot
alive
alive-ness
al-ka-li
al-ka-lies
al-ka-lis
al-ka-line
al-ka-lin-i-ty
al-ka-lize
al-ka-lized
al-ka-liz-ing
al-ka-li-za-tion

al-ka-loid
 al-ka-loi-dal
all-Amer-i-can
all-a-round
al-lay
 al-layed
 al-lay-ing
 al-lay-er
al-le-ga-tion
al-lege
 al-leged
 al-leg-ing
 al-lege-a-ble
 al-leg-ed-ly
al-le-giance
al-le-go-ry
 al-le-go-ries
 al-le-gor-ic
 al-le-gor-i-cal
 al-le-gor-i-cal-ly
 al-le-gor-ist
al-le-gret-to
al-le-gro
 al-le-gros
al-ler-gen
 al-ler-gen-ic
al-ler-gy
 al-ler-gies
 al-ler-gic
 al-ler-gist
al-le-vi-ate
 al-le-vi-at-ed
 al-le-vi-at-ing
 al-le-vi-a-tion
 al-le-vi-a-tor
 al-le-vi-a-tive
 al-le-vi-a-to-ry
al-ley
 al-leys
al-li-ance
al-lied
al-li-ga-tor
all--in-clu-sive
 all--in-cul-sive-ness
al-lit-er-ate
 al-lit-er-at-ed
 al-lit-er-at-ing
 al-lit-er-a-tive

al-lit-er-a-tive-ly
 al-lit-er-a-tive-ness
 al-lit-er-a-tion
al-lo-ca-ble
al-lo-cate
 al-lo-cat-ed
 al-lo-cat-ing
 al-lo-ca-tion
al-lo-cu-tion
al-log-a-mous
 al-log-a-my
al-lo-ge-ne-ic
al-lo-graph
 al-lo-graph-ic
al-lom-er-ism
 al-lom-er-ous
al-lo-path
al-lop-a-thy
 al-lo-path-ic
 al-lo-path-i-cal-ly
al-lop-a-thist
al-lo-phone
 al-lo-phon-ic
al-lo-pu-ri-nol
al-lo-ste-ric
 al-lo-ste-ri-cal-ly
al-lot
 al-lot-ted
 al-lot-ting
 al-lot-ment
 al-lot-ta-ble
 al-lot-ter
al-lo-trope
 al-lo-trop-ic
 al-lo-trop-cal-ly
al-lot-ro-py
 al-lot-ro-pism
al-lo-trope
 al-lo-trop-ic
 al-lo-trop-i-cal-ly
al-low
 al-low-a-ble
 al-low-a-bly
 al-low-ed-ly
al-low-ance
 al-low-anced
 al-low-anc-ing
al-loy

all--pow-er-ful
all--pur-pose
all right
all-spice
al-lude
 al-lud-ed
 al-lud-ing
al-lure
 al-lured
 al-lur-ing
 al-lure-ment
 al-lur-er
 al-lur-ing-ly
al-lu-sion
 al-lu-sive
 al-lu-sive-ly
 al-lu-sive-ness
al-lu-via
al-lu-vi-al
al-lu-vi-um
 al-lu-viums
al-ly
al-lies
al-lied
 al-ly-ing
al-ma mat-er
al-ma-nac
al-man-dine
al-man-dite
al-mighty
 al-mighti-ness
al-mond
al-mo-ner
al-most
alms-giv-er
 alms-giv-ing
alms-house
al-ni-co
al-oe
aloft
alo-ha
alone
 alone-ness
along
along-shore
along-side
aloof
 aloof-ly

aloof-ness
al-o-pe-cia
al-paca
al-pen-glow
al-pen-stock
al-pes-trine
al-pha
al-pha-bet
al-pha-bet-ic
al-pha-bet-i-cal
al-pha-bet-i-cal-ly
al-pha-bet-i-za-tion
al-pha-bet-ize
al-pha-bet-ized
al-pha-bet-iz-ing
al-ready
al-so
al-tar
al-ter
al-ter-a-bil-ity
al-ter-a-ble
al-ter-ant
al-ter-a-tion
al-ter-a-tive
al-ter-cate
al-ter-cat-ing
al-ter-cat-ed
al-ter-ca-tion
al-ter e-go
al-ter-nate
al-ter-nat-ed
al-ter-nat-ing
al-ter-nate-ly
al-ter-na-tion
al-ter-na-tive
al-ter-na-tive-ly
al-ter-na-tive-ness
al-ter-na-tor
al-though
al-tim-e-ter
al-tim-e-try
al-ti-pla-no
al-ti-tude
al-to
al-to-cu-mu-lus
al-to-gether
al-to-re-lie-vo
al-to-stra-tus

al-tru-ism
al-tru-is-tic
al-tru-is-ti-cal-ly
al-tru-ist
al-lu-mi-na
alu-mi-nate
alu-mi-nif-er-ous
al-u-min-i-um
alu-mi-nous
alu-mi-num
alum-na
alum-nae
alum-nus
alum-ni
al-ve-o-lar
al-ve-o-lus
al-ve-o-li
al-ways
alys-sum
amain
amal-gam
amal-gam-a-ble
amal-gam-ate
amal-gam-at-ed
amal-gam-at-ing
amal-gam-a-tion
aman-u-en-ses
aman-u-en-ses
am-a-ryl-lis
amass
amass-ment
amass-er
am-a-teur
am-a-teur-ism
am-a-teur-ish
am-a-teur-ish-ly
am-a-teur-ish-ness
am-a-tive
am-a-tive-ness
am-a-tive-ly
am-a-to-ry
am-au-ro-sis
amaze
amazed
amaz-ing
amaz-ed-ly
amaz-ed-ness
amaze-ment

amaz-ing-ly
am-bas-sa-do-ri-al
am-ber
amber-gris
am-ber-jack
am-bi-dex-trous
am-bi-dex-trous-ly
am-bi-dex-ter-i-ty
am-bi-ance
am-bi-ence
am-bi-ent
am-big-u-ous
am-big-u-ous-ly
am-big-u-ous-ness
am-bi-gu-i-ty
am-bit
am-bi-tion
am-bi-tion-less
am-bi-tious
am-bi-tious-ly
am-bi-tious-ness
am-biv-a-lence
am-biv-a-lent
am-biv-a-lent-ly
am-bi-ver-sion
am-bi-ver-sive
am-bi-vert
am-ble
am-bled
am-bling
am-bler
am-blyg-o-nite
am-bly-opia
am-bo-cep-tor
am-bro-sia
am-bro-sial-ly
am-bro-sial
am-bro-type
ambs-ace
am-bu-la-crum
am-bu-lance
am-bu-la-to-ry
am-bu-lant
am-bu-late
am-bu-lat-ed
am-bu-lat-ing
am-bu-la-tion
am-bus-cade

am-bus-cad-ed
am-bus-cad-ing
am-bus-cad-er
am-bush
am-bush-ment
am-bush-er
ameba
amel-io-rate
amel-io-rat-ed
amel-io-rat-ing
amel-io-ra-ble
amel-io-ra-tion
amel-ior-a-tive
amel-io-ra-tor
amen
ame-na-ble
ame-na-bil-i-ty
ame-na-ble-ness
ame-na-bly
amend
amend-a-ble
amend-er
amend-ment
amends
amend-i-ty
amend-i-ties
amerce
amerced
amerc-ing
amerce-a-ble
amerce-ment
amerce-er
Amer-i-ca
Amer-i-can
Amer-i-cana
Amer-i-can-ism
am-e-thyst
am-e-thys-tine
am-e-tro-pia
ami-a-ble
ami-a-bil-i-ty
ami-a-bly
ami-a-ble-ness
ami-ca-ble
am-i-ca-bil-i-ty
am-i-ca-bly
am-i-ca-ble-ness
am-ice

amid
amidst
am-ide
amid-ic
amid-ships
ami-go
amine
amino acid
ami-no-ac-id-uria
ami-no-py-rine
amir
amiss
am-i-to-sis
am-i-tot-ic
am-i-tot-i-cal-ly
am-i-ty
am-me-ter
am-mi-no
am-mon-nia
am-mon-ic
am-mo-ni-ac
am-mo-ni-um
am-mo-ni-un chlo-ride
am-mu-ni-tion
am-ne-sia
am-ne-sic
am-nes-tic
am-nes-ty
am-ni-on
am-ni-ons
am-ni-on-ic
am-nia
am-ni-ot-ic
a-moe-ba
a-moe-bae
a-moe-bas
a-moe-bic
a-moe-ban
a-moe-boid
a-mok
a-mong
a-mongst
a-mon-til-la-do
a-mor-al
a-mo-ral-i-ty
a-mor-al-ism
a-mor-al-ly
amo-ret-to

am-or-ist
am-o-rous
am-o-rous-ly
am-o-rous-ness
a-mor-phism
a-mor-phous
a-mor-phous-ness
a-mor-phous-ly
am-or-tize
am-or-tized
am-or-tiz-ing
am-or-ti-za-tion
am-or-tiz-able
a-mount
a-mour
am-per-age
am-pere
am-per-sand
am-phet-a-mine
am-phib-ia
am-phib-i-an
am-phib-i-ous
am-phib-i-ous-ly
am-phib-i-ous-ness
am-phi-the-a-ter
am-phi-the-at-ric
am-pho-ra
am-phe-rae
am-phe-ras
am-ple
am-pler
am-plest
am-ple-ness
am-ply
am-pli-fy
am-pli-fied
am-pli-fy-ing
am-pli-fi-ca-tion
am-pli-fi-er
am-pli-tude
am-pul
am-pu-tate
am-pu-tat-ed
am-pu-tat-ing
am-pu-ta-tion
am-pu-tee
a-muck
am-u-let

a-muse
 a-mused
 a-mus-ing
 a-muse-ment
 a-mus-ed
am-yl-ase
a-nach-ro-nism
 a-nach-ro-nis-tik
 a-nach-ro-nis-ti-cal-ly
 a-nach-ro-nous
an-a-con-da
an-aer-obe
an-aes-the-sia
an-aes-thet-ic
an-a-gram
 an-a-gram-mat-ic
 an-a-gram-mat-i-cal
 ana-gram-ma-tize
 ana-gram-ma-tized
 ana-gram-ma-tiz-ing
a-nal
an-a-lects
an-al-ge-sic
al-a-log
 an-a-log-i-cal
 an-a-log-i-cal-ly
a-nal-o-gize
 a-nal-o-gized
 a-nal-o-giz-ing
a-nal-o-gy
 a-nal-o-gies
 a-nal-o-gous
a-nal-y-sis
 a-nal-y-ses
an-a-lyst
 an-a-lyt-ic
 an-a-lyt-ics
an-a-lyze
 an-a-lyzed
 an-a-lyz-ing
 an-a-lyz-a-ble
 an-a-ly-za-tion
 an-a-lyz-er
an-a-pest
an-a-pes-tic
an-ar-chism
an-ar-chis-tic
an-ar-chy

an-ar-chic
an-ar-chi-cal
a-nath-e-ma
 a-nath-e-mas
 a-nath-e-ma-tize
 a-nath-e-ma-tized
 a-nath-e-ma-tiz-ing
 a-nath-e-mat-iz-a-tion
a-nat-o-mize
 a-nat-o-mized
 a-nat-o-mizing
 a-nat-o-mi-za-tion
a-nat-o-my
 a-nat-o-mies
 an-a-tom-i-cal
 an-a-tom-i-cal-ly
 a-nat-o-mist
an-ces-tor
 an-ces-tral
 an-ces-tress
 an-ces-try
an-chor
 an-chor-age
an-cho-ress
an-cho-rite
an-cho-vy
an-cient
 an-cient-ly
 an-cient-ness
an-cil-lary
an-dan-te
and-i-ron
an-dro-gen
 an-drog-y-nous
 an-drog-y-ny
an-dros-ter-one
an-ec-dote
 an-ec-dot-age
 an-ec-do-tal
 an-ec-dot-ist
a-ne-mia
 a-ne-mic
an-e-mom-e-ter
an-e-mom-e-try
a-nem-o-ne
an-er-oid
an-es-the-sia
 an-es-thet-ic

an-es-the-tize
an-es-the-tized
an-es-the-tiz-ing
an-eu-rysm
 an-eu-rism
 an-eu-rys-mal
a-new
an-ga-ry
an-gel
 an-gel-ic
 an-gel-i-cal
 an-gel-i-cal-ly
an-gel-i-ca
an-ger
an-gi-na
 an-gi-na pec-to-ris
an-gi-o-sperm
 an-gi-o-sper-mous
an-gle
an-gler
an-gle-worm
an-gling
an-go-ra
an-gos-tu-ra bark
an-gry
 an-gri-ly
 an-gri-ness
ang-strom u-nit
an-guish
an-gu-lar
 an-gu-lar-i-ty
 an-gu-lar-ly
 an-gu-lar-ness
an-hy-dride
an-hy-drous
an-i-line
an-i-mad-vert
 an-i-mad-ver-sion
an-i-mal
 an-i-mal-cule
 an-i-mal-cu-lar
 an-i-mal-ism
 an-i-mal-i-ty
 an-i-mal-ize
 an-i-mal-ized
 an-i-mal-iz-ing
an-i-mate
 an-i-mat-ed

an-i-mat-ing
an-i-ma-tion
a-ni-ma-to
an-i-mism
an-i-mis-tic
an-i-mos-i-ty
an-i-mus
an-i-on
an-ise
an-i-seed
an-i-sette
an-kle
an-kle-bone
an-klet
an-ky-lose
an-ky-losed
an-ky-los-ing
an-ky-lo-sis
an-ky-lot-ic
an-nal-ist
an-nal-is-tic
an-nals
an-neal
an-ne-lid
an-nel-i-dan
an-nex
an-nex-a-tion
an-nex-a-tion-ist
an-ni-hi-late
an-ni-hi-lat-ed
an-ni-hi-lat-ing
an-ni-hi-la-tion
an-ni-hi-la-tor
an-ni-ver-sa-ry
an-ni-ver-sa-ries
an-no Dom-i-ni
an-no-tate
an-no-tat-ed
an-no-tat-ing
an-no-ta-tion
an-no-ta-tor
an-nounce
an-nounced
an-nounc-ing
an-nounce-ment
an-nounc-er
an-noy
an-noy-ance

an-noy-er
an-nu-al
an-nu-i-ty
an-nu-i-tant
an-nul
an-nulled
an-nul-ling
an-nul-ment
an-nu-lar
an-nu-lar-i-ty
an-nu-lar-ly
an-nu-late
an-nu-let
an-nu-lus
an-nu-lus-es
an-nun-ci-a-tion
an-nun-ci-ate
an-nun-ci-at-ed
an-nun-ci-at-ing
an-nun-ci-a-tor
an-ode
an-od-ic
an-o-dyne
a-noint
a-noint-er
a-noint-ment
a-nom-a-ly
a-nom-a-lism
a-nom-a-lous
a-nom-a-lous-ly
a-nom-a-lous-ness
an-o-mie
an-o-my
an-o-nym
a-non-y-mous
a-no-nym-i-ty
a-non-y-mous-ly
a-non-y-mous-ness
a-noph-e-les
an-oth-er
an-ox-ia
an-ser-ine
an-swer
an-swer-a-ble
ant-ac-id
ant-tag-o-nist
an-tag-o-nism
an-tag-o-nis-tic

an-tag-o-nis-ti-cal-ly
an-tag-o-nize
an-tag-o-nized
an-tag-o-niz-ing
ant-arc-tic
an-te
an-ted
an-te-ing
ant-eat-er
an-te--bel-lum
an-te-ced-ence
an-te-ced-ent
an-te-cede
an-te-ced-ed
an-te-ced-ing
an-te-ce-dent-ly
an-te-cham-ber
an-te-choir
an-te-date
an-te-dat-ed
an-te-dat-ing
an-te-di-lu-vi-an
an-te-lope
an-te-lopes
an-te me-rid-i-em
an-ten-na
an-ten-nae
an-ten-nas
an-te-pe-nult
an-te-pe-nul-ti-mate
an-te-ri-or
an-te-room
an-them
an-ther
an-ther-id-i-um
an-thol-o-gy
an-thol-o-gies
an-thol-o-gist
an-thol-o-gize
an-thol-o-giz-ing
an-tho-zo-an
an-thra-cene
an-thra-cite
an-thra-cit-ic
an-thrax
an-thra-ces
an-thro-po-cen-tric
an-thro-po-gen-e-sis

an-thro-poid
an-thro-pol-o-gy
  an-thro-po-log-ic
  an-thro-po-log-i-cal
  an-thro-pol-o-gist
an-thr-pom-e-try
  an-thro-po-met-ric
an-ti-air-craft
an-ti-bi-o-sis
an-ti-bi-ot-ic
  an-ti-bod-y
  an-ti-bod-ies
an-tic
an-ti-christ
an-tic-i-pate
  an-tic-i-pat-ed
  an-tic-i-pat-ing
  an-tic-i-pa-tion
  an-tic-i-pa-tive
  an-tic-i-pa-to-ry
an-ti-cler-i-cal
  an-ti-cler-i-cal-ism
an-ti-cli-max
  an-ti-cli-mac-tic
an-ti-cli-nal
  an-ti-cline
an-ti-cy-clone
an-ti-dote
  an-ti-dot-al
an-ti-fed-er-al
  an-ti-fed-er-al-ist
  an-ti-fed-er-al-ism
an-ti-freeze
an-ti-gen
an-ti-he-ro
an-ti-his-ta-mine
an-ti-log-a-rithm
an-ti-ma-cas-sar
an-ti-mis-sile
an-ti-mo-ny
an-ti-pas-to
an-tip-a-thy
an-ti-phon
  an-tiph-o-nal
an-ti-pode
an-ti-quar-i-an
  an-ti-quar-y
  an-ti-quar-ies

an-ti-quate
  an-ti-quat-ed
  an-ti-quat-ing
  an-ti-quat-ed
an-tique
  an-tiqed
  an-tiq-uing
  an-tique-ly
  an-tique-ness
an-tiq-ui-ty
  an-tiq-ui-ties
an-ti-Sem-i-tism
an-ti-sep-sis
an-ti-sep-tic
an-ti-se-rum
an-ti-slav-er-y
an-ti-so-cial
an-tith-e-sis
  an-tith-e-ses
an-ti-thet-i-cal
an-ti-tox-in
  an-ti-tox-in
an-ti-trust
ant-ler
  ant-ler-ed
an-to-nym
an-trum
an-tra
a-nus
an-vil
anx-i-e-ty
  anx-i-e-ties
anx-ious
  anx-ious-ness
an-y
an-y-bod-y
  an-y-bod-ies
an-y-how
an-y-more
an-y-one
an-y-place
an-y-thing
an-y-way
an-y-where
an-y-wise
a-or-ta
  a-or-tas
  a-or-tae

a-or-tal
a-or-tic
a-pace
a-pache
a-part
a-part-heid
a-part-ment
ap-a-thy
  ap-a-thet-ic
  ap-a-thet-i-cal-ly
ape
a-per-ri-tif
ap-er-ture
a-pex
  a-pex-es
  a-pi-ces
ap-i-cal
a-pha-sia
a-phe-li-on
a-phe-lia
a-phid
a-phis
a-phi-des
aph-o-rism
  aph-o-rist
aph-ro-dis-i-ac
a-pi-an
a-pi-ar-i-an
a-pi-a-rist
a-pi-ary
  a-pi-ar-ies
a-pi-cul-ture
  a-pi-cul-tur-al
  a-pi-cul-tur-ist
a-piece
ap-ish
  ap-ish-ly
  ap-ish-ness
a-plomb
a-poc-a-lypse
  a-poc-a-lyp-tic
a-poc-o-pe
a-poc-ry-phal
ap-o-gee
a-po-lit-i-cal
a-pol-o-get-ics
  a-pol-o-gist
a-pol-o-gize

a-pol-o-gized
a-pol-o-giz-ing
a-pol-o-gy
a-pol-o-gies
a-pol-o-get-ic
a-pol-o-get-i-cal
ap-o-plec-tic
ap-o-plex-y
a-port
a-pos-ta-sy
a-pos-ta-sies
a-pos-tate
a-pos-ta-tize
a-pos-ta-tized
a-pos-to-tiz-ing
a pos-te-ri-o-ri
a-pos-tle
a-pos-tle-ship
a-pos-to-late
ap-os-tol-ic
ap-os-tol-i-cal
a-pos-tro-phe
a-poth-e-cary
a-poth-e-car-ies
ap-o-thegm
ap-o-phthegm
ap-o-theg-mat-ic
a-poth-e-o-sis
a-poth-e-o-ses
a-poth-e-o-size
a-poth-e-o-sized
a-poth-e-o-siz-ing
ap-pall
ap-palled
ap-pal-ling
ap-pal-ling-ly
ap-pa-rat-us
ap-pa-rat-us-es
ap-par-el
ap-par-ent
ap-pa-ri-tion
ap-pa-ri-tion-al
ap-peal
ap-peal-a-ble
ap-peal-er
ap-peal-ing-ly
ap-pear
ap-pear-ance

ap-pease
ap-peased
ap-peasing
ap-pease-ment
ap-peas-a-ble
ap-peas-er
ap-pel-lant
ap-pel-late
ap-pel-la-tion
ap-pel-la-tive
ap-pend
ap-pen-dage
ap-pend-ant
ap-pen-dec-to-my
ap-pen-di-ci-tis
ap-pen-dix
ap-pen-dix-es
ap-pen-di-ces
ap-per-cep-tion
ap-per-cep-tive
ap-per-tain
ap-pe-tite
ap-pe-tiz-er
ap-pe-tiz-ing
ap-plaud
ap-plause
ap-ple
ap-ple-jack
ap-pli-ance
ap-pli-ca-ble
ap-pli-ca-bil-i-ty
ap-pli-ca-ble-ness
ap-pli-cant
ap-pli-ca-tion
ap-pli-ca-tive
ap-pli-ca-to-ry
ap-pli-ca-tor
ap-plied
ap-ply
ap-ply-ing
ap-point
ap-point-a-ble
ap-point-ee
ap-point-er
ap-point-ment
ap-por-tion
ap-por-tion-ment
ap-pose

ap-posed
ap-pos-ing
ap-po-site
ap-po-si-tion
ap-po-si-tion-al
ap-pos-i-tive
ap-praise
ap-prais-al
ap-praised
ap-praiser
ap-prais-ing
ap-pre-ci-a-ble
ap-pre-ci-a-bly
ap-pre-ci-ate
ap-pre-ci-at-ed
ap-pre-ci-at-ing
ap-pre-ci-a-tion
ap-pre-ci-a-tive
ap-pre-hend
ap-pre-hen-si-ble
ap-pre-hen-sion
ap-pre-hen-sive
ap-pren-tice
ap-pren-tic-ed
ap-pren-tic-ing
ap-pren-tice-ship
ap-prise
ap-prised
ap-pris-ing
ap-prize
ap-proach
ap-proach-a-bil-i-ty
ap-proach-a-ble
ap-pro-ba-tion
ap-pro-ba-tive
ap-pro-ba-to-ry
ap-pro-pri-ate
ap-pro-pri-at-ed
ap-pro-pri-at-ing
ap-pro-pri-ate-ly
ap-pro-pri-a-tor
ap-pro-pri-a-tion
ap-pro-pri-a-tive
ap-prox-i-mate
ap-prox-i-mate-ly
ap-prox-i-ma-tion
ap-pur-te-nance
ap-pur-te-nant

ap-ri-cot
a-pri-o-ri
a-pron
ap-ro-pos
apt
  apt-ly
  apt-ness
ap-ter-ous
ap-ti-tude
aq-ua
  aq-uas
  aq-uae
a-qua-cul-ture
aq-ua-ma-rine
aq-ua-naut
aq-ua-plane
aquar-ia
aquar-i-um
  aquar-i-ums
a-quat-ic
aq-ua-tint
aq-ue-duct
a-que-ous
aq-ui-line
ar-a-besque
ar-a-ble
a-rach-nid
  a-rach-ni-dan
ar-ba-lest
  ar-ba-lest-er
  ar-ba-list
ar-bi-ter
  ar-bi-tral
ar-bit-ra-ment
ar-bi-trar-y
  ar-bi-trar-i-ly
  ar-bi-trar-i-ness
ar-bi-trate
  ar-bi-trat-ed
  ar-bi-trat-ing
  ar-bi-tra-ble
  ar-bi-tra-tor
  ar-bi-tra-tion
ar-bor
ar-bo-re-al
ar-bo-res-cent
ar-bo-re-ta
  ar-bo-re-tum

ar-bo-re-tums
ar-bor-vi-tae
ar-bu-tus
arc
  arced
  arc-ing
ar-cade
ar-cane
arch
  arch-ly
  arch-ness
ar-cha-ic
ar-cha-ism
ar-cha-ist
ar-cha-is-tic
arch-an-gel
arch-bish-op
  arch-bish-op-ric
arch-dea-con
arch-di-o-cese
  arch-di-oc-e-san
arch-du-cal
arch-duch-ess
arch-duch-y
  arch-duch-ies
arch-duke
arch-en-e-my
  arch-en-e-mies
arch-er
  ar-cher-y
ar-che-type
ar-che-typ-al
ar-che-typ-i-cal
arch-fiend
ar-chi-e-pis-co-pal
  ar-chi-e-pis-co-pate
ar-chi-pel-a-goes
  ar-chi-pel-a-gos
ar-chi-tect
ar-chi-tec-ton-ic
ar-chi-tec-ture
ar-chi-trave
ar-chive
  ar-chi-val
  ar-chi-vist
ar-chon
arch-priest
arch-way

arc-tic
arc-tic cir-cle
ar-dent
  ar-dent-ly
ar-dor
ar-du-ous
  ar-du-ous-ly
  ar-du-ous-ness
ar-e-a
  ar-e-al
  ar-e-a-way
a-re-na
a-re-o-la
  a-re-o-lae
  a-re-o-las
ar-gent
ar-gen-tine
ar-gil
ar-gon
ar-go-sy
  ar-go-sies
ar-got
  ar-got-ic
ar-gue
  ar-gued
  ar-gu-ing
  ar-gu-a-ble
  ar-gu-er
  ar-gu-ment
  ar-gu-men-ta-tion
  ar-gu-men-ta-tive
ar-gyle
ar-gyll
a-ri-a
ar-id
  a-rid-i-ty
a-right
a-rise
  a-rose
  a-ris-en
  a-ris-ing
ar-is-toc-ra-cy
  ar-is-toc-ra-cies
aris-to-crat
  aris-to-crat-ic
a-rith-me-tic
  a-rith-met-i-cal
  a-rith-met-i-cal-ly

a-rith-me-ti-cian
ar-ma-da
ar-ma-dil-lo
ar-ma-ment
ar-ma-ture
ar-mi-stice
ar-moire
ar-mor
ar-mor-er
ar-mor-y
 ar-mor-ies
arm-pit
ar-my
 ar-mies
ar-ni-ca
a-ro-ma
ar-o-mat-ic
 ar-o-mat-i-cal
a-round
a-rouse
 a-roused
 a-rous-ing
ar-peg-gi-o
 ar-peg-gi-os
ar-raign
 ar-raign-ment
ar-range
 ar-ranged
 ar-rang-er
 ar-rang-ing
 ar-range-ment
ar-rant
 ar-rant-ly
ar-ras
ar-ray
ar-rear
ar-rest
 ar-rest-er
 ar-rest-or
ar-ri-val
ar-rive
 ar-rived
 ar-riv-ing
ar-ro-gant
 ar-ro-gat-ed
 ar-ro-gat-ing
 ar-ro-ga-tion
ar-row

ar-row-head
ar-row-root
ar-roy-o
 ar-roy-os
ar-se-nal
ar-se-nate
ar-se-nic
ar-son
 ar-son-ist
ar-te-ri-al
ar-te-ri-o-scle-ro-sis
ar-ter-y
 ar-ter-ies
ar-te-sian well
art-ful
 art-ful-ly
 art-ful-ness
ar-thri-tis
 ar-thrit-ic
ar-thro-pod
 ar-throp-o-dal
 ar-throp-o-dous
ar-ti-choke
ar-ti-cle
ar-tic-u-lar
ar-tic-u-late
 ar-tic-u-lat-ed
 ar-tic-u-lat-ing
 ar-tic-u-late-ly
 ar-tic-u-late-ness
 ar-tic-u-lar-tor
 ar-tic-u-la-tion
 ar-tic-u-la-to-ry
ar-te-fact
 ar-ti-fact
ar-ti-fice
 ar-tif-i-cer
ar-ti-fi-cial
 ar-ti-fi-ci-al-i-ty
 ar-ti-fi-cial-ly
 ar-ti-fi-cial-ness
ar-til-ler-y
 ar-til-ler-ist
ar-ti-san
art-ist
ar-tiste
 ar-tis-tic
 ar-tis-ti-cal-ly

art-ist-ry
art-less
 art-less-ly
 art-less-ness
art-y
 ar-ti-ness
as-bes-tos
 as-bes-tus
as-cend
 as-cend-ance
 as-cend-ence
 as-cend-an-cy
 as-cend-en-cy
 as-cend-ant
 as-cend-ent
as-cen-sion
as-cent
as-cer-tain
 as-cer-tain-a-ble
 as-cer-tain-ment
as-cet-ic
 as-cet-is-al
 as-cet-i-cism
as-cot
as-cribe
 as-cribed
 as-crib-ing
 as-crib-a-ble
a-sep-sis
a-sep-tic
a-sex-u-al
 a-sex-u-al-i-ty
 a-sex-u-al-ly
a-shamed
 a-sham-ed-ly
ash-en
ash-lar
 ash-ler
a-shore
ash-y
a-side
as-i-nine
a-skance
a-skew
a-slant
a-sleep
a-slope
a-so-cial

as-par-a-gus
as-pect
as-pen
as-per-i-ty
as-perse
  as-persed
  as-pers-ing
as-per-sion
as-phalt
  as-phal-tic
as-pho-del
as-phyx-ia
  as-phyx-i-ate
  as-phyx-i-at-ed
  as-phyx-i-at-ing
  as-phyx-i-a-tion
as-pic
as-pi-dis-tra
as-pir-ant
as-pi-rate
  as-pi-rat-ed
  as-pi-rat-ing
  as-pi-ra-tion
  as-pi-ra-tor
as-pire
  as-pired
  as-pir-ing
  as-pir-er
as-pi-rin
as-sail
  as-sail-a-ble
  as-sail-ant
as-sas-sin
as-sas-si-nate
  as-sas-si-nat-ed
  as-sas-si-na-tion
  as-sas-si-na-tor
as-sault
as-say
  as-say-er
as-sem-blage
as-sem-ble
  as-sem-bled
  as-sem-bling
  as-sem-bler
as-sem-bly
  as-sem-blies
as-sem-bly-man

as-sem-bly-men
as-sent
  as-sent-er
as-sert
  as-sert-er
  as-ser-tion
as-ser-tive
  as-ser-tive-ly
  as-ser-tive-ness
as-sess
  as-sess-a-ble
  as-sess-ment
  as-sess-or
as-set
as-si-du-i-ty
as-sid-u-ous
  as-sid-u-ous-ly
  as-sid-u-ous-ness
as-sign
  as-sign-a-bil-i-ty
  as-sign-a-ble
  as-sign-a-bly
as-sig-na-tion
as-sign-ee
  as-sign-ment
as-sist
  as-sist-ance
as-sis-tant
as-size
as-so-ci-ate
  as-so-ci-at-ed
  as-so-ci-at-ing
  as-so-ci-a-tion
  as-so-ci-a-tive
as-so-nance
as-sort
  as-sort-ed
  as-sort-ment
as-suage
  as-suaged
  as-suag-ing
  as-suage-ment
as-sume
  as-sumed
  as-sum-ing
  as-sump-tion
as-sur-ance
as-sure

as-sured
  as-sur-ing
  as-sur-er
  as-sur-ed-ly
as-ter
as-ter-isk
a-stern
as-ter-oid
  as-ter-oi-dal
asth-ma
  asth-mat-ic
a-stig-ma-tism
  as-tig-mat-ic
a-stir
as-ton-ish
  as-ton-ish-ing
  as-ton-ish-ing-ly
  as-ton-ish-ment
as-tound
  as-tound-ing
a-strad-dle
as-tra-khan
as-tral
a-stray
a-stride
as-trin-gent
  as-trin-gen-cy
as-tro-dome
as-tro-labe
as-trol-o-gy
  as-trol-o-ger
  as-tro-log-ic
  as-tro-log-i-cal
as-tro-naut
  as-tro-nau-tics
  as-tro-nau-ti-cal
as-tro-nom-ic
  as-tro-nom-i-cal-ly
as-tron-o-my
  as-tron-o-mer
as-tro-phys-ics
  as-tro-phys-i-cist
as-tute
  as-tute-ly
  as-tute-ness
a-sun-der
a-sy-lum
a-sym-me-try

asym-met-ric
asym-met-ri-cal
asym-met-ri-cal-ly
at-a-vism
at-a-vist
at-a-vis-tic
a-tax-ia
a-tax-ic
at-el-ier
ath-er-o-scle-ro-sis
a-thirst
ath-lete
ath-let-ic
ath-let-ics
a-thwart
a-tilt
at-las
at-las-es
at-mos-phere
at-oll
at-om
atom-ic
atom-i-cal
atom-i-cal-ly
ato-nal-i-ty
ato-nal
ato-nal-ly
a-tone
a-toned
a-ton-ing
a-tone-ment
a-ton-er
a-top
a-tri-um
a-tro-cious
a-tro-cious-ly
a-tro-cious-ness
a-troc-i-y
a-troc-i-ties
at-ro-phy
at-ro-phies
at-ro-phied
at-ro-pine
at-tach
at-tach-a-ble
at-tach-ment
at-tack
at-tain

at-tain-a-ble
at-tain-a-bil-i-ty
at-tain-a-ble-ness
at-tain-ment
at-tain-der
at-taint
at-tar
at-tempt
at-tempt-a-ble
at-tend
at-tend-ance
at-tend-ant
at-ten-tion
at-ten-tive
at-ten-u-ate
at-ten-u-at-ed
at-ten-u-at-ing
at-ten-u-a-tion
at-test
at-tes-ta-tion
at-tic
at-tire
at-tired
at-tir-ing
at-ti-tude
at-ti-tu-di-nize
at-ti-tu-di-nized
at-ti-tu-di-niz-ing
at-tor-ney
at-tract
at-tract-a-ble
at-trac-tive
at-tract-or
at-trac-tion
at-tri-bute
at-tri-but-ed
at-tri-but-ing
at-tri-but-a-ble
at-tri-bu-tion
at-trib-u-tive
at-tri-tion
at-tune
at-tuned
at-tun-ing
a-typ-i-cal
a-typ-ic
a-typ-i-cal-ly
au-burn

au cou-rant
auc-tion
auc-tion-eer
au-da-cious
au-da-cious-ness
au-dac-i-ty
au-di-ble
au-di-ble-ness
au-di-bly
au-di-ence
au-di-o
au-di-o-vis-u-al
au-dit
au-di-tion
au-dit-or
au-di-to-rium
au-di-to-ry
au-ger
aug-ment
aug-ment-a-ble
aug-ment-er
aug-men-ta-tion
aug-ment-a-tive
au-grat-in
au-gur
au-gu-ry
au-gu-ries
au-gust
au-gust-ly
au-gust-ness
auk
auld lang syne
au na-tu-rel
aunt
au-ra
au-ras
au-rae
au-ral
au-ral-ly
au-re-ate
au-re-ole
au-re-voir
au-ri-cle
au-ric-u-lar
au-rif-er-ous
au-ro-ra
au-ro-ra bor-e-al-is
aus-cul-tate

aus-cul-tat-ed
aus-cul-tat-ing
aus-cul-ta-tion
aus-tere
aus-ter-i-ty
aus-ter-i-ties
aus-tral
au-then-tic
au-then-ti-cat-ed
au-then-ti-cat-ing
au-then-ti-ca-tion
au-then-ti-ca-tor
au-thor
au-thor-i-tar-i-an
au-thor-i-tar-i-an-ism
au-thor-i-ta-tive
au-thor-i-ty
au-thor-i-ties
au-thor-ize
au-thor-ized
au-thor-iz-ing
au-thor-i-za-tion
au-thor-ship
au-to
au-to-bi-og-ra-phy
au-to-bi-og-ra-phies
au-to-bi-og-ra-pher
au-toc-ra-cy
au-toc-ra-cies
au-to-crat
au-to-crat-ic
au-to-crat-i-cal
au-to-crat-i-cal-ly
au-toc-ra-cy
au-toc-ra-cies
au-to-graph
au-to-mat
au-to-mat-ic
au-to-ma-tion
au-to-mate
au-to-mat-ed
au-to-mat-ing
au-tom-a-tism
au-tom-a-ton
au-tom-a-tons
au-tom-a-ta
au-to-mo-bile
au-to-mo-tive

au-to-nom-ic
au-to-nom-i-cal-ly
au-ton-o-mous
au-ton-o-mous-ly
au-ton-o-my
au-ton-o-mies
au-ton-o-mist
au-top-sy
au-to-sug-ges-tion
au-tumn
au-tum-nal
aux-il-ia-ry
aux-il-ia-ries
a-vail
a-vail-a-bil-i-ty
a-vail-a-ble-ness
a-vail-ably
av-a-lanche
av-a-lanched
av-a-lanch-ing
a-vant-garde
av-a-rice
av-a-ri-cious
av-a-ri-cious-ly
av-a-ri-cious-ness
a-vast
av-a-tar
a-ve
a-venge
a-venged
a-veng-ing
a-veng-er
av-e-nue
a-ver
a-verred
a-ver-ring
a-ver-ment
av-er-age
av-er-aged
av-er-ag-ing
a-verse
a-verse-ly
a-ver-sion
a-vert
a-vi-ar-y
avi-ar-ies
a-vi-a-tion
a-vi-a-tor

av-id
a-vid-i-ty
av-id-ly
av-o-ca-do
av-o-ca-tion
a-void
avoid-a-ble
a-void-ance
a-vow
a-vow-er
a-vow-al
a-vowed
a-wait
a-wake
a-woke
a-wak-ed
a-wak-ing
a-wak-en
awak-en-ing
a-ward
a-ware
a-ware-ness
awe
awed
aw-ing
a-weigh
awe-some
awe-struck
aw-ful
aw-ful-ly
aw-ful-ness
awk-ward
awk-ward-ly
awl
awn
awned
awn-less
awn-ing
a-wry
ax-i-al
ax-i-al-ly
ax-i-om
ax-is
ax-le
a-zal-ea

bab-bitt
bab-ble
  bab-bled
  bab-bling
  bab-bler
babe
ba-bel
ba-be-sia
bab-e-si-a-sis
ba-boon
ba-bu
ba-bul
ba-bush-ka
ba-by
  ba-bies
  ba-bied
  ba-by-ing
  ba-by-hood
  ba-by-ish
baby blue--eyes
baby carriage
baby farm
baby grand
baby's breath
ba-by--sit
  ba-by--sat
  ba-by--sit-ting
  ba-by--sit-ter
baby talk
bac-cu
bac-ca-lau-re-ate
bac-ca-rat
bac-cha-nal
  bac-cha-na-li-an
bac-chant
bac-chant-te
bac-chic
back
bach-e-lor
  bach-e-lor-hood
bachelor's button
bac-il-lar-y
bac-cil-lus
  bac-cil-li
bac-i-tra-cin
back
back-ache
back away

back-bencher
back-bite
  back-bit
  back-bit-ten
  back-bit-er
back-board
back-bone
back--check
back-coun-try
back-court
back-court-man
back-cross
back-dive
back down
back-drop
back-field
back-fire
  back-fired
  back-fir-ing
back--formation
back-gam-mon
back-ground
background music
back-hand
  back-hand-ed
back-hoe
back-house
back-ing
back judge
back-lash
back-log
back matter
back mutation
back off
back out
back-pack
back-ped-al
back-rest
back room
back-saw
back-scat-ter
back-seat
back-side
back-slap
back-slide
  back-slid
  back-slid-den
  back-slid-ing

back-slid-er
back-spin
back-stage
back-stairs
back-stay
back-stitch
back-stop
back-stretch
back-stroke
back-swept
back swimmer
back-swing
back-sword
back-talk
back-track
back-up
back-ward
  back-wards
  back-ward-ness
back-wash
back-water
back-woods
  back-woods-man
back-yard
ba-con
bac-ter-emia
bac-ter-ia
  bac-ter-i-um
  bac-te-ri-al
  bac-te-ri-al-ly
bac-te-ri-cide
  bac-te-ri-ci-dal
bac-ter-in
bac-te-rio-cin
bac-te-ri-ol-o-gy
  bac-te-ri-ol-o-gist
  bac-te-ri-o-log-i-cal
bac-te-ri-ol-y-sis
bac-te-ri-o-phage
bac-te-rio-sta-sis
bac-te-rio-stat
bac-te-ri-uria
bac-te-rize
  bac-te-rized
  bac-te-rizing
bac-te-roid
bad
bad blood

bad-der-locks
bad-die
bade
badge
  badged
  badg-ing
badg-er
bad-i-nage
bad-land
  bad-lands
bad-ly
bad-min-ton
bad--mouth
bad-tem-pered
baf-fle
  baf-fled
  baf-fling
  baf-fler
baffling wind
bag
  bagged
  bag-ging
ba-gasse
bag-a-telle
ba-gel
bag-ful
bag-gage
bag-gy
  bag-gi-er
  bag-gi-est
bag-man
bagn-io
bag of waters
bag-pipe
  bag-pi-per
ba-guette
bag-wig
bag-worm
bah
bail
bail-able
bail-ee
bai-ley
bail-lie
bail-iff
bail-i-wick
bail-ment
bail-or

bails-man
  bails-men
bairn
bait
bai-za
bake
  baked
  bak-ing
bak-er
  bak-er-y
  bak-er-ies
baker's dozen
bakers' yeast
bak-ing pow-der
bak-ing so-da
bak-sheesh
  bak-shish
bal-a-lai-ka
bal-ance
  bal-anced
  bal-anc-ing
  bal-anc-er
balance beam
balance of payments
balance of power
balance of terror
balance of trade
balance sheet
balance wheel
bal-as
bal-boa
bal-brig-gan
bal-co-ny
  bal-co-nies
bald
  bald-ly
  bald-ness
bald cypress
bald eagle
bal-der-dash
bald--faced
bald-head
bald-pate
bal-dric
bale
  baled
  bal-ing
ba-leen

bale-fire
bale-ful
  bale-ful-ly
balk
  balk-er
bal-kan-ize
  bal-kan-ized
  bal-kan-iz-ing
  bal-kan-i-za-tion
balk-line
balk-y
  balk-i-er
  balk-i-est
ball
bal-lad
  bal-lade
  bal-lad-eer
  bal-lad-ry
bal-lade
bal-lad-eer
bal-lad-ist
bal-lad-ry
ballad stanza
ball--and--socket joint
bal-last
ball-bear-ing
ball boy
ball-car-ri-er
ball-cock
ball control
bal-le-ri-na
bal-let
ballet d' ac-tion
bal-let-o-mane
bal-let-o-ma-nia
ball--flower
ball hawk
bal-lis-ta
bal-lis-tic
  bal-lis-tics
  bal-lis-ti-cian
ballistic missile
bal-lis-to-car-dio-gram
ball lightning
ball of fire
bal-lon
bal-lo-net
bal-lon-ne

bal-loon
bal-loon-ing
bal-loon-ist
balloon sail
balloon tire
balloon vine
bal-lot
bal-lot-ed
bal-lot-ing
bal-lotte-ment
ball park
ball--point pen
ball-room
ball up
ball valve
bal-ly-hoo
bal-ly-rag
balm
bal-ma-caan
bal-mor-al
balm-y
balm-ier
balm-i-est
balm-i-ly
balm-i-ness
ba-lo-ney
bal-sa
bal-sam
bal-sam fir
balsam poplar
bal-us-ter
bal-us-trade
bam-bi-no
bam-bi-nos
bam-boo
bamboo curtain
bam-boo-zle
bam-boo-zled
bam-boo-zling
bam-boo-zler
ban
banned
ban-ning
ba-nal
ba-nal-i-ty
ban-nan-a
banana oil
banana seat

banana split
ba-nau-sic
band
band-age
band-aged
band-ag-ing
ban-dana
ban-dan-na
band-box
ban-deau
ban-deaux
band-ed
ban-de-ri-lla
ban-de-ri-lle-ro
ban-de-role
ban-di-coot
ban-dit
ban-dits
ban-dit-ti
ban-dit-ry
band-lead-er
band-mas-ter
ban-dog
band-o-leer
ban-do-lier
ban-dore
band razor
band saw
band shell
bands-man
bands-men
band-stand
band-wa-gon
band-width
ban-dy
ban-died
ban-dy--leg-ged
bane
bane-ber-ry
bane-ful
ban-ful-ness
bang
ban-ga-lore torpedo
bang away
bang-kok
ban-gla-desh
ban-gle
ban-ish

ban-ish-ment
ban-i-ster
ban-jo
bank
bank-able
bank acceptance
bank annuities
bank-book
bank discount
bank-er
banker-s bill
bank holiday
bank-ing
bank line
bank money
bank-note
bank paper
bank rate
bank-roll
bank-rupt
bank-rupt-cy
bank-rupt-cies
bank shot
bank-sia
bank-side
ban-ner
ban-ner-et
ban-ne-rol
ban-nock
banns
ban-quet
ban-quet-ter
banquet room
ban-quette
ban-shee
ban-tam
ban-tam-weight
ban-ter
ban-ter-er
ban-ter-ing-ly
bant-ling
ban-yan
ban-zal
ba-o-bab
bap-tism
bap-tis-mal
baptismal name
baptism of fire

bap-tist
  bap-tist-ery
  bap-tis-ter-ies
bap-tize
  bap-tized
  bap-tiz-er
  bap-tiz-ing
bar
  barred
  bar-ring
bar-a-thea
barb
bar-bar-ian
bar-bar-ic
bar-ba-rism
bar-bar-i-ty
  bar-bar-i-ties
bar-ba-rize
  bar-ba-rized
  bar-ba-riz-ing
bar-ba-rous
bar-bate
barbe
bar-be-cue
  bar-be-cued
  bar-be-cu-ing
barbed
barbed wore
bar-bel
bar-bel-late
bar-ber
bar-ber-ry
  bar-ber-ries
bar-ber-shop
barber's itch
bar-bet
bar-bi-can
bar-bi-cel
bar-bi-tal
bar-bi-tone
bar-bi-tu-rate
  bar-bi-tur-ic
bar-ti-tu-ric acid
bar-bule
bar-busse
barb-wire
bar car
bar-ca-role

bar chart
bard
bard-ol-a-ter
bare
  bar-er
  bar-est
  bare-ness
bare-back
bare bones
bare-faced
bare-foot
ba-rege
bare-hand-ed
bare-head-ed
bare-knuck-le
bare-ly
barf
bar-fly
bar-gain
  bar-gain-er
bargain basement
bargain counter
barge
  barg-ed
  barg-ing
barge-board
barg-ee
barge-man
bar graph
bar hop
bar-iat-rics
bar-ic
ba-ri-lla
bar-ite
bar-i-tone
bar-i-um
barium sulfate
bark
bark beetle
bar-keep-er
bar-ken-tine
bark-er
barky
bar-ley
bar-ley--bree
bar-ley-corn
bar-low
barm

bar-maid
bar-man
  bar-men
bar-mitz-vah
barm-y
barn
bar-na-cle
barn dance
barn lot
barn owl
barn raising
barn-storm
  barn-storm-er
  barn-storm-ing
barn-yard
baro-gram
bar-o-graph
ba-rom-et-er
  bar-o-met-ric
  bar-o-met-ric-al
barometric pressure
bar-on
  ba-ro-ni-al
bar-on-age
bar-on-ess
bar-on-et
  bar-on-et-age
  bar-on-et-cy
ba-rong
ba-ro-ni-al
bar-o-ny
  bar-o-nies
ba-roque
baro-re-cep-tor
ba-rouche
bar pilot
barque
bar-quen-tine
bar-rack
barracks bag
bar-ra-coon
bar-ra-cou-ta
bar-ra-cu-da
  bar-ra-cu-das
bar-rage
  bar-raged
  bar-rag-ing
barrage balloon

bar-ra-mun-da
bar-ran-ca
bar-ra-tor
bar-ra-try
  bar-ra-tries
  bar-ra-tor
  bar-ra-trous
bar-rel
  bar-reled
  bar-relled
  bar-rel-ling
barrel chair
bar-rel-ful
bar-rel-house
barrel organ
barrel roll
bar-ren
  bar-ren-ly
  bar-ren-ness
bar-rette
bar-ri-cade
  bar-ri-cad-ed
  bar-ri-cad-ing
bar-ri-er
barrier reef
bar-ring
bar-ri-o
  bar-ri-os
bar-ris-ter
bar-room
bar-row
barrow boy
bar sinister
bar-ten-der
bar-ter
  bar-ter-er
bar-ti-zan
bar-ware
bary-pn
ba-ry-ta
bar-yte
bary-tone
ba-sal
basal body
basal cell
basal metabolic rate
basal metabolism
ba-salt

bas-cule
base
base-ball
base-board
base-born
base burner
base component
base exchange
base hit
base-less
base-lev-el
base-line
base-ment
basement membrane
ba-sen-ji
base on balls
base path
base pay
base runner
bash
ba-shaw
bash-ful
  bash-ful-ly
  bash-ful-ness
ba-sic
  ba-si-cal-ly
basic process
basic slag
basic training
ba-sid-io-my-cete
ba-sid-io-spore
ba-sid-i-um
ba-si-fy
ba-sil
bas-i-lar
basilar membrane
ba-sil-i-cia
bas-i-lisk
basil thyme
ba-sin
bas-i-net
ba-sip-e-tal
ba-sis
bask
bas-ket
bas-ket-ball
basket case
basket fern

basket--handle arch
basket hilt
basket--of--gold
bas-ket-ry
basket star
basket weave
bas-ket-work
ba-so-phil
ba-so-phil-ia
ba-so-phil-ic
bas-re-lief
bass
bass clef
bass drum
bas-set hound
bass fiddle
bass horn
bas-si-net
bass-ist
bas-so
bas-soon
bas-so pro-fun-do
bas-so--re-lie-vo
bass viol
bass-wood
bast
bas-tard
bas-tard-ize
bastard wing
bas-tardy
baste
  bast-ed
  bast-ing
bas-tille
bas-ti-na-do
bas-ti-on
  bas-ti-oned
bast ray
bat
  bat-ted
  bat-ting
  bat-ter
bat-boy
batch
bate
  bat-ed
  bat-ing
bat-fish

bat-fowl	bat-tle	beachboy
bath	bat-tled	beach break
bath chair	bat-tling	beach buggy
bathe	bat-tle--ax	beach-comb-er
bathed	battle cruiser	beach flea
bath-ing	battle cry	beach-front
bath-er	bat-tle dore	beach grass
ba-thet-ic	battle fatigue	beach-head
bath-house	bat-tle-field	beach pea
bath-i-nette	bat-tle-front	beach plum
bathing beauty	bat-tle-ground	beach-side
bathing suit	battle group	beach wagon
bath mat	bat-tle-ment	beach-wear
batho-lith	battle royal	beachy
ba-thom-e-ter	bat-tle-ship	bea-con
ba-thos	bat-tle-wag-on	bead
bath-robe	bat-tue	bead-ed
bath-room	bat-ty	bead-like
bath salts	bat-ti-er	bea-dle
bath-tub	bat-ti-est	bead-roll-beads-man
bathtub gin	bau-ble	bead-work
bath-wa-ter	baid	beady
bathy-al	bau-drons	bead-y
bathy-met-ric	baulk	bead-i-er
ba-thym-e-try	baux-ite	bead-i-est
bathy-pe-lag-ic	baw-bee	bea-gle
bath-y-scaphe	baw-cock	beak
bath-y-sphere	bawd	beaked
ba-tik	bawd-y	beak-er
bat-ing	bawd-i-er	beam
ba-tiste	bawd-i-est	beam-ed
bat-man	bawl	beam--ends
bat-on	bawl out	beam-ish
ba-tra-chi-an	bay	beamy
ba-trach-tox-in	ba-ya-dere	bean
bats-man	bay-antler	bean-ball
batt	bay-ber-ry	bean curd
bat-tai-lous	bay leaf	bean-ie
bat-ta-lia	bay-o-net	beano
bat-tal-ion	bay-o-net-ted	bean sprouts
bat-te-ment	bay-o-net-ing	bean tree
bat-ten	bay-ou	bear
bat-ter	bay rum	bear-ing
bat-te-rie	bay window	bear-a-ble
battering ram	ba-zaar	bear-a-bly
bat-tery	ba-zoo-ka	bear-er
bat-ting	beach	bear-bait-ing
batting average	beach ball	bear-ber-ry

beard
  beard-ed
  beard-less
bear down
beard-tongue
bear grass
bear hug
bearing rein
bear-ish
be-ar-naise sauce
bear out
bear-skin
bear up
beast
  beast-li-ness
  beast-ly
  beast-li-er
  beast-li-est
beast epic
beast fable
beas-tings
beast-ly
beast of burden
beat
  beat-en
  beat-ing
  beat-er
be-a-tif-ic
beatific vision
be-at-i-fy
  be-at-i-fied
  be-at-i-fi-ca-tion
beat-ing
be-at-i-tude
beat-nik
beat out
beau
  beaus
  beaux
beau geste
beau-te-ous
  beau-te-ous-ly
beau-ti-cian
beau-ti-ful
beau-ti-ful-ly
beautiful people
beau-ti-fy
  beau-ti-fied

beau-ti-fy-ing
beau-ti-fi-ca-tion
beau-ti-fi-er
beau-ti-ful
beau-ti-ful-ly
beau-ty
beauty bush
beauty shop
beauty spot
beaux-arts
beaux esprits
bea-ver
bea-ver-board
be-bop
be-calm
be-cause
beck-on
be-cloud
be-come
  be-com-ing
  be-com-ing-ly
bed
  bed-ded
  bed-ding
be-daub
be-daz-zle
  be-daz-zled
  be-daz-zling
  be-daz-zle-ment
bed-bug
bed-clothes
be-deck
be-dev-il
  be-dev-iled
  be-dev-il-ing
  be-dev-il-ment
be-dew
bed-fast
bed-fel-low
be-dim
  be-dimmed
  be-dim-ming
bed-lam
bed-pan
be-drag-gle
  be-drag-gled
  be-drag-gling
bed-rid-den

bed-rock
bed-room
bed-sore
bed-spread
bed-spring
bed-time
bee-bread
beech
beef
beef-eat-er
beef-steak
beef-y
  beef-i-er
  beef-i-est
bee-hive
bee-line
beer-y
  beer-i-er
  beer-i-est
beest-ings
bees-wax
bee-tle
  bee-tled
  bee-tling
bee-tle-browed
be-fall
  be-fall-en
  be-fall-ing
be-fit
  be-fit-ted
  be-fit-ting
be-fog
  be-fogged
  be-fog-ging
be-fore
be-fore-hand
be-foul
be-friend
be-fud-dle
  be-fud-dled
  be-fud-dling
beg
  beg-ged
  beg-ging
be-get
  be-get-ten
  be-got
  be-got-ten

beg-gar
  beg-gar-dom
  beg-gar-hood
  beg-gar-ly
be-gin
  be-gan
  be-gun
  be-gin-ning
  be-gin-ner
be-go-ni-a
be-grime
  be-grimed
  be-grim-ing
be-grudge
  be-grudged
  be-grudg-ing
  be-grudg-ing-ly
be-guile
  be-guiled
  be-guil-ing
  be-guil-er
be-half
be-have
  be-haved
  be-hav-ing
be-hav-ior
  be-hav-ior-ism
  be-hav-ior-ist
  be-hav-ior-is-tic
be-head
be-he-moth
be-hest
be-hind
be-hind-hand
be-hold
  be-hold-ing
  be-hold-er
  be-hold-en
be-hoove
  be-hooved
  be-hoov-ing
beige
be-ing
be-la-bor
be-lat-ed
  be-lat-ed-ly
  be-lat-ed-ness
be-lay

be-lay-ed
be-lay-ing
belch
bel-dam
be-lea-quer
bel-fry
  bel-fries
be-lie
  be-lied
  be-ly-ing
be-lief
be-lieve
  be-lieved
  be-liev-ing
  be-liev-a-ble
  be-liev-er
be-lit-tle
  be-lit-tled
  be-lit-tling
bel-la-don-na
bell-boy
bell bouy
belle
belles let-tres
bell-hop
bel-li-cose
  bel-li-cos-i-ty
bel-lig-er-ence
  bel-lig-er-en-cy
  bel-lig-er-ent
  bel-lig-er-ent-ly
bel-low
  bel-lows
bell-weth-er
bel-ly
  bel-lies
  bel-lied
  bel-ly-ing
bel-ly-ache
  bel-ly-ach-ing
bel-ly-but-ton
be-long
  be-long-ings
be-loved
be-low
belt
  belt-ed
  belt-way

be-lu-ga
be-mire
  be-mired
  be-mir-ing
be-moan
be-muse
  be-mused
  be-mus-ing
bench
bend
  bend-ing
  bend-er
be-neath
ben-e-dict
ben-e-dic-tion
ben-e-fac-tion
ben-e-fac-tor
  ben-e-fac-tress
ben-e-fice
  ben-e-ficed
  ben-e-fic-ing
be-nef-i-cence
be-nef-i-cent
be-ne-fi-cial
  ben-e-fi-cial-ly
  ben-e-fi-ci-ar-ies
ben-e-fit
  ben-e-fit-ed
  ben-e-fit-ing
be-nev-o-lence
  be-nev-o-lent
  be-nev-o-lent-ly
be-night-ed
be-nign
  be-nig-ni-ty
  be-nig-ni-ties
  be-nign-ly
be-nig-nant
  be-nig-nan-cies
  be-nig-nan-cy
ben-i-son
ben-ny
  ben-nies
be-numb
bent
ben-zene
ben-zine
ben-zo-ate

ben-zo-in
ben-zol
be-queath
be-quest
be-rate
  be-rat-ed
  be-rat-ing
be-reave
  be-reaved
  be-reav-ing
be-reft
be-ret
ber-ga-mot
ber-i-ber-i
berke-li-um
ber-ry
  ber-ries
  ber-ried
  ber-ry-ing
ber-serk
berth
ber-tha
ber-yl
be-ryl-li-um
be-seech
  be-seeched
  be-seech-ing
  be-seech-ing-ly
be-set
  be-set-ting
be-shrew
be-side
  be-sides
be-siege
  be-sieged
  be-sieg-ing
  be-sieg-er
be-smear
be-smirch
bes-om
be-sot
  be-sot-ted
  be-sot-ting
be-spat-ter
be-speak
  be-speak-ing
best
bes-tial

bes-tial-ly
bes-ti-al-i-ty
bes-ti-al-i-ties
be-stir
  be-stirred
  be-stir-ring
be-stow
  be-stow-al
be-strew
be-stride
  be-strid-den
  be-strid-ing
bet
  bet-ted
  bet-ting
be-ta
be-take
  be-tak-en
  be-tak-ing
be-ta rays
be-ta-tron
be-tel
beth-el
be-tide
  be-tid-ed
  be-tid-ing
be-to-ken
be-tray
  be-tray-al
  be-tray-er
be-troth
  be-troth-al
  be-troth-ed
bet-ter
bet-ter-ment
bet-tor
be-tween
be-twixt
bev-el
  bev-eled
  bev-el-ing
bev-er-age
bev-y
  bev-ies
be-wail
be-ware
be-wil-der
  be-wil-der-ing-ly

be-wil-der-ment
be-witch
  be-witch-er
  be-witch-ery
  be-witch-ing
  be-witch-ing-ly
  be-witch-ment
be-yond
be-zique
bi-an-nu-al
bi-as
  bi-ased
  bi-as-ing
bi-ax-i-al
  bi-ax-i-al-ly
bi-be-lot
Bi-ble
  Bib-li-cal
  Bib-li-cal-ly
bib-li-og-ra-phy
  bib-li-og-ra-phies
  bib-li-o-graphic
bib-li-o-ma-ni-a
  bib-li-o-ma-ni-ac
bib-li-o-phile
bib-u-lous
bi-cam-er-al
bi-car-bo-nate
bi-ce-te-nary
  bi-cen-te-nar-ies
bi-cen-ten-ni-al
bi-ceps
bi-chlo-ride
bick-er
bi-con-cave
bi-con-vex
bi-cus-pid
  bi-cus-pi-dal
  bi-cus-pi-date
bi-cy-cle
  bi-cy-cled
  bi-cy-cling
  bi-cy-cler
  bi-cy-clist
bid
  bid-den
  bid-da-ble
  bid-der

bid-dy
  bid-dies
bide
  bid-ed
  bid-ing
bi-en-ni-al
  bi-en-ni-al-ly
bier
bi-fid
bi-fo-cal
  bi-fo-cals
bi-fur-cate
  bi-fur-cat-ed
  bi-fur-cat-ing
  bi-fur-ca-tion
big
  big-ger
  big-gest
big-a-my
  big-a-mies
  big-a-mist
  big-a-mous
big-heart-ed
big-horn
bight
big-no-ni-a
big-ot
  big-ot-ed
  big-ot-ed-ly
  big-ot-ry
  big-ot-ries
bi-jou
  bi-joux
bi-ju-gous
bi-ki-ni
bi-lat-er-al
  bi-lat-er-al-ly
bil-ber-ry
  bil-ber-ries
bilge
bil-i-ary
bi-lin-gual
bil-ious
bilk
bill
  bil-led
  bil-ling
bil-la-bong

bill-board
bil-let
bil-let-doux
bill-fold
bill-hook
bil-liards
bil-lings-gate
bil-lion
  bil-lion-are
  bil-lionth
bil-low
  bil-low-y
  bil-low-ier
  bil-low-i-est
bil-ly goat
bi-met-al-lism
  bi-met-al-list
  bi-me-tal-lic
bi-month-ly
  bi-month-lies
bi-na-ry
bi-nate
bin-au-ral
bind
  bind-ing
bind-er
bind-ery
  bind-er-ies
binge
bin-go
bin-na-cle
bi-noc-u-lar
bi-no-mi-al
bio-chem-is-try
  bio-chem-i-cal
  bio-chem-ist
bi-o-cide
bi-o-e-col-o-gy
bi-o-en-gi-neer-ing
bi-o-gen-e-sis
  bi-o-ge-net-ic
bi-og-ra-phy
  bi-og-ra-pher
  bi-o-graph-ic
  bi-o-graph-i-cal
  bi-o-graph-i-cal-ly
bi-ol-o-gy
  bi-o-log-i-cal

bi-ol-o-gist
bi-o-met-rics
bi-o-nom-ics
bi-o-phys-ics
  bi-o-phys-i-cal
  bi-o-phys-i-cist
bi-op-sy
  bi-op-sies
bi-o-sphere
bi-o-tin
bi-par-ti-san
bi-par-tite
  bi-par-ti-tion
bi-ped
  bi-ped-al
bi-plane
bi-po-lar
  bi-po-lar-i-ty
birch
  birch-en
bird-bath
bird-brain
  bird-brained
bird-call
bird-ie
bird-lime
bird-man
bird's-eye
bi-ret-ta
birth-day
birth-mark
birth-place
birth-right
birth-stone
bis-cuit
bi-sect
  bi-sec-tion
  bi-sec-tor
bi-sex-u-al
bish-op
  bish-op-ric
bis-muth
bi-son
bisque
bis-ter
  bis-tered
bis-tro
  bis-tros

bi-sul-fide
bitch
bite
  bit-ten
  bit-ing
  bit-ing-ly
bit-stock
bit-ter
  bit-ter-ish
  bit-ter-ly
  bit-ter-ness
bit-tern
bit-ter-root
bit-ters
bit-ter-sweet
bi-tu-men
bi-tu-mi-nous coal
bi-va-lent
  bi-va-lence
bi-valve
  bi-val-vu-lar
biv-ou-ac
  biv-ou-acked
  biv-ou-ack-ing
bi-week-ly
  bi-week-lies
bi-year-ly
bi-zarre
  bi-zarre-ly
  bi-zarre-ness
blab
  blab-bed
  blab-bing
  blab-ber
  blab-ber-mouth
black-ball
black-ber-ry
  black-ber-ries
black-bird
black-board
black-en
black-guard
black-head
black-ing
black-jack
black-list
black-mail
black-out

black-smith
black-snake
black-top
blad-der
blade
  blad-ed
blame
  blamed
  blam-ing
  blam-a-ble
  blame-a-ble
  blame-ful
  blame-less
  blame-less-ly
  blame-less-ness
blame-wor-thy
  blame-wor-thi-ness
blanch
  blanc-er
  blanch-ing
blanc-mange
bland
  bland-ly
  bland-ness
blan-dish
  blan-dish-er
  blan-dish-ment
blank
  blank-ly
  blank-ness
blan-ket
blare
  blared
  blar-ing
blar-ney
blas-pheme
  blas-phemed
  blas-phem-ing
  blas-phem-er
  blas-phem-ies
blas-phe-my
blast-ed
bas-tu-la
blat
  blat-ted
  blat-ting
bla-tant
  bla-tan-cy

bla-tant-ly
blath-er
blaze
  blazed
  blaz-ing
bla-zer
bleach
bleach-er
bleak
  bleak-ly
  bleak-ness
blear
  bleary
  blear-i-ness
bleed
  bleed-ing
  bleed-er
blem-ish
blench
blend
  blend-ed
  blend-ing
  blend-er
bless
  bless-ed
  bles-sing
  bless-ed-ness
blind
  blind-ing
  blind-ing-ly
  blind-ly
  blind-ness
blind-fold
blind-man's bluff
blink-er
bliss
  bliss-ful
  bliss-ful-ly
  bliss-ful-ness
blis-ter
  blis-ter-y
blithe
  blithe-ly
blithe-some
  blithe-some-ly
blitz-krieg
bliz-zard
block

block-er
block-ade
block-ad-ed
block-ad-ing
block-ad-er
block-bus-ter
block-head
block-house
block-ish
block-ish-ly
blocky
blond
blood-curd-ling
blood bank
blood-ed
blood-hound
blood-less
blood-less-ly
blood-less-ness
blood-let-ting
blood pres-sure
blood re-la-tion
blood-shed
blood-shot
blood-stone
blood-suck-er
blood-thirst-y
blood-thirst-i-ly
bloody
blood-i-er
blood-i-est
blood-ied
blood-y-ing
blood-i-ly
blood-i-ness
bloom-ers
bloom-ing
bloom-ing-ly
bloop-er
blos-som
blot
blot-ted
blot-ting
blotch
blotchy
blot-ter
blow
blown

blow-ing
blow-er
blow-fly
blow-flies
blow-gun
blow-hole
blow-out
blow-pipe
blow-torch
blow-up
blow-y
blowz-y
blub-ber
blub-bery
blu-cher
bludg-eon
blue
blu-er
blu-est
blue-ness
blue-bell
blue-ber-ry
blue-ber-ries
blue-bird
blue-blood-ed
blue-bon-net
blue-coat
blue-col-lar
blue-fish
blue-grass
blue-jac-ket
blue-nose
blue-pen-cil
blue-print
blu-et
blu-ing
blun-der
blun-der-er
blun-der-ing-ly
blun-der-buss
blunt
blunt-ly
blunt-ness
blur
blur-red
blur-ring
blur-ry
blush

blushed
blush-ing
blush-ing-ly
blus-ter
blus-ter-er
blus-ter-ing-ly
blus-ter-ous
blus-ter-y
bo-a
board-er
board-walk
boast
boas-ter
boast-ful
boast-ful-ness
boast-ing-ly
boat-house
boat-man
boat-swain
bob
bob-bed
bob-bing
bob-bin
bob-ble
bob-bled
bob-bling
bob-by-pin
bob-cat
bob-o-link
bob-sled
bob-tail
bob-white
bock
bode
bod-ed
bod-ing
bod-ice
bod-i-ly
bod-kin
bod-y
bod-ied
bod-y-ing
bod-y-guard
bog
bog-gy
bog-ging
bo-gey
bog-gle

bog-gled
bog-gling
bog-gler
bo-gus
bo-gy
boil-er
bois-ter-ous
bois-ter-ous-ly
bois-ter-ous-ness
bo-la
bo-las
bold
bold-ly
bold-ness
bold-face
bo-le-ro
bol-lix
boli-worm
boll weevil
bo-lo
bo-lo-gna
bo-lo-ney
bol-ster
bol-ster-er
bolt
bolt-ed
bolt-er
bom-bard
bom-bard-ment
bom-bar-dier
bom-bast
bom-bas-tic
bom-bas-ti-cal-ly
bomb-er
bomb-proof
bomb-shell
bomb-sight
bo-na fide
bo-nan-za
bon-bon
bond-age
bond-ed
bond-man
bond-men
bonds-men
bone
boned
bon-ing

bone-head
bon-er
bon-fire
bon-go
bon-gos
bon-gies
bon-ho-mie
bo-ni-to
bon-net
bon-ny
bon-sai
bo-nus
bo-nus-es
bon voy-age
bon-y
bon-i-er
bon-i-est
boo
booed
boo-ing
boo-by
boo-bies
boo-by trap
boo-dle
boo-hoo
boo-hooed
boo-hoo-ing
book
book-bind-er
book-case
book-end
book-ie
book-ish
book-ish-ness
book-keep-ing
book-keep-er
book-let
book-mak-er
book-mark
book-mo-bile
book-plate
book-sell-er
book-sell-ing
book-stall
book-worm
boo-me-rang
boon docks
boon-dog-gle

boor
boor-ish
boor-ish-ness
boost
boost-er
boot-black
boot-ee
boot-jack
boot-leg
boot-legged
boot-leg-ging
boot-leg-ger
boot-less
boot-less-ly
boot-less-ness
boot-lick
boot-lick-er
boo-ty
boo-ties
booze
booz-er
booz-y
booz-i-er
booz-i-est
bo-rax
bor-der
bor-der-ed
bor-der-ing
bor-der-land
bor-der-line
bore
bored
bor-ing
bor-er
bo-re-al
bore-dom
bo-ric
bo-ron
bor-ough
bor-row
bor-row-er
borsch
bosh
bosk-y
bos-om
boss-ism
boss-y
boss-i-er

boss-i-est
boss-i-ness
bo-sun
bot-a-ny
 bo-tan-i-cal
 bot-a-nist
 bot-a-nize
botch
 botchy
 botch-i-er
 botch-i-est
both-er
 both-er-some
bot-tle
 bot-tled
 bot-tling
 bot-tle-ful
 bot-tler
bot-tle-neck
bot-tom
 bot-tom-less
bot-u-lism
bou-doir
bouf-fant
bough
bought
bouil-lon
boul-der
boul-e-vard
bounce
 bounced
 bounc-ing
bound
bound-a-ry
 bound-a-ries
bound-er
bound-less
 bound-less-ness
boun-te-ous
 boun-te-ous-ness
boun-ti-ful
boun-ty
 boun-ties
bou-quet
bour-bon
bour-geois
bour-geoi-sie
bou-tique

bou-ton-niere
bo-vine
bow-el
bow-er
bow-ery
bow-ie
bow-ing
bow-knot
bowl
bow-leg
 bow-leg-ged
bowl-er
bow-line
bow-ling
bow-man
 bow-men
bow-string
box
 box-ful
 box-fuls
box-car
box-er
box-ing
box of-fice
boy
 boy-hood
 boy-ish
 boy-ish-ly
 boy-ish-ness
boy-cott
boy-friend
boy-sen-ber-ry
 boy-sen-ber-ries
brace
 bra-ced
 brac-ing
brace-let
 brac-er
 bra-ces
brack-en
brack-et
brack-ish
 brack-ish-ness
bract
brad
 brad-ded
 brad-ding
brae

brag
 brag-ged
 brag-ging
brag-gart
braid
 braid-er
 braid-ing
braille
brain-child
brain-less
brain-pow-er
brain-storm
 brain-storm-ing
brain-wash-ing
brain-y
 brain-i-er
 brain-i-est
braise
 braised
 brais-ing
brake
 braked
 brak-ing
brake-man
 brake-men
bram-ble
 bram-bly
branch
 branch-ed
brand
 brand-er
brand-ish
brand-new
bran-dy
 bran-dies
 bran-died
 bran-dy-ing
bra-sier
bras-se-rie
 bras-se-ries
bras-siere
brassy
 brass-i-er
 brass-i-est
brat
 brat-tish
 brat-ty
bra-va-do

brave
braved
brav-ing
brave-ness
brav-ery
brav-er-ies
bra-vo
bra-vos
bra-vu-ra
brawl
braw-ler
brawn
brawn-i-ness
brawny
brawn-i-er
brawn-i-est
bra-zen
bra-zier
breach
bread
bread=ed
breadth-ways
bread-win-ner
break
break-ing
break-a-ble
break-age
break-a-way
break-down
brak-er
break-fast
break-neck
break-through
break-up
breast-bone
breast-plate
breath
breathe
breathed
breath-ing
breath-er
breath-ing
breath-tak-ing
breath-tak-ing-ly
breathy
breath-i-er
breath-i-est
breech-es

breech-load-er
bred
breed
breed-ing
breeze
breezy
breez-i-er
breez-i-est
breez-i-ness
breth-ren
bre-vet
bre-vet-ted
bre-vet-ting
bre-vi-a-ry
bre-vi-a-ries
brev-i-ty
brew
brew-er
brew-ery
brew-er-ies
bri-ar
bri-ary
bribe
bribed
brib-ing
brib-a-ble
birb-ery
brib-er-ies
bric-a-brac
brick-lay-er
brick-lay-ing
brick-work
bride
brid-al
bride-groom
brides-maid
bridge
bri-dle
bri-dled
bri-dling
brief
brief-ly
brief-ing
bri-er
bri-gade
bri-a-dier
brig-an-tine
bright

bright-ly
bright-ness
bright-en
bril-liance
bril-lian-cy
bril-liant
brim
brimmed
brim-ming
brim-stone
brine
briny
bring
bring-ing
brink
bri-oche
bri-quet
bri-quette
brisk
brisk-ly
brisk-ness
bris-ket
bris-tle
bris-tled
britch-es
brit-tle
broach
broached
broach-ing
broad-cast
broad-cast-ed
broad-cast-ing
broad-cloth
broad-mind-ed
broad-side
bro-cade
bro-cad-ed
bro-cad-ing
broc-co-li
bro-chure
broil-er
bro-ken
bro-ker
bro-ker-age
bro-mide
bro-mine
bron-chi
bron-chi-al

bron-chi-tis
bron-chue
bron-co
bron-cos
bron-to-saur
bronze
bronz-ed
bronz-ing
brooch
brood
brood-ing
brook
broom-stick
broth-el
broth-er
broth-er-in-law
broth-ers-in-law
broth-er-ly
brow-beat
brow-beat-en
brow-beat-ing
brown
brown-ie
browse
browsed
brows-ing
bru-in
bruise
bruis-ed
bruis-er
bruis-ing
brunch
bru-net
brusque
bru-tal
bru-tal-i-ty
bru-tal-ize
bru-tal-ized
bru-tal-iz-ing
bru-tal-i-za-tion
brut-ish
bub-ble
bub-bled
bub-bling
bub-bler
bu-bon-ic plague
buc-ca-neer
buck-a-roo

buck-board
buck-et
buck-et-ed
buck-et-ing
buck-eye
buck-le
buck-saw
buck-shot
buck-skin
buck-tooth
buck-teeth
buck-toothed
buck-wheat
bu-col-ic
bud
bud-ded
bud-ding
bud-dy
budge
budg-et
buff-er
buf-fet
buf-fet-ed
buf-fet = ing
buf-foon
buf-foon-ery
buf-foon-er-ies
buf-foon-ish
bug
bugged
bug-ging
bug-a-boo
bug-gy
bug-gi-er
bug-gi-est
bu-gle
bu-gled
bu-gling
bu-gler
build
build-er
build-ing
built--in
built-up
bulb
bul-ba-ceous
bul-bar
bul-bous

bulge
bulged
bulg-ing
bulgy
bulk-head
bulk-y
bulk-i-er
bulk-i-est
bulk-i-ly
bulk-i-ness
bull-dog
bull-doze
bull-dozed
bull-doz-ing
bull-doz-er
bul-let
bul-le-tin
bul-let-proof
bull-fight
bull-fight-er
bull-fight-ing
bull-finch
bull-head-ed
bul-lion
bull-pen
bull's-eye
bul-ly
bul-lies
bul-lied
bul-ly-ing
bul-rush
bul-wark
bum
bum-mer
bum-mest
bum-ble-bee
bump-er
bump-kin
bump-tious
bump-tious-ness
bump-y
bump-i-er
bump-i-est
bunch
bunchy
bunch-i-er
bunch-i-est
bun-co

bun-combe
bun-dle
  bun-dled
  bun-dling
bun-ga-low
bun-gle
  bun-gled
  bun-gling
  bun-gler
bun-ion
bunk-er
bunk-house
bun-ko
bun-kum
bun-ny
  bun-nies
bun-ting
bu-oy
buoy-an-cy
  buoy-ant
  buoy-ant-ly
bur-ble
bur-den
bur-den-some
bur-dock
bu-reau
  bu-reaus
  bu-reaux
  bu-reauc-ra-cy
  bu-reauc-ra-cies
  bu-reau-crat
  bu-reau-crat-ic
bu-rette
bur-geon
burg-er
bur-gess
bur-glar
  bur-glar-ize
  bur-glar-ized
  bur-glar-iz-ing
  bur-gla-ries
  bur-gla-ry
bur-gle
  bur-gled
  bur-gling
bur-i-al
bur-lap
bur-lesque

bur-lesqued
bur-les-quing
bur-les-quer
bur-ly
  bur-li-er
  bur-li-est
  bur-li-ness
burn
  burn-ed
  burnt
  burn-ing
  burn-a-ble
  burn-er
bur-nish
  bur-nish-er
bur-noose
burn-sides
burp
burr
  burred
  bur-ring
bur-ro
  bur-ros
bur-row
  bur-row-er
bur-sa
  bur-sae
  bur-sal
bur-sar
  bur-sa-ri-al
  bur-sa-ry
  bur-sa-ries
bur-si-tis
burst
  burst-ing
  burst-er
bur-y
  bur-ied
  bur-y-ing
bus
  bus-ed
  bus-ing
bus-boy
bus-by
  bus-bies
bushed
bush-el
bu-shi-do

bush-ing
bush-man
  bush-men
bush-mas-ter
bush-rang-er
bush-whack
  bush-whack-er
  bush-whack-ing
bush-y
  bush-i-er
  bush-i-est
  bush-i-ness
bus-i-ly
busi-ness
busi-ness-like
busi-ness-man
  busi-ness-men
  busi-ness-wom-an
bus-kin
  bus-kined
bus-tard
bus-tle
  bus-tled
  bus-tling
  bus-tler
bus-y
bu-ta-di-ene
bu-tane
butch-er
butch-ery
  butch-er-ies
but-ler
butte
but-ter
but-tery
but-tock
but-ton
but-tress
bu-ty-ric
bux-om
buy
  bought
  buy-ing
buz-zard
buzz-er
by-gong
by-law
byte

ca-bal
  ca-balled
  ca-ball-ing
cab-a-la
  cab-a-lis-tic
  cab-a-lis-ti-cal
ca-bal-le-ro
ca-ba-na
cab-a-ret
cab-bage
cab-by
  cab-bies
ca-ber
cab-in
cab-i-net
cab-i-net-mak-er
cab-i-net-work
ca-ble
  ca-bled
  ca-bling
ca-ble-gram
cab-o-chon
ca-boo-dle
ca-boose
cab-ri-o-let
ca-ca-o
cach-a-lot
cache
  cached
  cach-ing
ca-chet
ca-cique
cack-le
ca-coph-o-ny
  ca-coph-o-nics
cac-tus
  cac-tus-es
cac-ti
cad
  cad-dish
ca-das-tral
  ca-das-tral-ly
ca-das-tre
ca-dav-er
  ca-dav-er-ic
  ca-dav-er-ine
  ca-dav-er-ous
cad-die

cad-died
cad-dis
cad-dis fly
cad-dish
  cad-dish-ly
  cad-dish-ness
cad-dis-worm
cad-dy
  cad-dies
cade
ca-delle
ca-dence
  ca-denced
ca-den-cy
ca-dent
ca-den-tial
ca-den-za
ca-det
  ca-det-ship
cadge
  cadged
  cadg-er
  cadg-ing
cad-mi-um
ca-dre
ca-du-ceus
  ca-du-cean
  ca-du-cei
ca-du-ci-ty
ca-du-cous
cae-cal
cae-ci-lian
cae-si-um
caes-pi-tose
cae-su-ra
  cae-su-rae
ca-fe
caf-e-te-ria
caf-e-to-ri-um
caf-feine
  caf-fein-ic
caf-tan
cage
  caged
cage-ling
ca-gey
cai-man
caird

cairn
cairn-gorm
cais-son
cai-tiff
ca-jole
  ca-jole-ment
  ca-jol-er
  ca-jol-ery
cake
  caked
cal-a-bash
cal-a-boose
cal-a-mine
ca-lam-i-ty
  ca-lam-i-ties
  ca-lam-i-tous
cal-cic
cal-ci-fy
  cal-ci-fied
  cal-ci-fy-ing
  cal-ci-fi-ca-tion
cal-ci-mine
cal-cite
cal-ci-um
cal-cu-la-ble
  cal-cu-la-bil-i-ty
cal-cu-late
  cal-cu-lat-ed
  cal-cu-lat-ing
  cal-cu-la-tion
cal-cu-la-tor
cal-cu-lus
  cal-cu-lus-es
cal-dron
cal-en-dar
cal-ends
calf
cal-i-ber
cal-i-brate
  cal-i-brat-ed
  cal-i-brat-ing
  cal-i-bra-tion
cal-i-co
  cal-i-coes
cal-i-per
ca-liph
  cal-iph-ate
cal-is-then-ics

cal-lig-ra-pher
cal-lig-ra-phy
call-ing
cal-li-o-pe
cal-lous
cal-loused
cal-low
cal-lus
cal-lus-es
calm
ca-lor-ic
cal-o-rie
cal-o-ries
cal-o-rif-ic
cal-u-met
cal-um-ny
calve
calved
ca-lyp-so
ca-lyp-sos
ca-lyx
ca-lyx-es
cal-y-ces
ca-ma-ra-de-rie
cam-ber
cam-bi-um
cam-bric
cam-el
ca-mel-lia
cam-eo
cam-era
cam-i-sole
cam-o-mile
cam-ou-flage
cam-ou-flaged
cam-ou-flag-ing
cam-paign
cam-pa-ni-le
cam-pa-ni-les
camp-er
cam-phor
cam-pus
cam-pus-es
camp-y
cam-shaft
can
canned
can-ning

ca-nal
ca-naled
ca-nal-ing
ca-nard
ca-nar-y
ca-nas-ta
can-can
can-cel
can-celed
can-cel-ing
can-cel-la-tion
can-cer
can-de-la-brum
can-did
can-di-da-cy
can-di-da-cies
can-di-date
can-died
can-dle
can-dor
can-dy
can-dies
can-died
can-dy-ing
cane
ca-nine
can-is-ter
can-ker
can-ker-ous
can-na-bis
canned
can-ner
can-nery
can-ner-ies
can-ni-bal
can-non
can-not
can-ny
can-nier
ca-noe
can-on
ca-non-i-cal
can-on-ize
can-on-ized
can-on-i-za-tion
can-o-py
can-ta-loup
can-ta-loupe

can-ta-lope
can-tan-ker-ous
can-ta-ta
can-teen
can-ter
can-ti-cle
can-ti-lev-er
can-to
can-tos
can-ton
can-tor
can-vas
can-yon
ca-pa-bil-i-ty
cap-pa-bil-i-ties
ca-pa-ble
ca-pa-bly
ca-pa-cious
ca-pac-i-tate
ca-pac-i-tat-ed
ca-pac-i-tat-ing
ca-pac-i-ty
ca-pac-i-ties
ca-per
ca-pi-as
cap-il-lar-i-ty
cap-il-lar-y
cap-il-lar-ies
cap-i-tal
cap-i-ta-tion
ca-pit-u-late
ca-pit-u-lat-ed
ca-pit-u-lat-ing
ca-pit-u-la-tor
ca-pon
ca-pote
ca-pric-cio
ca-price
ca-pri-cious
ca-pri-cious-ly
cap-ri-ole
cap-ri-oled
cap-ri-ol-ing
cap-size
cap-stan
cap-stone
cap-sule
cap-su-lar

cap-tain
  cap-tain-cy
cap-tion
cap-tious
  cap-tious-ness
cap-ti-vate
cap-tive
  cap-tiv-i-ty
  cap-tiv-i-ties
cap-tor
cap-ture
  cap-tured
  cap-tur-ing
  cap-tur-er
car-a-cole
  car-a-coled
  car-a-col-ing
car-a-cul
ca-rafe
car-a-mel
car-a-pace
car-at
car-a-van
car-a-van-sa-ry
  car-a-van-sa-ries
car-a-vel
car-a-way
car-bide
car-bine
car-bo-hy-drate
car-bo-lat-ed
car-bol-ic
car-bon
car-bo-na-ceous
car-bo-nate
  car-bo-na-tion
car-bon di-ox-ide
car-bon-if-er-ous
car-bon-ize
  car-bon-ized
  car-bon-iz-ing
  car-bon-i-za-tion
car-bon mon-ox-ide
car-boy
car-bun-cle
car-bu-re-tor
car-ca-jou
car-cass

car-cin-o-gen
  car-cin-o-gen-ic
car-ci-no-ma
  car-ci-no-mas
  car-ci-no-ma-ta
car-da-mom
car-di-ac
car-di-gan
car-di-nal
car-di-o-graph
  car-di-og-ra-phy
ca-reen
ca-reer
care-ful
  care-ful-ly
  care-ful-ness
care-less
  care-less-ly
  care-less-ness
ca-ress
  ca-ress-ing-ly
car-et
care-worn
car-go
  car-goes
  car-gos
car-hop
car-i-bou
car-i-ca-ture
  car-i-ca-tured
  car-i-ca-tur-ing
  car-i-ca-tur-ist
car-ies
car-il-lon
  car-il-lonned
  car-i-lon-ning
  car-i-lon-neur
car-mine
car-nage
car-nal
  car-nal-i-ty
  car-nal-ly
car-na-tion
car-nel-ian
car-ni-val
car-ni-vore
  car-niv-o-rous
  car-niv-o-rous-ly

car-niv-o-rous-ness
car-om
ca-rot-id
ca-rous-al
ca-rouse
  ca-roused
  ca-rous-ing
  ca-rous-er
car-ou-sel
carp
car-pen-ter
  car-pen-try
car-pet
car-pet-ing
car-pus
car-riage
car-ri-er
car-ri-ole
car-rot
car-roty
car-ry
  car-ried
  car-ry-ing
cart
cart-age
carte-blanche
car-tel
car-ti-lage
  car-ti-lag-i-nous
car-tog-ra-phy
  car-tog-ra-pher
  car-to-graph-ic
car-ton
car-toon
  car-toon-ist
car-tridge
cart-wheel
carve
car-vel
car-y-at-id
  car-y-at-ids
  car-y-at-i-des
ca-sa-ba
cas-cade
  cas-cad-ed
  cas-cad-ing
ca-sein
case-mate

case-mat-ed
case-ment
case-ment-ed
case-work
case-work-er
cash-ew
cash-ier
cash-mere
cas-ing
ca-si-no
cas-ket
cas-sa-ba
cas-sa-va
cas-se-role
cas-sette
cas-si-no
cas-sock
cas-socked
cas-so-wary
cas-so-war-ies
cast
cast-ing
cas-ta-net
cast-a-way
caste
cas-tel-lat-ed
cast-er
cas-ti-gate
cas-ti-gat-ed
cas-ti-gat-ing
cas-ti-ga-tion
cas-ti-ga-tor
cast i-ron
cas-tle
cas-tor
cas-trate
cas-trat-ed
cas-trat-ing
cas-trat-er
cas-tra-tion
cas-u-al
cas-u-al-ty
cas-u-al-ties
cas-u-ist
cas-u-is-tic
cas-u-ist-ry
cas-ist-ries
cas-u-ist

cas-u-ist-ic
cas-u-ist-ry
cas-u-ist-ries
cat-a-clysm
cat-a-cly-mal
cat-a-comb
cat-a-falque
cat-a-lep-sy
cat-a-lep-tic
cat-a-log
cat-a-loged
cat-a-log-ing
cat-a-log-er
cat-a-log-ist
ca-tal-pa
ca-tal-y-sis
ca-tal-y-ses
cat-a-lyt-ic
cat-a-lyst
cat-a-lyze
cat-a-lyzed
cat-a-lyz-ing
cat-a-ma-ran
cat-a-pult
cat-a-ract
ca-tarrh
ca-tas-tro-phe
cat-as-troph-ic
catch
caught
catch-ing
catch-er
catch-up
catch-y
catch-i-er
catch-i-est
cat-e-chism
cat-e-chis-mal
cat-e-chiz
cat-e-chu-men
cat-e-gor-i-cal
cat-e-gor-i-cal-ly
cat-e-go-ry
cat-a-go-ries
cat-e-gor-ize
cat-e-gor-ized
cat-e-gor-iz-ing
ca-ter

ca-ter-er
cat-er-pil-lar
ca-ter-waul
cat-fish
cat-fish-es
cat-gut
ca-thar-sis
ca-thar-ses
ca-thar-tic
ca-the-dral
cath-e-ter
cath-ode
cat-i-on
cat-nap
cat-napped
cat-nap-ping
cat-nip
cat's-paw
cat-sup
cat-tail
cat-tle
cat-ty
cat-tier
cat-ti-est
cat-ti-ly
cat-ti-ness
cat-ty-cor-ner
cau-cus
cau-cus-es
cau-cused
cau-cus-ing
cau-dal
cau-date
cau-dat-ed
cau-dle
caul-dron
cau-li-flow-er
caulk
caulk-er
caus-al
caus-al-ly
cau-sal-i-ty
cau-sal-i-ties
cause-way
caus-tic
caus-ti-cal-ly
cau-ter-ize
cau-ter-ized

cau-ter-iz-ing
cau-ter-i-za-tion
cau-ter-y
cau-ter-ies
cau-tion
cau-tion-ary
cau-tious
cav-al-cade
cav-a-lier
cav-a-lier-ly
cav-al-ry
cave
ca-ve-at
cav-ern
cav-ern-ous
cav-ier
cav-il
cav-iled
cav-il-ing
cav-i-ty
cav-i-ties
ca-vort
cay-enne
cay-man
cay-mans
cay-use
ce-cum
ce-dar
cede
ced-ed
ced-ing
ce-dil-la
ceil-ing
cel-an-dine
cel-a-brant
cel-e-brate
cel-e-brat-ed
cel-e-brat-ing
cel-e-bra-tion
cel-e-bra-tor
ce-leb-ri-ty
ce-leb-ri-ties
ce-ler-i-ty
cel-er-y
ce-les-tial
ce-li-ac
cel-i-ba-cy
cel-i-bate

cel-lar
cel-lo
cel-los
cel-list
cel-lo-phane
cel-lu-lar
cel-lule
cel-lu-lose
ce-ment
cem-e-ter-y
ce-no-bite
cen-o-taph
cen-ser
cen-sor
cen-so-ri-al
cen-sor-ship
cen-so-ri-ous
cen-so-ri-ous-ly
cen-so-ri-ous-ness
cen-sure
cen-sured
cen-sur-ing
cen-sur-er
cen-sus
cen-sus-es
cen-sused
cen-sus-ing
cen-tare
cen-taur
cen-te-nar-i-an
cen-te-na-ry
cen-te-nar-ies
cen-ten-ni-al
cen-ter
cen-ti-are
cen-ti-grade
cen-ti-gram
cen-ti-li-ter
cen-ti-me-ter
cen-tral
cen-tral-ize
cen-tral-ized
cen-tral-iz-ing
cen-trif-u-gal
cen-tri-fuge
cen-trip-e-tal
cen-tu-ri-an
cen-tu-ry

cen-tu-ries
ce-ram-ic
ce-ram-ics
ce-re-al
cer-e-bel-lum
cer-e-bral
cer-e-brum
cer-e-mo-ni-al
cer-e-mo-no-al-ism
cer-e-mo-ny
cer-e-mo-nies
ce-rise
ce-ric
ce-ri-um
cer-tain
cer-tain-ty
cer-tain-ties
cer-tif-i-cate
cer-tif-i-ca-tion
cer-ti-fy
cer-ti-fied
cer-ti-fy-ing
cer-ti-tude
ce-ru-le-an
cer-vi-cal
cer-vix
cer-vix-es
cer-vi-ces
ces-sa-tion
ces-sion
cess-pool
ce-ta-cean
ce-ta-ceous
chafe
chafed
chaf-ing
chaf-er
chaff
chaf-fer
chaff-er-er
cha-grin
cha-grined
cha-grin-ing
chain re-ac-tion
chair-man
chair-men
chaise-longue
chal-et

chal-ice
chalk
  chalky
chal-lenge
  chal-lenged
  chal-leng-ing
cham-ber
cham-ber-maid
cha-me-le-on
cham-ois
cham-pagne
cham-pi-on
  cham-pi-on-ship
chance-ful
chan-cel-lor
chanc-y
  chanc-i-er
  chanc-i-est
chan-de-lier
change
  changed
  chang-ing
  chang-a-ble
chan-nel
chan-ti-cleer
cha-os
cha-ot-ic
cha-pa-re-jos
chap-ar-ral
cha-peau
  cha-peaux
chap-el
chap-e-ron
chap-fall-en
chap-lain
chap-let
chap-ter
char
  charred
  char-ring
char-ac-ter
char-ac-ter-is-tic
  char-ac-ter-is-ti-cal-ly
char-ac-ter-ize
  char-ac-ter-ized
  char-ac-ter-iz-ing
  char-ac-ter-i-za-tion
  char-ac-ter-iz-er

cha-rade
char-coal
charge
  charged
  charg-ing
  charg-er
char-i-ot
  char-i-ot-eer
cha-ris-ma
char-i-ta-ble
  char-i-ta-ble-ness
  char-i-ta-bly
char-i-ty
  char-i-ties
cha-riv-a-ri
char-la-tan
  char-la-tan-ism
char-ley horse
charm
char-nel
char-ter
char-treuse
char-wom-an
chary
  char-i-er
  char-i-est
chase
  chased
  chas-ing
  chas-er
chasm
chas-sis
chaste
  chaste-ly
chas-ten
chas-tise
  chas-tised
  chas-tis-ing
  chas-tis-ment
  chas-tis-er
  chas-ti-ty
chat
  chat-ted
  chat-ting
cha-teau
  cha-teaux
chat-e-laine
chat-tel

chat-ter
chat-ter-box
chat-ty
  chat-ti-er
  chat-ti-est
  chat-ti-ly
  chat-ti-ness
chauf-feur
chau-vin-ist
  chau-vin-ism
  chau-vin-is-tic
cheap
  cheap-ly
  cheap-ness
  cheap-en
cheap-skate
cheat
check-er-board
check-list
check-mate
  check-mat-ed
  check-mat-ing
check-out
check-point
check-room
check-up
ched-dar
cheek-bone
cheek-y
  cheek-i-er
  cheek-i-est
  cheek-i-ness
cheer-ful
  cheer-ful-ly
  cheer-ful-ness
cheer-lead-er
cheer-less
  cheer-less-ly
  cheer-less-ness
chee-y
  cheer-i-er
  cheer-i-est
  cheer-i-ly
  cheer-i-ness
cheese-burg-er
cheese-cake
cheese-cloth
chees-y

chees-i-er
chees-i-est
chees-i-ness
chee-tah
chem-i-cal
  chem-i-cal-ly
che-mise
chem-ist
chem-is-try
chem-o-ther-a-py
che-nille
cher-ish
che-root
cher-ry
  cher-ries
cher-ub
  cher-ubs
  cher-u-bim
  che-ru-bic
cher-vil
chess-man
  chess-men
chest-nut
chest-y
  chest-i-er
  chest-i-est
chev-ron
chew
  chew-er
chi-a-ro-scu-ro
chi-can-ery
  cha-can-er-ies
chi-chi
chick-a-dee
chic-ken
chic-ken-heart-ed
chic-le
chic-o-ry
  chic-o-ries
chide
  chid-ed
chief
  chief-ly
chief-tain
chif-fon
chif-fo-nier
chi-gnon
chil-blain

chil-dren
child-bear-ing
child-birth
child-hood
child-ish
  child-ish-ly
  child-like
chili
  chil-ies
chill
  chill-ing-ly
chill-y
  chill-i-er
  chill-i-est
  chill-i-ness
chi-me-ra
chi-mer-ic
  chi-mer-i-cal
  chi-mer-i-cal-ly
  chi-mer-i-cal-ness
chim-ney
chim-pan-zee
chin
  chinned
  chin-ning
chi-na
chi-no
  chi-nos
chi-noi-se-rie
chintz-y
  chintz-i-er
  chintz-i-est
chip
  chipped
  chip-ping
chip-munk
chip-per
chi-rog-ra-pher
chi-rog-ra-phy
chi-rop-o-dist
chi-ro-prac-tic
chi-ro-prac-tor
chis-el
  chis-eled
  chis-el-ing
  chis-el-er
chit-chat
chi-tin

chit-ter-ling
chiv-al-ry
  chiv-al-ries
  chiv-al-ric
  chiv-al-rous
  chiv-al-rous-ly
  chiv-al-rous-ness
chlo-rine
chlo-ro-form
clo-ro-phyll
chock-full
choc-o-late
choice
  choice-ly
  choice-ness
choir-boy
choke
  choked
  chok-ing
  chok-er
chol-er
chol-era
chol-er-ic
cho-les-te-rol
choose
  chose
  cho-sen
  choos-ing
choos-y
  choos-i-er
  choos-i-est
chop
  chopped
  chop-ping
chop-per
  chop-pi-ness
chop-py
  chop-pi-er
  chop-i-est
chop-sticks
chop su-ey
cho-ral
  cho-ral-ly
cho-rale
chord
  chord-al
cho-rea
cho-re-og-ra-phy

cho-re-og-ra-pher
cho-re-o-graph-ic
cho-ric
chor-is-ter
chor-tle
chor-tled
chor-tling
cho-rus
cho-rus-es
cho-rused
cho-rus-ing
chos-en
chow-der
chow mein
chrism
Christ
chris-ten
chris-ten-ing
Chris-tian
Chris-ti-an-i-ty
Chris-ti-an-i-ties
Christ-mas
chro-mate
chro-mat-ic
chro-mat-i-cal-ly
chro-mat-ics
chro-ma-tin
chro-mic
chro-mi-um
chro-mo
chro-mus
chro-mo-lith-o-graph
chro-mo-some
chro-mo-sphere
chron-ic
chron-i-cal-ly
chron-i-cle
chron-i-cled
chron-i-cling
chron-i-cler
chron-o-log-i-cal
chron-o-log-i-cal-ly
chro-no-lo-gy
chro-nol-o-gies
chro-nol-o-gist
chro-nom-e-ter
chron-o-met-ric
chrys-a-lis

chry-sa-lis-es
chry-sal-i-des
chry-san-the-mum
chrys-o-lite
chub-by
chub-bi-er
chub-bi-est
chub-bi-ness
chuck-full
chuck-le
chuck-led
chuck-ling
chuk-ker
chum-my
chum-mi-er
chum-mi-est
chunk
chunky
chunk-i-er
chunk-i-est
church
church-li-ness
church-ly
church-go-er
church-man
church-men
church-war-den
church-yard
churl-ish
churl-ish-ly
churl-ish-ness
churn-er
chut-ney
chutz-pah
ci-bo-ri-um
ci-bo-ria
ci-ca-da
ci-ca-das
ci-ca-dea
cic-a-trix
cic-a-tri-ces
cic-a-trize
cic-a-trized
cic-a-triz-ing
cic-e-ro-ne
ci-der
ci-gar
cig-a-rette

cil-ia
cil-i-ar-y
cil-i-ate
cin-cho-na
cinc-ture
cin-der
cin-e-ma
cin-e-mas
cin-e-mat-ic
cin-e-ma-to-graph
cin-e-ma-tog-ra-phy
cin-e-rar-i-um
cin-na-bar
cin-na-mon
cinque-foil
ci-on
ci-pher
cir-ca
cir-ca-di-an
cir-cle
cir-cled
cir-cling
cir-clet
cir-cuit
cir-cu-i-tous
cir-cu-i-tous-ly
cir-cu-i-tous-ness
cir-cu-lar
cir-cu-lar-ize
cir-cu-lar-ized
cir-cu-lar-iz-ing
cir-cu-lar-i-za-tion
cir-cu-la-tion
cir-cu-late
cir-cu-lat-ed
cir-cu-lat-ing
cir-cu-la-tive
cir-cu-la-tor
cir-cu-la-to-ry
cir-cum-am-bi-ent
cir-cum-cise
cir-cum-cised
cir-cum-cis-ing
cir-cum-cis-er
cir-cum-ci-sion
cir-cum-fer-ence
cir-cum-fer-en-tial
cir-cum-flex

cir-cum-flu-ent
cir-cum-fuse
  cir-cum-fus-ing
  cir-cum-fu-sion
cir-cum-lo-cu-tion
  cir-cum-lo-cu-to-ry
cir-cum-nav-i-gate
  cir-cum-nav-i-gat-ed
  cir-cum-nav-i-gat-ing
  cir-cum-nav-i-ga-tion
  cir-cum-nav-i-ga-tor
cir-cum-scribe
  cir-cum-scribed
  cir-cum-scrib-ing
  cir-cum-scrib-er
  cir-cum-lo-scrip-tion
  cir-cum-scrip-tive
cir-cum-spect
cir-cum-stance
  cir-cum-stan-tial
  cir-cum-stan-ti-al-i-ty
  cir-cum-stan-ti-at-ed
  cir-cum-stan-ti-at-ing
  cir-cum-stan-ti-a-tion
cir-cum-vent
  cir-cum-ven-tion
  cir-cum-ven-tive
cir-cus
  cir-cus-es
cir-rho-sis
  cir-rhot-ic
cir-rus
cis-tern
cit-a-del
cite
  cit-ed
  cit-ing
ci-ta-tion
cith-a-ra
cit-i-zen
  cit-i-zen-ship
cit-i-zen-ry
  cit-i-zen-ries
cit-rate
cit-ric
cit-ron
cit-ron-el-la
cit-rus

cit-tern
city
  cit-ies
ci-ty-state
civ-et
civ-ic
  civ-ics
civ-il
ci-vil-ian
ci-vil-i-ty
  ci-vil-i-ties
civ-i-li-za-tion
civ-i-lize
  civ-i-lized
  civ-i-liz-ing
clab-ber
claim
  claim-a-ble
  claim-ant
  claim-er
clair-voy-ance
  clair-voy-ant
clam
  clammed
  clam-ming
clam-bake
clam-bar
clam-my
  clam-mi-er
  clam-mi-est
  clam-mi-ly
  clam-mi-ness
clam-or
  clam-or-ous
clan
  clan-nish
clan-des-tine
clang-or
  clang-or-ous
clans-man
  clans-men
clap
  clapped
  clap-ping
clap-board
clap-per
clap-trap
claque

clar-et
clar-i-fy
  clar-i-fied
  clar-i-fy-ing
  clar-i-fi-ca-tion
clar-i-net
  clar-i-net-ist
clar-i-on
clar-i-ty
class-a-ble
clas-sic
  clas-si-cal
  clas-si-cal-ly
clas-si-cism
  clas-si-cist
clas-si-fy
  clas-si-fied
  clas-si-fy-ing
  clas-si-fi-er
  clas-si-fi-ca-tion
class-mate
class-room
class-y
  class-i-er
  class-i-est
clat-ter
clause
  claus-i-cle
claus-tro-pho-bia
clav-i-chord
clav-i-cle
cla-vier
clay
  clay-ey
clay-more
clean-cut
clean-er
clean-ly
  clean-li-er
  clean-li-est
  clean-li-ness
cleanse
  cleansed
  cleans-ing
  cleans-er
clean-up
clear
  clear-ly

clear-ness
clear-ance
clear-cut
clear-ing
clear-sight-ed
cleav-age
cleave
cleaved
cleav-ing
cleav-er
clef
cleft
clem-en-cy
clem-ent
clere-sto-ry
clere-sto-riees
cler-gy
cler-gies
cler-gy-man
cler-gy-men
cler-ic
cler-i-cal
cler-i-cal-ism
cler-i-cal-ist
clev-er
clev-er-ly
clev-er-ness
clev-is
clev-is-es
clew
cli-ent
cli-en-tele
cliff-hang-er
cli-mac-ter-ic
cli-mate
cli-mat-ic
cli-mat-i-cal
climb
climb-a-ble
climb-er
clinch-er
cling
cling-ing
cling-ing-ly
cling-er
clin-ic
clin-i-cal
clin-i-cal-ly

clink-er
clip
clipped
clip-ping
clip-per
clique
cliqu-ey
cliqu-ish
clit-o-ris
clo-a-ca
clo-a-cae
clo-a-cal
clob-ber
clock-wise
clock-work
clod
clod-dish
clod-dy
clog
clog-ged
clog-ging
clois-ter
clois-tral
close
closed
clos-ing
clos-est
close-ly
close-ness
close-fist-ed
close-mouthed
clos-et
clos-et-ed
clos-et-ing
close-up
clo-sure
clot
clot-ted
clot-ting
clothe
clothed
cloth-ing
clothes-horse
clothes-line
clothes-pin
cloth-ier
cloth-ing
clo-ture

cloud-burst
cloud-y
cloud-i-er
cloud-i-est
cloud-i-ly
cloud-i-ness
clo-ven
clo-ver
clo-ver-leaf
clown
clown-ish
cloy
cloy-ing-ly
club
clubbed
club-bing
club-foot
club-house
clump
clumpy
clum-sy
clum-si-er
clum-si-est
clum-si-ly
clum-si-ness
clus-ter
coach-man
coach-men
co-ag-u-late
co-ag-u-lat-ed
co-ag-u-lat-ing
co-ag-u-la-tion
co-a-lesce
co-a-lesced
co-a-les-cing
co-a-les-cence
co-a-les-cent
co-a-li-tion
coarse
coars-er
coars-est
coars-en
coarse-ly
coast-er
coast-line
coat-ing
co-au-thor
coax

coax-ing-ly
co-balt
cob-ble
cob-bled
cob-bling
cob-bler
cob-ble-stone
co-bra
cob-web
cob-webbed
cob-web-by
co-ca
co-caine
coc-cyx
coc-cy-ges
coc-cyg-e-al
coch-le-a
cock-ade
cock-a-too
cock-crow
cock-er span-iel
cock-eyed
cock-fight
cock-le
cock-le-bur
cock-le-shell
cock-ney
cock-neys
cock-pit
cock-roach
cocks-comb
cock-sure
cock-tail
cocky
cock-i-er
cock-i-est
cock-i-ness
co-coa
co-co-nut
co-coon
cod
cod-fish
cod-dle
cod-dled
cod-dling
code
cod-ed
cod-ing

co-deine
codg-er
cod-i-cil
cod-i-fy
cod-i-fied
cod-i-fy-ing
cod-i-fi-ca-tion
cod-liv-er oil
co-ed
co-ed-u-ca-tion
coe-len-ter-ate
co-e-qual
co-erce
co-erced
co-er-cing
co-er-ci-ble
co-er-cion
co-er-cive
co-ex-ist
co-ex-ist-ence
co-ex-ist-ent
cof-fee
cof-fee-house
cof-fee-pot
cof-fer
cof-fin
co-gent
co-gen-cy
co-gent-ly
cog-i-tate
cog-i-tat-ed
cog-i-tat-ing
cog-i-ta-ble
cog-i-ta-tive
cog-nac
cog-nate
cog-ni-tion
cog-ni-tive
cog-ni-zance
cog-ni-zant
cog-wheel
co-hab-it
co-hab-i-ta-tion
co-here
co-hered
co-her-ing
co-her-ent
co-her-ence

co-her-en-cy
co-her-ent-ly
co-he-sion
co-he-sive
co-hes-sive-ly
co-hes-sive-ness
co-hort
coif-feur
coif-fure
coif-fured
coif-fur-ing
coin-age
co-in-cide
co-in-cid-ed
co-in-cid-ing
co-in-ci-dence
co-in-ci-den-tal
co-in-ci-den-tal-ly
co-i-tion
co-i-tus
co-i-tal
coke
coked
cok-ing
co-la
col-an-der
cold-blood-ed
cole-slaw
col-ic
col-icky
col-i-se-um
co-li-tis
col-lab-o-rate
col-lab-o-rat-ed
col-lab-o-rat-ing
col-lab-o-ra-tion
col-lab-o-ra-tor
col-lage
col-lapse
col-lapsed
col-laps-ing
col-lap-si-ble
col-lar
col-lar-bone
col-late
col-lat-ed
col-lat-ing
col-la-tion

col-la-tor
col-lat-er-al
col-league
col-lect
col-lect-i-ble
col-lec-tor
col-lect-ed
col-lec-tion
col-lec-tive
col-lec-tive-ly
col-lect-tiv-i-ty
col-lec-tiv-ism
col-lec-tiv-ize
col-lec-tiv-iz-ing
col-lec-tiv-i-za-tion
col-lege
col-le-gi-al
col-le-gian
col-le-giate
col-lide
col-lid-ed
col-lid-ing
col-li-sion
col-li-mate
col-li-mat-ed
col-li-mat-ing
col-li-ma-tion
col-lo-cate
col-lo-cat-ed
col-lo-cat-ing
col-lo-ca-tion
col-loid
col-lo-qui-al
col-lo-qui-al-ly
col-lo-qui-al-ism
col-lo-quy
col-lo-quies
col-lu-sion
col-lu-sive
co-logne
co-lon
colo-nel
co-lo-ni-al
co-lo-ni-al-ism
co-lo-ni-al-ist
col-o-nist
col-o-nade
col-o-ny

col-o-nies
col-o-nize
col-o-nized
col-o-niz-ing
col-o-niz-er
col-o-ni-za-tion
col-or
col-or-er
col-or-less
col-or-a-tion
col-or-blind
col-or-blind-ness
col-or-cast
col-ored
col-or-fast
col-or-ful
col-or-ing
co-los-sal
co-los-sus
co-los-si
colt-ish
col-um-bine
col-umn
co-lum-nar
co-lumned
col-um-nist
co-ma
co-mas
co-ma-tose
com-bat
com-bat-ed
com-bat-ing
com-bat-ant
com-ba-tive
comb-er
com-bi-na-tion
com-bi-na-tion-al
com-bi-na-tive
com-bine
com-bined
com-bin-ing
com-bin-a-ble
com-bin-er
com-bo
com-bos
com-bust-ti-ble
com-bus-ti-bil-i-ty
con-bus-tion

com-bus-tive
come
com-ing
come-back
co-me-di-an
co-me-di-enne
come-down
com-e-dy
com-e-dies
come-ly
come-li-ness
come-on
com-er
com-et
come-up-pance
com-fort
com-fort-a-ble
com-fort-a-bly
com-fort-er
com-fy
com-fi-er
com-fi-est
com-ic
com-i-cal
com-ing
com-i-ty
com-i-ties
com-ma
com-mas
com-mand
com-man-dant
com-man-deer
com-mand-er
com-mand-er-ship
com-mand-ment
com-man-do
com-man-dos
com-mem-o-rate
com-mem-o-rat-ed
com-mem-o-rat-ing
com-mem-o-ra-ble
com-mem-o-ra-tion
com-mem-o-ra-tive
com-mem-o-ra-to-ry
com-mence
com-menced
com-menc-ing
com-mence-ment

com-mend
  com-mend-a-ble
  com-mend-a-bly
com-men-da-tion
  com-mend-a-to-ry
com-men-su-rate
  com-men-su-rate-ly
  com-men-su-ra-tion
com-ment
com-men-tary
  com-men-tar-ies
  com-men-ta-tor
com-merce
com-mer-cial
  com-mer-cial-ism
  com-mer-cial-ize
  com-mer-cial-ized
  com-mer-cial-iz-ing
com-mie
com-mis-er-ate
  com-mis-er-at-ed
  com-mis-er-at-ing
  com-mis-er-a-tion
  com-mis-er-a-tive
com-mis-sar
com-mis-sar-y
  com-mis-sar-ies
com-mis-sion
  com-mis-sioned
com-mis-sion-er
com-mit
  com-mit-ted
  com-mit-ting
  com-mit-ment
com-mit-tee
  com-mit-tee-man
  com-mit-tee-wo-man
com-mode
com-mo-di-ous
com-mod-i-ty
  com-mod-i-ties
com-mo-dore
com-mon
com-mon-al-ty
  com-mon-al-ties
com-mon-place
com-mons
com-mon-wealth

com-mo-tion
com-mu-nal
  com-mu-nal-i-ty
com-mune
  com-muned
  com-mun-ing
com-mu-ni-cant
com-mu-ni-cate
  com-mu-ni-cat-ed
  com-mu-ni-cat-ing
  com-mu-ni-ca-ble
  com-mu-ni-ca-tive
  com-mu-ni-ca-tion
com-mun-ion
  com-mun-ism
  com-mun-ist
com-mu-ni-ty
  com-mu-ni-ties
com-mu-nize
  com-mu-nized
  com-mu-niz-ing
com-mu-ta-tion
com-mu-ta-tor
com-mute
  com-mut-ed
  com-mut-ing
  com-mut-a-ble
com-mut-er
com-pact
com-pan-ion
  com-pan-ion-a-ble
  com-pan-ion-ship
com-pa-ny
  com-pa-nies
com-par-a-ble
  com-par-a-bil-ity
com-par-a-tive
com-pare
  com-pared
  com-par-ing
com-par-i-son
com-part-ment
  com-part-men-tal
  com-part-ment-ed
  com-part-men-tal-ize
com-pass
com-pas-sion
  com-pas-sion-ate

com-pat-ible
  com-pat-i-bly
  com-pat-i-bil-i-ty
com-pa-tri-ot
com-peer
com-pel
  com-pelled
  com-pel-ling
com-pem-di-ous
  com-pen-di-um
com-pen-sate
  com-pen-sat-ed
  com-pen-sat-ing
  com-pen-sa-tive
  com-pen-sa-tor
  com-pen-sa-to-ry
com-pen-sa-tion
com-pete
  com-pet-ed
  com-pet-ing
com-pet-i-tor
com-pe-tence
com-pe-ten-cy
com-pe-tent
com-pe-ti-tion
com-pet-i-tive
com-pile
  com-piled
  com-pil-ing
  com-pi-la-tion
com-pla-cence
  com-pla-cen-cy
  com-pla-cent
com-plain
com-plain-ant
com-plaint
com-plai-sance
  com-plai-sant
com-plect-ed
com-ple-ment
  com-ple-men-tal
  com-ple-men-ta-ry
com-plete
  com-plet-ed
  com-plet-ing
  com-plet-a-ble
com-ple-tion
com-plex

com-plex-ion
com-plex-ioned
com-plex-i-ty
com-plex-i-ties
com-pli-ance
com-pli-an-cy
com-pli-ant
com-pli-cate
com-pli-cat-ed
com-pli-cat-ing
com-pli-ca-tion
com-plic-i-ty
com-plic-i-ties
com-pli-ment
com-pli-men-ta-ri-ly
com-ply
com-plied
com-ply-ing
com-po-nent
com-port
com-port-ment
com-pose
com-posed
com-pos-ing
com-pos-er
com-pos-ite
com-po-si-tion
com-post
com-po-sure
com-pote
com-pound
com-pre-hend
com-pre-hend-i-ble
com-pre-hen-si-ble
com-pre-hen-si-bly
com-pre-hen-sion
com-pre-hen-sive
com-press
com-presed
com-press-i-ble
com-press-i-bil-ity
com-pres-sion
com-pres-sor
com-prise
com-prised
com-pris-ing
com-pro-mise
com-pro-mised

com-pro-mis-ing
comp-trol-ler
com-pul-sion
com-pul-sive
com-pul-so-ry
com-punc-tion
com-pute
com-put-ed
com-put-ing
com-pu-ta-tion
com-pu-ter
com-put-er-ize
com-put-er-ized
com-put-er-iz-ing
com-put-er-i-za-tion
com-rade
com-rade-ship
com-sat
con
conned
con-ning
con-cave
con-ceal
con-ceal-a-ble
con-ceal-ment
con-cede
con-ced-ed
con-ced-ing
con-ceit
con-ceit-ed
con-ceive
con-ceived
con-ceiv-ing
con-ceiv-a-ble
con-ceiv-a-bly
con-cen-trate
con-cen-tra-ted
con-cen-trat-ing
con-cen-tra-tive
con-cen-tra-tion
con-cen-tric
con-cen-tri-cal
con-cen-tric-i-ty
con-cept
con-cep-tu-al
con-cep-tion
con-cep-tive
con-cep-tu-al-ize

con-cep-tu-al-ized
con-cep-tu-al-iz-ing
con-cern
con-cerned
con-cern-ing
con-cert
con-cert-ed
con-cer-ti-na
con-cert-mas-ter
con-cer-to
con-ces-sion
con-ces-sion-aire
conch
conchs
con-cil-i-ate
con-cil-i-at-ed
con-cil-i-at-ing
con-cil-i-a-tion
con-cil-i-a-to-ry
con-cise
con-cise-ness
con-cise-ly
con-clave
con-clude
con-clud-ed
con-clud-ing
con-clu-sion
con-clu-sive
con-coct
con-coc-tion
con-com-i-tant
con-com-i-tance
con-cord
con-cord-ance
con-cord-ant
con-course
con-crete
con-cret-ed
con-cret-ing
con-cre-tion
con-cre-tive
con-cu-bine
con-cur
con-curred
con-cur-ring
con-cur-rence
con-cur-rent
con-cus-sion

con-cus-sive
con-demn
  con-dem-na-ble
  con-dem-na-tion
  con-dem-na-to-ry
con-dense
  con-densed
  con-dens-ing
  con-den-sa-ble
  con-den-sa-tion
  con-dens-er
con-de-scend
  con-de-scend-ing
  con-de-scen-sion
con-di-ment
con-di-tion
  con-di-tion-al
  con-di-tion-er
  con-di-tion-ed
con-dole
  con-doled
  con-dol-ing
  con-do-la-to-ry
  con-do-ler
con-do-lence
con-dom
con-do-min-i-um
con-done
  con-doned
  con-don-ing
  con-do-na-tion
con-dor
con-duce
  con-duced
  con-duc-ing
con-duct
  con-duct-i-bil-i-ty
  con-duct-i-ble
con-duct-ance
con-duc-tion
con-fer-ence
  con-fer-en-tial
con-fess
  con-fess-ed-ly
con-fes-sion
  con-fes-sion-al
con-fes-sor
con-fet-ti

con-fi-dant
  con-fi-dante
con-fide
  con-fid-ed
  con-fid-ing
con-fi-dence
  con-fi-dent
con-fi-den-tial
con-fig-u-ra-tion
  con-fig-u-ra-tion-al
con-fine
  con-fined
  con-fin-ing
  con-fine-ment
con-firm
  con-firm-a-ble
  con-fir-ma-tion
  con-fir-ma-tive
  con-fir-ma-to-ry
con-fir-med
  con-firm-ed-ly
  con-firm-ed-ness
con-fis-cate
  con-fis-cat-ed
  con-fis-cat-ing
  con-fis-ca-tion
  con-fis-ca-tor
  con-fis-ca-to-ry
con-fla-gra-tion
con-flict
  con-flict-ing
  con-flic-tive
  con-flic-tion
con-flu-ence
  con-flu-ent
con-flux
con-form
  con-form-ist
  con-form-ism
  con-form-a-ble
  con-form-a-bly
  con-form-ance
con-for-ma-tion
con-form-i-ty
  con-form-i-ties
con-found
  con-found-ed
  con-found-ed-ly

con-front
  con-fron-ta-tion
con-fuse
  confused
  con-fus-ing
  con-fus-ed-ly
  con-fus-ed-ness
con-fu-sion
con-fute
  con-futed
  con-fut-ing
  con-fu-ta-tion
con-ga
  con-gas
con-geal
  con-geal-ment
con-gen-ial
  con-ge-ni-al-i-ty
  con-gen-ial-ly
con-gen-i-tal
con-ger
  con-ge-ries
con-gest
  con-ges-tion
  con-ges-tive
con-glom-er-ate
  con-glom-er-at-ing
  con-glom-er-a-tion
con-grat-u-late
  con-grat-u-lat-ed
  con-grat-u-lat-ing
  con-grat-u-la-tor
  con-grat-u-la-to-ry
  con-grat-u-la-tion
con-gre-gate
  con-gre-gat-ed
  con-gre-gat-ing
con-gre-ga-tion
  con-gre-ga-tion-al
con-gress
  con-gres-sion-al
con-gress-man
  con-gress-men
  con-gress-wom-an
  con-gress-wom-en
con-gru-ent
  con-gru-ent-ly
  con-gru-ence

con-gru-en-cy
con-gru-en-cies
con-gru-i-ty
con-gru-i-ties
con-gru-ous
con-gru-ous-ly
con-ic
con-i-cal
co-ni-fer
con-jec-ture
con-jec-tured
con-jec-tur-ing
con-jec-tur-al
con-join
con-joint
con-joint-ly
con-ju-gal
con-ju-gal-ly
con-ju-gate
con-ju-gat-ed
con-ju-gat-ing
con-ju-ga-tion
con-ju-ga-tive
con-junc-tion
con-junc-tive
con-jur-a-tion
con-jure
con-jured
con-jur-ing
con-jur-er
con-nect
con-nec-tor
con-nec-tion
con-nec-tive
con-nip-tion
con-nive
con-nived
con-niv-ing
con-niv-ance
con-nois-seur
con-note
con-not-ed
con-not-ing
con-no-ta-tion
con-no-ta-tive
con-nu-bi-al
con-ni-bi-al-ly
con-quer

con-quer-a-ble
con-quer-or
con-quest
con-quis-ta-dor
con-quis-ta-dors
con-quis-ta-dor-es
con-san-quin-e-ous
con-san-quin-i-ty
con-science
con-sci-en-tious
con-sci-en-tious-ly
con-scious
con-scious-ly
con-scious-ness
con-script
con-scrip-tion
con-se-crate
con-se-crat-ed
con-se-crat-ing
con-se-cra-tive
con-se-cra-tion
con-sec-u-tive
con-sec-u-tive-ly
con-sen-sus
con-sent
con-sent-er
con-se-quence
con-se-quent
con-se-quent-ly
con-se-quen-tial
con-se-quen-ti-al-i-ty
con-se-quen-tial-ly
con-ser-va-tion
con-ser-va-tion-al
con-ser-va-tion-ist
con-serv-a-tive
con-serv-a-tism
con-ser-va-tive-ly
con-serv-a-to-ry
con-serv-a-to-ries
con-serve
con-served
con-serv-ing
con-serv-a-ble
con-serv-er
con-sid-er
con-sid-er-a-ble
con-sid-er-a-bly

con-sid-er-ate
con-sid-er-a-tion
con-sid-er-ing
con-sign
con-sign-er
con-sign-or
con-sign-ment
con-sign-ee
con-sist
con-sist-en-cy
con-sist-en-cies
con-sist-ence
con-sist-ent
con-sist-ent-ly
con-sis-to-ry
con-sis-to-ries
con-so-la-tion
con-sol-a-to-ry
con-sole
con-soled
con-sol-ing
con-sol-a-ble
con-sol-i-date
con-sol-i-dat-ed
con-sol-i-dat-ing
con-sol-i-da-tion
con-so-nant
con-so-nance
con-so-nant-ly
con-so-nan-tal
con-sort
con-sor-ti-um
con-sor-tia
con-spic-u-ous
con-spic-u-ous-ly
con-spic-u-ous-ness
con-spire
con-spired
con-spir-ing
con-spir-a-cy
con-spir-a-cies
con-spir-a-tor
con-spir-a-to-ri-al
con-spir-er
con-spir-ing-ly
con-sta-ble
con-sta-ble-ship
con-stab-u-lar-y

con-stab-u-lar-ies
con-stant
 con-stan-cy
con-stant-ly
con-stel-la-tion
con-ster-na-tion
con-sti-pate
 con-sti-pa-tion
con-stit-u-en-cy
 con-stit-u-en-cies
con-stit-u-ent
con-sti-tute
con-sti-tu-tion
 con-sti-tu-tion-al
 con-sti-tu-tion-al-i-ty
 con-sti-tu-tion-al-ly
con-strain
 con-strain-a-ble
 con-strained
con-straint
con-strict
 con-stric-tive
 con-stric-tion
con-stric-tor
con-struct
 con-struc-tor
con-struc-tion
 con-struc-tion-al
con-struc-tive
 con-struc-tive-ly
 con-struc-tive-ness
con-strue
 con-strued
 con-stru-ing
 con-stru-a-ble
 con-stru-er
con-sul
 con-su-lar
 con-sul-ship
con-su-late
con-sult
 con-sul-ta-tion
con-sult-ant
con-sume
 con-sumed
 con-sum-ing
 con-sum-a-ble
con-sum-er

con-sum-mate
 con-sum-mat-ed
 con-sum-mat-ing
 con-sum-mate-ly
 con-sum-ma-tion
con-sump-tion
com-sump-tive
con-tact
con-ta-gion
 con-ta-gious
 con-ta-gious-ness
con-tain
 con-tain-a-ble
con-tain-er
con-tain-ment
con-tam-i-nate
 con-tam-i-nat-ed
 con-tam-i-nat-ing
 con-tam-i-nant
 con-tam-i-na-tion
 con-tam-i-na-tive
 con-tam-i-na-tor
con-tem-plate
 con-tem-plat-ed
 con-tem-plat-ing
 con-tem-pla-tion
 con-tem-pla-tive
con-tem-po-ra-ne-ous
con-tem-po-rar-y
 con-tem-po-rar-ies
con-tempt
 con-tempt-i-ble
 con-tempt-i-bly
con-temp-tu-ous
 con-temp-tu-ous-ly
con-tend
 con-tend-er
con-tent
 con-tent-ment
con-tent-ed
 con-tent-ed-ly
 con-tent-ed-ness
con-ten-tion
con-ten-tious
 con-ten-tious-ly
 con-ten-tious-ness
con-ter-mi-ous
con-test

con-test-a-ble
con-test-er
con-test-ant
con-text
con-tig-u-ous
 con-ti-gu-i-ty
 con-ti-gu-i-ties
 con-tig-u-ous-ly
 con-tig-u-ous-ness
con-ti-nence
 con-ti-nen-cy
con-ti-nent
 con-ti-nent-ly
 con-ti-nen-tal
con-tin-gent
 con-tin-gen-cies
 con-tin-gent-ly
con-tin-u-al
 con-tin-u-al-ly
con-tin-u-ance
con-tin-ue
 con-tin-ued
 con-tin-u-ing
 con-tin-u-a-tion
 con-tin-u-er
con-ti-nu-i-ty
 con-ti-nu-i-ties
con-tin-u-ous
 con-tin-u-ous-ly
con-tin-u-um
 con-tin-ua
con-tort
 con-tor-tion
 con-tor-tive
 con-tor-tion-ist
con-tour
con-tra-band
can-tra-cep-tive
 con-tra-cep-tion
con-tract
 con-tract-ed
 con-tract-i-ble
 con-trac-tu-al
con-trac-tion
 con-trac-tive
 con-trac-tile
con-trac-tor
con-tra-dict

con-tra-dict-a-ble
con-tra-dic-tion
con-tra-dic-to-ry
con-tra-dis-tinc-tion
con-trail
con-tral-to
  con-tral-tos
  con-tral-ti
con-trap-tion
con-tra-pun-tal
con-tra-ri-wise
con-tra-ry
  con-tra-ries
  con-tra-ri-ly
  con-tra-ri-ness
con-trast
  con-trast-a-ble
  con-trast-ing-ly
con-tra-vene
  con-tra-vened
  con-tra-ven-ing
  con-tra-ven-er
  con-tra-ven-tion
con-trib-ute
  con-trib-ut-ed
  con-trib-ut-ing
  con-trib-ut-a-ble
  con-trib-u-tor
  con-trib-u-tory
con-tri-bu-tion
con-trite
  con-trite-ly
  con-trite-ness
  con-tri-tion
con-trive
  con-triv-ed
  con-triv-ing
  con-triv-ance
con-trol
  con-trolled
  con-trol-ling
  con-trol-la-ble
con-trol-ler
  con-trol-ler-ship
con-tro-ver-sy
  con-tro-ver-sies
  con-tro-ver-sal
  con-tro-ver-sial-ly

con-tro-vert
con-tu-me-ly
  con-tu-me-lies
con-tuse
  con-tused
  con-tus-ing
  con-tu-sion
co-nun-drum
cov-va-lesce
  con-va-lesced
  con-va-les-cing
con-va-les-cence
  con-va-les-cent
con-vec-tion
con-vene
  con-vened
  con-ven-ing
  con-ven-er
con-ven-ience
con-ven-ient
  con-ven-ient-ly
con-vent
con-ven-tion
  con-ven-tion-al
  con-ven-tion-al-ism
  con-ven-tion-al-ist
  con-ven-tion-al-i-ty
  con-ven-tion-al-i-ties
  con-ven-tion-al-ize
  con-ven-tion-al-ized
  con-ven-tion-al-iz-ing
con-verge
  con-verged
  con-verg-ing
  con-ver-gence
  con-ver-gen-cy
  con-ver-gent
con-ver-sant
con-ver-sa-tion
  con-ver-sa-tion-al
  con-ver-sa-tion-al-ist
con-verse
  con-versed
  con-vers-ing
  con-verse-ly
con-ver-sion
con-vert
con-vert-er

con-vert-i-ble
  con-vert-i-bil-i-ty
  con-vert-i-bly
con-vex
  con-vex-ly
  con-vex-i-ty
con-vey
  con-vey-a-ble
con-vey-ance
con-vey-er
  con-vey-or
con-vict
con-vic-tion
  con-vic-tion-al
con-vince
  con-vinced
  con-vinc-ing
  con-vinc-er
  con-vinc-i-ble
con-viv-i-al
  con-viv-i-al-i-ty
  con-viv-i-al-ly
con-vo-ca-tion
  con-vo-ca-tion-al
con-voke
  con-voked
  con-vok-ing
  con-vok-er
con-vo-lute
  con-vo-lut-ed
  con-vo-lut-ing
  con-vo-lute-ly
  con-vo-lu-tion
con-voy
con-vulse
  con-vulsed
  con-vuls-ing
con-vul-sion
  con-vul-sive
  con-vul-sive-ly
co-ny
coo
  cooed
  coo-ing
  coo-ing-ly
cook-book
cook-er-y
  cook-e-ries

cook-out
cool
  cool-ish
  cool-ly
  cool-ness
cool-ant
cool-er
coo-lie
  coo-lies
coon-skin
coop-er
coop-er-age
co-op-er-ate
  co-op-er-at-ed
  co-op-er-at-ing
co-op-er-a-tion
co-op-er-a-tive
  co-op-er-a-tive-ly
co-opt
co-op-ta-tion
co-or-di-nate
  co-or-di-nat-ed
  co-or-di-nat-ing
  co-or-di-nate-ly
  co-or-di-na-tor
  co-or-di-na-tion
coo-tie
cop
  copped
  cop-ping
cope-stone
co-pi-lot
co-pi-ous
  co-pi-ous-ly
  co-pi-ous-ness
cop-out
cop-per
  cop-per-y
cop-per-head
cop-per-plate
cop-pice
cop-ra
copse
cop-u-la
  cop-u-las
  cop-u-lae
  cop-u-lar
cop-u-late

cop-u-lat-ed
cop-u-lat-ing
cop-u-la-tion
cop-u-la-tive
cop-u-la-tive-ly
copy
  cop-ies
  cop-ied
  cop-y-ing
cop-y-book
cop-y-cat
cop-y-ist
cop-y-right
co-quet
  co-quet-ted
  co-quet-ting
co-quet-ry
  co-quet-ries
co-quette
  co-quet-tish
  co-quet-tish-ly
cor-a-cle
cor-al
cor-bel
cord-age
cor-date
  cor-date-ly
cor-dial
  cor-dial-i-ty
  cor-dial-ness
  cor-dial-ly
cor-dil-le-ra
cord-ite
cor-don
cor-do-van
cor-du-roy
cord-wood
core
  cored
  cor-ing
co-re-la-tion
co-re-spond-ent
co-ri-an-der
cor-ker
cork-screw
corn-cob
cor-nea
  cor-ne-al

cor-ner
cor-ner-stone
cor-net
  cor-net-ist
corn-flow-er
cor-nice
corn-starch
cor-nu-co-pi-a
corn-y
  corn-i-er
  conr-i-est
co-rol-la
cor-ol-lar-y
  cor-ol-lar-ies
co-ro-na
  co-ro-nas
  co-ro-nae
cor-o-nar-y
cor-o-na-tion
cor-o-ner
  cor-o-ner-ship
cor-o-net
  cor-o-net-ed
cor-po-ral
cor-po-rate
  cor-po-rate-ly
  cor-po-ra-tive
cor-po-ra-tion
cor-po-rat-ism
cor-po-re-al
  cor-po-re-al-i-ty
  cor-po-re-al-ness
corps
corpse
corps-man
  corps-men
cor-pu-lent
  cor-pu-lence
  cor-pu-len-cy
cor-pus
cor-pus-cle
  cor-pus-cu-lar
cor-ral
  cor-ralled
  cor-ral-ling
cor-rect
  cor-rect-a-ble
  cor-rect-i-ble

cor-rect-ness
cor-rec-tor
cor-rec-tion
cor-rec-tion-al
cor-rec-tive
cor-re-late
cor-re-lat-ed
cor-re-lat-ing
cor-re-la-tion
cor-rel-a-tive
cor-re-spond
cor-re-spond-ing
cor-re-spond-ing-ly
cor-re-spond-ence
cor-re-spond-ent
cor-ri-dor
cor-ri-gi-ble
cor-ri-gi-bil-i-ty
cor-ri-gi-bly
cor-rob-o-rate
cor-rob-o-rat-ed
cor-rob-o-rat-ing
cor-rob-o-ra-tion
cor-rob-o-ra-tive
cor-rob-o-ra-to-ry
cor-rode
cor-rod-ed
cor-rod-ing
cor-rod-i-ble
cor-ro-sion
cor-ro-sive
cor-ru-gate
cor-ru-gat-ed
cor-ru-gat-ing
cor-ru-ga-tion
cor-rupt
cor-rupt-er
cor-rup-ti-ble
cor-rup-ti-bil-i-ty
cor-rupt-ly
cor-rupt-ness
cor-rup-tion
cor-sage
cor-sair
cor-set
cor-set-ed
cor-tex
cor-ti-ces

cor-ti-cal
cor-ti-sone
co-run-dum
co-sig-na-to-ry
cos-met-ic
cos-mic
cos-mi-cal-ly
cos-mog-o-ny
cos-mog-o-nies
cos-mo-gon-ic
cos-mog-o-nist
cos-mog-o-ny
cos-mog-o-nist
cos-mog-ra-phy
cos-mog-ra-phies
cos-mog-ra-pher
cos-mo-graph-ic
cos-mol-o-gy
cos-mol-o-gies
cos-mo-log-ic
cos-mol-o-gist
cos-mo-naut
cos-mo-pol-i-tan
cos-mo-pol-i-tan-ism
cos-mop-o-lite
cos-mos
cost-ly
cost-li-er
cost-li-est
cost-li-ness
cost--plus
cos-tume
cos-tumed
cos-tum-ing
cos-tum-er
co-sy
co-si-er
cos-i-est
co-te-rie
co-ter-mi-nous
co-til-lion
cot-tage
cot-ter
cot-ton
cot-ton-y
cot-ton-mouth
cot-ton-seed
cot-ton-tail

cot-ton-wood
couch
coun-cil
coun-cil-or
coun-cil-man
coun-cil-lor-ship
count
count-a-ble
count-down
coun-te-nance
coun-te-nanced
coun-te-nanc-ing
coun-te-nanc-er
count-er
coun-ter-act
coun-ter-ac-tion
coun-ter-ac-tive
coun-ter-at-tack
coun-ter-charge
coun-ter-charged
coun-ter-char-ging
coun-ter-claim
coun-ter-claim-ant
coun-ter-clock-wise
coun-ter-cul-ture
coun-ter-es-pi-o-nage
coun-ter-feit
coun-ter-feit-er
coun-ter-in-tel-li-gence
coun-ter-mand
coun-ter-meas-ure
coun-ter-of-fen-sive
coun-ter-pane
coun-ter-part
coun-ter-point
coun-ter-poise
coun-ter-poised
coun-ter-pois-ing
coun-ter-rev-o-lu-tion
coun-ter-sign
coun-ter-sig-na-ture
coun-ter-sink
coun-ter-sank
coun-ter-sunk
coun-ter-spy
coun-ter-spies
coun-ter-weight
coun-tees

count-less
coun-tri-fied
coun-try
 coun-tries
coun-try-man
 coun-try-men
 coun-try-wom-an
 coun-try-wom-en
coun-try-side
coun-ty
 coun-ties
coup
 coups
coup-le
 coup-led
 coup-ling
coup-ler
cou-pon
cour-age
 cou-ra-geous
cour-i-er
course
 coursed
 cours-ing
cours-er
cour-te-ous
 cour-te-ous-ly
cour-te-sy
 cour-te-sies
court-house
cour-ti-er
court-ly
 court-li-er
 court-li-est
 court-li-ness
court-mar-tial
 courts-mar-tial
 court-mar-tialed
 court-mar-tial-ling
court-room
court-ship
court-yard
cous-in
 cous-in-hood
 cous-in-ly
cou-tu-rier
cov-e-nant
 cov-e-nan-ter

cov-e-nan-tor
cov-er
 cov-ered
 cov-er-ing
 cov-er-less
cov-er-age
cov-er-all
cov-er-let
cov-ert
 cov-ert-ly
 cov-ert-ness
cov-er-up
cov-et
 cov-et-a-ble
 cov-et-er
cov-et-ous
 cov-et-ous-ly
cov-ey
cow-ard
 cow-ard-ly
 cow-ard-li-ness
cow-ard-ice
cow-boy
cow-er
 cow-er-ing-ly
cow-hide
cowl
 cowled
cow-lick
cowl-ing
cow-man
 cow-men
co-work-er
cow-poke
cow-pox
cow-ry
 cow-rie
 cow-ries
cox-swain
coy
 coy-ly
 coy-ness
coy-o-te
coz-en
 coz-en-age
 coz-en-er
co-zy
 co-zi-er

co-zi-est
co-zi-ly
co-zi-ness
crab
 crabbed
 crab-bing
 crab-by
 crab-bed-ly
 crab-bed-ness
crack-down
crack-er
crack-ing
crack-le
 crack-led
 crack-ling
crack-up
cra-dle
 cra-dled
 cra-dling
crafts-man
 crafts-man-ship
crafty
 craft-i-er
 craft-i-est
 craft-i-ly
 craft-i-ness
crag
 crag-ged
 crag-gy
 crag-gi-ness
cram
 crammed
 cram-ming
 cram-mer
cran-ber-ry
 cran-ber-ries
crane
 craned
 cran-ing
cra-ni-um
 cra-ni-ums
 cra-nia
 cra-ni-al
 cra-ni-ate
 cra-ni-al-ly
crank-case
crank-shaft
crank-y

crank-i-er
crank-i-est
crank-i-ly
crank-i-ness
cran-ny
cran-nies
cran-nied
crash-land
crass
crass-ly
crass-ness
crate
crat-ed
crat-ing
cra-ter
cra-ter-al
cra-tered
cra-vat
crave
craved
crav-ing
crav-er
crav-ing-ly
craw-fish
crawl
crawl-y
crawl-ing-ly
crawl-er
cray-fish
cray-on
craze
craz-ing
cra-zy
cra-zi-er
cra-zi-est
cra-zi-ly
cra-zi-ness
creak
creak-i-ly
creak-i-ness
creaky
creak-i-er
creak-i-est
cream
cream-i-ly
cream-i-ness
cream-y
cream-i-er

cream-i-est
cream-er
cream-er-y
cream-er-ies
crease
creased
creas-ing
creas-y
creas-i-er
creas-i-est
cre-ate
cre-at-ed
cre-at-ing
cre-a-tion
cre-a-tion-al
cre-a-tive
cre-a-tive-i-ty
cre-a-tor
crea-ture
cre-dence
cre-den-tial
cre-den-za
cred-i-ble
cred-i-bil-i-ty
cred-i-bly
cred-it
cred-it-a-ble
cred-it-a-bil-i-ty
cred-it-a-bly
cred-i-tor
cre-do
cre-dos
cred-u-lous
creek
creel
creep
crept
creep-ing
creepy
creep-i-er
creep-i-est
creep-i-ness
creep-er
cre-mate
cre-mat-ed
cre-mat-ing
cre-ma-tion
cre-ma-tor

cre-ma-to-ry
cre-ma-to-ri-um
cre-o-sote
crepe
creped
crep-ing
cre-pus-cu-lar
cres-cen-do
cres-cent
crest
crest-ed
crest-less
crest-fall-en
cre-ta-ceous
cre-tin-ism
cre-tonne
cre-vasse
crev-ice
crew-el
crib
cribbed
crib-bing
crib-ber
crib-bage
crick-et
cri-er
crim-i-nal
crim-i-nal-i-ty
crim-i-nal-ly
crim-i-nol-o-gy
crim-i-nol-o-gist
crimpy
crimp-i-er
crimp-i-est
crim-son
cringe
cringed
cring-ing
crin-kle
crin-kled
crin-kling
crin-kly
crin-kli-er
crin-kli-est
crip-ple
crip-pled
crip-pling
cri-sis

cri-ses
crisp
crisp-er
crisp-ness
crispy
crisp-i-er
crisp-i-est
criss-cross
cri-te-ri-on
cri-te-ria
crit-ic
crit-i-cal
crit-i-cal-ly
crit-i-cal-ness
crit-i-cism
crit-i-cize
crit-i-cized
crit-i-ciz-ing
crit-i-ciz-a-ble
cri-tique
crit-er
croak-y
croak-i-er
croak-i-est
croak-er
cro-chet
cro-cheted
cro-chet-ing
cro-chet-er
crock-ery
croc-o-dile
cro-cus
cro-cus-es
crois-sant
cro-ny
cro-nies
crook-ed
croon-er
crop
cropped
crop-ping
crop-per
cro-quette
cross-bar
cross-bones
cross-bow
cross-bred
cross-breed

cross-breed-ing
cross-coun-try
cross-cut
cross-ex-am-ine
cross-ex-am-ined
cross-ex-am-in-ing
cross-fer-ti-li-za-tion
cross-ing
cross-pol-li-na-tion
cross-pol-li-nate
cross-pur-pose
cross-ref-er-ence
cross-stitch
cross-ways
crotch-ety
crotch-et-i-ness
crouch
croup
croupy
crou-pi-er
crou-ton
crow-bar
crow's--foot
crow's--feet
crow's--nest
cru-cial
cru-ci-al-i-ty
cru-cial-ly
cru-ci-ble
cru-ci-fix
cru-ci-fix-ion
cru-ci-form
cru-ci-fy
cru-ci-fied
cru-ci-fy-ing
crude
crud-er
crud-est
crude-ly
crude-ness
cru-di-ty
cru-di-ties
cru-el
cru-el-ly
cru-el-ness
cru-el-ty
cru-et
cruise

cruised
cruis-ing
cruis-er
crul-ler
crum-ble
crum-bled
crum-bling
crum-bly
crum-my
crum-mi-er
crum-mi-est
crum-pet
crum-ple
crum-pled
crum-pling
crum-pler
crum-ply
crum-pli-er
crum-pli-est
crunchy
crunch-i-er
crunch-i-est
cru-sade
cru-sad-er
crush-er
crush-ing
crush-ing-ly
crus-ta-cean
crust-y
crust-i-er
crust-i-est
crust-i-ly
crust-i-ness
crux
crux-es
cru-ces
cry
cried
cry-ing
cry-ba-by
cry-o-gen-ics
cry-o-sur-gery
crypt
crypt-al
crypt-a-nal-y-sis
crypt-ic
cryp-ti-cal
cryp-ti-cal-ly

cryp-to-gram
cryp-to-graph
  cryp-tog-ra-phy
  cryp-to-graph-ic
  cryp-tog-ra-pher
crys-tal
crys-tal-line
crys-tal-lize
  crys-tal-lized
  crys-tal-liz-ing
  crys-tal-liz-er
  crys-tal-liz-a-ble
  crys-tal-li-za-tion
cub-by
  cub-bies
cu-by-hole
cube
  cubed
  cub-ing
cu-bic
cu-bi-cle
cub-ism
cu-bit
cuck-old
  cuck-old-ry
cuck-oo
  cuck-oos
  cuck-ooed
  cuck-oo-ing
cu-cum-ber
cud-dle
  cud-dled
  cud-dling
  cud-dle-some
  cud-dly
  cud-dli-er
  cud-dli-est
cudg-el
  cudg-eled
  cudg-el-ing
cue
  cued
  cu-ing
cui-sine
cul-de-sac
  culs-de-sac
cu-li-nary
cul-mi-nant

cul-mi-nate
  cul-mi-nat-ed
  cul-mi-nat-ing
  cul-mi-na-tion
cu-lottes
cul-pa-ble
  cul-pa-bil-i-ty
  cul-pa-bly
cul-prit
cult
  cul-tic
cul-ti-vate
  cul-ti-vat-ed
  cul-ti-vat-ing
  cul-ti-va-tion
  cul-ti-va-ble
  cul-ti-vat-a-ble
cul-ti-va-tor
cul-tur-al
cul-ture
  cul-tured
  cul-tur-ing
cul-vert
cum-ber
  cum-ber-some
cum-brance
cum lau-de
cum-mer-bound
cum-mu-late
  cum-mu-lat-ed
  cum-mu-lat-ing
  cum-mu-la-tion
  cum-mu-la-tive
cu-mu-lo-nim-bus
  cu-mu-lo-nim-bus-es
cu-mu-lus
  cu-mu-lous
cu-ne-i-form
cum-ni-lin-gus
cun-ning
  cun-ning-ly
  cun-ning-ness
cup
  cupped
  cup-ping
cup-board
cup-cake
cup-ful

cup-fuls
cu-pid-i-ty
cu-po-la
cur-a-ble
  cur-a-bil-i-ty
  cur-a-bly
cu-rate
cur-a-tive
cu-ra-tor
  cu-ra-to-ri-al
  cu-ra-tor-ship
curb-ing
curb-stone
cur-dle
  cur-dled
  cur-dling
cure
  cured
  cur-ing
  cur-er
cure-all
cur-few
cu-ria
  cu-ri-ae
cu-ri-al
cu-rie
cu-ri-o
  cu-ri-os
cu-ri-os-i-ty
  cu-ri-os-i-ties
cu-ri-ous
cu-ri-um
curl
  curl-er
curl-i-cue
curl-ing
curly
  curl-i-er
  curl-i-est
  curl-i-ness
cur-rant
cur-ren-cy
  cur-ren-cies
cur-rent
cur-ric-u-lum
  cur-ric-u-lums
  cur-ric-u-la
  cur-ric-u-lar

cur-rish
cur-ry
  cur-ries
  cur-ried
  cur-ry-ing
  cur-ri-er
cur-ry-comb
curse
cur-sive
  cur-sive-ly
cur-so-ry
  cur-so-ri-ly
  cur-so-ri-ness
curt
cur-tail
  cur-tail-ment
cur-tain
curt-sy
  curt-sies
  curt-sied
  curt-sy-ing
cur-va-ceous
cur-va-ture
curve
  cruved
  curv-ing
  curv-ed-nesss
cur-vi-lin-e-ar
cush-ion
cush-y
  cush-i-er
  cush-i-est
cus-pid
  cus-pi-dal
cus-pi-date
  cus-pi-dat-ed
cus-pi-da-tion
cus-pi-dor
cuss-ed
  cuss-ed-ly
  cuss-ed-ness
cus-tard
cus-to-di-al
cus-to-dian
  cus-to-di-an-ship
cus-to-dy
  cus-to-dies
cus-tom

cus-tom-ary
  cus-tom-ar-ies
  cus-tom-ar-i-ly
  cus-tom-ari-ness
cus-tom-built
cus-tom-er
cus-tom-ize
  cus-tom-ized
  cos-tom-iz-er
  cus-tom-iz-ing
cus-tom-made
cut-abil-i-ty
cu-ta-ne-ous
  cu-ta-ne-ous-ly
cut-away
cut-back
cutch
cute
  cut-er
  cut-est
  cute-ly
  cute-ness
cute-sy
  cute-si-er
  cute-si-est
cu-ti-cle
  cu-tic-u-lar
cu-tin
  cu-tin-ized
cu-tis
cut-lass
cut-ler
cut-lery
cut-let
cut-line
cut-ta-ble
cut-ter
cut-throat
cut-ting
  cut-ting-ly
cut-tle
cut-tle-fish
cut-up
cu-vette
cy-an
cy-an-a-mide
cy-a-nate
cy-an-ic

cy-a-nide
cy-a-nine
cy-a-nite
cy-a-no
cy-ano-gen
cy-a-nosed
cy-a-no-sis
cy-an-urate
cy-ber-nat-ed
cy-ber-na-tion
cy-ber-net-ic
  cy-ber-net-ics
cy-borg
cy-cad-e-oid
cy-ca-sin
cy-cla-mate
cyc-la-men
cy-cle
cy-clic
  cy-cli-cal
  cy-cli-cal-ly
cy-clom-e-ter
cy-clone
cy-clo-rama
  cy-clo-ram-ic
cy-clo-tron
cyg-net
cyl-in-der
  cy-lin-dric
  cy-lin-dri-cal
cym-bal
  cym-bal-ist
cyn-ic
  cyn-i-cism
cyn-i-cal
  cyn-i-cal-ly
cy-no-sure
cy-pher
cy-press
cyst
  cys-tic
cys-tic fi-bro-sis
cy-tol-o-gy
  cy-tol-o-gist
czar
czar-das
czar-e-vitch
cza-ri-na

dab
dabbed
dab-bing
dab-ble
dab-bled
dab-bing
dab-bler
dac-tyl
dac-tyl-ic
dad-dy--long-legs
daf-fo-dil
daf-fy
daf-fi-er
daf-fi-est
dag-ger
da-guerre-o-type
dahl-ia
dai-ly
dai-lies
dain-ty
dain-ti-er
dain-ti-est
dain-ties
dain-ti-ly
dain-ti-ness
dai-qui-ri
dair-y
dair-ies
dair-y-man
dair-y-men
da-is
dai-sy
dai-sies
dal-ly
dal-lied
dal-ly-ing
dal-li-ance
dam-age
dam-aged
dam-ag-ing
dam-age-a-ble
dam-a-scene
dam-a-scened
dam-a-scen-ing
dam-ask
damn
dam-na-ble
dam-na-ble-ness

dam-na-bly
dam-na-tion
damned
damp-en
damp-er
dam-sel
dam-son
dan-de-li-on
dan-der
dan-dle
dan-dled
dan-dling
dan-druff
dan-dy
dan-dies
dan-di-er
dan-di-est
dan-dy-ism
dan-ger
dan-ger-ous
dan-ger-ous-ly
dan-ger-ous-ness
dan-gle
dan-gled
dan-gling
dan-gler
dank
dank-ly
dank-ness
dan-seuse
dan-seus-es
dap-per
dap-ple
dap-pled
dap-pling
dare
dared
dar-ing
dare-dev-il
dar-ing-ly
dark
dark-ish
dark-ly
dark-ness
dark-en
dark-ling
dark-room
dar-ling

dar-ling-ly
dar-ling-ness
darn-er
dart-er
dash-board
dash-er
da-shi-ki
dash-ing
dash-ing-ly
das-tard
das-tard-li-ness
das-tard-ly
da-ta
da-ta-ma-tion
date
dat-ed
dat-ing
dat-a-ble
dat-er
date-less
date-line
da-tive
da-tum
da-tu-ra
daub
daub-er
daugh-ter
daugh-ter-less
daugh-ter-ly
daugh-ter--in--law
daugh-ters--in--law
daunt
daunt-less
daunt-less-ly
daunt-less-ness
dau-phin
da-ven
dav-en-port
da-vit
daw-dle
daw-dled
daw-dling
daw-dler
dawn
day-bed
day-break
day-dream
day-dream-er

day-light
day-time
daze
  dazed
  daz-ing
  daz-ed-ly
  daz-ed-ness
daz-zle
  daz-zled
  daz-zling
  daz-zler
  daz-zling-ly
de-acid-i-fy
dea-con
  dea-con-ry
  dea-con-ship
dea-con-ess
de-ac-ti-vate
  de-ac-ti-va-tion
  de-ac-ti-va-tor
dead-beat
dead-en
  dead-ened
  dead-en-er
  dead-en-ing
  dead-en-ing-ly
dead-end
dead-light
dead-line
dead-lock
dead-ly
  dead-li-er
  dead-li-est
  dead-li-ness
dead-pan
dead-weight
dead-wood
de-aer-ate
  de-aer-a-tion
deaf
  deaf-ish
  deaf-ly
  deaf-ness
deaf-en
  deaf-ened
  deaf-en-ing
  deaf-en-ing-ly
deaf-mute

deal
  dealt
  deal-ing
  deal-er
de-alate
  de-alat-ed
deal-er-ship
deal-fish
de-am-i-nase
de-am-i-nate
dean-ery
dean-ship
dear
  dear-ly
  dear-ness
dearth
death
  death-less
  death-ly
death-blow
death-trap
death-watch
de-ba-cle
de-bar
  de-barred
  de-bar-ring
  de-bar-ment
de-bark
  de-bar-ka-tion
de-base
  de-based
  de-bas-ing
  de-base-ment
  de-bas-er
de-bate
  de-bat-ed
  de-bat-ing
  de-bat-a-ble
  de-bat-er
de-bauch
  de-bauch-er
  de-bauch-ment
  de-bauch-ery
  de-bauch-er-ies
deb-au-chee
de-ben-ture
de-bil-i-tate
  de-bil-i-tat-ed

de-bil-i-tat-ing
de-bil-i-ta-tion
de-bil-i-ty
  de-bil-i-ties
deb-it
deb-o-nair
de-bris
debt-or
de-bunk
  de-bunk-er
de-but
deb-u-tante
de-cade
dec-a-dent
  dec-a-dence
  dec-a-dent-ly
dec-a-gon
dec-a-gram
dec-a-he-dron
  dec-a-he-drons
de-cal
de-camp
  de-camp-ment
de-cant
  de-cant-er
de-cap-i-tate
  de-cap-i-tat-ed
  de-cap-i-tat-ing
  de-cap-i-ta-tion
dec-a-pod
de-cath-lon
de-cay
de-crease
  de-creased
de-ceit
  de-ceit-ful
  de-ceit-ful-ly
  de-ceit-ful-ness
de-ceive
  de-ceived
  de-ceiv-ing
  de-ceiv-er
  de-ceiv-ing-ly
  de-ceiv-a-ble
de-cel-er-ate
  de-cel-er-at-ed
  de-cel-er-at-ing
  de-cel-er-a-tion

de-cen-cy
  de-cen-cies
de-cen-ni-al
  de-cen-ni-al-ly
de-cent
  de-cent-ly
de-cen-tral-ize
  de-cen-tral-ized
  de-cen-tral-iz-ing
  de-cen-tral-i-za-tion
de-cep-tion
  de-cep-tive
  de-cep-tive-ly
  de-cep-tive-ness
dec-i-bel
de-cide
  de-cid-ed
  de-cid-ing
  de-cid-a-ble
  de-cid-ed-ly
  de-cid-ed-ness
de-cid-u-ous
  de-cid-u-ous-ly
dec-i-mal
dec-i-mate
  dec-i-mat-ed
  dec-i-mat-ing
  dec-i-ma-tion
de-ci-pher
  de-ci-pher-a-ble
de-ci-sion
de-ci-sive
  de-ci-sive-ly
  de-ci-sive-ness
deck-le edge
de-claim
  dec-la-ma-tion
  de-clam-a-tory
de-clare
  de-clared
  de-clar-ing
  de-clar-a-tive
  de-clar-a-to-ry
  de-clar-er
  dec-la-ra-tion
de-clas-si-fy
  de-clas-si-fied
  de-clas-si-fy-ing

de-clen-sion
dec-li-na-tion
de-cline
  de-clined
  de-clin-ing
  de-clin-a-ble
de-cliv-i-ty
  de-cliv-i-ties
de-code
  de-cod-ed
  de-cod-ing
  de-cod-er
de-com-pose
  de-com-posed
  de-com-pos-ing
  de-com-po-si-tion
de-com-press
  de-com-pres-sion
de-con-tam-i-nate
  de-con-tam-i-nat-ed
  de-con-tam-i-nat-ing
  de-con-tam-i-na-tion
de-con-trol
  de-con-trolled
  de-con-trol-ling
de-cor
dec-o-rate
  dec-o-rat-ed
  dec-o-rat-ing
  dec-o-ra-tion
  dec-o-ra-tive
  dec-o-ra-tive-ly
  dec-o-ra-tor
dec-o-rous
  dec-o-rous-ly
de-co-rum
de-coy
de-crease
  de-creased
  de-creas-ing
  de-creas-ing-ly
de-cree
  de-creed
  de-cree-ing
de-crep-it
  de-crep-i-tude
  de-crep-it-ly
de-cre-scen-do

de-cre-scen-dos
de-cry
  de-cried
  de-cry-ing
  de-cri-al
ded-i-cate
  ded-i-cat-ed
  ded-i-cat-ing
  ded-i-ca-to-ry
  ded-i-ca-tive
  ded-i-ca-tion
de-duce
  de-duc-i-ble
de-duct
  de-duct-i-ble
de-duc-tion
  de-duc-tive
  de-duc-tive-ly
deep
  deep-ly
  deep-ness
deep-en
deep-root-ed
deep-seat-ed
deer-skin
de-es-ca-late
  de-es-ca-lat-ed
  de-es-ca-lat-ing
  de-es-ca-la-tion
de-face
  de-faced
  de-fac-ing
  de-face-ment
  de-fac-er
de fac-to
de-fame
  de-famed
  de-fam-ing
  def-a-ma-tion
  de-fam-a-to-ry
  de-fam-er
de-fault
  de-fault-er
de-feat
de-feat-ism
  de-feat-ist
def-e-cate
  def-e-cat-ed

def-e-cat-ing
def-e-ca-tion
de-fect
de-fec-tion
de-fec-tor
de-fec-tive
de-fec-tive-ly
de-fec-tive-ness
de-fend
de-fend-er
de-fend-ant
de-fense
de-fense-less
de-fense-less-ly
de-fense-less-ness
de-fen-si-ble
de-fen-si-bil-i-ty
de-fen-si-bly
de-fen-sive
de-fen-sive-ly
de-fer
de-ferred
de-fer-ring
de-fer-ment
def-er-ence
def-er-en-tial
def-er-en-tial-ly
de-fi-ance
de-fi-ant
de-fi-ant-ly
de-fi-cient
de-fi-cien-cy
de-fi-cien-cies
de-fi-cient-ly
def-i-cit
de-file
de-filed
de-fil-ing
de-fine
de-fined
de-fin-ing
de-fin-er
de-fin-a-ble
de-fin-a-bly
def-i-nite
def-i-nite-ly
def-i-nite-ness
def-i-ni-tion

de-fin-i-tive
de-fin-i-tive-ly
de-flate
de-flat-ed
de-flat-ing
de-fla-tion
de-fla-tion-ary
de-flect
de-flec-tion
de-flec-tive
de-flec-tor
de-flow-er
de-fo-li-ate
de-fo-li-at-ed
de-fo-li-at-ing
de-for-est
de-for-est-a-tion
de-form
de-for-ma-tion
de-formed
de-form-i-ty
de-form-i-ties
de-fraud
de-fray
de-fray-al
de-fray-ment
de-fray-a-ble
de-frost
de-frost-er
deft
deft-ly
deft-ness
de-funct
de-fy
de-fied
de-fy-ing
de-fi-er
de-gen-er-ate
de-gen-er-at-ed
de-gen-er-at-ing
de-gen-er-ate-ly
de-gen-er-a-cy
de-gen-er-a-tion
de-gen-er-a-tive
de-grade
de-graded
de-grad-ing
deg-ra-da-tion

de-gree
de-his-cence
de-his-cent
de-hy-drate
de-hy-drat-ed
de-hy-drat-ing
de-hy-dra-tion
de-i-fy
de-i-fied
de-i-fy-ing
de-i-fi-ca-tion
de-i-fi-er
deign
de-ist
de-ism
de-is-tic
de-is-ti-cal
de-i-ty
de-i-ties
de-ject-ed
de-jec-ted-ly
de-jec-tion
de ju-re
de-lay
de-lay-er
de-lec-ta-ble
de-lec-ta-ble-ness
de-lec-ta-bly
de-lec-ta-tion
del-e-gate
del-e-gat-ed
del-e-gat-ing
del-e-ga-tion
de-lete
de-let-ed
de-let-ing
de-le-tion
del-e-te-ri-ous
de-lib-er-ate
de-lib-er-at-ed
de-lib-er-at-ing
de-lib-er-ate-ly
de-lib-er-ate-ness
de-lib-er-a-tion
de-lib-er-a-tive
de-lib-er-a-tor
del-i-ca-cy
del-i-ca-cies

del-i-cate
  del-i-cate-ly
  del-i-cate-ness
del-i-ca-tes-sen
de-li-cious
  de-li-cious-ly
  de-li-cious-ness
de-lim-it
  de-lim-i-ta-tion
de-lin-e-ate
  de-lin-e-at-ed
  de-lin-e-at-ing
  de-lin-e-a-tion
  de-lin-e-a-tor
de-lin-quent
  de-lin-quen-cy
  de-lin-quen-cies
de-lir-i-um
  de-lir-i-ums
  de-lir-ia
  de-lir-i-ous
  de-lir-i-ous-ly
de-liv-er
  de-liv-er-a-ble
  de-liv-er-er
de-liv-er-ance
de-liv-ery
  de-liv-er-ies
de-louse
  de-loused
  de-lous-ing
del-phin-i-um
del-ta
del-toid
de-lude
  de-lud-ed
  de-lud-ing
  de-lud-er
  de-lu-sive
  de-lu-so-ry
  de-lu-sive-ly
del-uge
  del-uged
  del-ug-ing
de-lu-sion
de-luxe
delve
  delved

delv-ing
dem-a-gogue
  dem-a-gogu-ery
  dem-a-gog-ic
  dem-a-gog-i-cal
de-mand
  de-mand-er
de-mar-ca-tion
de-mean
de-mean-or
de-ment-ed
de-men-tia
de-mer-it
dem-i-god
de-mise
  de-mised
  de-mis-ing
dem-i-tasse
de-mo-bi-lize
  de-mo-bi-lized
  de-mo-bi-liz-ing
  de-mo-bi-li-za-tion
de-moc-ra-cy
  de-moc-ra-cies
dem-o-crat
dem-o-crat-ic
  dem-o-crat-i-cal-ly
de-moc-ra-tize
  de-moc-ra-tized
  de-moc-ra-tiz-ing
  de-moc-ra-ti-za-tion
de-mog-ra-phy
  de-mog-ra-pher
  dem-o-graph-ic
de-mol-ish
  de-mol-ish-er
  dem-o-li-tion
de-mon
  de-mon-ic
de-mon-e-tize
  de-mon-e-tized
  de-mon-e-tiz-ing
  de-mon-e-ti-za-tion
de-mo-ni-ac
  de-mo-ni-a-cal
de-mon-ol-o-gy
  de-mon-ol-o-gist
dem-on-strate

dem-on-strat-ed
dem-on-strat-ing
de-mon-stra-ble
de-mon-stra-bly
dem-on-stra-tion
de-mon-stra-tive
  de-mon-stra-tive-ly
  de-mon-stra-tive-ness
  dem-on-stra-tor
de-mor-al-ize
  de-mor-al-ized
  de-mor-al-iz-ing
  de-mor-al-i-za-tion
  de-mor-al-iz-er
de-mote
  de-mot-ed
  de-mot-ing
  de-mo-tion
de-mur
  de-murred
  de-mur-ring
  de-mur-ral
  de-mur-er
  de-mur-est
  de-mure-ly
  de-mure-ness
de-mur-rage
de-nat-u-ral-ize
  de-nat-u-ral-ized
  de-nat-u-ral-iz-ing
  de-nat-u-ral-i-za-tion
de-na-ture
  de-na-tured
  de-na-tur-ing
den-drite
den-dro-lite
den-drol-o-gy
den-e-ga-tion
de-ni-al
de-ni-er
den-im
den-i-zen
de-nom-i-nate
  de-nom-i-nat-ed
  de-nom-i-nat-ing
de-nom-i-na-tion
  de-nom-i-na-tion-al
  de-nom-i-na-tion-al-ism

de-nom-i-na-tive
de-nom-i-na-tor
de-note
  de-not-ed
  de-not-ing
  de-no-ta-tion
de-noue-ment
de-nounce
  de-nounced
  de-noun-cing
  de-nounce-ment
  de-nun-ci-a-tion
  de-nun-ci-a-to-ry
dense
  den-ser
  den-sest
  dense-ly
  dense-ness
den-si-ty
  den-si-ties
den-tal
den-tate
den-ti-frice
den-tin
den-tist
den-tist-ry
den-ti-tion
den-ture
de-nude
  de-nud-ed
  de-nud-ing
  den-u-da-tion
de-nun-ci-ate
  de-nun-ci-at-ed
  de-nun-ci-at-ing
  de-nun-ci-a-tion
  de-nun-ci-a-to-ry
de-ny
  de-nied
  de-ny-ing
de-o-dor-ant
  de-o-dor-ize
  de-o-dor-ized
  de-o-dor-iz-ing
de-part
de-part-ed
de-part-ment
  de-part-men-tal

de-par-ture
de-pend
  de-pend-ence
de-pend-a-ble
  de-pend-a-bly
  de-pend-a-bil-i-ty
de-pend-en-cy
  de-pend-en-cies
de-pend-ent
de-pict
  de-pic-tion
de-pil-a-to-ry
  de-pil-a-to-ries
de-plete
  de-plet-ed
  de-plet-ing
  de-ple-tion
de-plor-a-ble
  de-plor-a-bly
de-plore
  de-plored
  de-plor-ing
de-ploy
  de-ploy-ment
de-po-nent
de-pop-u-late
  de-pop-u-lat-ed
  de-pop-u-lat-ing
  de-pop-u-la-tion
de-port
  de-por-ta-tion
de-port-ment
de-pose
  de-posed
  de-pos-ing
  de-pos-a-ble
de-pos-it
  de-pos-i-tor
dep-o-si-tion
  de-pos-i-to-ry
de-pot
de-prave
  de-praved
  de-prav-ing
  de-prav-i-ty
dep-re-cate
  dep-re-cat-ed
  dep-re-cat-ing

  dep-re-cat-ing-ly
  dep-re-ca-tion
dep-re-ca-to-ry
de-pre-ci-ate
  de-pre-ci-at-ed
  de-pre-ci-at-ing
  de-pre-ci-a-tion
  de-pre-ci-a-to-ry
  de-pre-ci-a-tor
dep-re-date
  dep-re-dat-ed
  dep-re-dat-ing
  dep-re-da-tion
de-press
de-pres-sant
de-pressed
de-pres-sion
de-prive
  de-prived
  de-priv-ing
  dep-ri-va-tion
depth
dep-u-ta-tion
de-pute
  de-put-ed
  de-put-ing
dep-u-tize
  dep-u-tized
  dep-u-tiz-ing
dep-u-ty
  dep-u-ties
  dep-u-ty-ship
de-rail
  de-rail-ment
de-range
  de-ranged
  de-rang-ing
  de-range-ment
der-e-lict
  der-e-lic-tion
de-ride
  de-rid-ed
  de-rid-ing
de-ri-sion
de-ri-sive
  de-ri-sive-ly
  de-ri-so-ry
der-i-va-tion

de-riv-a-tive
de-rive
  de-rived
  de-riv-ing
  de-riv-a-ble
der-ma
  der-mal
der-ma-tol-o-gy
  der-ma-to-log-i-cal
  der-ma-tol-o-gist
der-mis
der-o-gate
  der-o-gat-ed
  der-o-gat-ing
  der-o-ga-tion
de-rog-a-to-ry
  de-rog-a-to-ri-ly
der-rick
der-rin-ger
der-vish
des-cant
de-scend
  de-scend-a-ble
de-scend-ant
de-scent
de-scribe
  de-scribed
  de-scrib-ing
  de-scriba-ble
  de-scrib-er
de-scrip-tion
  de-scrip-tive
  de-scrip-tive-ly
  de-scrip-tive-ness
de-scry
  de-scried
  de-scry-ing
des-e-crate
  des-e-crat-ed
  des-e-crat-ing
  des-e-cra-tion
de-seg-re-gate
  de-seg-re-gat-ed
  de-seg-re-gat-ing
  de-seg-re-ga-tion
des-ert
de-sert
  de-sert-er

de-ser-tion
de-serve
  de-served
  de-serv-ing
  de-serv-ed-ly
des-ha-bille
des-ic-cate
  des-ic-cat-ed
  des-ic-cat-ing
  des-ic-ca-tion
  des-ic-ca-tive
de-sid-er-a-tum
de-sign
des-ig-nate
  des-ig-nat-ed
  des-ig-nat-ing
  des-ig-na-tion
  des-ig-na-tive
  des-ig-na-tor
de-sign-ed-ly
de-sign-er
de-sign-ing
de-sire
  de-sired
  de-sir-ing
  de-sir-a-ble
  de-sir-a-bil-i-ty
  de-sir-a-bly
  de-sir-ous
de-sist
des-o-late
  des-o-lat-ed
  des-o-lat-ing
  des-o-late-ly
  des-o-la-tion
de-spair
  de-spair-ing
  de-spair-ing-ly
des-per-a-do
  des-per-a-does
des-per-ate
  des-per-ate-ly
  des-per-ate-ness
  des-per-a-tion
des-pi-ca-ble
  des-pi-ca-bly
de-spise
  de-spised

de-spis-ing
de-spite
de-spoil
  de-spoil-er
  de-spo-li-a-tion
de-spond
  de-spond-en-cy
  de-spond-ence
  de-spond-ent
  de-spond-ent-ly
des-pot
  des-pot-ic
  des-pot-i-cal-ly
  des-pot-ism
des-sert
des-ti-na-tion
des-tine
  des-tined
  des-tin-ing
des-ti-ny
  des-ti-nies
des-ti-tute
  des-ti-tu-tion
de-stroy
de-stroy-er
de-struc-tion
  de-struct-i-ble
  de-struct-i-bil-i-ty
de-struc-tive
  de-struc-tive-ly
  de-struc-tive-ness
des-ue-tude
des-ul-to-ry
  des-ul-to-ri-ly
de-tach
  de-tach-a-ble
de-tached
de-tach-ment
de-tail
  de-tailed
de-tain
  de-tain-ment
  de-tain-er
de-tect
  de-tect-a-ble
  de-tec-tion
de-tec-tive
de-tec-tor

de-ten-tion
de-ter
  de-terred
  de-ter-ring
de-ter-gent
de-te-ri-o-rate
  de-te-ri-o-rat-ed
  de-te-ri-o-rat-ing
  de-te-ri-o-ra-tion
de-ter-mi-na-ble
de-ter-mi-nant
de-ter-ni-nate
de-ter-mi-na-tion
  de-ter-mi-na-tive
de-ter-mine
  de-ter-mined
  de-ter-min-ing
  de-ter-min-er
de-ter-mined
  de-ter-mined-ly
de-ter-min-ism
  de-ter-min-ist
de-ter-rent
  de-ter-rence
de-test
  de-test-a-ble
  de-test-a-bly
de-tes-ta-tion
de-throne
  de-throned
  de-thron-ing
  de-throne-ment
det-o-nate
  det-o-nat-ed
  det-o-nat-ing
  det-o-na-tion
  det-o-na-tor
de-tour
de-tract
  de-trac-tion
  de-trac-tor
det-ri-ment
  det-ri-men-tal
  det-ri-men-tal-ly
de-tri-tus
deuce
deu-te-ri-um
de-val-u-ate

de-val-u-at-ed
de-val-u-at-ing
de-val-u-a-tion
dev-as-tate
dev-as-tat-ed
dev-as-tat-ing
dev-as-ta-tion
de-vel-op
  de-vel-op-ment
de-vel-op-er
de-vi-ate
  de-vi-at-ed
  de-vi-at-ing
  de-vi-ant
  de-vi-a-tion
de-vice
dev-il
  dev-il-ment
  dev-il-try
  dev-il-tries
  dev-il-ry
dev-il-ish
  dev-il-ish-ly
  dev-il-ish-ness
de-vi-ous
  de-vi-ous-ly
  de-vi-ous-ness
de-vise
  de-vised
  de-vis-ing
  de-vis-a-ble
  de-vis-al
  de-vi-see
  de-vi-sor
de-void
de-volve
  de-volved
  de-volv-ing
  dev-o-lu-tion
de-vote
  de-vot-ing
de-vot-ed
  de-vot-ed-ly
dev-o-tee
de-vo-tion
  de-vo-tion-al
de-vour
  de-vour-er

de-vour-ing-ly
de-vout
  de-vout-ly
  de-vout-ness
dew-drop
dew-lap
dewy
  dew-i-er
  dew-i-est
  dew-i-ness
dew-y-eyed
dex-ter-ous
  dex-ter-i-ty
  dex-ter-ous-ly
dex-trose
di-a-be-tes
  di-a-bet-ic
di-a-bol-ic
  di-a-bol-i-cal
  di-a-bol-i-cal-ly
di-a-crit-ic
di-a-crit-i-cal
  di-a-crit-i-cal-ly
di-a-dem
di-ag-nose
  di-ag-nosed
  di-ag-nos-ing
  di-ag-no-sis
  di-ag-no-ses
  di-ag-nos-tic
  di-ag-nos-ti-cian
di-ag-o-nal
  di-ag-o-nal-ly
di-a-gram
  di-a-gramed
  di-a-gram-ing
  di-a-gram-mat-ic
  di-a-gram-mat-i-cal
di-al
  di-aled
  di-al-ing
di-a-lect
  di-a-lec-tal
di-a-lec-tic
  di-a-lec-ti-cal
  di-a-lec-ti-cian
di-a-logue
di-am-e-ter

di-a-met-ric
di-a-met-ric-al
di-a-met-ric-al-ly
dia-mond
dia-per
di-aph-a-nous
di-a-phragm
di-ar-rhea
di-a-ry
di-as-to-le
di-as-tol-ic
di-a-ther-mic
di-a-tom
di-a-ton-ic
dib-ble
dib-bled
dib-bling
di-chot-o-my
di-chot-o-mous
di-cho-tom-ic
dic-tate
dic-ta-tion
dic-ta-tor
dic-ta-to-ri-al
dic-ta-to-ri-al-ly
dic-tion-ary
dic-tum
di-dac-tic
di-dac-ti-cally
di-er-e-ses
di-e-tary
di-e-tet-ic
di-e-tet-i-cal
di-e-tet-i-cal-ly
di-e-tet-ics
di-e-ti-cian
dif-fer-ence
dif-fer-enced
dif-fer-en-cing
dif-fer-ent
dif-fer-ent-ly
dif-fer-en-tial
dif-fer-en-tial-ly
dif-fer-en-ti-ate
dif-fer-en-ti-at-ed
dif-fi-cult
dif-fi-cult-ly
dif-fi-dence

dif-fi-dent
dif-fi-dent-ly
dif-fuse
dif-fused
dif-fus-ing
dif-fuse-ness
dif-fu-sion
di-gest
di-gest-er
di-gest-i-ble
di-gest-i-bil-i-ty
di-ges-tion
dig-ger
dig-gings
dig-it-al
dig-i-tal-is
dig-ni-fied
dig-ni-fy
dig-ni-fy-ing
dig-ni-tary
dig-ni-tar-ies
dig-ni-ty
di-gress
di-gres-sion
di-gres-sive
di-he-dral
di-lap-i-dat-ed
di-lap-i-da-tion
dil-a-ta-tion
di-late
di-lat-ed
di-lat-ing
di-lat-a-ble
di-la-tion
dil-a-to-ry
dil-a-to-ri-ly
di-lem-ma
dil-et-tan-te
dil-et-tan-tes
dil-i-gence
dil-i-gent
dil-i-gent-ly
dil-ly-dal-ly
di-lute
di-lut-ed
di-lut-ing
di-lute-ness
di-men-sion

di-men-sion-al
di-min-ish
di-min-ish-a-ble
di-min-u-en-do
di-min-u-en-dos
dim-i-nu-tion
di-min-u-tive
di-min-u-tive-ness
dim-ple
dim-pled
dim-pling
din-er
di-nette
din-ghy
din-ghies
din-gy
din-gi-er
din-gi-est
din-gi-ness
din-ner
di-no-saur
di-o-cese
di-oc-e-san
di-o-ram-a
diph-the-ri-a
di-plo-ma
di-plo-ma-cy
di-plo-ma-cies
dip-lo-mat
dip-lo-mat-ic
dip-lo-mat-i-cal-ly
dip-per
dip-so-ma-nia
dip-so-ma-ni-ac
dire
dir-er
dir-est
dire-ness
di-rect
di-rect-ness
di-rec-tion
di-rec-tion-al
di-rec-tive
di-rect-ly
di-rec-tor
di-rec-to-ri-al
di-rec-tor-ship
di-rec-to-rate

di-rec-to-ry
di-rec-to-ries
dis-a-ble
dis-a-bling
dis-a-bil-i-ty
dis-a-ble-ment
dis-a-buse
dis-a-bused
dis-a-bus-ing
dis-ad-van-tage
dis-ad-van-taged
dis-af-fect
dis-af-fec-tion
dis-af-fect-ed
dis-a-gree
dis-a-gree-ing
dis-a-gree-a-ble
dis-a-gree-ment
dis-al-low
dis-al-low-ance
dis-ap-pear
dis-ap-pear-ance
dis-ap-point
dis-ap-point-ment
dis-ap-pro-ba-tion
dis-ap-prove
dis-ap-prov-al
dis-arm
dis-ar-ma-ment
dis-ar-range
dis-ar-ranged
dis-ar-rang-ing
dis-ar-ray
dis-as-sem-ble
dis-as-ter
dis-as-trous
dis-as-trous-ly
dis-a-vow
dis-a-vow-al
dis-band
dis-band-ment
dis-bar
dis-barred
dis-bar-ring
dis-be-lieve
dis-be-lief
dis-be-liev-er
dis-burse

dis-bursed
dis-burs-ing
dis-burs-er
dis-cern-ing
dis-cern-ment
dis-charge
dis-charged
dis-charg-ing
dis-char-ger
dis-ci-ple
dis-ci-ple-ship
dis-ci-pline
dis-ci-plines
dis-ci-pli-nary
dis-claim-er
dis-close
dis-closed
dis-clos-er
dis-clo-sure
dis-coid
dis-col-or
dis-col-or-a-tion
dis-com-fit
dis-com-fi-ture
dis-com-fort
dis-com-mode
dis-com-mod-ing
dis-com-pose
dis-com-posed
dis-com-pos-ing
dis-con-cert
dis-con-cert-ed
dis-con-nect
dis-con-nec-tion
dis-con-so-late
dis-con-tent
dis-con-tent-ed
dis-con-tin-ue
dis-con-tin-ued
dis-con-tin-u-ing
dis-con-tin-u-ous
dis-cord
dis-cord-ance
dis-cord-ant-ly
dis-count
dis-cour-age
dis-cour-ag-ing
dis-course

dis-coursed
dis-cours-ing
dis-cour-te-ous
dis-cour-te-sy
dis-cov-er
dis-cov-er-a-ble
dis-cov-er-er
dis-cov-er-y
dis-cov-er-ies
dis-cred-it
dis-cred-it-a-bly
dis-creet
dis-crep-an-cy
dis-crep-an-cies
dis-crete
dis-cre-tion
dis-cre-tion-ary
dis-crim-i-nate
dis-crim-i-nate-ly
dis-crim-i-na-to-ry
dis-crim-i-na-tor
dis-cur-sive
dis-cur-sive-ly
dis-cur-sive-ness
dis-cus
dis-cus-es
dis-cuss
dis-cuss-i-ble
dis-cus-sion
dis-dain
dis-dain-ful
dis-dain-ful-ly
dis-ease
dis-eased
dis-eas-ing
dis-em-bark
dis-em-body
dis-em-bod-ied
dis-em-bod-y-ing
dis-em-bow-el
dis-em-bow-eled
dis-em-bow-el-ing
dis-en-chant
dis-en-chant-ment
dis-en-cum-ber
dis-en-fran-chise
dis-en-fran-chised
dis-en-fran-chis-ing

dis-en-gage
  dis-en-gaged
  dis-en-gag-ing
dis-en-tan-gle
  dis-en-tan-gled
  dis-en-tan-gling
dis-es-tab-lish
dis-fa-vor
dis-fig-ure
  dis-fig-ured
  dis-fig-ur-ing
  dis-fig-ure-ment
dis-fran-chise
  dis-fran-chised
  dis-fran-chis-ing
dis-gorge
  dis-gorged
  dis-gorg-ing
dis-grace
  dis-graced
  dis-grac-ing
dis-grace-ful
  dis-grace-ful-ly
dis-grun-tle
  dis-grun-tled
  dis-grun-tling
dis-guise
  dis-guised
  dis-guis-ing
  dis-guis-er
dis-gust
  dis-gust-ed
  dis-gust-ing
dis-ha-bille
dis-har-mo-ny
  dis-har-mo-nies
dis-heart-en
dis-hev-eled
dis-hon-est
  dis-hon-est-ly
  dis-hon-es-ty
  dis-hon-es-ties
dis-hon-or
dis-hon-or-a-ble
  dis-hon-or-a-bly
dis-il-lu-sion
dis-in-cline
  dis-in-clined

dis-in-fect
dis-in-her-it
dis-in-te-grate
dis-in-ter-es-ted
  dis-in-ter-est-ed-ly
dis-junc-tion
dis-loy-al
  dis-loy-al-ty
dis-o-be-di-ence
dis-or-der-ly
dis-o-ri-ent
dis-pas-sion
dis-pen-sa-tion
dis-pos-a-ble
dis-qual-i-fy
dis-qui-et
dis-re-spect
  dis-re-spect-ful
dis-rup-tive
  dis-rupt-er
dis-sat-is-fy
  dis-sat-is-fy-ing
dis-sem-blance
dis-sem-i-nate
  dis-sem-i-nat-ing
  dis-sem-i-na-tor
dis-sent
dis-ser-tate
  dis-ser-ta-ting
  dis-ser-ta-tion
dis-serv-ice
dis-si-dent
dis-sim-i-lar
  dis-sim-i-lar-i-ty
dis-sim-i-late
  dis-sim-i-lat-ing
  dis-sim-i-la-tive
dis-si-pate
  dis-si-pa-tion
dis-so-nance
dis-so-nant
dis-suade
  dis-sua-sion
  dis-sua-sive
dis-tance
dis-taste
  dis-taste-ful-ly
dis-tem-per

dis-til-late
dis-till-ery
dis-tinc-tion
dis-tin-guish
dis-tract
  dis-tract-ing
dis-trib-ute
  dis-trib-ut-ed
  dis-tri-bu-tion
  dis-tri-u-tor
dis-u-nite
di-van
di-verge
  di-ver-gence
  di-ver-gent
di-verse
di-ver-sion
div-i-dend
di-vi-sor
di-vulge
  di-vulg-ing
  di-vul-gence
do-a-ble
doc-tor-ate
doc-u-ment
dod-der
dog-ma
dog-mat-ic
  dog-mat-i-cal
dol-drums
dol-or-ous
dol-phin
do-mes-tic
do-mes-ti-cate
do-mes-tic-i-ty
dom-i-cile
  dom-i-cil-ing
dom-i-nance
dom-i-nant
dom-i-neer
do-min-ion
dop-ey
  dop-i-est
  dop-i-ness
dor-mant
dor-mer
dor-mi-to-ry
dos-age

dos-si-er
dou-ble-faced
dou-ble-take
dou-ble-time
doubt-a-ble
douche
dow-a-ger
dow-el
down-ward-ly
doz-ing
doz-en
drab-ness
drag-gle
drag-on
drain-age
dra-mat-ics
dra-per-y
dread-ful
drib-ble
  drib-bled
  drib-bling
  drib-bler
drill-ing
dri-ly
driv-el
  driv-eled
  driv-el-ing
driz-zle
  driz-zling
  driz-zly
drom-e-dar-y
droop
  droop-y
  droop-i-er
  droop-i-est
drop-per
dross
drought
  drought-y
  drought-i-er
  drought-i-est
drowned
drowse
  drowsed
  drows-ing
  drow-si-ness
drudge
drug-gist

dru-id
drum-mer
drunk-ard
drunk-en
  drunk-en-ly
  drunk-en-ness
dry-ad
du-al
  du-al-i-ty
du-al-ism
  du-al-ist
  du-al-is-tic
du-bi-ous
  du-bi-e-ty
  du-bi-ous-ly
  du-bi-ous-ness
du-bi-ta-ble
  du-bi-ta-tion
du-cal
duc-at
duch-ess
duchy
duck-bill
duck-ling
duct-less
duc-tile
  duc-til-i-ty
duct-ing
duct-ule
dud-geon
du-el
  du-eled
  du-el-ing
  du-el-ist
du-et
dui-ker
duke-dom
dul-cet
  dul-cet-ly
dul-ci-fy
  dul-ci-fy-ing
  dul-ci-mer
dull-ish
  dull-ish-ly
dumb-bell
dum-found
  dumb-foun-der
dump-ing

dump-ish
dump-ling
dunce
dung
dun-ga-ree
dun-geon
du-o-dec-i-mal
du-o-de-num
  du-o-de-na
  du-o-de-nal
du-pli-cate
  du-pli-cat-ing
  du-pli-ca-tor
du-plic-i-ty
du-ra-ble
  du-ra-bil-ity
  du-ra-bly
dur-ance
du-ra-tion
dur-ing
du-ti-a-ble
du-ti-ful
  du-ti-ful-ly
  du-ti-ful-ness
dwarf
  dwarf-ish
dwell
  dwelled
  dwell-ing
dwin-dle
  dwin-dled
  dwin-dling
dye-stuff
dy-ing
dy-nam-ic
  dy-nam-i-cal
  dy-na-mism
dy-na-mite
dy-na-mo
dy-nas-ty
  dy-nas-ties
dyne
dys-en-tery
dys-func-tion
dys-pep-sia
dys-pep-tic
  dys-pep-ti-cal
dys-tro-phy

ea-ger
 ea-ger-ly
 ea-ger-ness
ea-gle
ea-gle eyed
ea-glet
ear-ache
ear-drum
earl-dom
ear-ly
 ear-li-er
 ear-li-est
ear-mark
ear-muff
earn
 earn-er
ear-nest
 ear-nest-ly
 ear-nest-ness
earn-ings
ear-phone
ear-ring
earth-en
earth-ly
 earth-li-er
 earth-li-est
earth-quake
earth-y
ear-wax
ease
 eased
 eas-ing
ea-sel
ease-ment
eas-i-ly
 eas-i-ness
east-er-ly
east-ern
east-ern-most
east-ward
eas-y
 eas-i-er
 eas-i-est
eas-y-go-ing
eat
ebb
eb-on-y
 eb-on-ies

e-bul-lience
e-bul-lient
e-bul-li-tion
ec-cen-tric
 ec-cen-tri-cal-ly
ec-cen-tric-i-ty
 ec-cen-tric-i-ties
ec-cle-si-as-tic
 ec-cle-si-as-ti-cal
 ec-cle-si-as-ti-cal-ly
ech-e-lon
e-chi-no-derm
ech-o
e-cho-ic
e-clair
ec-lec-tic
 ec-lec-ti-cal-ly
 ec-lec-ti-cism
e-clipse
 e-clipsed
 e-clips-ing
e-clip-tic
e-col-o-gy
 e-c-o-log-ic
 e-c-o-log-i-cal
 e-col-o-gist
e-co-nom-ic
 e-co-nom-i-cal
e-co-nom-ics
e-con-o-mist
e-con-o-mize
 e-con-o-mized
 e-con-o-miz-ing
 e-con-o-miz-er
e-con-o-my
 e-con-o-mies
ec-o-sys-tem
ec-ru
ec-sta-sy
 ec-sta-sies
ec-stat-ic
 ec-stat-i-cal
ec-to-morph
 ec-to-mor-phic
ec-to-plasm
ec-u-men-i-cal
ec-u-men-ic
 ec-u-men-i-cal-ly

ec-u-men-ism
ec-ze-ma
e-de-ma
 e-de-ma-ta
e-den-tate
edg-y
ed-i-ble
e-dict
ed-i-fice
ed-i-fy
 ed-i-fied
 ed-i-fy-ing
 ed-i-fi-ca-tion
ed-it
e-di-tion
ed-i-tor
 ed-i-tor-ship
ed-i-to-ri-al
 ed-i-to-ri-al-ly
 ed-i-to-ri-al-ize
 ed-i-to-ri-al-lized
ed-u-cate
 ed-u-cat-ed
 ed-u-cat-ing
 ed-u-ca-ble
ed-u-ca-tion
 ed-u-ca-tion-al
ed-u-ca-tor
e-duce
 e-duced
 e-duc-ing
 e-duc-i-ble
 e-duc-tion
educ-tor
edul-co-rate
 edul-co-rated
 edul-co-rat-ing
eel
 eel-like
 eel-ly
eel-grass
ee-rie
 ee-ri-er
 ee-ri-est
 ee-ri-ly
 ee-ri-ness
ef-face
 ef-faced

ef-face-ment
ef-fac-er
ef-fac-ing
ef-fect
ef-fec-tive
ef-fec-tive-ness
ef-fec-tive-ly
ef-fec-tu-al
ef-fec-tu-al-i-ty
ef-fec-tu-al-ly
ef-fec-tu-al-ness
ef-fec-tu-ate
ef-fec-tu-at-ed
ef-fec-tu-at-ing
ef-fec-tu-a-tion
ef-fem-i-nate
ef-fem-i-na-cy
ef-fem-i-na-cies
ef-fem-i-nate-ly
ef-fer-ent
ef-fer-ent-ly
ef-fer-vesce
ef-fer-vesced
ef-fer-vesc-ing
ef-fete
ef-fete-ly
ef-fete-ness
ef-fi-ca-cious
ef-fi-ca-cy
ef-fi-ca-cies
ef-fi-cien-cy
ef-fi-cien-cies
ef-fi-cient
ef-fi-cient-ly
ef-fi-gy
ef-fi-gies
ef-flo-resce
ef-flu-ent
ef-flu-ence
ef-flu-vi-um
ef-flu-via
ef-flu-vi-ums
ef-flu-vi-al
ef-fort
ef-fort-less
ef-fort-less-ly
ef-fron-ter-y
ef-fron-ter-ies

ef-ful-gent
ef-ful-gence
ef-fuse
ef-fused
ef-fus-ing
ef-fu-sion
ef-fu-sive
ef-fu-sive-ly
egal-i-tar-i-an
egal-i-tar-i-an-ism
egg-nog
egg-plant
e-go
e-gos
e-go-cen-tric
e-go-ism
e-go-ist
e-go-is-tic
e-go-tism
e-go-tis-tic
e-go-tis-ti-cal
e-gre-gious
e-gre-gious-ly
e-gress
e-gret
ei-der-down
eight
eighth
eight-ball
eight-fold
eight-y
eight-ies
eight-i-eth
ei-ther
e-jac-u-late
e-jac-u-lat-ed
e-jac-u-lat-ing
e-jac-u-la-tion
e-ject
e-jec-tion
e-ject-ment
e-jec-tor
eke
eked
ek-ing
e-lab-o-rate
e-lab-o-rat-ed
e-lab-o-rat-ing

e-lab-o-rate-ly
e-lab-o-ra-tion
e-lapse
e-lapsed
e-laps-ing
e-las-tic
e-las-ti-cal-ly
e-las-tic-i-ty
e-late
e-lat-ed
e-lat-ing
e-la-tion
el-bow
el-bow-room
el-der
eld-er-ship
el-der-ly
eld-er-li-ness
eld-est
e-lect
e-lec-tion
e-lec-tion-eer
e-lec-tive
e-lec-tor
e-lec-tor-ate
e-lec-tric
e-lec-tri-cal
e-lec-tri-cal-ly
e-lec-tri-cian
e-lec-tric-i-ty
e-lec-tri-fy
e-lec-tri-fied
e-lec-tri-fy-ing
e-lec-tri-fi-ca-tion
elec-tro-car-di-o-graph
e-lec-tro-cute
e-lec-tro-cut-ed
e-lec-tro-cut-ing
e-lec-tro-cu-tion
e-lec-trode
e-lec-tro-dy-nam-ics
e-lec-trol-y-sis
e-lec-tro-lyze
e-lec-tro-lyzed
e-lec-tro-lyz-ing
e-lec-tro-lyte
e-lec-tro-lyt-ic
e-lec-tro-mag-net

e-lec-tro-mag-net-ism
e-lec-tro-mag-net-ic
e-lec-tron
e-lec-tron-ic
e-lec-tron-ics
e-lec-tron-i-cal-ly
e-lec-tro-plate
e-lec-tro-plat-ed
e-lec-tro-plat-ing
e-lec-tro-ther-a-py
e-lec-trum
el-ee-mos-y-nar-y
el-e-gant
el-e-gance
el-e-gan-cy
el-e-gant-ly
el-e-gy
el-e-gies
el-e-gi-ac
el-e-gist
el-e-gize
el-e-gized
el-e-giz-ing
el-e-ment
el-e-men-tal
el-e-men-tal-ly
el-e-men-ta-ry
el-e-men-ta-ri-ly
el-e-phant
el-e-phan-tine
el-e-vate
el-e-vat-ed
el-e-vat-ing
el-e-va-tion
el-e-va-tor
e-lev-en
e-lev-enth
elf
e-lic-it
el-i-gi-ble
el-i-gi-bil-i-ty
el-i-gi-bly
e-lim-i-nate
e-lim-i-nat-ed
e-lim-i-nat-ing
e-lim-i-na-tion
e-lim-i-na-tor
e-lite

e-lit-ism
e-lit-ist
e-lix-ir
el-lipse
el-lip-sis
el-lip-ses
el-lip-ti-cal
el-lip-tic
el-lip-ti-cal-ly
el-o-cu-tion
el-o-cu-tion-ary
el-o-cu-tion-ist
e-lon-gate
e-lon-gat-ed
e-lon-gat-ing
e-lon-ga-tion
e-lope
el-o-quence
el-o-quent
el-o-quent-ly
else-where
e-lu-ci-date
e-lu-ci-dat-ed
e-lu-ci-dat-ing
e-lu-ci-da-tion
e-lu-ci-da-tor
e-lude
e-iud-ed
e-lud-ing
e-lu-sion
e-lu-sive
e-lu-sive-ly
e-lu-sive-ness
elv-ish
e-ma-ci-ate
e-ma-ci-at-ed
e-ma-ci-at-ing
e-ma-ci-a-tion
em-a-nate
em-a-nat-ed
em-a-nat-ing
em-a-na-tion
e-man-ci-pate
e-man-ci-pat-ed
e-man-ci-pat-ing
e-man-ci-pa-tor
e-mas-cu-late
e-mas-cu-lat-ed

e-mas-cu-lat-ing
e-mas-cu-la-tion
em-balm
em-balm-er
em-balm-ment
em-bank-ment
em-bar-go
em-bar-goes
em-bar-goed
em-bar-go-ing
em-bark
em-bar-ka-tion
em-bark-ment
em-bar-rass
em-bar-rass-ing-ly
em-bar-rass-ment
em-bas-sy
em-bas-sies
em-bat-tle
em-bat-tled
em-bat-tling
em-bat-tle-ment
em-bed
em-bed-ded
em-bed-ding
em-bel-lish
em-bel-lish-ment
em-ber
em-bez-zle
em-bez-zled
em-bez-zling
em-bez-zle-ment
em-bez-zler
em-bit-ter
em-bit-ter-ment
em-bla-zon
em-bla-zon-er
em-blaz-on-ment
em-bla-zon-ry
em-blem
em-blem-at-ic
em-blem-at-i-cal
em-bod-y
em-bod-ied
em-bod-y-ing
em-bod-i-ment
em-bold-en
em-bo-lism

em-bo-lus
em-bos-om
em-boss
  em-boss-ment
em-bou-chure
em-brace
  em-braced
  em-brac-ing
em-broi-der
  em-broi-dery
  em-broi-der-ies
em-broil
  em-broil-ment
em-bry-o
  em-bry-os
  em-bry-on-ic
em-bry-ol-o-gy
em-cee
  em-ceed
  em-cee-ing
e-mend
em-er-ald
e-merge
  e-merged
  e-merg-ing
  e-mer-gence
  e-mer-gent
e-mer-gen-cy
  e-mer-gen-ies
e-mer-i-tus
em-er-y
e-met-ic
em-i-grant
em-i-grate
  em-i-grat-ed
  em-i-grat-ing
  em-i-gra-tion
em-i-nence
em-i-nent
  em-i-ent-ly
em-i-nent do-main
em-is-sary
  em-is-sar-ies
e-mis-sion
  e-mis-sive
e-mit
  e-mit-ted
  e-mit-ting

e-mit-ter
e-mol-lient
e-mol-u-ment
e-mote
  e-mot-ed
  e-mot-ing
  e-mo-tive
emo-tion
  emo-tion-al
  emo-ton-al-ly
emo-tion-al-ism
em-pan-el
em-pa-thize
  em-pa-thized
  em-pa-thiz-ing
em-pa-thy
  em-pa-thet-ic
  em-path-ic
em-per-or
em-pha-sis
  em-pha-ses
em-pha-size
  em-pha-sized
  em-pha-siz-ing
em-phat-ic
  em-phat-i-cal-ly
em-phy-se-ma
em-pire
  em-pir-i-cal
  em-pir-i-cal-ly
em-pir-i-cism
  em-pir-i-cist
em-place-ment
em-ploy
  em-ploy-a-ble
  em-ploy-ee
  em-ploy-er
  em-ploy-ment
em-pori-um
  em-po-ri-ums
  em-po-ria
em-pow-er
em-press
emp-ty
  emp-ti-er
  emp-ti-est
  emp-tied
  emp-ty-ing

emp-ti-ly
emp-ti-ness
emp-ty--hand-ed
emp-ty--head-ed
e-mu
em-u-late
  em-u-lat-ed
  em-u-lat-ing
  em-u-la-tion
e-mul-si-fy
  e-mul-si-fied
  e-mul-si-fy-ing
  e-mul-si-fi-ca-tion
  e-mul-si-fi-er
emul-sion
  emul-sive
en-a-ble
  en-a-bled
  en-a-bling
en-act
e-nam-el
  e-nam-eled
  e-nam-el-ing
  e-nam-el-er
e-nam-el-ware
en-am-or
  en-am-ored-ness
en-camp
  en-camp-ment
en-cap-su-late
  en-cap-su-lat-ed
  en-cap-su-lat-ing
  en-cap-sule
en-case
  en-cased
  en-cas-ing
en-ceinte
en-ceph-a-li-tis
  en-ceph-a-lit-ic
en-ceph-a-lon
  en-ceph-a-la
en-chant
  en-chant-er
  en-chant-ress
en-chant-ing
  en-chant-ing-ly
en-chant-ment
en-chi-la-da

en-cir-cle
  en-cir-cled
  en-cir-cling
  en-cir-cle-ment
en-clave
en-close
  en-closed
  en-clos-ing
en-clo-sure
en-code
  en-cod-ed
  en-cod-ing
en-co-mi-ast
en-com-pass
  en-com-pass-ment
en-core
en-coun-ter
en-cour-age
  en-cour-aged
  en-cour-ag-ing
  en-cour-ag-ing-ly
en-croach
  en-croach-er
  en-croach-ment
en-crust
  en-crus-ta-tion
en-cum-ber
  en-cum-brance
en-cy-clo-pe-di-a
  en-cy-clo-pe-dic
  en-cy-clo-pe-di-cal
  en-cy-clo-pe-di-cal-ly
en-cyst
en-dan-ger
  en-dan-ger-ment
en-dear
  en-dear-ment
en-dea-vor
en-dem-ic
  en-dem-i-cal
  en-dem-i-cal-ly
end-ing
end-less
  end-less-ly
  end-less-ness
end-most
en-do-crine
  en-do-cri-nol-o-gy

en-do-crin-o-log-ic
en-do-crin-o-log-i-cal
en-do-cri-nol-o-gist
en-dog-e-nous
en-dorse
  en-dorsed
  en-dors-ing
  en-dor-see
  en-dor-ser
  en-dorse-ment
en-do-sperm
en-dow
  en-dow-ment
en-due
  en-dued
  en-du-ing
en-dur-ance
en-dure
  en-dured
  en-dur-ing
  en-dur-a-ble
  en-dur-a-bly
  en-dur-ing-ness
end-ways
en-e-ma
en-e-my
  en-e-mies
en-er-get-ic
  en-er-get-i-cal
  en-er-get-i-cal-ly
en-er-gize
  en-er-gized
  en-er-giz-ing
  en-er-gi-zer
en-er-gy
  en-er-gies
en-er-vate
  en-er-vat-ed
  en-er-vat-ing
  en-er-va-tion
en-fee-ble
  en-fee-bled
  en-fee-bling
  en-fee-ble-ment
en-fi-lade
  en-fi-lad-ed
  en-fi-lad-ing
en-fold

en-force
  en-forced
  en-forc-ing
  en-force-a-ble
  en-force-ment
  en-forc-er
en-fran-chise
  en-fran-chised
  en-fran-chis-ing
  en-fran-chise-ment
en-gage
  en-gaged
  en-gag-ing
  en-gage-ment
en-gen-der
en-gine
  en-gi-neer
en-gorge
  en-gorged
  en-gorg-ing
  en-gorge-ment
en-grave
  en-graved
  en-grav-ing
  en-grav-er
en-gross
  en-grossed
  en-gross-er
  en-gross-ing
  en-gross-ing-ly
  en-gross-ment
en-gulf
  en-gulf-ment
en-hance
  en-hanced
  en-hanc-ing
  en-hance-ment
e-nig-ma
  en-ig-mat-ic
  en-ig-mat-i-cal
  en-ig-mat-i-cal-ly
en-join
  en-join-er
  en-join-ment
en-joy
  en-joy-a-ble
  en-joy-a-ble-ness
  en-joy-a-bly

en-joy-ment
en-large
en-larged
en-larg-ing
en-large-a-ble
en-larg-er
en-large-ment
en-light-en
en-light-en-ment
en-list
en-list-ed
en-list-ment
en-liv-en
en-liv-en-er
en-mesh
en-mi-ty
en-mi-ties
en-no-ble
en-no-bled
en-no-bling
en-no-ble-ment
en-no-bler
en-nui
e-nor-mi-ty
e-nor-mi-ties
e-nor-mous
e-nor-mous-ly
e-nor-mous-ness
e-nough
en-plane
en-planed
en-plan-ing
en-rage
en-raged
en-rag-ing
en-rap-ture
en-rap-tured
en-rap-tur-ing
en-rich
en-rich-er
en-rich-ment
en-roll
en-roll-ment
en route
en-sconce
en-sconced
en-sconc-ing
en-sem-ble

en-shrine
en-shrin-ing
en-shroud
en-sign
en-si-lage
en-si-laged
en-si-lag-ing
en-slave
en-slaved
en-slav-ing
en-slave-ment
en-slav-er
en-snare
en-snared
en-snar-ing
en-snare-ment
en-snar-er
en-snar-ing-ly
en-sue
en-sued
en-su-ing
en-su-ing-ly
en-sure
en-sured
en-sur-ing
en-sur-er
en-tail
en-tail-er
en-tail-ment
en-tan-gle
en-tan-gled
en-tan-gling
en-tan-gle-ment
en-tan-gler
en-tente
en-ter
en-ter-a-ble
en-ter-i-tis
en-tr-prise
en-ter-pris-ing
en-ter-pris-ing-ly
en-ter-tain
en-ter-tain-er
en-ter-tain-ing
en-ter-tain-ing-ly
en-ter-tain-ment
en-thrall
en-thralled

en-thrall-ing
en-thrall-ment
en-throne
en-throned
en-thron-ing
en-throne-ment
en-thuse
en-thused
en-thus-ing
en-thu-si-asm
en-thu-si-ast
en-thu-si-as-tic
en-thu-si-as-ti-cal-ly
en-tice
en-ticed
en-tic-ing
en-tice-ment
en-tic-er
en-tic-ig-ly
en-tire
en-tire-ly
en-tire-ness
en-tire-ty
en-tire-ties
en-ti-tle
en-ti-tled
en-ti-tling
en-ti-tle-ment
en-ti-ty
en-ti-ties
en-to-mol-o-gy
en-to-mol-o-gies
en-to-mo-log-ic
en-to-mo-log-i-cal
en-to-mo-log-i-cal-ly
en-to-mol-o-gist
en-tou-rage
en-trails
en-train
en-train-er
en-trance
en-trance-way
en-tranced
en-tranc-ing
en-trance-ment
en-tranc-ing-ly
en-trant
en-trap

en-trapped
en-trap-ping
en-trap-ment
en-treat
en-treat-ing-ly
en-treat-ment
en-treat-y
en-tree
en-trench
en-trench-ment
en-tre-pre-neur
en-tre-pre-neur-i-al
en-tre-pre-neur-ship
en-tro-py
en-trust
en-trust-ment
en-try
en-tries
en-twine
en-twined
en-twin-ing
e-nu-mer-ate
e-nu-mer-at-ed
e-nu-mer-at-ing
e-nu-mer-a-tion
e-nu-mer-a-tive
e-nu-mer-a-tor
e-nun-ci-ate
e-nun-ci-at-ed
e-nun-ci-at-ing
e-nun-ci-a-tion
e-nun-ci-a-tive
e-nun-ci-a-tor
en-u-re-sis
en-u-ret-ic
en-vel-op
en-vel-oped
en-vel-op-ing
en-vi-a-ble
en-vi-a-ble-ness
en-vi-a-bly
en-vi-ous
en-vi-ous-ly
en-vi-ous-ness
en-vi-ron
en-vi-ron-ment
en-vi-ron-men-tal
en-vi-ron-men-tal-ly

en-vi-rons
en-vis-age
en-vis-aged
en-vis-ag-ing
en-vi-sion
en-voy
en-vy
en-vies
en-vied
en-vy-ing
en-vi-er
en-vy-ing-ly
en-zyme
en-zy-mat-ic
en-zy-mat-i-cal-ly
e-on
ep-au-let
e-phed-rine
e-phem-er-al
e-phem-er-al-ness
e-phem-er-al-ly
ep-ic
ep-i-cal
ep-i-cen-ter
ep-i-cure
epi-cu-re-an
ep-i-dem-ic
ep-i-dem-i-cal-ly
ep-i-der-mis
ep-i-der-mal
ep-i-der-mic
ep-i-glot-tis
ep-i-gram
ep-i-logue
ep-i-log
epis-co-pa-cy
epsi-co-pa-cies
epis-co-pal
epis-co-pa-lian
epis-co-pa-lian-ism
epis-co-pate
ep-i-sode
ep-i-sod-ic
ep-i-sod-i-cal
ep-i-sod-i-cal-ly
e-pis-te-mol-o-gy
e-psi-te-mo-log-i-cal
e-pis-te-mol-o-gist

e-pis-tle
e-pis-to-lar-y
ep-i-taph
ep-i-taph-ic
ep-i-taph-ist
ep-i-thet
ep-i-thet-ic
ep-i-thet-i-cal
e-pit-o-me
epit-o-mize
epit-o-mized
epit-o-miz-ing
ep-och
ep-och-al
ep-ox-y
ep-ox-y res-in
ep-si-lon
eq-ua-ble
eq-ua-bil-i-ty
eq-ua-ble-ness
eq-ua-bly
e-qual
e-qualed
e-qual-ling
e-qual-ly
e-qual-ness
e-qual-i-tar-i-an
e-qual-i-tar-i-an-ism
e-qual-i-ty
e-qual-i-ties
e-qual-ize
e-qual-ized
e-qual-iz-ing
e-qual-i-za-tion
e-qual-iz-er
e-qua-nim-i-ty
e-quate
e-quat-ed
e-quat-ing
e-qua-tion
e-qua-tion-al
e-qua-tion-al-ly
e-qua-tor
e-qua-to-ri-al
e-qua-to-ri-al-ly
e-ques-tri-an
e-ques-tri-enne
e-qui-dis-tance

e-qui-dis-tant
e-qui-dis-tant-ly
e-qui-lat-er-al
e-qui-li-brate
e-qui-li-brat-ed
e-qui-li-brat-ing
e-qui-li-bra-tion
e-qui-l-bra-tor
e-qui-lib-ri-um
e-qui-lib-ri-ums
e-qui-lib-ria
e-quine
e-qui-noc-tial
e-qui-nox
e-quip
e-quipped
e-quip-ping
e-quip-per
eq-ui-page
e-quip-ment
e-qui-poise
eq-ui-ta-ble
eq-ui-ta-ble-ness
eq-ui-ta-bly
eq-ui-ty
eq-ui-ties
e-quiv-a-lance
e-quiv-a-len-cy
e-quiv-a-lent
e-quiv-a-lent-ly
e-quiv-o-cal
e-quiv-o-cal-ly
e-quiv-o-cal-ness
e-quiv-o-cate
e-quiv-o-cat-ed
e-quiv-o-cat-ing
e-quiv-o-ca-tor
e-quiv-o-ca-tion
e-ra
e-rad-i-cate
e-rad-i-cat-ed
e-rad-i-cat-ing
e-rad-i-ca-ble
e-rad-i-ca-tion
e-rad-i-ca-tive
e-rad-i-ca-tor
e-rase
e-rased

e-ras-ing
e-ras-a-bil-i-ty
e-ras-a-ble
e-ras-er
e-ras-ure
e-rect
e-rect-a-ble
e-rect-er
e-rec-tive
e-rect-ly
e-rect-ness
e-rec-tile
e-rec-til-i-ty
e-rec-tion
e-rec-tor
er-go
er-mine
e-rode
e-rod-ed
e-rod-ing
e-rog-e-nous
e-ro-sion
e-rot-ic
e-rot-i-cal-ly
e-rot-i-cism
err
err-ing-ly
er-rand
er-rant
er-rant-ly
er-rat-ic
er-rat-i-cal-ly
er-ra-tum
er-ra-ta
er-ro-ne-ous
er-ro-ne-ous-ly
er-ro-ne-ous-ness
er-ror
er-ror-less
er-satz
erst-while
er-u-dite
er-u-dite-ly
er-u-dite-ness
er-u-di-tion
e-rupt
e-rup-tion
e-rup-tive

e-rup-tive-ly
e-rup-tive-ness
es-ca-lade
es-ca-lad-ed
es-ca-lad-ing
es-ca-lad-er
es-ca-late
es-ca-lat-ed
es-ca-lat-ing
es-ca-la-tion
es-ca-la-tor
es-cal-lop
es-ca-pade
es-cape
es-caped
es-cap-ing
es-cap-er
es-ca-pee
es-cap-ist
es-cap-ism
es-carp-ment
es-chew
es-chew-al
es-chew-er
es-cort
es-cri-toire
es-crow
es-cutch-eon
es-cutch-eoned
e-soph-a-gus
es-o-ter-ic
es-o-ter-i-cal
es-o-ter-i-cal-ly
es-pal-ier
es-pe-cial
es-pe-cial-ly
es-pe-cial-ness
es-pi-o-nage
es-pla-nade
es-pouse
es-poused
es-pous-ing
es-pous-er
es-pous-al
es-pres-so
es-prit
es-prit de corps
es-py

es-pied
es-py-ing
es-quire
  es-quired
  es-quir-ing
es-say
  es-say-er
  es-say-ist
es-sence
es-sen-tial
  es-sen-ti-al-i-ty
  es-sen-tial-ly
  es-sen-tial-ness
es-tab-lish
  es-tab-lish-er
  es-tab-lish-ment
es-tate
es-teem
es-thete
  es-thet-ic
es-ti-ma-ble
  es-ti-ma-ble-ness
  es-ti-ma-bly
es-ti-mate
  es-ti-mat-ed
  es-ti-mat-ing
  es-ti-ma-tive
  es-ti-ma-tor
es-ti-ma-tion
es-trange
  es-tranged
  es-trang-ing
  es-trange-ment
  es-tran-ger
es-trus
es-tu-ar-y
  es-tu-ar-ies
  es-tu-ar-i-al
etch
  etch-er
  etch-ing
e-ter-nal
  e-ter-nal-ly
e-ter-ni-ty
e-ter-nize
  e-ter-nized
  e-ter-niz-ing
  e-ter-ni-za-tion

eth-a-nol
e-ther
e-the-re-al
  e-the-re-al-i-ty
  e-the-re-al-ly
  e-the-re-al-ness
e-the-re-al-ize
  e-the-re-al-ized
  e-the-re-al-iz-ing
  e-the-re-al-i-za-tion
eth-ic
  eth-i-cal
  eth-i-cal-ly
  eth-ics
eth-nic
  eth-ni-cal
  eth-ni-cal-ly
eth-nol-o-gy
eth-yl
eti-ol-o-gy
  eti-o-log-ist
  eti-o-log-i-cal
  eti-o-log-i-cal-ly
et-i-quette
e-tude
et-y-mol-o-gy
  et-y-mol-o-gies
  et-y-mo-log-ic
  et-y-mo-log-i-cal
  et-y-mol-o-gist
eu-ca-lyp-tus
  eu-ca-lyp-tus-es
  eu-ca-lyp-ti
eu-gen-ic
eu-lo-gise
  eu-lo-gized
  eu-lo-giz-ing
  eu-lo-gis-tic
  eu-lo-gis-ti-cal-ly
eu-nuch
eu-phe-mism
  eu-phe-mist
  eu-phe-mis-tic
  eu-phe-mis-ti-cal
  eu-phe-mis-ti-cal-ly
eu-phe-mize
  eu-phe-mized
  eu-phe-miz-ing

eu-pho-ni-ous
  eu-pho-ni-ous-ly
  eu-pho-ni-ous-ness
eu-pho-ny
  eu-phon-ic
  eu-phon-i-cal
  eu-phon-i-cal-ly
  eu-pho-ria
  eu-phor-ic
eu-re-ka
eu-tha-na-sia
e-vac-u-ate
  e-vac-u-at-ed
  e-vac-u-at-ing
  e-vac-u-a-tion
  e-vac-u-a-tive
  e-vac-u-a-tor
e-vac-u-ee
e-vade
  e-vad-ed
  e-vad-ing
  e-vad-a-ble
  e-vad-er
  e-vad-ing-ly
e-val-u-ate
  e-val-u-at-ed
  e-val-u-at-ing
  e-val-u-a-tion
  e-val-u-a-tor
ev-a-nesce
  ev-a-nesced
  ev-a-nesc-ing
ev-a-nes-cent
  ev-a-nes-cence
  ev-a-nes-cent-ly
e-van-gel
  evan-gel-i-cal
  evan-gel-ic
  evan-gel-i-cal-ism
  evan-gel-i-cal-ly
  evan-gel-i-cal-ness
evan-ge-lism
  evan-ge-lis-tic
  evan-ge-lis-ti-cal-ly
evan-ge-list
evan-ge-lize
  evan-ge-lized
  evan-ge-liz-ing

evan-ge-li-za-tion
evan-ge-liz-er
e-vap-o-rate
e-vap-o-rat-ed
e-vap-o-rat-ing
e-vap-o-ra-ble
e-vap-o-ra-tion
e-vap-o-ra-tive
e-vap-o-ra-tor
e-va-sion
e-va-sive
e-va-sive-ly
e-va-sive-ness
e-ven
e-ven-ly
e-ven-ness
e-ven-hand-ed
eve-ning
e-vent
e-vent-ful
event-ful-ly
event-ful-ness
e-ven-tu-al
e-ven-tu-al-ly
e-ven-tu-al-i-ty
e-ven-tu-al-i-ties
e-ven-tu-ate
e-ven-tu-at-ed
e-ven-tu-at-ing
ev-er
ev-er-green
ev-er-last-ing
ev-er-last-ing-ly
ev-er-last-ing-ness
ev-er-more
e-vert
e-ver-si-ble
e-ver-sion
eve-ry
eve-ry-body
eve-ry-day
eve-ry-one
eve-ry-thing
eve-ry-where
e-vict
e-vic-tion
e-vic-tor
ev-i-dence

ev-i-denced
ev-i-denc-ing
ev-i-dent
ev-i-dent-ly
ev-i-den-tial
ev-i-den-tial-ly
e-vil
e-vince
e-vinced
e-vinc-ing
e-vin-ci-ble
e-vis-cer-ate
e-vis-cer-at-ed
e-vis-cer-at-ing
e-vis-cer-a-tion
e-voke
e-voked
e-vok-ing
ev-o-ca-tion
ev-o-lu-tion
ev-o-lu-tion-al
ev-o-lu-tion-ary
ev-o-lu-tion-ism
ev-ol-lu-tion-ist
e-volve
e-volved
e-volv-ing
e-volv-a-ble
e-volve-ment
e-volv-er
ew-er
ex-ac-er-bate
ex-ac-er-bat-ed
ex-ac-er-bat-ing
ex-ac-er-ba-tion
ex-act
ex-act-a-ble
ex-ac-tor
ex-act-ing
ex-act-ing-ly
ex-act-ing-ness
ex-act-i-tude
ex-act-ly
ex-ag-ger-ate
ex-ag-ger-at-ed
ex-ag-ger-at-ing
ex-ag-ger-a-tion
ex-ag-ger-a-tor

ex-alt
ex-alt-er
ex-al-ta-tion
ex-alt-ed
ex-alt-ed-ly
ex-alt-ed-ness
ex-am
ex-am-i-na-tion
ex-am-ine
ex-am-ined
ex-am-in-ing
ex-am-in-a-ble
ex-am-in-er
ex-am-i-nee
ex-am-ple
ex-am-pled
ex-am-pling
ex-as-per-ate
ex-as-per-at-ed
ex-as-per-at-ing
ex-as-per-a-tion
ex-ca-vate
ex-ca-vat-ed
ex-ca-cat-ing
ex-ca-va-tion
ex-ca-va-tor
ex-ceed
ex-ceed-ing
ex-ceed-ing-ly
ex-cel
ex-celled
ex-cel-ling
ex-cel-lence
ex-cel-len-cy
ex-cel-len-cies
ex-cel-lent
ex-cel-lent-ly
ex-cel-si-or
ex-cept
ex-cept-ing
ex-cep-tion
ex-cep-tion-a-ble
ex-cep-tion-al
ex-cerpt
ex-cess
ex-ces-sive
ex-ces-sive-ly
ex-ces-sive-ness

ex99

ex-change
 ex-changed
 ex-chang-ing
 ex-change-a-bil-i-ty
 ex-change-a-ble
 ex-chan-ger
ex-cheq-uer
ex-cise
 ex-cised
 ex-cis-ing
 ex-cis-a-ble
 ex-ci-sion
ex-cit-a-ble
 ex-cit-a-bil-i-ty
 ex-cit-a-bly
 ex-ci-ta-tion
ex-cite
 ex-cit-ed
 ex-cit-ing
ex-cit-ed
 ex-cit-ed-ly
 ex-cit-ed-ness
ex-cite-ment
ex-cit-ing
 ex-cit-ing-ly
ex-claim
ex-cla-ma-tion
 ex-clam-a-to-ry
 ex-clam-a-to-ri-ly
ex-clude
ex-clu-sion
ex-clu-sive
 ex-clu-sive-ly
 ex-clu-sive-ness
 ex-clu-siv-i-ty
ex-com-mu-ni-cate
ex-co-ri-ate
 ex-co-ri-at-ed
 ex-co-ri-at-ing
 ex-co-ri-a-tion
ex-cre-ment
 ex-cre-men-tal
ex-cres-cence
 ex-cres-cent
ex-cre-ta
 ex-cre-tal
ex-crete
 ex-cret-ed

ex-cret-ing
ex-cre-tion
ex-cru-ci-ate
 ex-cru-ci-at-ed
 ex-cru-ci-at-ing
 ex-cru-ci-at-ing-ly
 ex-cru-ci-a-tion
ex-cul-pate
 ex-cul-pat-ed
 ex-cul-pat-ing
 ex-cul-pa-tion
 ex-cul-pa-to-ry
ex-cur-sion
 ex-cur-sion-al
 ex-cur-sion-ary
 ex-cur-sion-ist
ex-cur-sive
 ex-cur-sive-ly
 ex-cur-sive-ness
ex-cus-a-to-ry
ex-cuse
ex-e-cra-ble
 ex-e-cra-ble-ness
 ex-e-cra-bly
ex-e-crate
 ex-e-crat-ed
 ex-e-crat-ing
 ex-e-cra-tive
 ex-e-cra-tor
ex-e-cra-tion
ex-e-cute
 ex-e-cut-ed
 ex-e-cut-ing
 ex-e-cut-a-ble
 ex-e-cut-er
ex-e-cu-tion
ex-e-cu-tion-er
ex-ec-u-tive
 ex-ec-u-tive-ly
ex-ec-u-tor
 ex-ec-u-tor-ship
ex-e-ge-sis
ex-em-pli-fy
 ex-em-pli-fied
 ex-em-pli-fy-ing
 ex-em-pli-fi-a-ble
 ex-em-pli-fi-ca-tion
ex-empt

ex-emp-tion
ex-er-cise
 ex-er-cised
 ex-er-cis-ing
 ex-er-cis-er
ex-ert
ex-er-tion
ex-fo-li-ate
 ex-fo-li-at-ed
 ex-fo-li-at-ing
 ex-fo-li-a-tion
ex-hal-la-tion
ex-hale
 ex-haled
 ex-hal-ing
 ex-hal-ant
ex-haust
ex-hib-it
 ex-hib-it-a-ble
 ex-hib-i-tor
 ex-hib-i-to-ry
ex-hi-bi-tion
 ex-hi-bi-tion-ism
 ex-hi-bi-tion-ist
 ex-hi-bi-tion-is-tic
ex-hil-a-rate
ex-hort
 ex-hor-ta-tive
 ex-hor-ta-to-ry
 ex-hort-er
 ex-hort-ing-ly
ex-hor-ta-tion
ex-hume
 ex-humed
 ex-hum-ing
ex-i-gen-cy
 ex-i-gen-cies
ex-i-gent
 ex-i-gent-ly
ex-ile
 ex-iled
ex-ist
 ex-ist-ence
 ex-ist-ent
ex-is-ten-tial
 ex-is-ten-tial-ly
ex-it
ex li-bris

ex-o-dus
ex of-fi-ci-o
ex-og-a-my
  ex-og-a-mous
ex-og-e-nous
  ex-og-e-nous-ly
ex-on-er-ate
ex-or-bi-tant
  ex-or-bi-tance
  ex-or-bi-tant-ly
ex-or-cise
  ex-or-cised
  ex-or-cis-ing
  ex-or-cism
  ex-or-cist
ex-o-tic
  ex-ot-i-cal-ly
  ex-ot-i-cism
ex-pand
  ex-pand-er
ex-panse
  ex-pan-si-ble
ex-pan-sion
  ex-pan-sion-ism
  ex-pan-sion-ist
ex-pan-sive
  ex-pan-sive-ly
  ex-pan-sive-ness
ex-pa-ti-ate
  ex-pa-ti-at-ed
  ex-pa-ti-at-ing
  ex-pa-ti-a-tion
ex-pa-tri-ate
  ex-pa-tri-at-ed
  ex-pa-tri-at-ing
  ex-pa-tri-a-tion
ex-pect
  ex-pect-a-ble
  ex-pect-a-bly
  ex-pect-ing-ly
ex-pect-an-cy
  ex-pect-an-cies
ex-pect-ant
  ex-pect-ant-ly
ex-pec-ta-tion
ex-pec-to-rate
  ex-pec-to-rat-ed
  ex-pec-to-rat-ing

ex-pec-to-ra-tion
ex-pe-di-en-cy
  ex-pe-di-ent
  ex-pe-di-ent-ly
ex-pe-dite
  ex-pe-dit-ed
  ex-pe-dit-ing
  ex-pe-dit-er
ex-pe-di-tion
  ex-pe-di-tion-ary
ex-pe-di-tious
  ex-pe-di-tious-ly
ex-pel
  ex-pelled
  ex-pel-ling
ex-pend
  ex-pend-a-ble
  ex-pend-a-bil-i-ty
ex-pend-i-ture
ex-pense
  ex-pen-sive
  ex-pen-sive-ly
  ex-pen-sive-ness
ex-pe-ri-ence
  ex-pe-ri-enced
  ex-pe-ri-enc-ing
ex-pe-ri-en-tial
  ex-pe-ri-en-tial-ly
ex-per-i-ment
  ex-per-i-men-ta-tion
  ex-per-i-men-tal
  ex-per-i-men-tal-ism
  ex-per-i-men-tal-ist
  ex-per-i-men-tal-ly
ex-pert
  ex-pert-ly
  ex-pert-ness
ex-per-tise
ex-pi-ra-tion
  ex-pir-a-to-ry
ex-pire
  ex-pired
  ex-pir-ing
ex-plain
  ex-plain-a-ble
  ex-plain-er
ex-pla-na-tion
  ex-plan-a-to-ry

ex-plan-a-to-ri-ly
ex-ple-tive
ex-pli-ca-ble
ex-pli-cate
  ex-pli-cat-ed
  ex-pli-cat-ing
  ex-pli-ca-tion
  ex-pli-ca-tive
  ex-pli-ca-tor
ex-plic-it
  ex-plic-it-ly
  ex-plic-it-ness
ex-plode
  ex-plod-ed
  ex-plod-ing
  ex-plod-er
ex-ploit
  ex-ploit-a-ble
  ex-ploi-ta-tion
  ex-ploit-er
  ex-ploit-ive
ex-plore
  ex-plo-ra-tion
  ex-plor-a-to-ry
  ex-plor-er
ex-plo-sion
ex-plo-sive
  ex-plo-sive-ly
  ex-plo-sive-ness
ex-po-nent
  ex-po-nen-tial
  ex-po-nen-tial-ly
ex-port
  ex-port-a-ble
  ex-por-ta-tion
  ex-port-er
ex-pose
  ex-posed
  ex-pos-ing
  ex-pos-er
ex-po-si-tion
  ex-pos-i-tor
  ex-pos-i-to-ry
ex post fac-to
ex-pos-tu-late
ex-po-sure
ex-pound
  ex-pound-er

ex-press
ex-press-er
ex-press-i-ble
ex-pres-sion
ex-pres-sive
ex-pres-sive-ly
ex-pres-sive-ness
ex-press-ly
ex-press-way
ex-pro-pri-ate
ex-pro-pri-at-ing
ex-pro-pri-a-tor
ex-pro-pri-a-tion
ex-pul-sion
ex-pul-sive
ex-punge
ex-pur-gate
ex-pur-ga-to-ry
ex-pur-ga-to-ri-al
ex-qui-site
ex-qui-site-ly
ex-qui-site-ness
ex-tant
ex-tem-po-ra-ne-ous
ex-tem-po-rize
ex-tem-po-rized
ex-tem-po-riz-ing
ex-tem-po-ri-za-tion
ex-tem-po-riz-er
ex-tend
ex-tend-i-bil-i-ty
ex-tend-i-ble
ex-tend-ed
ex-tend-ed-ly
ex-tend-ed-ness
ex-tend-er
ex-ten-si-ble
ex-ten-si-bil-i-ty
ex-ten-sion
ex-ten-sion-al
ex-ten-sive
ex-ten-sive-ly
ex-ten-sive-ness
ex-tent
ex-ten-u-ate
ex-te-ri-or
ex-te-ri-or-ly
ex-ter-mi-nate

ex-ter-mi-nat-ed
ex-ter-mi-nat-ing
ex-ter-mi-na-tion
ex-ter-mi-na-tor
ex-ter-nal
ex-ter-nal-ly
ex-tinct
ex-tinc-tion
ex-tin-guish
ex-tin-guish-a-ble
ex-tin-guish-er
ex-tin-guish-ment
ex-tir-pate
ex-tir-pat-ed
ex-tir-pat-ing
ex-tir-pa-tion
ex-tir-pa-tive
ex-tol
ex-tol-ler
ex-tol-lingly
ex-tol-ment
ex-tort
ex-tor-ter
ex-tor-tive
ex-tor-tion
ex-tra
ex-tract
ex-tract-a-ble
ex-trac-tive
ex-trac-tor
ex-trac-tion
ex-tra-cur-ric-u-lar
ex-tra-dite
ex-tra-ne-ous
ex-tra-ne-ous-ly
ex-tra-ne-ous-ness
ex-traor-di-nary
ex-traor-di-nar-i-ly
ex-trap-o-late
ex-trap-o-lat-ed
ex-trap-o-lat-ing
ex-trap-o-la-tion
ex-tra-sen-so-ry
ex-tra-ter-res-tri-al
ex-tra-ter-ri-to-ri-al
ex-trav-a-gance
ex-trav-a-gan-cy
ex-trav-a-gant

ex-trav-a-gant-ly
ex-trav-a-gan-za
ex-treme
ex-treme-ly
ex-treme-ness
ex-trem-ist
ex-trem-ism
ex-trem-i-ty
ex-trem-i-ties
ex-tri-cate
ex-tri-cat-ed
ex-tri-cat-ing
ex-tri-ca-ble
ex-tri-ca-tion
ex-trin-sic
ex-tro-vert
ex-tro-ver-sion
ex-trude
ex-u-ber-ance
ex-u-ber-ant
ex-u-ber-ant-ly
ex-ude
ex-ud-ed
ex-ud-ing
ex-u-da-tion
ex-ult
ex-ult-ant
ex-ult-ant-ly
ex-ul-at-tion
ex-ult-ing-ly
ex-ur-ban-ite
eye
eyed
eye-ing
eye-ball
eye-glass
eye-glass-es
eye-hole
eye-lash
eye-let
eye-lid
eye-o-pen-er
eye-o-pen-ing
eye-wit-ness
eyre
ey-rie
ey-ry
ey-ries

fa-ble
 fa-bled
fab-ric
fab-ri-cant
fab-ri-cate
 fab-ri-cated
 fab-ri-cat-ing
 fab-ri-ca-tion
fab-u-lar
fab-u-list
fab-u-lous
 fab-u-lous-ly
 fab-u-lous-ness
fa-cade
 fa-cades
face
 faced
 fac-ing
face card
face--lift
fac-et
 fac-et-ed
fa-ce-ti-ae
fa-ce-tious
 fa-ce-tious-ly
 fa-ce-ti-ous-ness
fa-cial
 fa-cial-ly
fac-ile
 fac-ile-ly
 fac-ile-ness
fa-cil-i-tate
 fa-cil-i-tat-ed
 fa-cil-i-ta-tive
 fa-cil-i-ta-tor
fa-cil-i-ty
 fa-cil-i-ties
fac-ing
fac-sim-i-le
fact
 fac-tic-i-ty
fac-tion
 fac-tion-al
 fac-tion-al-ism
 fac-tion-al-ly
fac-ti-tious
 fac-ti-tious-ly
 fac-ti-tious-ness

fac-tor
 fac-tor-able
 fac-tored
 fac-tor-ing
fac-to-ry
 fac-to-ries
fac-to-tum
fac-tu-al
 fac-tu-al-i-ty
 fac-tu-al-ly
 fac-tu-al-ness
fac-ul-ty
fad
 fad-dish
 fad-dish-ness
 fad-dism
 fad-dist
fade
 fad-ed
 fad-ing
fa-er-ie
 fa-ery
 fa-er-ies
fag
 faggged
 fag-ging
fag-got
fag-ot
Fahr-en-heit
fail-ing
 fail-ing-ly
fail-safe
fail-ure
faint
 faint-ish
 faint-ish-ness
 faint-ly
 faint-ness
faint-heart-ed
 faint-herat-ed-ly
 faint-heart-ed-ness
fair
 fir-ness
fair-ground
fair-ly
fair-mind-ed
 fair-mind-ed-ness
fair--trade

fair-y
 fair-ies
fair-y-like
fair-y tale
faith
faith-ful
 faith-ful-less
fake
 faked
 fak-ing
 fak-er
fal-con
fal-con-ry
fall
 fall-en
 fall-ing
fal-la-cious
 fal-la-cious-ly
 fal-la-cious-ness
fal-la-cy
 fal-la-cies
fall-guy
fal-li-ble
 fal-li-bly
fail-ing star
fall-out
 fallings-out
 falling-outs
fal-low
 fal-low-ness
false
 fals-er
 fals-est
false-hood
fal-si-fy
 fal-si-fi-ca-tion
 fal-si-fied
 fal-si-fi-er
 fal-si-fy-ing
fal-si-ty
 fal-si-ties
fal-ter
 fal-tered
 fal-ter-er
 fal-ter-ing
 fal-ter-ing-ly
fame
 famed

fa-mil-ial
fa-mil-iar
  fa-mil-iar-ly
  fa-mil-iar-ness
fa-mil-i-ar-i-ty
  fa-mil-iar-ize
  fa-mil-iar-iz-ing
fam-ily
  fam-i-lies
fam-ine
fam-ish
  fam-ished
  fam-ish-ment
fa-mous
  fa-mous-ly
  fa-mous-ness
fan
  fan-like
  fanned
  fan-ner
  fan-ning
fa-nat-ic
  fa-nat-i-cal
fa-nat-i-cism
fa-nat-i-cize
  fa-nat-i-cized
fan-ci-er
fan-ci-ful
  fan-ci-ful-ly
  fan-ci-ful-ness
fan-cy
  fan-cied
  fan-cies
  fan-ci-est
  fan-ci-ly
  fan-ci-ness
  fan-cy-ing
fan-cy-work
fan-fare
fang
  fanged
fan-light
fan-tas-tic
  fan-tas-ti-cal
  fan-tas-ti-cal-i-ty
  fan-tas-ti-cal-ly
fan-ta-sy

fan-ta-sies
far
  far-ther
  far-thest
  fur-ther
  fur-thest
far-a-way
farce
  farced
  farc-ing
far-ci-cal
  far-ci-cal-ly
fare
  fared
  far-ing
fare-well
far-fetched
far-flung
far-gone
farm
farm-er
farm-hand
farm-house
farm-ing
farm-land
farm-yard
far-off
far-reach-ing
  far-reach-ing-ly
far-see-ing
far-sight-ed
  far-sight-ed-ly
far-ther
far-ther-most
far-thest
fas-ci-a
  fas-ci-ae
fas-ci-cle
  fas-ci-cled
fas-ci-nate
  fas-ci-nat-ed
  fas-ci-nat-ing
fas-ci-na-tion
fas-cism
  fas-cist
  fa-scis-tic
fash-ion
fash-ion-ble

fast
fas-ten
  fas-ten-er
  fas-ten-ing
fas-tid-i-ous
  fas-ti-di-ous-ly
fat
  fat-ter
  fat-test
fa-tal
  fa-tal-ly
fa-tal-ism
  fa-tal-ist
fa-tal-i-ty
  fa-tal-i-ties
fate
  fat-ed
  fat-ing
fate-ful
  fate-ful-ly
  fate-ful-ness
fa-ther
fa-ther-hood
  fa-ther-ly
fa-ther-in-law
  fa-thers-in-law
fa-ther-land
fath-om
  fath-om-a-ble
  fath-om-less
fa-tique
  fa-tiqued
  fa-tiq-uing
fat-i-ga-ble
fat-ten
  fat-ten-er
fat-ty
  fat-ti-er
  fat-ti-est
  fat-ti-ness
  fat-tish
fa-tu-i-ty
  fa-tui-ties
fat-u-ous
  fat-u-ous-ly
  fat-u-ous-ness
fau-cet
fault

fault-find-er
fault-find-ing
fault-less
fault-less-ly
fault-less-ness
fault-y
fault-i-er
fault-i-est
fault-i-ly
fau-na
fau-nas
fau-nae
faux pas
fa-vor
fa-vor-ing-ly
fa-vor-a-ble
fa-vor-ably
fa-vored
fa-vored-ly
fa-vored-ness
fa-vor-ite
fa-vor-it-ism
fawn
faze
fazed
faz-ing
fe-al-ty
fear
fear-ful
fear-ful-ly
fear-ful-ness
fear-less
fear-less-ly
fear-less-ness
fear-some
fear-some-ly
fear-some-ness
fea-si-ble
fea-si-bil-i-ty
fea-si-ble-ness
fea-si-bly
feast
feat
feath-er
fea-thered
feath-er-bed-ding
fea-ture
fea-tured

fea-tur-ing
fea-ture-ness
fe-brile
fe-ces
fe-cal
feck-less
fe-cund
fe-cun-di-ty
fe-cun-date
fe-cun-dat-ed
fe-cun-da-tion
fed-er-al
fed-er-al-ism
fed-er-li-ist
fed-er-al-ize
fed-er-al-ized
fed-er-al-iz-ing
fed-er-al-i-za-tion
fed-er-al-ly
fed-er-ate
fed-er-at-ed
fed-er-at-ing
fed-er-a-tion
fee
fee-ble
fee-bler
fee-blest
fee-bly
fee-ble-mind-ed
fee-ble-mind-ed-ness
feed
fed
feed-ing
feed-er
feed-back
feel
feel-ing
feel-er
feel-ing
feel-ing-ly
feel-ing-ness
feign
feigned
feign-ed-ly
feign-er
feign-ing-ly
feint
feist-y

feist-i-er
feist-i-est
fe-lic-i-tate
fe-lic-i-tat-ed
fe-lic-i-tat-ing
fe-lic-i-ta-tion
fe-lic-i-tous
fe-lic-i-tous-ly
fe-lic-i-ty
fe-lic-i-ties
fe-line
fe-line-ly
fe-line-i-ty
fell
fel-la-ti-o
fel-low
fel-low-ship
fe-lon
fel-o-ny
fel-o-nies
fe-lo-ni-ous
fe-lo-ni-ous-ly
fe-male
fem-i-nine
fem-i-nine-ly
fem-i-nine-ness
fem-i-nin-i-ty
fem-i-nism
fem-i-nist
fem-i-nis-tic
fem-i-nize
fem-i-nized
fem-i-niz-ing
fe-mur
fe-murs
fem-o-ra
fem-o-ral
fen
fen-ny
fen-ni-er
fen-ni-est
fence
fecned
fenc-ing
fenc-er
fen-der
fe-ral
fer-ment

fer-ment-a-ble
fer-men-ta-tion
fern
fern-er-y
fern-er-ies
fe-ro-cious
fe-ro-cious-ly
fe-ro-ci-ty
fer-ret
fer-ret-er
fer-ro-con-crete
fer-ro-mag-net-ic
fer-ru-gi-nous
fer-rule
fer-ry
fer-ries
fer-ry-boat
fer-ry-man
fer-tile
fer-tile-ly
fer-tile-ness
fer-til-i-ty
fer-ti-li-za-tion
fer-ti-li-za-tion-al
fer-ti-lize
fer-ti-lized
fer-ti-liz-ing
fer-ti-liz-a-ble
fer-ti-liz-er
fer-vent
fer-ven-cy
fer-vid
fer-vid-ly
fer-vid-ness
fer-vor
fes-ter
fes-ti-val
fes-tive
fes-tive-ly
fes-tive-ness
fes-tiv-i-ty
fes-toon
fes-toon-ery
fes-toon-er-ies
fe-tal
fetch
fetch-er
fetch-ing

fetch-ing-ly
fete
fet-id
fet-id-ly
fet-id-ness
fet-ish
fet-ish-ism
fet-ish-ist
fet-ish-is-tic
fet-lock
fet-ter
fet-tle
fe-tus
fe-tus-es
feud
feud-ist
feu-dal
feu-dal-ism
feu-dal-ist
feu-dal-is-tic
feu-dal-i-za-tion
feu-dal-ize
feu-dal-ized
feu-dal-iz-ing
fe-ver
fe-ver blis-ter
fe-ver-ish
fe-ver-ish-ly
fe-ver-ish-ness
fe-ver-ous
fe-ver-ous-ly
few
few-ness
fez-zes
fi-as-co
fi-as-cos
fi-as-coes
fi-at
fib
fi-ber
fi-bered
fi-ber-board
fi-ber-glass
fi-bril
fi-bril-la-tion
fi-broid
fi-brous
fib-u-la

fib-u-las
fib-u-lae
fick-le
fick-le-ness
fic-tion
fic-tion-al
fic-tion-al-ly
fic-ti-tious
fid-dle
fid-dler
fid-dled
fi-del-i-ty
fidg-et
fidg-ety
field-er
field-glass
fiend
fiend-ish
fiend-ish-ly
fiend-ish-ness
fierce
fierce-ly
fierce-ness
fier-y
fier-i-er
fier-i-est
fier-i-ly
fier-i-ness
fif-teen
fif-teenth
fifth
fif-ti-eth
fif-ty
fif-ties
fight
fight-er
fig-ment
fig-u-ra-tion
fig-u-ra-tive
fig-u-ra-tive-ly
fid-u-ra-tive-ness
fig-ure
fig-ured
fig-ur-ing
fig-ur-er
fig-ure-head
fig-ur-ine
fil-a-ment

fil-a-men-ta-ry
fil-a-ment-ed
fil-a-men-tous
filch
file
  filed
  fil-ing
fi-let
fi-let mi-gnon
fil-i-al
  fil-i-al-ly
fil-i-bus-ter
fil-i-gree
  fil-i-greed
  fil-i-gree-ing
  fil-lings
fill-er
fil-let
fill-ing
fil-lip
fil-ly
  fil-lies
film-strip
film-y
  film-i-er
  film-i-est
  film-i-ness
fil-ter
filth
  filth-i-ness
  filthy
  filth-i-er
  filth-i-est
fin
  finned
  fin-ning
  fin-less
  fin-like
fi-na-gled
  fi-na-gling
  fi-na-gler
fi-nal
fi-na-le
fi-nal-ist
fi-nal-i-ty
  fi-nal-i-ties
fi-nal-ize
  fi-nal-ized

fi-nal-iz-ing
fi-nal-ly
fi-nance
  fi-nanced
  fi-nanc-ing
  fi-nan-cial
  fi-nan-cial-ly
fin-an-cier
finch
find
  found
  find-ing
find-er
fine
  fin-er
  fin-est
  fine-ly
  fine-ness
fin-er-y
  fin-er-ies
fi-nesse
  fi-nessed
  fi-ness-ing
fin-ger
fin-ger-bowl
fin-ger-ing
fin-ger-nail
fin-ger-print
fin-i-al
fin-i-cal
  fin-i-cal-ly
fin-ick-y
  fin-ick-ing
fin-is
  fin-is-es
fin-ish
  fin-ished
  fin-ish-er
fi-nite
  fi-nite-ly
  fi-nite-ness
fire
  fired
  fir-ing
  fir-er
fire-arm
fire-ball
fire-brand

fire-bug
fire-crack-er
fire-fight-er
fire-fly
  fire-flies
fire-man
fire-place
fire-plug
fire-pow-er
fire-proof
fire-side
fire-trap
fire-wa-ter
fire-wood
fire-works
fir-ing-squad
firm
  firm-ly
  firm-ness
fir-ma-ment
first-born
first-hand
first-ling
first-ly
first-rate
first-string
fis-cal
  fis-cal-ly
fish-er
fish-er-man
  fish-er-men
fish-er-y
  fish-er-ies
fish-hook
fish-ing
fish-wife
  fish-wived
fish-y
  fish-i-er
  fish-i-est
fis-sle
fis-sion
fis-sure
  fis-sured
  fis-sur-ing
fist-ic
fist-i-cuff
fit

fit-ter
fit-test
fit-ted
fit-ting
fit-ly
fit-ness
fit-ful
fit-ful-ly
fit-ful-ness
fit-ting
fit-ting-ly
fit-ting-ness
five-fold
five-and-ten
fix
fix-a-ble
fixed
fix-ed-ly
fix-er
fix-a-tion
fix-a-tive
fix-ings
fix-i-ty
fix-i-ties
fix-ture
fiz-zle
fiz-zled
fiz-zling
fiz-zy
fiz-zi-er
fiz-zi-est
flab-ber-gast
flab-by
flab-bi-er
flab-bi-est
flab-bi-ly
flab-bi-ness
flac-cid
flag
flagged
flag-ging
flag-el-lant
flag-el-lat-ed
flag-el-lat-ing
flag-el-la-tion
fla-gi-tious
flag-on
flag-pole

flag-rank
fla-grant
fla-grant-ly
flag-ship
flag-stone
flail
flair
flake
flaked
flak-ing
flak-y
flak-i-er
flak-i-est
flak-i-ness
flam-boy-ant
flam-boy-ance
flam-boy-an-cy
flam-boy-ant-ly
flame
flamed
falm-ing
flam-ing-ly
flam-ma-ble
flange
flank
flank-er
flan-nel-ette
flap
flapped
flap-ping
flap-per
flap-jack
flare
flared
flar-ing
flare-up
flash-back
flash-light
flash-i-er
flash-i-est
flash-i-ly
flash-i-ness
flask
flat
flat-ly
flat-ted
flat-ting
flat-ness

flat-car
flat-foot
flat-foot-ed
flat-foot-ed-ly
falt-ten
flat-ten-er
flat-ter
flat-ter-er
flat-ter-ing-ly
flat-ter-y
flat-ter-ies
flat-u-lent
flat-u-lence
flat-u-len-cy
flat-u-lent-ly
flat-ware
flaunt
flaunt-er
flaunt-ing-ly
flanty
flaunt-i-er
flaunt-i-est
flau-tist
fla-vor
fla-vored
fla-vor-less
fla-vor-ing
flaw-less
fla-zen
flax-seed
flay-er
flea-bite
flea-bit-ten
fleck
flec-tion
fledge
fledged
fledg-ing
fledg-ling
flee
fled
flee-ing
fleece
fleeced
fleec-ing
fleec-y
fleec-i-er
fleec-i-est

fleec-i-ness
fleet
  fleet-ly
  fleet-ness
fleet-ing
  fleet-ing-ly
  fleet-ing-ness
flesh-ly
  flesh-li-er
  flesh-li-est
flesh-pots
flesh-y
  flesh-i-ert
  flesh-i-est
flesh-i-ness
flex-i-ble
  flex-i-bil-i-ty
  flex-i-bly
flex-ion
flex-or
flex-ure
fib-ber-ti-gib-bet
flick-er
  flick-er-ing
fli-er
flight
  flight-less
flight-y
  flight-i-er
  flight-i-est
  flight-i-ly
  flight-i-ness
flim-flam
  flim-flammed
  flim-flam-ming
firm-sy
  firm-si-er
  firm-si-est
  firm-si-ly
  firm-si-ness
flinch
  flinch-er
  flinch-ing-ly
fin-ders
fling
  flung
  fling-ing
flint-y

flint-i-er
flint-i-est
flint-i-ness
flip
  flipped
  flip-ping
flip-flop
flip-pant
  flip-pan-cy
  flip-pant-ly
flip-per
flirt-er
flir-ta-tion
  flir-ta-tious
flit
  flit-ted
  flit-ting
  flit-ter
float-a-ble
float-a-tion
float-er
float-ing
floc-cu-lent
  floc-cu-lence
flocked
flood-gate
flood-light
  flood-lit
floor-ing
floor-walk-er
floo-zy
  floo-zies
flop
  flopped
  flop-ping
  flop-per
flop-house
flop-py
  flop-pi-er
  flop-pi-est
  flop-pi-ly
flo-ra
  flo-ras
  flo-rae
flo-ral
flo-res-cence
  flo-res-cent
flo-ret

flo-ri-cul-ture
  flo-ri-cul-tur-al
  flo-ri-cul-tur-ist
flor-id
  flo-rid-i-ty
  flor-id-ly
  flor-id-ness
flo-rist
floss
  flossy
  floss-i-er
  floss-i-est
flo-ta-tion
flo-til-la
flot-sam
flounce
  flounced
  flounc-ing
floun-der
flour-y
  flour-i-er
  flour-i-est
flour-ish
  flou-rish-ing
flow-er
  flow-ered
  flow-er-ing
flow-ery
  flow-er-i-ness
flub
  flubbed
  flub-bing
fluc-tu-ate
  fluc-tu-at-ed
  fluc-tu-at-ing
  fluc-tu-a-tion
flue
  flu-ent
  flu-ency
  flu-ent-ly
fluff
  fluff-i-ness
  fluff-y
  fluff-i-er
  fluff-i-est
flu-id
  flu-id-ly
  flu-id-ness

fluke
fluky
fluk-i-er
fluk-i-est
flum-mer-y
flum-mer-ies
flun-ky
flunk-ies
flu-o-resce
flu-o-resced
flu-o-resc-ing
flu-o-res-cence
flu-o-res-sent
flur-ry
flur-ries
flur-ried
flur-ry-ing
flus-ter
flute
flut-ed
flut-ing
flut-ist
flut-ter
flut-ter-er
flut-ter-ing-ly
flut-tery
flut-ter-i-er
flut-ter-i-est
flux-ion
fly-brown
fly-by-night
fly-er
fly-ing
fly-leaf
fly-leaves
fly-pa-per
fly-speck
fly-wheel
foal
foam
foam-i-ness
foam-y
foam-i-er
foam-i-est
fob
fobbed
fob-bing
fo-cal

fo-cal-lize
fo-cal-lized
fo-cal-iz-ing
fo-cus
fo-cus-es
fo-cus-ing
fo-cus-er
fod-der
foe-tus
foe-tal
fog
fogged
fog-ging
fog-gy
fog-gi-er
fog-gi-est
fog-gi-ly
fog-gi-ness
fog-horn
fo-gy
fo-gies
fo-gy-ish
foi-ble
fold-er
fol-de-rol
fo-li-a-ceous
fo-li-age
fo-li-ate
fo-li-at-ed
fo-li-at-ing
fol-li-a-tion
fo-li-o
fo-li-os
fol-li-oed
fo-li-o-ing
folk-lore
folk-lor-ist
flok-sy
flok-si-er
flok-si-est
flok-si-ness
folk-ways
fol-li-cle
fol-lic-u-lar
fol-low
fol-low-er
fol-low-ing
fol-ly

fol-lies
fo-ment
fo-men-ta-tion
fo-ment-er
fon-dant
fon-dle
fond-led
fon-dling
fon-dler
fond-ly
fond-ness
fon-due
food-stuff
fool-er-y
fool-er-ies
fool-har-dy
fool-har-di-ness
fool-proof
fools-cap
foot-age
foot-ball
foot-board
foot-can-dle
foot-ed
foot-fall
foot-hill
foot-hold
foot-ing
foot-lights
foot-loose
foot-note
foot-not-ed
foot-not-ing
foot-path
foot-print
foot-sore
foot-step
foot-stool
foot-wear
foot-work
foo-zle
foo-zled
foo-zling
fop
fop-pery
fop-per-ies
fop-pish
fop-pish-ly

fop-pish-ness
for-age
  for-aged
  for-ag-ing
for-ay
for-bear
  for-bore
  for-borned
  for-bear-ing
  for-bear-ance
  for-bear-ing-ly
for-bid
  for-bade
  for-bid-den
  for-bid-ding
  for-bid-ding-ness
force
  forced
  forc-ing
  forc-a-ble
  force-less
  forc-er
force-ful
  force-ful-ly
  force-ful-ness
for-ceps
for-ci-ble
  for-ci-bly
ford-a-ble
  fore-arm
fore-bear
fore-bode
  fore-bod-ed
  fore-bod-ing
  fore-bod-er
fore-brain
fore-cast
  fore-cast-ed
  fore-cast-ing
  fore-cast-er
fore-close
  fore-closed
  fore-clos-ing
  fore-clo-sure
fore-fa-ther
fore-fin-ger
fore-foot
  fore-feet

fore-front
fore-gath-er
fore-go
  fore-went
  fore-gone
  fore-go-ing
fore-ground
fore-hand
fore-hand-ed
  fore-hand-ed-ness
fore-head
for-eign
  for-eign-er
  for-eign-ness
fore-know
  fore-knew
  fore-known
  fore-know-ing
  fore-knowl-edge
fore-leg
fore-lock
fore-man
  fore-men
fore-most
fore-noon
fo-ren-sic
fore-or-dain
fore-quar-ter
fore-run
  fore-ran
  fore-run-ning
fore-run-ner
fore-see
  fore-saw
  fore-seen
  fore-see-ing
  fore-see-a-ble
  fore-se-er
fore-shad-ow
  fore-shad-ow-er
fore-sight
  fore-sight-ed
  fore-sight-ed-ness
fore-skin
for-est
fore-stall
for-est-a-tion
for-es-ter

for-es-try
fore-taste
  fore-tast-ed
  fore-tast-ing
fore-tell
  fore-told
  fore-tell-ing
  fore-tell-er
fore-thought
for-ev-er
for-ev-er-more
fore-warn
fore-word
for-feit
  for-feit-er
for-fei-ture
for-gath-er
forge
  forged
  forg-ing
  forg-er
for-ger-y
  fog-er-ies
for-get
  for-got
  for-got-ten
  for-get-ting
  for-get-ta-ble
  for-get-ter
for-get-ful
  for-get-ful-ly
  for-get-ful-ness
for-give
  for-gave
  for-giv-en
  for-giv-ing
  for-giv-a-ble
  for-give-ness
  for-giv-er
for-go
  for-went
  for-gone
  for-go-ing
  for-go-er
fork-loft
for-lorn
  for-lorn-ly
  for-lorn-ness

for-mal
  for-mal-ly
for-mal-ism
for-mal-i-ty
  for-mal-i-ties
for-mal-ize
  for-mal-ized
  for-mal-iz-ing
  for-mal-i-za-tion
for-mat
for-ma-tion
form-a-tive
for-mer
for-mer-ly
for-mi-da-ble
  for-mi-da-ble-ness
  for-mi-da-bly
form-less
  form-less-ly
  form-less-ness
for-mu-la
  for-mu-las
  for-mu-lae
for-mu-lar-y
  for-mu-lar-ies
for-mu-late
  for-mu-lat-ed
  for-mu-lat-ing
  for-mu-la-tion
  for-mu-la-tor
for-ni-cate
  for-ni-cat-ed
  for-ni-cat-ing
  for-ni-cat-or
  for-ni-ca-tion
for-sake
  for-soke
  for-sak-en
  for-sak-ing
  for-sak-en-ly
for-swear
  for-swore
  for-sworn
  for-swear-ing
  for-swear-er
fort
forte
forth-com-ing

forth-right
  forth-right-ness
forth-with
for-ti-fi-ca-tion
for-ti-fy
  for-ti-fied
  for-ti-fy-ing
  for-ti-fi-er
for-tis-si-mo
for-ti-tude
fort-night
for-night-ly
  for-night-lies
for-tress
for-tu-i-tous
  for-tu-i-tous-ly
  for-tu-i-tous-ness
for-tu-nate
  for-tu-nate-ly
for-tune
for-tune-tell-er
  for-tune-tell-ing
for-ty
  for-ties
for-ty-nin-er
fo-rum
  fo-rums
  fo-ra
for-ward
  for-ward-er
  for-ward-ly
  for-ward-ness
fos-sil
fos-sil-ize
  fos-sil-ized
  fos-sil-iz-ing
  fos-sil-i-za-tion
fos-ter
  fos-tered
  fos-ter-ing
fought
fou-lard
found
foun-da-tion
  foun-da-tion-al
found-er
found-ling
found-ry

found-ries
foun-tain
foun-tain-head
four-flush-er
four-square
four-teen
  four-teenth
fourth
  fourth-ly
fowl
  fowl-er
fox-hole
  fox-i-er
  fox-i-est
  fox-i-ly
  fox-i-ness
foy-er
fra-cas
  fra-cas-es
frac-tion
  frac-tion-al
frac-tious
  frac-tious-ly
frac-ture
  frac-tured
  frac-tur-ing
frag-ile
  fra-gil-i-ty
frag-ment
  frag-ment-al
  frag-men-ter-i-ness
  frag-men-tary
frag-men-ta-tion
frag-ment-ize
  frag-ment-ized
  frag-ment-iz-ing
fra-grance
  fra-grant
  fra-grant-ly
frail
  frail-ty
  frail-ness
frame
  framed
  fram-ing
  fram-er
frame-up
frame-work

franc
fran-chise
  fran-chised
frank
  frank-er
  frank-ly
  frank-ness
frank-furt-er
frank-in-cense
fran-tic
  fran-ti-cal-ly
fra-ter-nal
  fra-ter-nal-ly
fra-ter-ni-ty
  fra-ter-ni-ties
frat-er-nize
frat-ri-cide
  frat-ri-cid-al
fraud-u-lent
  fraud-u-lence
fraught
fraz-zle
  fraz-zled
  fraz-zling
freak
  freak-ish
freck-le
  freck-led
  freck-li-er
free
  fre-er
  free-ly
free-bie
free-boot-er
free-dom
free-lance
  free-lanced
  free-lanc-ing
free-spoken
  free-spo-ken-ness
free-stone
  free-think-ing
free-way
free-wheel
freeze
  froze
  fro-zen
  freez-ing

freeze-dry
  freeze-dried
  freeze-dry-ing
freez-er
fre-net-ic
  fre-net-i-cal-ly
fren-zy
  fren-zies
  fren-zied
  fren-zy-ing
fre-quen-cy
  fre-quen-cies
fre-quent
  fre-quent-er
  fre-quent-ly
fre-quen-ta-tive
fres-co
  fres-coes
  fres-cos
  fres-coed
  fres-co-ing
fresh
  fresh-ly
  fresh-ness
fresh-en
  fresh-en-er
fresh-et
fresh-man
  fresh-men
fret
  fret-ted
fret-work
fri-ary
  fri-ar-ies
fric-as-see
  fric-as-seed
fric-tion
  fric-tion-al
friend
  friend-less
friend-ly
  friend-li-er
  friend-li-est
frieze
fright-ful
  fright-ful-ly
frig-id
  fri-gid-i-ty

  frig-id-ly
  frig-id-ness
frilly
  frill-i-er
  frill-i-est
fringe
  fringed
  fring-ing
frip-pery
  frip-per-ies
frisky
  frisk-i-er
fit-ter
friv-o-lous
  fri-vol-i-ty
frizz
  friz-zi-ness
  friz-zi-er
friz-zle
  friz-zled
  friz-zling
frol-ic
  frol-ick-ed
  frol-ick-ing
frol-ic-some
front-age
  fron-tal-ly
fron-tier
frost
  frost-ed
frost-bite
  frost-bit
  frost-bit-ten
  frost-bit-ting
frost-ing
frost-y
  frost-i-er
froth
  froth-i-ness
  frothy
  froth-i-er
  froth-i-est
frou-frou
fro-ward
frown
  frown-ing-ly
frow-zy
  frow-zi-er

fro-zen
 fro-zen-ly
 fro-zen-ness
fruc-ti-fy
 fruc-ti-fied
 fruc-ti-fy-ing
 fruc-ti-fi-ca-tion
fru-gal
 fru-gal-i-ty
 fru-gal-i-ties
 fru-gal-ly
fruit-ful
 fruit-ful-ly
fru-i-tion
 fruit-less-ly
fruity
frump
 frump-ish
 frump-i-est
frus-trate
 frus-trat-ed
 frus-trat-ing
 frus-tra-tion
fry
 fried
 fry-ing
fry-er
fud-dle
 fud-dled
 fud-dling
fudge
 fudged
 fudg-ing
fu-el
 fu-eled
 fu-el-ing
fu-gi-tive
 fu-gi-tive-ly
ful-crum
 ful-crums
 ful-cra
ful-fill
 ful-filled
 ful-fil-ling
 ful-fil-ment
full
 full-ness
 ful-ly

full-back
ful-mi-nate
 ful-mi-nat-ed
 ful-mi-nat-ing
 ful-mi-na-tion
ful-some
 ful-some-ly
fum-ble
 fum-bled
 fum-bling
 fum-bler
fume
 fumed
 fum-ing
 fum-ing-ly
fu-mi-gate
 fu-mi-gat-ed
 fu-mi-gat-ing
func-tion
 func-tion-less
func-tion-al
 func-tion-al-ly
func-tion-ary
 func-tion-ar-ies
fun-da-men-tal
 fun-da-men-tal-ly
 fun-da-men-tal-ism
 fun-da-men-tal-ist
fu-ner-al
fu-ner-re-al
fun-gi-cide
 fun-gi-cid-al
 fun-gi-cid-al-ly
fun-gous
fun-gus
 fun-gi
 fun-gus-es
funic-u-lar
funk-y
 funk-i-er
 funk-i-est
fun-nel
 fun-neled
 fun-nel-ing
fun-ny
 fun-ni-er
 fun-ni-est
fur

furred
fur-ring
fur-bish
fu-ri-ous
 fu-ri-ous-ly
fur-long
fur-lough
fur-nace
fur-nish
fur-nish-ings
fur-ni-ture
for-row
fur-ry
 fur-ri-er
 fur-ri-est
fur-ther
fur-ther-more
fur-ther-most
fur-thest
fur-tive
 fur-tive-ly
fu-ry
 fu-ries
fuse
 fused
fu-see
fu-se-lage
fu-si-bil-i-ty
fu-si-ble
fu-si-form
fu-si-lade
 fu-si-lad-ed
 fu-si-lad-ing
fu-sion
fussy
 fuss-i-er
 fuss-i-est
 fuss-i-ly
fus-tian
fus-ty
fu-tile
fu-til-i-ty
 fu-til-i-ties
fu-ture
fu-tur-ism
fu-tur-is-tic
fu-tu-ri-ty
fuzz-y

gab
  gabbed
  gab-ber
gab-ar-dine
gab-ble
  gab-bled
  gab-bler
  gab-bling
gab-by
  gab-bi-er
  gab-bi-est
gab-ble
  gab-bled
  gab-bling
gad
  gad-ded
  gad-ding
gad-a-bout
gad-fly
  gad-flies
gad-get
  gad-ge-teer
  gad-get-ry
gaffe
  gaf-fer
gag
  gagged
  gag-ging
ga-ga
gai-e-ty
  gai-e-ties
gai-ly
gain-ful
gain-say
  gain-said
  gain-say-ing
  gain-say-er
  gain-says
gait
ga-la
ga-lac-tic
gal-ax-y
  gal-a-xies
gal-lant
gal-lant-ry
  gal-lant-ries
gal-late
gal-ler-y

gal-ler-ied
gal-ler-ies
gal-ley
  galleys
gal-li-cism
gal-li-cize
  gal-li-ci-za-tion
  gal-li-cized
  gal-li-ciz-ing
gal-li-mau-fry
  gal-li-mau-fries
gall-ing
gal-li-vant
gal-lon
  gal-lon-age
gal-loon
gal-lop
gal-lows
  gal-lows-es
gall-stone
ga-loot
ga-lop
ga-lore
ga-losh
  ga-loshed
gal-van-ic
gal-va-nism
gal-va-nize
  gal-va-nized
gal-va-nom-e-ter
gal-va-no-scope
gal-yak
gam
  gammed
  gam-ming
gamba
gam-ba-do
  gam-ba-does
  gam-ba-dos
gam-bit
gam-ble
  gam-bled
  gam-bling
  gam-bler
gam-boge
gam-bol
gam-brel
game

gamed
gam-er
gam-est
gam-ing
game-fish
game fowl
game-keep-er
gam-elan
game-ly
game-ness
game of chance
game of skill
game-some
game-ster
gamet
gam-ete
  ga-met-ic
  ga-met-i-cal-ly
game theory
gam-in
gamine
gam-ing
gam-ma
gamma ray
gam-mer
gam-mon
gamo-gen-e-sis
  gamo-ge-net-ic
  gamo-ge-net-i-cal-ly
gam-ut
gam-y
  gam-i-er
  gam-i-est
  gam-i-ly
  gam-i-ness
gan-der
gang
gang-er
gang hook
gang-land
gan-gling
gan-gli-on
  gan-glia
  gan-gli-on-at-ed
  gan-gli-ons
gan-gly
  gan-gli-er
  gan-gli-est

gang-plank
gang-plow
gang-rel
gan-grene
 gan-grened
 gan-gren-ing
 gan-gre-nous
gang-ster
gangue
gang up
gang-way
gan-is-ter
gan-ja
gan-net
gan-oid
gant-e-lope
gant-let
gant-line
gan-try
 gan-tries
gap
 gapped
 gap-ping
gape
 gap-er
gape-worm
gapped scale
gar
ga-rage
 ga-raged
 ga-rag-ing
ga-rage-man
garage sale
garb
gar-bage
gar-ble
 gar-bled
 gar-bler
 gar-bling
gar-board
gar-boil
gar-con
garde-man-ger
gar-den
 gar-dened
 gar-den-er
 gar-den-ful
 gar-den-ing

garden apartment
garden city
garden cress
garden heliotrope
gar-de-nia
garden-variety
garde-robe
gar-dy-loo
gar-fish
gar-gan-tu-an
gar-get
 gar-gety
gar-gle
 gar-gled
 gar-gling
gar-goyle
 gar-goyled
gar-i-bal-di
gar-ish
gar-land
gar-lic
gar-lic salt
gar-ment
gar-ner
 gar-nered
 gar-ner-ing
gar-net
garnet paper
gar-ni-er-ite
gar-nish
gar-nish-ee
 gar-nish-eed
 gar-nish-ee-ing
gar-nish-ment
gar-ni-ture
gar-pike
gar-ret
gar-ri-son
 gar-ri-soned
 gar-ri-son-ing
garrison cap
Gar-ri-son finish
gar-rote
 gar-rot-ed
 gar-rot-ing
 gar-rot-er
gar-ru-lous
 gar-ru-lous-ly

gar-ru-lous-ness
gar-ter
garter snake
garth
gar-vey
gas
gassed
 gass-es
 gas-sing
gas-bag
gas chamber
gas-con
gas-con-ade
 gas-con-ad-er
gas-e-ous
 gas-eous-ness
gas fitter
gas gangrene
gash
gas-hold-er
gas-house
gas-i-fy
 gas-i-fied
 gas-ifi-er
 gas-i-fy-ing
 gas-i-fi-ca-tion
 gas-i-fi-er
gas-ket
gas-kin
gas-light
gas-lit
gas log
gas mask
gas oil
gas-olier
gas-o-line
gas-om-e-ter
gas-operated
gasp
gasp-er
gas plant
gas-ser
gas-sy
 gas-si-er
 gas-si-est
 gas-si-ness
gas-tric
gas-ti-tis

gas-tro-in-tes-ti-nal
gas-tron-o-my
  gas-tro-nom-ic
  gas-tro-nom-i-cal
  gas-tro-nom-i-cal-ly
gas-works
gate-crash-er
  gate-crash-ing
gate-house
gate-keep-er
gate-post
gate-way
gath-er
  gath-er-ing
gauche
gau-cho
gaud-y
  gaud-i-er
  gaud-i-est
  gaud-i-ly
  gaud-i-ness
gauge
  gauged
  gaug-ing
gaunt-let
gauze
  gauz-i-er
  gauz-i-est
  gauz-i-ness
  gauzy
gay-e-ty
gaze
  gazed
  gaz-er
  gaz-ing
ga-ze-bo
  ga-ze-bos
  ga-ze-boes
ga-zelle
ga-zette
gaz-et-teer
gear-box
gear-ing
gear-shift
gear-wheel
gee
  geed
  gee-ing

gee-zer
gei-sha
gel
  gelled
  gel-ling
gel-a-tin
gel-lat-i-nous
ge-la-tion
geld
  geld-ed
  geld-ing
  gelt
gel-id
gem
  gemmed
  gem-ming
gem-i-nate
  gem-i-nat-ed
  gem-i-nat-ing
  gem-i-nate-ly
  gem-i-na-tion
gem-ol-o-gy
  gem-o-log-i-cal
  gem-ol-o-gist
gem-stone
gen-darme
gen-der
gene
ge-ne-al-o-gy
  ge-ne-a-log-i-cal
  ge-ne-al-o-gist
gen-er-al
gen-er-al-is-si-mo
  gen-er-al-is-si-mos
gen-er-al-ist
gen-er-al-i-ty
  gen-er-al-i-ties
gen-er-al-ize
  gen-er-al-ized
  gen-er-al-iz-ing
  gen-er-al-i-za-tion
  gen-er-al-iz-er
gen-er-ate
  gen-er-at-ed
  gen-er-at-ing
  gen-er-a-tive
  gen-er-a-tive-ly
gen-er-a-tion

gen-er-a-tor
ge-ner-ic
  ge-ner-i-cal
  ge-ner-i-cal-ly
gen-er-ous
gen-er-os-i-ty
  gen-er-os-i-ties
gen-e-sis
ge-net-ic
  ge-net-i-cal-ly
ge-net-ics
  ge-net-i-cist
gen-ial
  ge-ni-al-i-ty
ge-nie
  ge-nies
  ge-nii
gen-i-tal
gen-i-ta-lia
gen-i-tals
gen-ius
  gen-ius-es
gen-o-cide
  gen-o-ci-dal
gen-re
gen-teel
gen-tian
gen-tile
gen-til-i-ty
  gen-til-i-ties
gen-tle
  gen-tler
  gen-tlest
  gen-tly
gen-tle-folk
gen-tle-man
  gen-tle-men
gen-tle-wom-an
  gen-tle-wom-en
gen-try
gen-u-flect
  gen-u-flec-tion
  gen-u-flec-tor
gen-u-ine
ge-nus
  gen-e-ra
  ge-nus-es
ge-o-cen-tric

ge-o-cen-tri-cal-ly
ge-o-chem-is-try
ge-o-chem-i-cal
ge-o-chem-ist
ge-ode
ge-o-des-ic
ge-o-gra-phy
ge-o-gra-phies
ge-o-gra-pher
ge-o-gra-phic
ge-o-graph-i-cal
ge-ol-o-gy
ge-ol-o-gies
ge-o-log-ic
ge-o-log-i-cal
ge-o-log-i-cal-ly
ge-ol-o-gist
ge-o-met-ric
ge-om-e-try
ge-om-e-tries
ge-o-phys-ics
ge-o-phys-i-cal
ge-o-phys-i-cist
ge-o-pol-i-tic
ge-o-pol-i-tics
ge-o-pol-o-tic
ge-o-po-lit-i-cal
ge-o-po-lit-i-cal-ly
ge-o-ther-mal
ger-bil
ger-i-at-ric
ger-i-at-rics
ger-i-a-tri-cian
ger-i-at-rist
ger-mane
ger-mi-cide
ger-mi-cid-al
ger-mi-nate
ger-mi-nat-ed
ger-mi-nat-ing
ger-mi-na-tion
ger-on-tol-o-gy
ger-on-tol-o-gist
ger-ry-man-der
ger-und
ges-so
ges-tate
ges-tat-ed

ges-tat-ing
ges-ta-tion
ges-tic-u-late
ges-tic-u-lat-ed
ges-tic-u-lat-ing
ges-tic-u-la-tion
ges-tic-u-la-tive
ges-tic-u-la-to-ry
ges-tic-u-la-tor
ges-ture
ges-tured
ges-tur-ing
ges-tur-er
ge-sund-heit
get-a-way
gew-gaw
gey-ser
ghast-ly
ghast-li-er
ghast-li-est
ghast-li-ness
gher-kin
ghet-to
ghe-tos
ghet-toes
ghost-ly
ghost-li-er
ghost-li-est
ghost-li-ness
ghost-write
ghost-wrote
ghost-writ-ten
ghost-writ-ting
ghoul
gi-ant
gib-ber-ish
gib-bon
gibe
gib-er
gib-ing-ly
gib-let
gid-dy
gid-di-er
gid-di-est
gid-di-ly
gid-di-ness
gi-gan-tic
gi-gan-tism

gig-gle
gig-gled
gig-gling
gig-gler
gig-gly
gig-gli-er
gig-gli-est
gig-o-lo
gild-ed
gilt-edged
gim-crack
gim-let
gim-mick
gin-ger
gin-ger-bread
gin-ger-ly
gin-ger-li-ness
gin-ger-snap
gin-ger-y
ging-ham
gird-er
gir-dle
gir-dled
gir-dling
girl-hood
girl-ish
girth
gist
give
gave
giv-en
giv-ing
give-and-take
give-a-way
giz-zard
gla-cial
gla-cier
glad
glad-der
glad-dest
glad-ly
glad-ness
glad-den
glad-i-a-tor
glad-i-a-to-ri-al
glad-i-o-lus
glad-i-o-lus-es
glad-i-o-la

glad-some
glam-or-ize
  glam-or-ized
  glam-or-iz-ing
  glam-or-i-za-tion
  glam-or-i-zer
glam-or-ous
  glam-or-ous-ly
  glam-or-ous-ness
glam-our
glance
  glanced
  glanc-ing
glan-du-lar
glare
  glared
  glar-ing
  glar-i-ness
  glar-y
  glar-i-er
  glar-i-est
glass-blow-ing
  glass-blow-er
glass-ful
glass-ware
glass-y
  glass-i-er
  glass-i-est
  glass-i-ly
  glass-i-ness
glau-co-ma
glaze
  glazed
  glaz-ing
gla-zier
gleam
  gleam-ing
  gleam-y
glean
  glean-er
  glean-ing
glee
  glee-ful
  glee-ful-ly
  glee-ful-ness
glen-gar-ry
glib
  glib-ber

glib-best
glib-ly
glib-ness
glide
  glid-ed
  glid-ing
glim-mer
glimpse
  glimpsed
glis-san-do
  glis-san-di
  glis-san-dos
glis-ten
glit-ter
gloam-ing
gloat
  gloat-er
  gloat-ing
glob
glo-bal
  glob-al-ly
globe-trot-ter
  globe-trot-ting
glob-u-lar
glob-ule
glock-en-spiel
gloom-y
  gloom-i-er
  gloom-i-est
  gloom-i-ly
  gloom-i-ness
glo-ri-fy
  glo-ri-fied
  glo-ri-fy-ing
  glo-ri-fi-ca-tion
  glo-ri-fi-er
glo-ri-ous
  glo-ri-ous-ly
  glo-ri-ou-ness
glo-ry
  glo-ries
  glo-ried
  glo-ry-ing
glos-sa-ry
glos-sa-ries
glossy
  gloss-i-er
  gloss-i-est

gloss-i-ly
gloss-i-ness
glot-tis
  glot-tis-es
  glot-ti-des
glove
  gloved
  glov-ing
glow
  glow-er
  glow-ing
glow-worm
glu-cose
glue
  glued
  glu-ing
glum
  glum-mer
  glum-mest
glut
  glut-ted
  glut-ting
glu-ten
glu-ti-nous
glut-ton
glut-ton-ous
  glut-tony
glyc-er-in
  glyc-er-ine
glyc-er-ol
gnarl
  gnarled
  gnarly
  gnarl-i-er
  gnarl-i-est
gnash
gnat
gnaw
  gnawed
  gnaw-ing
gneiss
gnome
gnu
  gnus
goad-ed
go-a-head
goal-keep-er
goat-ee

goat-herd
goat-skin
gob-ble
  gob-bled
  gob-bling
gob-ble-dy-ween
gob-let
gob-lin
go-cart
god-child
  god-chil-dren
  god-daugh-ter
  god-son
god-dess
good-fa-ther
god-head
god-less
  god-less-ness
god-like
god-ly
  god-li-er
  god-li-est
  god-li-ness
god-mo-ther
god-par-ent
god-send
go-get-ter
gog-gle
  gog-gled
  gog-gling
gog-gle-eyed
gog-gles
go-ing
goi-ter
gold-brick
gold-en
gold-smith
go-nad
gon-do-la
gon-do-lier
gon-er
gon-or-rhea
goo-ber
good-by
  good-bye
good-for-noth-ing
good-heart-ed
good-ish

good-look-ing
good-ly
  good-li-er
  good-li-est
good-na-tured
good-ness
good-tem-pered
good-y
  good-ies
goof-off
goof-y
  goof-i-er
  goof-i-est
  goof-i-ness
goose-ber-ry
  goose-ber-ries
gore
  gored
  gor-ing
gorge
  gorged
  gorg-ing
gor-geous
  gor-geous-ly
  gor-geous-ness
gor-y
  gor-i-er
  gor-i-est
gos-ling
gos-pel
gos-sa-mer
  gos-sa-mery
  gos-sa-mer-i-er
  gos-sa-mer-i-est
gos-sip
  gos-sip-ing
  gos-sipy
gouge
  gouged
  goug-ing
  goug-er
gou-lash
gourd
gour-met
  gour-mets
gout
  gouty
  gout-i-er

gout-i-est
gov-ern
  gov-ern-a-ble
gov-ern-ess
gov-ern-ment
  gov-ern-men-tal
gov-er-nor
  gov-er-nor-ship
gow-and
gowned
grab
  grabbed
  grab-bing
  grab-ber
grace
  graced
  grac-ing
grace-ful
  grace-ful-ly
  grace-ful-ness
grace-less
gra-cious
gra-da-tion
grade
  grad-ed
  grad-ing
grad-er
gra-di-ent
grad-u-al
  grad-u-al-ly
  grad-u-al-ness
grad-u-ate
  grad-u-at-ed
  grad-u-at-ing
  grad-u-ation
graf-fi-to
  graf-fi-ti
graft
  graft-age
  graft-er
  graft-ing
gra-ham
grain
grain-y
  grain-i-er
  grain-i-est
  grain-i-ness
gram

gram-mar
gram-mar-i-an
gram-mat-i-cal
gram-mat-i-cal-ly
gra-na-ry
gra-na-ries
grand
grand-ly
grand-child
grand-daugh-ter
gran-dee
gran-deur
grand-fa-ther
gran-dil-o-quence
gran-dil-o-quent
gran-di-ose
gran-di-ose-ly
grand-moth-er
grand-par-ent
grand-son
grand-stand
grange
grang-er
gran-ite
gra-nat-ic
gran-ny
gran-nies
gran-u-lar
gran-u-lar-i-ty
gran-u-late
gran-u-lat-ed
gran-u-lat-ing
gran-u-la-tion
gran-ule
grape-fruit
grape-vine
graph-ic
graph-i-cal
graph-i-cal-ly
graph-ite
graph-ol-o-gy
graph-ol-o-gist
grap-nel
grap-ple
grap-pled
grap-pling
grap-pler
grass

grass-y
grass-i-er
grass-i-est
grass-hop-per
grass-land
grate
grat-ed
grat-ing
grate-ful
grate-ful-ly
grate-ful-ness
grat-i-fy
grat-i-fied
grat-i-fy-ing
gra-tis
grat-i-tude
gra-tu-i-tous
gra-tu-i-ty
gra-tu-i-ties
grave
graved
grav-en
grav-ing
grav-er
grave-ly
grave-ness
grav-el
grav-eled
grav-el-ing
grav-el-ly
grave-stone
grave-yard
grav-i-tate
grav-i-tat-ed
grav-i-tat-ing
grav-i-ta-tion
grav-i-ta-tion-al
grav-i-ty
grav-i-ties
gra-vy
grav-ies
gray
gray-ly
gray-ness
gray-ling
graze
grazed
graz-ing

grease
greas-ed
greas-ing
greas-y
greas-i-er
greas-i-ness
great
great-ly
great-coat
great-heart-ed
greed-y
greed-i-er
greed-i-est
greed-i-ly
greed-i-ness
green-back
green-er-y
green-er-ies
green-gro-cer
green-horn
green-house
green-hous-es
green-ing
green-ish
green-ish-ness
green-sward
greet
greet-er
greet-ing
gre-gar-i-ous
gre-gar-i-ous-ly
gre-gar-i-ous-ness
grem-lin
gren-a-dier
gren-a-dine
grey
grey-ly
grey-ness
grid-dle
grid-dle-cake
grid-i-ron
grief
griev-ance
grieve
grieved
griev-ing
griev-ous
griev-ous-ly

grif-fin
grif-fon
grill
gril-lage
grille
grill-room
grim
grim-mer
grim-mest
grim-ly
grim-ness
grim-ace
grim-aced
grim-ac-ing
grime
grimed
grim-ing
grim-y
grim-i-er
grim-i-est
grim-i-ly
grim-i-ness
grin
grin-ned
grin-ning
grin-ner
grind
ground
grind-ing
grind-er
grind-stone
grin-go
grin-gos
grip
gripped
grip-ping
gripe
griped
grip-er
grippe
gris-ly
gris-li-er
gris-li-est
gris-li-ness
gris-tle
gris-tly
gris-tli-er
gris-tli-est

grit
grit-ted
grit-ting
grit-ty
grit-ti-er
grit-ti-est
grit-ti-ly
grit-ti-ness
griz-zled
griz-zly
griz-zli-er
griz-zli-est
griz-zlies
groan
groan-er
gro-cer
gro-cer-y
gro-cer-ies
grog-gy
grog-gi-er
groin
grom-met
groom
groove
grooved
groov-er
groov-y
groov-i-er
groov-i-est
grope
groped
grop-ing
gros-grain
gross
gross-es
gross-ness
gro-tesque
gro-tesque-ly
gro-tesque-ness
grot-to
grot-toes
grot-tos
grouch
grouchy
grouch-i-er
grouch-i-est
ground-er
ground-less

ground-less-ly
ground-less-ness
ground-ling
ground-nut
ground-work
group-ie
grouse
groused
grous-ing
grous-er
grov-el
grov-eled
grov-el-er
grow
grow-ing
grow-er
growl
growl-er
grown-up
growth
grub
grubbed
grub-bing
grub-ber
grub-by
grub-bi-er
grub-bi-est
grub-stake
grub-staked
grub-stak-ing
grudge
grudged
grudg-ing
grudg-ing-ly
gru-el
gru-el-ing
grue-some
grue-some-ly
gruff
gruff-ly
gruff-ness
grum-ble
grum-bled
grum-bling
grum-bler
grump-y
grump-i-er
grump-i-ness

grunt
grunt-er
grunt-ing
gua-no
gua-nos
guar-an-tee
guar-an-teed
guar-an-tee-ing
guar-an-tor
guar-an-ty
guar-an-ties
guar-an-ty-ing
guard-ed
guard-ed-ly
guard-house
guard-i-an
guards-man
guards-men
gua-va
gu-ber-na-to-ri-al
gudg-eon
guer-ril-la
gue-ril-la
guess
gues-ser
guess-work
guest
guf-faw
guid-ance
guide
guid-ed
guid-ing
guide-book
guide-post
gui-don
guid-hall
guile
guile-ful
guile-ful-ly
guile-less
guile-less-ly
guil-lo-tine
guil-lo-tined
guil-lo-tin-ing
guilt
guilt-less
guilt-less-ly
guilt-y

guilt-i-er
guilt-i-ness
guin-ea
guise
gui-tar
gui-tar-ist
gul-let
gul-li-ble
gul-li-bil-i-ty
gul-li-bly
gul-ly
gul-lies
gul-lied
gum
gummed
gum-ming
gum-bo
gum-bos
gum-drop
gum-my
gum-mi-er
gum-mi-ness
gump-tion
gum-shoe
gum-shoed
gun
gunned
gun-ning
gun-boat
gun-fight
gun-fight-er
gun-fire
gun-man
gun-men
gun-ner
gun-ner-y
gun-ny
gun-nies
gun-ny-bag
gun-pow-der
gun-stock
gun-wale
gup-py
gup-pies
gur-gle
gur-gled
gur-gling
gu-ru

gush-er
gush-ing
gush-y
gush-i-er
gush-i-est
gus-set
gus-ta-to-ry
gus-to
gust-y
gust-i-er
gust-i-est
gut
gut-ted
gut-ter
gut-tur-al
gut-tur-al-ly
guz-zle
guz-zled
guz-zling
gym-na-si-um
gym-na-si-ums
gym-nast
gym-nas-tic
gym-nas-tics
gy-ne-col-o-gy
gy-ne-co-log-ic
gy-ne-col-o-gist
gyp
gypped
gyp-sum
gyp-sy
gyp-sies
gy-ral
gy-rate
gy-rat-ed
gy-rat-ing
gy-ra-tor
gy-ra-to-ry
gyr-fal-con
gy-roi-dal
gy-rom-e-ter
gy-ro-plane
gy-ro-scope
gy-ro-scop-ic
gy-rose
gy-rus
gyve
gyved

hab-da-lah
ha-be-as cor-pus
hab-er-dash-er
  hab-er-dash-ery
  hab-er-dash-er-ies
ha-ber-geon
habile
ha-bil-i-ment
ha-bil-i-tate
hab-it
hab-it-a-ble
  hab-it-able-ness
  hab-it-abil-i-ty
  hab-it-ably
ha-bi-tant
  ha-bi-tan
hab-i-ta-tion
hab-it-form-ing
ha-bit-u-al
  ha-bit-u-al-ly
  ha-bit-u-al-ness
ha-bit-u-ate
  ha-bit-u-at-ed
  ha-bit-u-at-ing
  ha-bit-u-a-tion
hab-i-tude
ha-bi-tue
hab-i-tus
Habs-burg
ha-cek
ha-cen-da-do
ha-chure
  ha-chured
  ha-chur-ing
ha-ci-en-da
  ha-ci-en-das
hack
hack-a-more
hack-beryry
hack-but
  hack-but-eer
  hack-but-ter
hack-ie
hack-le
  hack-led
  hack-ling
hack-ly
hack-man

hack-ma-tack
hack-ney
  hack-neyed
hack-saw
hack-work
had
ha-dal
had-dock
hade
Ha-des
hadj
hadn't
had-ron
  ha-dron-ic
hadst
hae
haem
hae-ma-tox-y-lon
hae-mo-glo-bin
hae-mo-phil-i-a
haet
haft
haf-ta-rah
hag
ha-gar
hag-fish
hag-gard
  hag-gard-ly
hag-gle
  hag-gled
  hag-gling
  hag-gler
ha-gi-ol-o-gy
  hag-i-ol-o-gies
  hag-i-ol-o-gist
hag-rid-den
haik
hai-ku
hail-fel-low
hail-stone
hail-storm
hair
hair ball
hair--breadth
hair-brush
hair-cell
hair-cloth
hair-cut

hair-do
hair-dress-er
hair-dress-ing
haired
hair follicle
hair-less
hair-line
hair-piece
hair-pin
hair--rais-er
hair--rais-ing
hair seal
hair shirt
hair space
hair-split-ter
  hair-split-ting
hair-spring
hair-streak
hair-stroke
hair-style
hair-styl-ing
hair-styl-ist
hair--trigger
hair-worm
hair-y
  hair-i-er
  hair-i-est
Hai-tian
hake
ha-kim
ha-la-la
ha-la-tion
hal-berd
hal-cy-on
hale
  haled
  hal-ing
half
half-and-half
half-back
half--baked
hald blood
half--blood-ed
half boot
half--bound
half--breed
half brother
half--caste

half cock
half--cocked
half crown
half dime
half--dol-lar
half eagle
half--evergreen
half gainer
half--hardy
half-heart-ed
  half-heart-ed-ly
half hitch
half hour
half--life
  half-lives
half--mast
half--moon
half note
half-pen-ny
half--pint
half plane
half rest
half sister
half-slip
half--sole
half sovereign
half--staff
half step
half--timber
halftime
half title
half-tone
half--track
half--truth
half voley
half-way
halfway house
half--wit
  half--wit-ted
hal-i-but
hal-i-to-sis
hall-mark
hal-lo
hal-low
  hal-lowed
hal-lu-ci-nate
  hal-lu-ci-nat-ed
  hal-lu-ci-nat-ing

hal-lu-ci-na-tion
  hal-lu-ci-na-to-ry
hal-lu-cin-o-gen
  hal-lu-cin-o-gen-ic
hal-lux
hall-way
ha-lo
  ha-los
  ha-loes
halo-phile
halt
  halt-ing
  halt-ing-ly
hal-ter
hal-ter-break
halve
  halved
  halv-ing
halv-ers
halves
hal-yard
ham-burg-er
ham-let
ham-mer
ham-mer-head
ham-mer-less
ham-mock
ham-my
  ham-mi-er
  ham-mi-est
hamp-er
ham-ster
ham-string
  ham-strung
  ham-string-ing
hand-bag
hand-ball
hand-bill
hand-book
hand-cuff
hand-ed
hand-ful
  hand-fuls
hand-i-cap
  hand-i-capped
  hand-i-cap-ping
  hand-i-cap-per
hand-i-craft

hand-i-ly
  handi-ness
hand-i-work
han-ker-chief
han-dle
  han-dled
  han-dling
  han-dler
han-dle-bar
hand-made
hand-maid-en
hand--me--down
hand-out
hand-pick
  hand-picked
hand-rail
hand-shake
hand-some
  hand-som-er
  hand-som-est
  hand-some-ly
  hand-some-ness
hand-spike
hand-spring
hand-to-hand
hand--to--mouth
hand-work
hand-writ-ing
handy
  hand-i-er
  hand-i-est
handy-man
  handy-men
hang
  hung
  hanged
  hang-ing
hang-ar
hang-dog
hang-er
hang-er--on
hang-man
  hanf-men
hang-nail
hang-out
hang-o-ver
hang--up
hank-er

han-som
hap-haz-ard
  hap-haz-ard-ly
  hap-haz-ard-ness
hap-less
  hap-less-ly
hap-ly
hap-pen
hap-pen-ing
hap-pen-stance
hap-pi-ness
hap-py
  hap-pi-er
  hap-pi-est
  hap-pi-ly
hap-py--go--lucky
hara-kiri
ha-rangue
  ha-rangued
  ha-rangu-ing
ha-rass
  ha-rass-ment
har-bin-ger
har-bor
hard--bit-ten
hard--boiled
hard--core
hard-cov-er
hard-en
  hard-en-er
hard hat
hard-head-ed
hard-heart-ed
har-di-hood
har-di-ness
hard-ly
  har-di-er
  har-di-est
  har-di-ly
hare-brained
hare-lip
har-em
har-le-quin
har-lot
  har-lot-ry
harm-ful
  harm-ful-ly
  harm-ful-ness

harm-less
  harm-less-ly
  harm-less-ness
har-mon-ic
  har-mon-i-cal-ly
har-mon-i-ca
har-mon-ics
har-mo-ni-ous
  har-mo-ni-ous-ly
har-mo-nize
  har-mo-nized
  har-mo-niz-ing
har-mo-ny
  har-mo-nies
har-ness
harp-ist
har-poon
harp-si-chord
har-py
  har-pies
har-que-bus
har-ri-dan
har-row
  har-row-ing
har-ry
  har-ried
  har-ry-ing
harsh
  harsh-ly
  harsh-ness
har-um-scar-um
har-vest
har-ves-ter
has--been
hash-ish
  hash-eesh
hasn't
has-sle
  has-sled
  has-sling
has-sock
has-ten
hasty
  hast-i-er
  hast-i-est
  hast-i-ness
hatch-ery
  hatch-er-ies

hatch-et
hatch-way
hate
  hat-ed
  hat-ing
  hat-er
hate-ful
  hate-ful-ly
  hate-ful-ness
ha-tred
hat-ter
haugh-ty
  haugh-ti-er
  haugh-ti-est
  haugh-ti-ly
  haught-ti-ness
haul
  haul-age
haunch
  haunch-es
haunt-ed
  haunt-ing
hau-teur
ha-ven
have--not
haven't
hav-er-sack
havers
hav-oc
hawk
  hawk-ish
haw-ser
hay-loft
hay-mak-er
hay-mow
hay-seed
hay-stack
hay-wire
haz-ard
  haz-ard-ous
  haz-ard-ous-ly
  haz-ard-ou-ness
haze
  hazed
  haz-ing
ha-zel
ha-zel-nut
hazy

ha-zi-er
ha-zi-est
ha-zi-ly
ha-zi-ness
head-ache
head-band
head-dress
head-er
head-first
head-fore-most
head-gear
head-hunt-er
head-ing
head-land
head-less
head-light
head-line
head-lined
head-lin-ing
head-long
head-mas-ter
head-mis-tress
head-most
head--on
head-piece
head-quar-ters
head-set
head-stone
head-strong
head-wait-er
head-wa-ter
head-way
head-wind
heady
head-i-er
head-i-est
head-i-ly
head-i-ness
heal-er
health-ful
health-ful-ly
healthy
health-i-er
health-i-est
health-i-ness
heaped
hear
heared

hear-ing
hear-er
hear-ken
hear-say
hearse
heart-ache
heart-break
heart-break-ing
heart-brok-en
heart-burn
heart-en
heart-felt
hearth-stone
heart-less
heart-less-ly
heart-less-ness
heart-rend-ing
heart-sick
heart-strings
heart--to--heart
hearty
heart-i-er
heart-i-est
heart-i-ly
heart-i-ness
heat-ed
heat-er
heath
hea-then
heave
heaved
heav-ing
heav-en
heav-en-ly
heav-en-ward
heav-en-wards
heavy
heav-i-er
heav-i-est
heav-i-ly
heav-i-ness
heavy--du-ty
heavy--hand-ed
heavy-weight
heck-le
heck-led
heck-ling
heck-ler

hect-are
hec-tic
hec-ti-cal-ly
hec-to-gram
hec-to-li-ter
hec-to-me-ter
hedge
hedged
hedg-ing
hedg-er
he-do-nism
he-do-nist
he-do-nis-tic
hee-haw
hefty
heft-i-er
heft-i-est
he-ge-mo-ny
he-ge-mo-nies
heg-e-mon-ic
he-gi-ra
heif-er
height-en
height-en-er
hei-nous
hei-nous-ly
hei-nous-ness
heir-ess
heir-loom
heist
he-li-cop-ter
he-li-um
he-lix
he-li-ces
he-lix-es
hell--bent
hell-cat
hel-lion
hell-ish
hell-ish-ly
hell-ish-ness
hel-lo
hel-los
helm
helm-less
hel-met
hel-met-ed
helms-man

helms-men
help-er
help-ful
help-ful-ly
help-ful-ness
help-ing
help-less
help-less-ly
help-less-ness
help-mate
hel-er--skel-ter
hem
hemmed
hem-ming
he--man
he--men
hemi-sphere
hemi-spher-ic
hemi-sper-i-cal
hem-lock
he-mo-glo-bin
he-mo-phil-ia
hem-or-rhage
hem-or-rhag-ing
hem-or-rhag-ic
hem-or-rhoid
hem-or-rhoid-al
hemp-en
hem-stitch
hence-forth
hench-man
hench-men
hench-man-ship
hen-na
hen-peck
hep-a-ti-tis
her-ald
he-ral-dic
her-ald-ry
her-ald-ries
herb-age
her-biv-o-rous
Her-cu-le-an
herd-er
herds-man
herds-men
here-af-ter
he-red-i-tary

he-red-i-tar-i-ly
he-red-i-tar-i-ness
he-red-i-ty
he-red-i-ties
here-in
here-of
her-e-sy
her-e-sies
her-e-tic
he-ret-i-cal
he-ret-i-cal-ly
here-to
here-to-fore
here-upon
here-with
her-i-ta-ble
her-i-ta-bil-i-ty
her-i-ta-bly
her-i-tage
her-maph-ro-dite
her-maph-ro-dit-ic
her-maph-ro-dit-ism
her-met-ic
her-met-i-cal
her-met-i-cal-ly
her-mit
her-mit-age
her-nia
her-ni-al
her-ni-a-tion
he-ro
he-roes
he-ro-ic
he-ro-ical
he-ro-ical-ly
her-o-in
her-o-ine
her-o-ism
her-on
her-ring-bone
her-ring-boned
her-ring-bon-ing
her-self
hes-i-tant
hes-i-tan-cy
hes-i-tan-cies
hes-i-tant-ly
hes-i-tate

hes-i-tat-ed
hes-i-tat-ing
hes-i-tat-er
hes-i-ta-tor
hes-i-tat-ing-ly
hes-i-ta-tion
het-ero-dox
het-ero-doxy
het-er-o-ge-neous
het-er-o-ge-ne-ity
het-er-o-ge-neous-ly
het-ero-sex-u-al
het-ero-sex-u-al-i-ty
hew
hewed
hewn
hew-ing
hew-er
hexa-gon
hex-ag-o-nal
hex-ag-o-nal-ly
hey-day
hey-dey
hi-a-tus
hi-a-tus-es
hi-ba-chi
hi-ber-nate
hi-ber-nat-ed
hi-ber-nat-ing
hi-ber-na-tion
hi-bis-cus
hic-cup
hic-cuped
hic-cup-ing
hid-den
hid-den-ness
hide
hid
hid-den
hid-er
hide-bound
hid-eous
hid-eous-ly
hid-eous-ness
hide-out
hi-er-ar-chy
hi-er-ar-chies
hi-er-ar-chal

hi-er-ar-chic
hi-er-ar-chi-cal
hi-er-ar-chi-cal-ly
hi-ero-glyph
hi-ero-glyph-ic
hi-ero-glyph-i-cal
hi-ero-glyph-i-cal-ly
hi--fi
high-ball
high-born
high-boy
high-brow
high-browed
high-brow-ism
high-er--up
high-fa-lu-tin
high-fa-lu-ting
high--flown
high--grade
high--hand-ed
high--hand-ed-ly
high--hand-ed-ness
high--hat
high-land
high-light
high--mind-ed
high--mind-ed-ly
high--mind-ed-ness
high-ness
high--pressure
high--pressured
high--pressur-ing
high school
high seas
high--spir-it-ed
high--spir-it-ed-ly
high--spir-it-ed-ness
high--strung
high-tail
high--tension
high--toned
high-way
high-way-man
high-way-men
hi-jack
hi-jack-er
hi-jack-ing
hike

hiked
hik-ing
hik-er
hi-lar-i-ous
hi-lar-i-ous-ly
hi-lar-i-ous-ness
hi-lar-i-ty
hill-bil-ly
hill-bil-lies
hill-ock
hill-side
hill-top
hilly
hill-i-er
hill-i-est
him-self
hin-der
hin-der-er
hind-most
hind-quar-ter
hin-drance
hind-sight
hinge
hinged
hing-ing
hint-er
hint-ing-ly
hin-ter-land
hipped
hip-pie
hip-po
hip-pos
hip-po-drome
hip-po-pot-a-mus
hip-po-pot-a-mus-es
hip-po-pot-a-mi
hire-ling
hir-sute
hir-sute-ness
hiss
hiss-er
his-ta-mine
his-ta-min-ic
his-to-ri-an
his-tor-ic
his-tor-i-cal
his-tor-i-cal-ly
his-tor-i-cal-ness

his-to-ry
his-to-ries
his-tri-on-ic
his-tri-on-i-cal
his-tri-on-i-cal-ly
his-tri-on-ics
hit
hit-ting
hit--and--run
hitch
hitch-er
hitch-hike
hitch-hiked
hitch-hik-ing
hitch-hik-er
hith-er-to
hive
hived
hiv-ing
hoary
hoar-i-er
hoar-i-est
hoar-i-ness
hoard
hoard-er
hoard-ing
hoar-frost
hoarse
hoarse-ly
hoars-en
hoarse-ness
hoax
hoax-er
hob-ble
hob-bled
hob-bling
hob-by
hob-bies
hob-by-horse
hob-gob-lin
hob-nail
hob-nail-ed
hob-nob
hob-nobbed
hob-nob-bing
ho-bo
ho-boes
ho-bos

ho-bo-ism
hock-er
hock-ey
ho-cus-po-cus
hodge-podge
hoe
  hoed
  hoe-ing
hoe-down
hog
  hogged
  hog-ging
hog-gish
  hog-gish-ly
  hog-gish-ness
hogs-head
hog--tie
  hog--tied
  hog--ty-ing
hog-wash
hoi pol-loi
hoist-er
ho-kum
hold-er
hold-ing
hold-out
hold-over
hold-up
hole
  holed
  hol-ing
  holey
hol-i-day
ho-li-ness
Hol-land
hol-ler
hol-low
  hol-low-ly
  hol-low-ness
hol-ly
  hol-lies
hol-ly-hock
hol-mi-um
ho-lo-caust
ho-lo-gram
hol-o-graph
hol-ster
ho-ly

ho-li-er
ho-li-est
ho-lies
hom-age
hom-bre
  hom-bres
home-com-ing
home-less
  home-less-ness
home-ly
  home-li-er
  home-li-est
  home-li-ness
home-made
hom-er
home-sick
  home-sick-ness
home-spun
home-stead
  home-stead-er
home-ward
  home-wards
home-work
homey
hom-i-er
hom-i-est
hom-i-ness
hom-i-cide
hom-i-let-ics
hom-i-ly
  hom-i-lies
homing pigeon
hom-i-ny
ho-mo-ge-neous
  ho-mo-ge-ne-ity
  ho-mo-ge-neous-ness
ho-mog-e-nize
  ho-meg-e-nized
  ho-mog-e-niz-ing
ho-mo-graph
ho-mol-o-gous
  ho-mol-o-gy
  ho-mol-o-gies
hom-onym
  hom-onym-ic
ho-mo-phone
  ho-mo-pho-nic
ho-mo-sex-u-al

ho-mo-sex-u-al-i-ty
hone
  honed
  hon-ing
hon-est
  hon-est-ly
hon-es-ty
  hon-es-ties
hon-ey
  hon-eys
  hon-eyed
  hon-ied
  hon-ey-ing
hon-ey-bee
hon-ey-comb
hon-ey-moon
  hon-ey-moon-er
hon-ey-suck-le
  hon-ey-suck-led
hon-ky--tonk
hon-or
hon-or-able
  hon-or-ably
hon-o-rar-i-um
  hon-o-rar-i-ums
  hon-o-rar-i-a
hon-or-ary
hon-or-if-ic
hood-ed
hood-lum
hoo-doo
  hoo-doo-ism
hood-wink
  hood-wink-er
hoo-ey
hoof
  hoofs
  hooves
  hoofed
hooked
hook-er
hook-up
hoo-li-gan
  hoo-li-gan-ism
hoop
  hooped
  hoop-like
hoop-la

hoo-ray
hoose-gow
hoot
  hoot-er
  hoot-ing-ly
hop
  hopped
  hop-ping
  hop-er
hope-ful
  hope-ful-ly
  hope-ful-ness
hope-less
  hope-less-ly
  hope-less-ness
hop-head
hop-per
hop-scotch
horde
  hord-ed
  hord-ing
ho-ri-zon
hor-i-zon-tal
  hor-i-zon-tal-ly
hor-mone
  hor-mon-al
horn
  horned
  horn-like
  horny
  horn-i-er
  horn-i-est
hor-net
horn-swog-gle
  horn-swog-gled
  horn-swog-gling
hor-rol-o-gy
  ho-rol-o-ger
  ho-rol-o-gist
horo-scope
hor-ren-dous
  hor-ren-dous-ly
hor-ri-ble
  hor-ri-bly
hor-rid
  hor-rid-ly
  hor-rid-ness
hor-ri-fy

hor-ri-fied
hor-ri-fy-ing
hor-ri-fi-ca-tion
hor-ror
horse
  hors-es
  horsed
  hors-ing
horse-back
horse-fly
  horse-flies
horse-hair
horse-laugh
horse-men
  horse-man-ship
  horse-wom-an
  horse-wom-en
horse opera
horse-play
horse-pow-er
horse-rad-ish
horse-shoe
  horse-sho-er
horse-whip
  horse-whipped
  horse-whip-ping
hors-ey
  horsy
  hors-i-er
  hors-i-est
  hors-i-ly
  hors-i-ness
hor-ta-to-ry
hor-ti-cul-ture
  hor-ti-cul-tur-al
  hor-ti-cul-tur-ist
ho-san-na
hose
  hos-es
  hosed
  hos-ing
ho-siery
hos-pice
hos-pi-ta-ble
  hos-pi-ta-bly
hos-pi-tal
  hos-pi-tal-i-ty
  hos-pi-tal-i-ties

hos-pi-tal-iza-tion
hos-pi-tal-ize
  hos-pi-tal-ized
  hos-pi-tal-iz-ing
hos-tage
hos-tel
  hos-tel-ry
  hos-tel-ries
host-ess
hos-tile
  hos-tile-ly
hos-til-i-ty
  hos-til-i-ties
hos-tler
hot
  hot-ter
  hot-test
  hot-ly
hot-bed
hot--blood-ed
ho-tel
hot-head
  hot-head-ed
  hot-head-ed-ness
hot-house
hot-shot
hound
  hound-er
hour-glass
hour-ly
house
  hous-es
  housed
  hous-ing
house-boat
house-bro-ken
  house-break
  house-broke
  house-break-ing
house-fly
house-hold
house-keep-er
  house-keep-ing
house-maid
house-warm-ing
house-wife
  house-wives
  house-wife-ly

house-wif-ery
house-work
hous-ing
hov-el
  hov-eled
  hov-el-ing
hov-er
  hov-er-er
  hov-er-ing
how-ev-er
how-it-zer
  howl-er
how-so-ev-er
hoy-den
  hoy-den-ish
hob-bub
huck-le-ber-ry
  huck-le-ber-ries
huck-ster
hud-dle
  hud-dled
  hud-dling
  hud-dler
huffy
  huff-i-er
  huff-i-est
  huff-i-ly
  huff-i-ness
hug
  hugged
  hug-ging
  hug-ger
huge
  hug-er
  hug-est
  huge-ly
  huge-ness
hu-la
hulk-ing
hul-la-ba-loo
hum
  hummed
  hum-ming
  hum-mer
hu-man
  hu-man-ness
hu-mane
  hu-mane-ly

hu-man-ness
hu-man-ism
hu-man-ist
hu-man-ist-ic
hu-man-i-tar-i-an-ism
hu-man-i-ty
hu-man-i-ties
hu-man-ize
hu-man-ized
hu-man-iz-ing
hu-man-i-za-tion
hu-man-iz-er
hu-man-kind
hu-man-ly
hum-ble
  hum-bler
  hum-blest
  hum-bled
  hum-bling
  hum-ble-ness
  hum-bly
hum-bug
  hum-bugged
  hum-bug-ging
  hum-bug-ger
  hum-bug-gery
hum-ding-er
hum-drum
hu-mer-us
hu-mid
  hu-mid-ly
hu-mid-i-fy
  hu-mid-i-fied
  hu-mid-i-fy-ing
  hu-mid-i-fi-er
hu-mid-i-ty
hum-ming-bird
hum-mock
  hum-mocky
  hum-mock-i-er
  hum-mock-i-est
hu-mor
hu-mor-ist
  hu-mor-is-tic
hu-mor-ous
  hu-mor-ous-ly
  hu-mor-ous-ness
hump

humped
humpy
  hump-i-er
  hump-i-est
hump-back
hu-mus
hunch-back
  hunch-backed
hun-dred
hun-ger
hun-gry
  hun-gri-er
  hun-gri-est
  hun-gri-ly
  hun-gri-ness
hunt
  hunt-er
  hunt-ing
  hunt-ress
  hunts-man
  hunts-men
hur-dle
  hur-dled
  hur-dling
  hur-dler
hur-dy--gur-dy
  hur-dy--gur-dies
hurl-er
hurl-y--burl-y
  hurl-y--burl-ies
hur-rah
hur-ri-cane
hur-ry
  hur-ried
  hur-ry-ing
  hur-ried-ly
  hur-ry-ing-ly
hurt-ful
  hurt-ful-ly
  hurt-ful-ness
hurt-ing
hur-tle
  hur-tled
  hur-tling
hurt-less
hus-band
  hus-band-er
  hus-band-less

hus-band-ly
hus-band-man
hus-band-ry
hush
husk-er
husk-ing
husky
  husk-i-er
  husk-i-est
  husk-i-ly
  husk-i-ness
  husk-ies
hus-sar
hus-sy
  hussies
hus-tings
hus-tle
  hus-tled
  hus-tling
  hus-tler
hutch
hut-ment
huz-zah
  huz-za
hy-a-cinth
  hy-a-cin-thine
hy-a-line
hyaline cartilage
hy-a-lite
hy-a-loid
hy-a-lo-plasm
hy-al-uron-ic acid
hy-al-uron-i-dase
hy-brid
  hy-brid-ism
  hy-brid-i-ty
hybrid computer
hy-brid-ize
  hy-brid-ized
  hy-brid-iz-er
  hy-brid-iz-ing
  hy-brid-i-za-tion
hybrid perpetual rose
hybrid tea rose
hybrid vigor
hy-bris
hy-da-thode
hy-da-tid

hy-dra
hy-dras
hy-dae
hy-drase
hy-dras-tine
hy-dras-tis
hy-drate
hy-dra-ted
hy-dra-ting
hy-dra-tion
hy-dra-tor
hy-drau-lic
hy-drau-li-cal-ly
hy-drau-lics
hy-dra-zide
hy-dra-zine
hy-dric
hy-drid
hy-dri-od-ic acid
hy-dro-car-bon
hy-dro-cele
hy-dro-ce-phal-ic
hy-dro-chlo-ride
hy-dro-col-loid
hy-dro-dy-nam-ics
hy-dro-dy-na-mic
hy-dro-elec-tric
hy-dro-flu-or-ic acid
hy-dro-foil
hy-dro-form-ing
hy-dro-gen
hy-drog-e-nous
hy-drog-e-nase
hy-dro-ge-nate
hy-drog-ra-phy
hy-droid
hy-dro-ki-net-ic
hy-dro-lase
hy-drol-o-gy
hy-dro-ly-sate
hy-dro-ly-sis
hy-dro-lyze
hy-dro-mag-net-ic
hy-dro-man-cy
hy-dro-me-chan-ics
hy-drom-e-ter
hy-dro-met-ric
hy-dro-met-ri-cal

hy-drom-e-try
hy-dro-pho-bia
hy-dro-plane
hy-dro-plan-er
hy-dro-plan-ing
hy-dro-pon-ics
hy-dro-ther-a-py
hy-dro-ther-a-pist
hy-drous
hy-drox-ide
hy-drox-yl
hy-dro-zo-an
hy-e-na
hy-giene
hy-gien-ic
hy-gien-i-cal-ly
hy-gien-ist
hy-men
hy-me-ne-al
hy-me-ne-al-ly
hym-nal
hy-per-bo-la
hy-per-bo-le
hy-per-bo-lize
hy-per-bo-lized
hy-per-bo-liz-ing
hy-per-bol-ic
hy-phen
hy-phen-ate
hy-phen-at-ed
hy-phen-at-ing
hyp-no-sis
hyp-not-ic
hyp-no-tism
hyp-no-tist
hy-po
hy-po-chon-dria
hy-po-chon-dri-ac
hy-poc-ri-sy
hy-poc-ri-sies
hyp-o-crite
hy-po-der-mic
hy-po-ten-sion
hy-pot-e-nuse
hyp-ox-ia
hyp-sog-ra-phy
hys-te-ria
hys-ter-ics

iamb	ichthyoid	**ide-ol-o-gy**
iambs	**ici-cle**	**ideo-mo-tor**
iam-bus	**i-con**	**ides**
iam-bus-es	i-con-o-clasm	**id-i-o-cy**
iat-ric	i-con-o-clast	id-i-o-cies
i-bez	i-con-o-graphy	**id-i-om**
ibid	i-con-o-later	id-i-o-mat-ic
ibi-dem	i-con-o-latry	id-i-o-mat-i-cal-ly
ibis	**ic-ter-us**	**id-io-mor-phic**
ibis-es	icterical	**id-io-path-ic**
I-car-i-an	icteris	**id-io-plasm**
ice	**ico-nog-ra-pher**	id-i-o-syn-cra-sy
iced	**icon-o-graph-ic**	id-i-o-syn-cra-sies
ic-ing	**ico-nog-ra-phy**	id-i-o-syn-crat-ic
ice age	**id**	**id-i-ot**
ice ax	**i-de-a**	id-i-ot-ic
ice bag	**ideal**	id-i-ot-i-cal-ly
ice-berg	ide-al-less	**idle**
ice-blink	**ide-al-ize**	idled
ice-boat	ide-al-ized	idler
ice-bound	ide-al-iz-ing	idling
ice-box	ide-al-i-za-tion	**idol**
ice-breaker	**ide-al-ly**	**idol-a-ter**
ice cap	**idem**	**idol-a-trous**
ice--cold	**idem-po-tent**	**idol-a-try**
ice--cream	**iden-tic**	**idol-ize**
ice-fall	**iden-ti-cal**	**idyll**
ice floe	iden-ti-cal-ly	idyl-lic
ice fog	**iden-ti-fi-a-ble**	idyl-lic-al-ly
ice hockey	iden-ti-fy-ing	**ig-loo**
ice-house	iden-ti-fi-a-bly	**ig-ne-ous**
Ice-lan-dic	**iden-ti-fi-ca-tion**	**ig-nes-cent**
ice-man	**iden-ti-fy**	**ig-nite**
ice-men	iden-ti-fied	**ig-ni-tion;**
ice milk	iden-ti-fy-ing	**ig-ni-tron**
ice needle	iden-ti-fi-er	**ig-no-ble**
ice pack	**iden-ti-ty**	ig-no-bil-i-ty
ice pick	iden-ti-ties	ig-no-bly
ice plant	**identity card**	**ig-no-mi-ny**
ice point	**identity crisis**	ig-no-min-ies
ice show	**identity element**	ig-no-min-i-ous
ice--skate	**identity matrix**	ig-no-min-i-ous-ly
ice storm	**ideo-gram**	**ig-no-ra-mus**
ice water	**id-e-o-graph**	**ig-no-rance**
i-chor	id-e-o-graph-ic	**ig-no-rant**
ich-thy-ol-o-gy	id-e-o-graph-i-cal	ig-no-rance
ichthyological	id-e-o-graph-y	ig-no-rant-ly
ichthyologist	**ideo-log-i-cal**	**ig-no-ra-tio elen-chi**

ig-nore
  ig-nored
  ig-nor-ing
igua-na
iguan-odon
ike-ba-na
ikon
ilang-ilang
ile
il-e-itis
il-e-uj
il-e-us
ilex
il-i-ac
ilk
il-ka
ill
ill--ad-vised
  ill-ad-vis-ed-ly
il-la-tion
il-la-tive
il-laud-able
ill-be-ing
ill-bod-ing
ill--bred
il-le-gal
  il-le-gal-i-ty
  il-le-gal-ly
il-leg-i-ble
  il-leg-i-bil-i-ty
  il-leg-i-bly
il-le-git-i-mate
  il-le-git-i-ma-cy
  il-le-git-i-ma-cies
  il-le-git-i-mate-ly
ill--fat-ed
ill--fa-vored
ill--got-ten
ill--hu-mored
il-lib-er-al
il-lib-er-al-ism
il-lic-it
il-lim-it-able
il-liq-uid
il-lite
il-lit-er-a-cy
  il-lit-er-a-cies
il-lit-er-ate

ill--man-nered
ill-na-tured
ill-ness
il-log-i-c
il-log-i-cal
ill-sort-ed
ill-starred
ill-tem-pered
  ill-tem-pered-ly
ill-timed
ill-treat
ill--treat-ment
il-lume
il-lu-mi-nance
il-lu-mi-nant
il-lu-mi-nate
  il-lu-mi-nat-ed
  il-lu-mi-nat-ing
  il-lu-mi-na-tor
il-lu-mi-na-tion
il-lu-mine
  il-lu-mined
  il-lu-min-ing
ill-us-age
ill-use
il-lu-sion
  il-lu-sive
  il-lu-sive-ly
  il-lu-sive-ness
il-lu-sion-ary
il-lu-sion-is
il-lu-sive
il-lu-so-ry
il-lus-trate
  il-lus-trat-ed
  il-lus-trat-ing
il-lus-tra-tion
  il-lus-tra-tive
  il-lus-tra-tive-ly
  il-lus-tra-tor
il-lus-tri-ous
  il-lus-tri-ous-ly
il-lu-vi-al
il-lu-vi-ate
  il-lu-vi-at-ed
  il-lu-vi-at-ing
il-lu-vi-a-tion
il-lu-vi-um

ill will
ill--wish-er
il-ly
il-men-ite
Ilo-ca-no
im-age
  im-aged
image orthicon
im-ag-ery
image tube
imag-in-able
  imag-in-able-ness
  imag-in-ably
imag-i-nary
  imag-i-nar-ies
  imag-i-nar-i-ly
  imag-i-nar-i-ness
imaginary number
imaginary part
imaginary unit
imag-i-na-tion
  imag-i-na-tion-al
imag-i-na-tive
  imag-i-na-tive-ly
imag-ine
  imag-ined
  imag-in-ing
im-ag-ism
ima-go
imam
imam-ate
ima-ret
im-bal-ance
im-be-cile
  im-be-cil-ic
  im-be-cile-ly
  im-be-cil-i-ty
imbed
  imbed-ded
  im-bed-ding
im-bibe
im-bi-bi-tion
imbitter
imbosom
im-bri-cate
im-bri-ca-tion
im-bro-glio
imbrown

im-brue
  im-brued
  im-bru-ing
im-brute
im-bue
imdtly
im-id-az-ole
im-ide
im-i-do
im-ine
im-i-no
imip-ra-mine
imit
im-i-ta-ble
im-i-tate
  im-i-tat-ed
  im-i-tat-ing
  im-i-ta-tor
im-i-ta-tion
  im-i-ta-tive
im-mac-u-la-cy
im-mac-u-late
  im-mac-u-la-cy
  im-mac-u-late-ly
im-mane
im-ma-nent
  im-ma-nence
  im-ma-ne-cy
  im-ma-nent-ly
im-ma-te-ri-al
  im-ma-te-ri-al-ness
  im-ma-te-ri-al-i-ty
im-ma-te-ri-al-ism
im-ma-te-ri-al-i-ty
im-ma-te-ri-al-ize
im-ma-ture
  im-ma-ture-ly
  im-ma-ture-ness
  im-ma-tu-ri-ty
im-meas-ur-a-ble
  im-meas-ur-a-bly
im-me-di-a-cy
  im-me-di-a-cies
im-me-di-ate
  im-me-di-ate-ly
  im-me-di-ate-ness
immediate constituent
im-me-di-ate-ly

im-me-di-ate-ness
im-med-i-ca-ble
  im-med-i-ca-bly
im-me-mo-ri-al
  im-me-mo-ri-al-ly
im-mense
  im-mese-ly
  im-mese-ness
  im-men-si-ty
im-merge
  im-merged
im-merse
  im-mersed
  im-mers-ing
im-mer-sion
im-mesh
im-me-thod-i-cal
im-mi-grant
  im-mi-grat-ed
  im-mi-gra-tion
  im-mi-gra-tor
im-mi-grate
  im-mi-grat-ed
  im-mi-grat-ing
im-mi-nen-cy
im-mi-nent
  im-mi-nence
im-min-gle
im-mis-ci-ble
im-mit-i-ga-ble
im-mi-tance
im-mix
im-mo-bile
  im-mo-bil-i-ty
  im-mo-bi-lize
im-mod-er-a-cy
im-mod-er-ate
  im-mod-er-ate-ly
  im-mod-er-ate-ness
im-mod-est
  im-mod-est-ly
  im-mod-es-ty
im-mo-late
  im-mo-lat-ed
  im-mo-lat-ing
  im-mo-la-tion
  im-mo-la-tor
im-mor-al

im-mor-al-ist
im-mo-ral-i-ty
im-mor-al-ly
im-mor-tal
im-mor-tal-i-ty
im-mor-tal-ize
  im-mor-tal-iza-tion
  im-mor-tal-iz-er
im-mor-telle
im-mo-tile
im-mov-a-ble
  im-mov-a-bli-i-ty
  im-mov-a-bly
im-mune
im-mu-ni-ty
  im-mu-ni-ties
im-mu-nize
  im-mu-nized
  im-mu-niz-ing
  im-mu-ni-za-tion
im-mu-no-as-say
im-mu-no-dif-fu-sion
im-mu-no-elec-tro-pho-re-sis
im-mu-no-flu-o-res-cence
im-mu-no-gen-e-sis
im-mu-no-ge-net-ics
im-mu-no-ge-net-ic
im-mu-no-glob-u-lin
im-mu-no-he-ma-tol-o-gy
immunol
im-mu-nol-o-gy
im-mu-no-pa-thol-o-gy
im-mu-no-re-ac-tive
im-mu-no-sup-pres-sion
im-mu-no-ther-a-py
im-mure
  im-mured
  im-mur-ing
im-mu-ta-ble
  im-mu-ta-bil-i-ty
  im-mu-ta-bly
imp
im-pact
  im-pac-tion
im-pact-ed
im-pac-tor
im-paint
im-pair

im-pair-er
im-pair-ment
im-pa-la
im-pal-as
im-pal-ae
im-pale
im-paled
im-pal-ing
im-pale-ment
im-pal-er
im-pal-pa-ble
im-pal-pa-bil-i-ty
im-pal-pa-bly
im-pan-el
im-pan-eled
im-pan-el-ing
im-par-a-dise
im-par-i-ty
im-part
im-par-tial
im-par-ti-al-i-ty
im-par-tial-ly
im-par-ti-ble
im-pass-able
im-pass-abil-i-ty
im-pass-able-ness
im-pass-ably
im-passe
im-pas-si-ble
im-pas-si-bil-i-ty
im-pas-si-bly
im-pas-sion
im-pas-sioned
im-pas-sioned-ly
im-pas-sive
im-pas-sive-ly
im-pas-sive-ness
im-pas-siv-i-ty
im-paste
im-pas-to
im-pa-tience
im-pa-tient
im-pa-tient-ly
im-pawn
im-peach
im-peach-a-ble
im-peach-ment
im-pearl

im-pec-ca-ble
im-pec-ca-bil-i-ty
im-pec-ca-bly
im-pe-cu-nious
im-pe-cu-nious-ly
im-pe-cu-nious-ness
im-ped-ance
im-pede
im-ped-ed
im-ped-ing
im-ped-i-ment
im-ped-i-men-ta
im-pel
im-pelled
im-pel-ling
im-pend
im-pend-ing
im-pen-dent
im-pen-e-tra-bil-i-ty
im-pen-e-tra-ble
im-pen-e-tra-ble-ness
im-pen-e-tra-bly
im-pen-i-tence
im-pen-i-tent
im-pen-i-tent-ly
im-per-a-tive
im-per-a-tive-ly
im-per-a-tive-ness
im-pe-ra-tor
im-per-a-to-ri-al
im-per-ceiv-able
im-per-cep-ti-ble
im-per-cep-ti-bil-i-ty
im-per-cep-tive
im-per-cep-tive-ness
im-per-fect
im-per-fect-ly
im-per-fect-ness
im-per-fec-tion
im-per-fec-tive
im-per-fo-rate
im-pe-ri-al
im-pe-ri-al-ly
im-pe-ri-al-ism
im-pe-ri-al-ist
im-pe-ri-al-is-tic
im-pe-ri-al-is-ti-cal-ly
imperial moth

im-per-il
im-per-iled
im-per-il-ing
im-per-il-ment
im-pe-ri-ous
im-pe-ri-ous-ly
im-pe-ri-ous-ness
im-per-ish-able
im-per-ish-abil-i-ty
im-per-ish-able-ness
im-per-ish-ably
im-pe-ri-um
im-per-ma-nence
im-per-ma-nen-cy
im-per-ma-nent
im-per-ma-nent-ly
im-per-me-able
im-per-me-abil-i-ty
im-per-me-able-ness
im-per-me-ably
im-per-mis-si-ble
im-per-mis-si-bil-i-ty
im-per-mis-si-bly
im-per-son-al
im-per-son-al-i-ty
im-per-son-al-i-ties
im-per-son-al-ly
im-per-son-ate
im-per-son-at-ed
im-per-son-at-ing
im-per-son-a-tion
im-per-son-ator
im-per-ti-nence
im-per-ti-nen-cy
im-per-ti-nent
im-per-ti-nence
im-per-ti-nent-ly
im-per-turb-able
im-per-turb-ably
im-per-vi-ous
im-per-vi-ous-ly
im-per-vi-ous-ness
im-pe-tig-i-nous
im-pe-ti-go
im-pe-trate
im-pet-u-os-i-ty
im-pet-u-ous
im-pet-u-ous-ly

im-pet-u-ous-ness
im-pe-tus
im-pe-tus-es
im-pi-ety
im-pi-eties
im-pinge
im-pinged
im-ping-ing
im-pinge-ment
im-ping-er
im-pi-ous
im-pi-ous-ly
im-pi-ous-ness
imp-ish
im-pla-ca-ble
im-pla-ca-bil-i-ty
im-pla-ca-ble-ness
im-pla-ca-bly
im-plant
im-plan-ta-tion
im-plant-er
im-plau-si-ble
im-plau-si-bly
im-plau-si-bil-i-ty
im-ple-ment
im-ple-men-tal
im-ple-men-ta-tion
im-pli-cate
im-pli-cat-ed
im-pli-cat-ing
im-pli-ca-tion
im-plic-it
im-plic-it-ly
im-plic-it-ness
implicit differentiation
implicit function
im-plode
im-ploded
im-plod-ing
im-plore
im-plored
im-plor-ing
im-plo-ra-tion
im-plo-sion
im-plo-sive
im-ply
im-plied
im-ply-ing

im-po-lite
im-po-lite-ly
im-po-lite-ness
im-pol-i-tic
im-pol-i-tic-ly
im-pon-der-a-ble
im-pon-der-a-bil-i-ty
im-pon-der-a-bly
im-pone
im-poned
im-port
im-port-a-ble
im-port-er
im-por-tance
im-por-tant
im-por-tant-ly
im-por-tan-cy
im-por-tant
im-por-ta-tion
imported cabbageworm
imported fire ant
im-por-tu-nate
im-por-tu-nate-ly
im-por-tune
im-por-tuned
im-por-tun-ing
im-por-tu-ni-ty
im-pose
im-posed
im-pos-ing
im-pos-ter
im-po-si-tion
im-pos-si-bil-i-ty
im-pos-si-bil-i-ties
im-pos-si-ble
im-pos-si-bly
im-post
im-pos-tor
im-pos-tume
im-pos-ture
im-po-tence
im-po-ten-cy
im-po-tent
im-po-tent-ly
im-pound
im-pound-age
im-pound-ment
im-pov-er-ish

im-pov-er-ish-ment
im-prac-ti-ca-ble
im-prac-ti-ca-bil-i-ty
im-prac-ti-ca-ble-ness
im-prac-ti-ca-bly
im-prac-ti-cal
im-pre-cate
im-pre-cat-ed
im-pre-cat-ing
im-pre-ca-tion
im-pre-cise
im-pre-cis-ly
im-pre-ci-sion
im-pre-cis-ness
im-preg-na-ble
im-preg-na-bil-i-ty
im-preg-na-ble-ness
im-preg-na-bly
im-preg-nate
im-preg-nat-ed
im-preg-nat-ing
im-preg-na-tion
im-preg-n-tor
im-pre-sa
im-pre-sa-rio
im-pre-sa-ri-os
im-press
im-press-er
im-press-i-ble
im-press-ment
im-pres-sion
im-pres-sion-ist
im-pres-sion-a-ble
im-pres-sion-a-bly
im-pres-sion-ism
im-pres-sion-ist
im-pres-sion-is-tic
im-pres-sive
im-pres-sive-ly
im-pres-sive-ness
im-press-ment
im-pres-sure
im-prest
im-pri-ma-tur
im-pri-mis
im-print
im-print-er
im-pris-on

im-pris-on-ment
im-prob-a-bil-i-ty
im-prob-a-ble
im-prob-a-ble-ness
im-prob-a-bly
im-promp-tu
im-prop-er
im-prop-er-ly
im-prop-er-ness
improper fraction
improper integral
im-pro-pri-ety
im-pro-pri-eties
im-prov-able
im-prove
im-proved
im-prov-ing
im-prov-a-bil-i-ty
im-prov-a-ble
im-prove-ment
im-prov-i-dence
im-prov-i-dent
im-prov-i-dent-ly
im-pro-vi-sa-tion
im-pro-vi-sa-tion-al
im-prov-i-sa-tor
im-pro-vi-sa-to-re
im-pro-vise
im-pro-vised
im-pro-vis-ing
im-pro-vis-er
im-pru-dence
im-pru-dent
im-pru-dent-ly
im-pu-dic-i-ty
im-pugn
im-pugn-er
im-puis-sant
im-pulse
im-pul-sion
impulse buying
im-pul-sive
im-pu-ni-ty
im-pure
im-pure-ly
im-pure-ness
im-pu-ri-ty
im-pu-ri-ties

im-pu-ta-tion
im-pute
im-put-ed
im-put-ing
im-put-able
im-put-a-tion
im-put-a-tive
im-put-er
in
in-a-bil-i-ty
in ab-sen-tia
in-ac-ces-si-ble
in-ac-ces-si-bil-i-ties
in-ac-ces-si-ble-ness
in-ac-ces-si-bly
inac-cu-ra-cy
in-ac-cu-rate
in-ac-cu-rate-ly
in-ac-cu-ra-cy
in-ac-cu-ra-cies
in-ac-tion
in-ac-tive
in-ac-tive-ly
in-ac-tiv-i-ty
in-ad-e-quate
in-ad-e-qua-cies
in-ad-e-qua-cy
in-ad-e-quate-ly
in-ad-mis-si-ble
in-ad-mis-si-bly
in-ad-ver-tence
in-ad-ver-ten-cy
in-ad-ver-tent
in-ad-ver-tent-ly
in-ad-vis-able
in-alien-a-ble
in-alien-a-bly
in-al-ter-able
in-al-ter-able-ness
in-al-ter-abli-i-ty
in-al-ter-ably
in-am-o-ra-ta
in-am-o-ra-tas
in--and--in
inane
inane-ly
inane-ness
inan-i-ty

inan-i-ties
in-an-i-mate
in-a-ni-tion
inan-i-ty
in-ap-par-ent
in-ap-peas-able
in-ap-pe-tence
in-ap-pli-ca-ble
in-ap-po-site
in-ap-pre-cia-ble
in-ap-pre-cia-tive
in-ap-proach-able
in-ap-pro-pri-ate
in-ap-pro-pri-ate-ly
in-ap-pro-pri-ate-ness
in-apt
in-apt-ti-tude
in-apt-ly
in-apt-ness
in-ar-gu-able
in-ar-tic-u-late
in-ar-tic-u-late-ly
in-ar-tic-u-late-ness
in-ar-tis-tic
in-as-much as
in-at-ten-tion
in-at-ten-tive
in-at-ten-tive-ly
in-au-di-ble
in-au-gu-ral
in-au-gu-rate
in-au-gu-rat-ed
in-au-gu-rat-ing
in-au-gu-ra-tion
in-aus-pi-cious
in-aus-pi-cious-ly
in-au-then-tic
in--between
in-board
in-born
in-bound
inbounds line
in-breathe
in-bred
in-breed
in-breed-ing
in-cal-cu-la-ble
in-cal-cu-la-bly

in-ca-les-cence
in camera
in-can-desce
in-can-des-cence
in-can-des-cent
  in-can-des-cence
  in-can-des-cent-ly
in-can-descent lamp
in-can-ta-tion
in-ca-pa-ble
  in-ca-pa-bly
in-ca-pac-i-tate
  in-ca-pac-i-tat-ed
  in-ca-pac-i-tat-ing
in-ca-pac-i-ty
  in-ca-pac-i-ties
in-car-cer-ate
  in-car-cer-at-ed
  in-car-cer-at-ing
  in-car-cer-a-tion
in-car-di-na-tion
in-car-na-dine
  in-car-na-dined
  in-car-na-din-ing
in-car-nate
  in-car-nat-ed
  in-car-nat-ing
in-car-na-tion
incase
in-cau-tion
in-cau-tious
  in-cau-tious-ly
  in-cau-tious-ness
in-cen-di-a-rism
in-cen-di-ary
  in-cen-di-aries
in-cense
  in-censed
  in-ceas-ing
in-cen-tive
in-cep-tion
in-cer-ti-tude
in-ces-san-cy
in-ces-sant
  in-ces-sant-ly
in-cest
  in-ces-tu-ous
  in-ces-tu-ous-ly

in-ces-tu-ous-ness
inch
in chief
inch-meal
in-cho-ate
  in-cho-ate-ly
  in-cho-ate-ness
in-cho-ative
inch-worm
in-ci-dence
in-ci-dent
in-ci-den-tal
  in-ci-den-tal-ly
incidental music
in-cin-er-ate
  in-cin-er-at-ed
  in-cin-er-at-ing
  in-cin-er-a-tion
in-cin-er-a-tor
in-cip-i-ence
in-cip-i-en-cy
in-cip-i-ent
  in-cip-i-ent-ly
in-ci-pic
in-cise
  in-cised
  in-cis-ing
in-ci-sion
in-ci-sive
  in-ci-sive-ly
  in-ci-sive
  in-ci-sor
in-ci-ta-tion
in-cite
  in-cit-ed
  in-cit-ing
  in-cite-ment
  in-cit-er
in-ci-vil-i-ty
in-clem-en-cy
in-clem-ent
  in-clem-ent-ly
in-clin-able
in-cli-na-tion
in-cline
  in-clined
  in-clin-ing
  in-clin-er

inclined plane
in-cli-nom-e-ter
in-clip
inclose
in-clude
  in-clud-ed
  in-clud-ing
  in-clud-a-ble
  in-clu-sion
inclusion body
in-clu-sive
  in-clu-sive-ly
  in-clu-sive-ness
inclusive disjunction
inclusive of
in-co-erc-ible
incog
in-cog-i-tant
in-cog-ni-ta
in-cog-ni-to
  in-cog-ni-tos
in-cog-ni-zant
in-co-her-ence
in-co-her-ent
  in-co-her-ent-ly
in-com-bus-ti-ble
in-come
income account
imcome bond
income tax
in-com-ing
in-com-men-su-ra-ble
  in-com-men-su-ra-bly
in-com-men-su-rate
in-com-mode
in-com-mo-di-ous
in-com-mod-i-ty
in-com-mu-ni-ca-ble
in-com-mu-ni-ca-do
im-com-mu-ni-ca-tive
in-com-mut-able
in-com-pa-ra-ble
  in-com-pa-ra-bly
in-com-pat-i-bil-i-ty
in-com-pat-i-ble
  in-com-pat-i-bly
in-com-pe-tence
in-com-pen-ten-cy

in-com-pe-tent
in-com-pe-tent-ly
in-com-plete
in-com-plete-ly
in-com-plete-ness
in-com-ple-tion
in-com-pli-ant
in-com-pre-hen-si-ble
in-com-pre-hen-si-bly
in-com-pre-hen-sion
in-com-press-ible
in-com-put-able
in-con-ceiv-able
in-con-ceiv-ably
in-con-cin-ni-ty
in-con-clu-sive
in-con-clu-sive-ly
in-con-clu-sive-ness
in-con-dens-able
in-con-dite
in-con-for-mi-ty
in-con-gru-ence
in-con-gru-ent
in-con-gru-ity
in-con-gru-ous
in-con-gru-ous-ly
in-con-gru-ous-ness
in-con-gru-i-ties
in-con-scient
in-con-sec-u-tive
in-con-se-quent
in-con-se-quent
in-con-se-quen-tial
in-con-se-quen-tial-ly
in-con-sid-er-able
in-con-sid-er-ably
in-con-sid-er-ate
in-con-sid-er-ate-ly
in-con-sid-er-ate-ness
in-con-sis-tence
in-con-sis-ten-cy
in-con-sis-tent
in-con-sist-ent-ly
in-con-sol-able
in-con-sol-able-ness
in-con-sol-ably
in-con-so-nance
in-con-so-nant

in-con-spic-u-ous
in-con-spic-u-ous-ly
in-con-stant
in-con-stan-cy
in-con-stan-cies
in-con-stant-ly
in-con-sum-able
in-con-test-able
in-con-test-abil-i-ty
in-con-ti-nence
in-con-ti-nen-cy
in-con-ti-nent
in-con-ti-nent-ly
in-con-trol-la-ble
in-con-tro-vert-ible
in-con-ve-nience
in-con-ve-nien-cy
in-con-ve-nient
in-con-ve-nient-ly
in-con-ven-ienc-ing
in-con-vert-ible
in-con-vert-ibly
in-con-vinc-ible
in-co-or-di-nate
in-co-or-di-na-tion
in-cor-po-rate
in-cor-po-rat-ed
in-cor-po-rat-ing
in-cor-po-ra-tion
in-cor-po-ra-tor
in-cor-po-re-al
in-cor-po-re-ity
in-cor-rect
in-cor-rect-ly
in-cor-ri-gi-ble
in-cor-ri-gi-bil-i-ty
in-cor-ri-gi-ble-ness
in-cor-ri-gi-bly
in-cor-rupt
in-cor-rupt-ible
in-cor-rupt-ibil-i-ty
in-cor-rupt-ible-ness
in-cor-rupt-ibly
in-cor-rup-tion
in-crease
in-creased
in-creas-ing
in-creas-able

in-creas-ing-ly
in-crea-ate
in-cred-i-ble
in-cred-i-bil-i-ty
in-cred-i-ble-ness
in-cred-i-bly
in-cre-du-li-ty
in-cred-u-lous
in-cred-u-lous-ness
in-cred-u-lous-ly
in-cre-ment
in-cre-men-tal
in-cre-men-tal-ism
incremental repetition
in-cres-cent
in-crim-i-nate
in-crim-i-nat-ed
in-crim-i-nat-ing
in-crim-i-na-tion
in-crim-i-na-tor
in-crim-i-na-to-ry
in-cross
in-cross-bred
in-crust
in-crus-ta-tion
in-cu-bate
in-cu-bat-ed
in-cu-bat-ing
in-cu-ba-tion
in-cu-ba-tor
in-cu-bus
in-cu-bus-es
in-cul-cate
in-cul-cat-ed
in-cul-cat-ing
in-cul-ca-tion
in-cul-ca-tor
in-cul-pa-ble
in-cul-pate
in-cul-pat-ed
in-cul-pat-ing
in-cul-pa-tion
in-cult
in-cum-ben-cy
in-cum-ben-cies
in-cum-bent
in-cum-bent-ly
incumber

in-cu-na-ble
in-cu-nab-u-lum
in-cur
  in-curred
  in-cur-ring
in-cur-able
  in-cur-a-bil-i-ty
  in-cur-a-ble-ness
  in-cur-a-bly
in-cu-ri-ous
in-cur-rence
in-cur-rent
in-cur-sion
  in-cur-sive
in-cur-vate
in-curve
in-cus
in-cuse
in-da-ba
in-da-gate
in-da-mine
in-debt-ed
  in-debt-ed-ness
in-de-cen-cy
  in-den-cies
in-de-cent
  in-de-cent-ly
indecent assault
indecent exposure
in-de-ci-pher-able
in-de-ci-sion
in-de-ci-sive
  in-de-ci-sive-ly
  in-de-ci-sive-ness
in-de-clin-able
in-de-com-pos-able
in-de-co-rous
in-de-co-rum
in-deed
in-de-fat-i-ga-ble
  in-de-fat-i-ga-bil-i-ty
  in-de-fat-i-ga-ble-ness
  in-de-fat-i-ga-bly
in-de-fea-si-ble
in-de-fec-ti-ble
in-de-fen-si-ble
in-de-fin-able
  in-de-fin-abil-i-ty

in-de-fin-able-ness
in-de-fin-able
in-def-i-nite
  in-def-i-nite-ly
  in-def-i-nite-ness
indefinite integral
in-de-his-cent
in-del-i-ble
  in-del-i-bil-ity
  in-del-i-ble-ness
  in-del-i-bly
in-del-i-ca-cy
in-del-i-cate
  in-del-i-cate-ness
  in-del-i-cate-ly
in-dem-ni-fi-ca-tion
in-dem-ni-fy
  in-dem-ni-fied
  in-dem-ni-fy-ing
  in-dem-ni-fi-er
in-dem-ni-ty
  in-dem-ni-ties
in-de-mon-stra-ble
in-dene
in-dent
in-den-ta-tion
  in-dent-ed
in-den-ture
  in-den-tured
  in-den-tur-ing
indentured servant
in-de-pen-dence
in-de-pen-den-cy
in-de-pen-dent
  in-de-pen-dent-ly
indipendent assortment
independent variable
in--depth
in-de-scib-able
  in-de-scrib-abil-ity
  in-de-scrib-able-ness
  in-de-scrib-ably
in-de-struc-ti-ble
  in-de-struc-ti-bil-i-ty
  in-de-struc-ti-ble-ness
  in-de-struc-ti-bly
in-de-ter-min-able
in-det-mi-na-cy

indeterminacy principle
in-de-ter-mi-nate
  in-de-ter-mi-nat-ly
  in-de-ter-mi-na-tion
in-dex
  in-dex-er
  in-dex-es
  in-di-ces
index finger
index fossil
index number
index of refraction
In-dia
india ink
india rubber
indic
in-di-can
in-di-cant
in-di-cate
  in-di-cat-ed
  in-di-cat-ing
  in-di-ca-tion
in-dic-a-tive
  in-dic-a-tive-ly
in-di-ca-tor
  in-dic-a-tory
in-di-cia
in-dict
  in-dict-a-ble
  in-dict-er
  in-dict-or
  in-dict-ment
in-dif-fer-ence
in-dif-fer-en-cy
in-dif-fer-ent
  in-dif-fer-ent-ist
  in-dif-fer-ent-ly
in-dif-fer-ent-ism
in-di-gence
in-di-gene
in-dig-e-nous
  in-dig-e-nous-ly
  in-dig-e-nous-ness
in-di-gent
  in-di-gent-ly
in-di-gest-ed
in-di-gest-ible
  in-di-gest-ibil-i-ty

in-di-gest-ible-ness
in-di-ges-tion
in-di-ges-tive
in-dign
in-dig-nant
in-dig-ant-ly
in-dig-na-tion
in-dig-ni-ty
in-dig-ni-ties
in-di-go
in-di-goes
in-di-gos
indigo bunting
indigo plant
indigo snake
in-di-go-tin
in-di-rect
in-di-rect-ly
in-di-rect-ness
indirect cost
indirect evidence
indirect fire
in-di-rec-tion
indirect lighting
indirect object
indirect proof
indirect tax
in-dis-cern-ible
in-dis-ci-plin-able
in-dis-ci-pline
in-dis-ci-plined
in-dis-cov-er-able
in-dis-creet
in-dis-creet-ly
in-dis-creet-ness
in-dis-crete
in-dis-cre-tion
in-dis-crim-i-nate
in-dis-crim-i-nate-ly
in-dis-crim-i-nat-ing
in-dis-crim-i-na-tion
in-dis-cuss-ible
in-dis-pens-able
in-dis-pens-able-ness
in-dis-pens-abil-i-ty
in-dis-pens-ably
in-dis-pose
in-dis-posed

in-dis-pos-ing
in-dis-po-si-tion
in-dis-put-able
in-dis-so-cia-ble
in-dis-sol-u-ble
in-dis-sol-u-bil-i-ty
in-dis-sol-u-ble-ness
in-dis-sol-u-bly
in-dis-tinct
in-dis-tinc-tive
in-dis-tin-guish-able
in-dite
in-di-um
in-di-vert-ible
in-di-vid-u-al
in-di-vid-u-al-ly
in-di-vid-u-al-ism
in-di-vid-u-al-ist
in-di-vid-u-al-is-tic
in-di-vid-u-al-i-ty
in-di-vid-u-al-i-ties
in-di-vid-u-al-ize
in-di-vid-u-al-ized
in-di-vid-u-al-iz-ing
individual medley
in-di-vid-u-ate
in-di-vid-u-a-tion
in-di-vis-i-ble
in-doc-ile
in-doc-tri-nate
in-doc-tri-nat-ed
in-doc-tri-nat-ing
in-doc-tri-na-tion
in-doc-tri-na-tor
in-dole
in-dole-ace-tic acid
in-dole-bu-tyr-ic acid
in-do-lence
in-do-lent
in-do-lent-ly
in-do-meth-a-cin
in-dom-i-ta-ble
in-dom-i-ta-bil-i-ty
in-dom-ita-ble-ness
in-dom-i-ta-bly
in-do-ne-sian
in-door
in-doors

in-do-phe-nol
indorse
in-dox-yl
in-draft
in-drawn
in-du-bi-ta-ble
in-du-bi-ta-bil-i-ty
in-dubi-ta-ble-ness
in-du-bi-tab-ly
in-duce
in-duced
in-duce-ment
in-duc-er
in-duc-i-ble
in-duc-ing
in-duct
in-duct-ee
in-duc-tance
in-duc-tion
in-duc-tive
induction coil
induction heating
in-duc-tor
indue
in-dulge
in-dulged
in-dulg-ing
in-dul-gence
in-dul-gent
in-dul-gent-ly
in-du-line
in-dult
in-du-rate
in-dus
in-du-si-um
in-dus-tri-al
in-dus-tri-al-ly
in-dus-tri-al-ness
industrial arts
industrial engineering
in-dus-tri-al-ism
in-dus-tri-al-ize
in-dus-tri-al-ist
in-dus-tri-al-i-za-tion
in-dus-tri-al-ized
in-dus-tri-al-iz-ing
industrial melanism
industrial park

industrial psychology
industrial relations
industrial revolution
industrial school
industrial sociology
industrial union
in-dus-tri-ous
  in-dus-tri-ous-ly
in-dus-try
  in-dus-tries
in-dwell
in-dwell-ing
in-bri-ant
ine-bri-ate
  ine-bri-at-ed
  ine-bri-at-ing
  ine-bri-a-tion
  ine-bri-ety
in-ed-u-ca-ble
in-ef-fa-ble
  in-ef-fa-bil-i-ty
  in-ef-fa-ble-ness
  in-ef-fa-bly
in-ef-fec-tive
  in-ef-fec-tive-ly
  in-ef-fec-tive-ness
in-ef-fec-tu-al
  in-ef-fec-tu-al-i-ty
  in-ef-fec-tu-al-ly
  in-ef-fec-tu-al-ness
in-ef-fi-cient
  in-ef-fi-cien-cy
  in-ef-fi-cien-cies
  in-ef-ffi-cient-ly
in-e-gal-i-tar-i-an
in-elas-tic
inelastic collision
inelastic scattering
in-el-e-gance
in-el-e-gant
in-el-i-gi-ble
  in-el-i-gi-bil-i-ty
  in-el-i-gi-bly
in-el-o-quent
in-e-luc-ta-ble
in-elud-ible
in-enar-ra-ble
in-ept

in-ept-i-tude
  in-ept-ly
in-ept-ness
in-e-qual-i-ty
in-eq-ui-ta-ble
in-eq-ui-ty
  in-eq-ui-ties
in-equi-valve
in-erad-i-ca-ble
in-er-ran-cy
in-er-rant
in-ert
  in-ert-ly
  in-ert-ness
in-er-tia
  in-er-tial
inertial guidance
in-es-cap-a-ble
in-es-sen-tial
in-es-ti-ma-ble
  in-es-ti-ma-bly
in-ev-i-ta-ble
  in-ev-i-ta-bil-i-ty
  in-ev-i-ta-ble-ness
  in-ev-i-ta-ble-ness
  in-ev-i-ta-bly
in-ex-act
in-ex-cus-able
  in-ex-cus-able-ness
  in-ex-cus-ably
in-ex-haust-i-ble
  in-ex-haust-i-bil-i-ty
  in-ex-haust-i-ble-ness
  in-ex-haust-i-bly
in-ex-is-tence
in-ex-is-tent
in-ex-o-ra-ble
  in-ex-o-ra-bil-i-ty
  in-ex-o-ra-ble-ness
  in-ex-o-ra-bly
in-ex-pe-di-ence
in-ex-pe-di-en-cy
in-ex-pe-di-ent
in-ex-pen-sive
in-ex-pe-ri-ence
  in-ex-pe-ri-enced
in-ex-pert
  in-ex-per-ly

in-ex-pert-ness
in-ex-pert
  in-ex-pert-ly
  in-ex-pert-ness
in-ex-pi-a-ble
  in-ex-pi-a-ble-ness
  in-ex-pi-a-bly
in-ex-plain-able
in-ex-pli-ca-ble
  in-ex-pli-ca-bil-i-ty
  in-ex-pli-ca-ble-ness
  in-ex-pli-ca-bly
in-ex-plic-it
in-ex-press-ible
in-ex-press-ible-ness
in-ex-pres-sive
in-ex-pug-na-ble
in-ex-pung-ible
in ex-ten-so
in-ex-tin-guish-able
in ex-tre-mis
in-ex-tri-ca-ble
in-fal-li-ble
  in-fal-i-bil-i-ty
  in-fal-li-ble-ness
  in-fal-li-bly
in-fa-mous
  in-fa-mous-ly
  in-fa-mous-ness
in-fa-my
  in-fa-mies
in-fan-cy
  in-fan-cies
in-fant
  in-fant-hood
  in-fant-like
in-fan-ta
in-fan-te
in-fan-ti-cide
in-fan-tile
  in-fan-tine
  in-fan-til-i-ty
infantile paralysis
in-fan-til-ism
in-fan-tine
in-fan-try
  in-fan-tries
  in-fan-try-man

in-fan-try-men
infant school
in-farct
in-fare
in-fat-u-ate
  in-fat-u-at-ed
  in-fat-u-at-ing
  in-fat-u-at-ed-ly
  in-fat-u-a-tion
in-fau-na
in-fea-si-ble
in-fect
  in-fect-ed-ness
  in-fect-er
  in-fect-or
in-fec-tion
in-fec-tious
  in-fec-tious-ly
  in-fec-tious-ness
  in-fec-tive
infectious hepatitis
infectious mononucleosis
in-fec-tive
in-fe-lic-i-tous
in-fe-lic-i-ty
in-fer
  inferred
  in-fer-ring
  in-fer-a-ble
  in-fer-a-bly
  in-fer-ence
  in-fer-er
in-fer-en-tial
in-fe-ri-or
  in-fe-ri-or-i-ty
  in-fe-ri-or-ly
inferiority complex
in-fer-nal
infernal machine
in-fer-no
  in-fer-nos
in-fer-tile
in-fest
  in-fes-ta-tion
  in-fest-er
in-fi-del
in-fi-del-i-ty
  in-fi-del-i-ties

in-field
  in-field-er
infield hit
infield out
in-fight-ing
  in-fight-er
in-fil-trate
  in-fil-trat-ed
  in-fil-trat-ing
  in-fil-tra-tion
  in-fil-tra-tive
  in-fil-tra-tor
in-fi-nite
  in-fi-nite-ly
  in-fi-nite-ness
  in-fin-i-tude
in-fin-i-tes-i-mal
  in-fin-i-tes-i-mal-ty
infinitesimal calculas
in-fin-i-tive
  in-fin-i-tive-ly
in-fin-i-tude
in-fin-i-ty
  in-fin-i-ties
in-firm
  in-firm-lly
  in-firm-ness
in-fir-ma-ry
  in-fir-ma-ries
in-fir-mi-ty
  in-fir-mi-ties
in-fix
in fla-gran-te de-lic-to
in-flame
  in-flamed
  in-flam-ing
  in-flam-er
in-flam-ma-ble
  in-flam-ma-bil-i-ty
  in-flam-ma-ble-ness
  in-flam-ma-bly
in-flam-ma-tion
in-flam-ma-to-ry
in-flate
  in-flat-ed
  in-flat-ing
  in-flat-a-ble
  in-flat-ed-ness

in-fla-tor
in-flat-er
in-fla-tion
  in-fla-tion-ary
  in-fla-tion-ism
  in-fla-tion-ist
inflationary spiral
in-fla-tion-ism
in-flect
  in-flec-tion
  in-flec-tion-al
  in-flec-tion-al-ly
  in-flec-tion-less
  in-flec-tive
  in-flec-tor
inflection point
in-flexed
in-flex-i-ble
  in-flex-i-bil-i-ty
  in-flex-i-ble-ness
  in-flex-i-bly
in-flex-ion
in-flict
  in-flict-a-ble
  in-flict-er
  in-flict-or
  in-flic-tion
  in-flic-tive
in--flight
in-flo-res-cence
in-flow
in-flu-ence
  in-flu-enced
  in-flu-enc-ing
  in-flu-ence-a-ble
  in-flu-enc-er
  in-flu-en-tial
  in-flu-en-tial-ly
in-flu-en-za
  in-flu-en-zal
  in-flu-en-za-like
in-flux
in-fold
in-form
  in-formed
  in-for-mer
in-for-mal
  in-for-mal-i-ty

in-for-mal-ly
in-form-ant
in for-ma-pau-pe-ris
in-for-mat-ics
in-for-ma-tion
in-for-ma-tion-al
in-for-ma-tive
in-for-ma-tive-ly
in-for-ma-tive-ness
in-for-ma-to-ry
information retrieval
information science
information theory
in-for-ma-to-ry
in-formed
in-form-er
in-fra
in-fract
in-frac-tion
in-fra dig
in-fra-hu-man
in-fran-gi-bil-i-ty
in-fran-gi-ble
in-fran-gi-ble-ness
in-fran-gi-bly
in-fra-red
in-fra-son-ic
in-fra-spe-cif-ic
in-fra-struc-ture
in-fre-quence
in-fre-quen-cy
in-fre-quent
in-fre-quent-ly
in-fringe
in-fringed
in-fring-ing
in-fringe-ment
in-fring-er
in-fun-dib-u-lar
in-fun-dib-u-li-form
in-fun-dib-u-lum
in-fu-ri-ate
in-fu-ri-at-ed
in-fu-ri-at-ing
in-fu-ri-at-ing-ly
in-fu-ri-a-tion
in-fuse
in-fused

in-fus-ing
in-fus-er
in-fus-i-bil-i-ty
in-fus-i-ble
in-fu-sion
in-fu-sive
in-fu-so-ri-al
in-fu-so-ri-an
in-gath-er
in-gen-ious
in-gen-ious-ly
in-gen-ious-ness
in-ge-nue
in-ge-nu-ity
in-gen-u-ous
in-gen-u-ous-ly
in-gen-u-ous-ness
in-gest
in-ges-tion
in-ges-tive
in-ges-ta
in-gle
in-gle-nook
in-glo-ri-ous
in-glo-ri-ous-ly
in-glo-ri-ous-ness
in-got
ingot iron
in-grain
in-grained
in-grate
in-gra-ti-ate
in-gra-ti-at-ed
in-gra-ti-at-ing
in-gra-ti-a-tion
in-grat-i-tude
in-gre-di-ent
in-group
in-grow-ing
in-grown
in-growth
in-gui-nal
in-gur-gi-tate
in-gur-gi-tat-ed
in-gur-gi-tat-ing
in-gur-gi-ta-tion
in-gulf
in-hab-it

in-hab-it-a-ble
in-hab-i-ta-tion
in-hab-it-er
in-hab-it-ed
in-hab-it-an-cy
in-hab-it-ant
in-hal-ant
in-ha-la-tion
in-ha-la-tor
in-hale
in-haled
in-hal-ing
in-hal-er
in-har-mon-ic
in-har-mo-ni-ous
in-har-mo-ni-ous-ly
in-har-mo-ny
in-here
in-hered
in-her-ing
in-her-ence
in-her-ent
in-her-ent-ly
in-he-sion
in-her-it
in-her-i-tor
in-her-it-able
in-her-i-tance
inheritance tax
in-hib-it
in-hib-i-tive
in-hib-o-to-ry
in-hib-i-ter
in-hib-it-or
in-hi-bi-tion
in-hos-pi-ta-ble
in-hos-pi-tal-i-ty
in--house
in-hu-man
in-hu-man-i-ty
in-hu-mane
in-hume
in-im-i-cal
in-im-i-ta-ble
in-iq-ui-tous
in-iq-ui-ty
in-iq-ui-ties
in-i-tial

in-i-tialed
in-i-tial-ing
in-i-tial-ly
ini-tial-ism
ini-tial-ize
initial rhyme
initial side
initial teaching alphabet
in-i-ti-ate
 in-i-ti-at-ed
 in-i-ti-at-ing
 in-i-ti-a-tion
 in-i-ti-a-tor
in-i-ti-a-tive
ini-tia-to-ry
in-ject
 in-jec-tion
 in-jec-tor
in-jec-tant
in-jec-tor razor
in-ju-di-cious
in-junc-tion
 in-junc-tive
in-jure
 in-jured
 in-jur-ing
 in-ju-ri-ous
in-ju-ry
 in-ju-ries
in-jus-tice
ink
ink-ber-ry
ink-blot
ink-blot test
ink-horn
in-kle
ink-ling
ink-stand
ink-well
inky cap
inky
in-laid
in-land
in-land-er
in--law
in-lay
 in-laid
 in-lay-ing

in-let
in-li-er
in--line engine
in lo-co pa-ren-tis
in-ly
in-mate
in me-di-as res
in-me-mo-ri-an
in--mi-grant
in--migrate
 in--mi-gra-tion
in-most
in-nards
in-nate
in-ner
inner city
in-ner--di-rect-ed
inner ear
inner light
in-ner-most
inner planet
inner product
in-ner-sole
inner space
in-ner-spring
inner tub
in-ner-vate
 in-ner-vat-ed
 in-ner-vat-ing
 in-ner-va-tion
in-nerve
inn-hold-er
in-ning
inn-keep-er
in-no-cence
in-no-cen-cy
in-no-cent
 in-no-cent-ly
in-noc-u-ous
in-nom-i-nate
innominate artery
innominate bone
innominate vein
in-no-vate
 in-no-vat-ed
 in-no-vat-ing
 in-no-va-tion
in-no-va-tive

in-no-va-tor
in-nu-en-do
 in-nu-en-dos
 in-nu-en-does
in-nu-mer-a-ble
in-nu-mer-ous
in-nu-mer-a-bly
in-nu-tri-tion
in-ob-serv-ance
 in-ob-serv-ant
 in-ob-serv-ant-ly
in-oc-u-lant
in-oc-u-late
 in-oc-u-lat-ed
 in-oc-u-lat-ing
 in-oc-u-la-tion
 in-oc-u-la-tor
in-oc-u-lum
in-of-fen-sive
in-op-er-a-ble
in-op-er-a-tive
in-oper-cu-late
in-op-por-tune
 in-op-por-tun-i-ty
in order that
in-or-di-nate
in-or-gan-ic
in-os-cu-late
ino-si-tol
ino-tro-pic
in-pa-tient
in--per-son
in per-so-nam
in pet-to
in-phase
in-pour
in--print
in--pro-cess
in pro-pria per-so-na
in-put
in-quest
in-qui-e-tude
in-qui-line
in-quire
in-quiry
 in-quir-ies
in-quis-i-tive
in-quis-i-tor

in-quis-i-to-ri-al
in-quis-i-to-ri-al-ly
in-qui-si-tion
in-qui-si-tive
in-quis-i-tor
in re
in rem
in--res-i-dence
in-road
in-rush
in-sa-lu-bri-ous
in-sane
in-san-i-ty
in-san-i-ties
in-sa-tia-ble
in-sa-tia-bil-i-ty
in-sa-tia-bly
in-sa-ti-ate
in-scribe
in-scrip-tion
in-scrip-tive
in-scroll
in-scru-ta-ble
in-scru-ta-bil-i-ty
in-scru-ta-bly
in-sculp
in-seam
in-sect
in-sec-ta-ry
in-sec-ti-cid-al
in-sec-ti-cide
in-sec-ti-cid-al
in-sec-ti-fuge
in-sec-tile
in-sec-ti-vor
in-sec-tiv-o-rous
in-sec-tiv-o-ry
in-se-cure
in-se-cu-ri-ty
in-sem-i-nate
in-sem-i-nat-ed
in-sem-i-nat-ing
in-sem-i-na-tion
in-sem-i-na-tor
in-sen-sate
in-sen-si-ble
in-sen-si-tive
in-sen-si-tiv-i-ty

in-sen-ti-ent
in-sep-a-ra-ble
in-sep-a-ra-bil-i-ty
in-sep-a-ra-bly
in-sert
in-sert-er
in-ser-tion
in-ser-tion-al
in-ser-vice
in-ses-so-ri-al
in-set
in-set-ting
in-shore
in-side
inside address
inside of
inside out
in-sid-er
inside track
in-sid-i-ous
in-sight
in-sight-ful
in-sig-nia
in-sig-nif-i-cance
in-sig-nif-i-can-cy
in-sig-nif-i-cant
in-sig-nif-i-cance
in-sin-cere
in-sin-cer-i-ty
in-sin-cer-i-ties
in-sin-u-ate
in-sin-u-at-ed
in-sin-u-at-ing
in-sin-u-a-tor
in-sin-u-a-tion
in-sip-id
in-si-pid-i-ty
in-sip-id-ness
in-sist
in-sist-ence
in-sist-ent
in-so-bri-e-ty
in-so-cia-ble
in-so-cia-bil-i-ty
in-so-cia-bly
in-so-far
insofar as
insol

in-so-late
in-so-la-tion
in-sole
in-so-lence
in-so-lent
in-so-lence
in-sol-u-bi-lize
in-sol-u-bi-li-za-tion
in-sol-u-ble
in-sol-u-bil-i-ty
in-sol-u-bly
in-solv-a-ble
in-sol-vent
in-sol-ven-cy
in-som-nia
in-som-ni-ac
in-so-much
in-so-much as
insomuch that
in-sou-ci-ance
insoul
in-span
in-spect
in-spec-tion
inspection arms
in-spec-tor
inspectoral general
insphere
in-spi-ra-tion
in-spi-ra-tion-al
in-spi-ra-tor
in-spi-ra-to-ry
in-spire
in-spir-ing
in-spir-it
in-spis-sate
in-sta-bil-i-ty
in-sta-ble
in-sta-bil-i-ty
in-stall
in-stal-la-tion
in-stall-ment
installment plan
in-stance
in-stanced
in-stanc-ing
in-stan-cy
in-stan-ta-ne-ous

in-stan-ta-ne-ity
in-stan-ta-neous-ly
in-stant-ly
instant replay
in-star
in-state
  in-stat-ed
  in-stat-ing
  in-state-ment
in sta-tu-quo
in-stau-ra-tion
in-stead
instead of
in-step
in-sti-gate
  in-sti-gat-ed
  in-sti-gat-ing
  in-sti-ga-tion
  in-sti-ga-tor
in-still
in-stinct
in-stinc-tive
  in-stinc-tu-al
  in-stinc-tive-ly
in-sti-tute
  in-sti-tut-ed
  in-sti-tut-ing
  in-sti-tut-er
in-sti-tu-tion
  in-sti-tu-tion-al
in-sti-tu-tion-al-ism
  in-sti-tu-tion-al-ist
in-sti-tu-tion-al-ize
  in-sti-tu-tion-al-iza-tion
  in-sti-tu-tion-al-ized
  in-sti-tu-tion-al-iz-ing
in-sti-tu-tor
in-struct
in-struc-tion
in-struc-tive
in-struc-tor
in-stru-ment
in-stru-men-tal
in-stru-men-tal-ism
in-stru-men-ta-list
in-stru-men-tal-i-ty
in-stru-men-ta-tion
instrument flying

instrument landing
instrument panel
in-sub-or-di-nate
  in-sub-or-di-na-tion
in-sub-stan-tial
  in-sub-stan-ti-al-i-ty
in-suf-fer-a-ble
  in-suf-fer-a-bly
in-suf-fi-cience
in-suf-fi-cien-cy
in-suf-fi-cient
  in-suf-fi-cien-cy
in-suf-flate
  in-suf-fla-tion
in-su-lant
in-su-lar
  in-su-lar-i-ty
in-su-late
  in-su-lat-ed
  in-su-lat-ing
in-su-la-tion
in-su-la-tor
in-su-lin
insulin shock
in-sult
in-sup-port-able
  in-sup-port-able-ness
  in-sup-port-ably
in-sup-press-i-ble
  in-sup-press-ibly
in-sur-ance
insurance run
in-sure
  in-sured
  in-sur-ing
  in-sur-er
in-sur-gence
in-sur-gen-cy
in-sur-gent
in-sur-mount-able
in-sur-rec-tion
  in-sur-rec-tion-ary
in-sus-cep-ti-ble
in-tact
in-ta-glio
in-take
in-tan-gi-ble
  in-tan-gi-bil-i-ty

in-tan-gi-bly
in-te-ger
in-te-gra-ble
in-te-gral
  in-te-gral-ly
integral calculus
integral domain
in-te-grand
in-te-grate
  in-te-grat-ed
  in-te-grat-ing
integrated circuit
in-te-gra-tion
  in-te-gra-tion-ist
in-te-gra-tive
in-te-gra-tor
in-teg-ri-ty
in-teg-u-ment
in-tel-lect
in-tel-lec-tion
in-tel-lec-tive
in-tel-lec-tu-al
in-tel-lec-tu-al-ism
in-tel-lec-tu-al-ize
in-tel-li-gence
in-tel-li-gent
  in-tel-li-gent-ly
intelligence quotient
in-tel-li-genc-er
intelligence test
in-tel-li-gent
in-tel-li-gent-sia
in-tel-li-gi-ble
  in-tel-li-gi-bil-i-ty
  in-tel-li-gi-bly
in-tem-per-ance
in-tem-per-ate
in-tend
  in-tend-er
in-ten-dance
in-ten-dant
in-tend-ed
in-tend-ing
in-tend-ment
in-ten-er-ate
in-tense
  in-tense-ly
  in-tense-ness

in-ten-si-fy
in-ten-si-fied
in-ten-si-fy-ing
in-ten-si-fi-ca-tion
in-ten-si-fi-er
in-ten-sion
in-ten-si-ty
in-ten-si-ties
in-ten-sive
in-ten-sive-ly
in-ten-sive-ness
in-tent
in-ten-tion
in-ten-tion-al
in-ten-tion-al-ly
in-ten-tioned
in-ter
in-tera-bang
in-ter-act
in-ter-ac-tion
in-ter-ac-tant
in-ter-alia
in-ter ali-os
in-ter-atom-ic
in-ter-brain
in-ter-breed
in-ter-bred
in-ter-breed-ing
in-ter-ca-la-ry
in-ter-ca-late
in-ter-cede
in-ter-ced-ed
in-ter-ced-ing
in-ter-ced-er
in-ter-cel-lu-lar
in-ter-cel-lu-lar-ly
in-ter-cept
in-ter-cep-ter
in-ter-cept-or
in-ter-cep-tion
in-ter-cep-tive
in-ter-ces-sion
in-ter-change
in-ter-changed
in-ter-chang-ing
in-ter-chang-a-ble
in-ter-chng-a-bil-i-ty
in-ter-chang-a-bly

in-ter-clav-i-cle
in-ter-col-le-gi-ate
in-ter-co-lum-ni-a-tion
in-ter-com
in-ter-com-mun-i-cate
intercommunication system
in-ter-com-mu-nion
in-ter-con-nect
in-ter-con-nec-tion
in-ter-con-ti-nen-tal
in-ter-con-ver-sion
in-ter-cool-er
in-ter-cos-tal
in-ter-course
in-ter-crop
in-ter-cross
in-ter-cul-tur-al
in-ter-cur-rent
in-ter-cut
in-ter-de-nom-i-na-tion-al
in-ter-den-tal
in-ter-de-part-men-tal
inter-de-pend
in-ter-de-pen-dence
in-ter-de-pen-den-cy
in-ter-de-pend-ent
in-ter-dict
in-ter-dic-tion
in-ter-dif-fuse
in-ter-dig-i-tate
in-ter-dis-ci-pli-nary
in-ter-est
in-ter-est-ed
in-ter-est-ed-ly
interest group
in-ter-est-ing
in-ter-face
in-ter-fa-cial
in-ter-faith
in-ter-fas-cic-u-lar
in-ter-fere
in-ter-fer-ence
in-ter-fer-o-gram
in-ter-fer-om-e-ter
in-ter-fer-on
in-ter-fer-tile
in-ter-file
in-ter-fuse

in-ter-ga-lac-tic
in-ter-gen-er-a-tion-al
in-ter-ge-ner-ic
in-ter-gla-cial
in-ter-gov-ern-men-tal
in-ter-gra-du-tion
in-ter-grade
in-ter-group
in-ter-growth
in-ter-hemi-spher-ic
in-ter-im
in-ter-ion-ic
in-te-ri-or
interior decoration
interior decorator
interior designer
in-te-ri-or-ize
interior monologue
in-ter-ject
in-ter-jec-tion
in-ter-jec-to-ry
in-ter-lace
in-ter-lace-ment
in-ter-lam-i-nate
in-ter-lard
in-ter-lay-er
in-ter-leaf
in-ter-leaves
in-ter-leave
in-ter-leaved
in-ter-leav-ing
in-ter-li-brary
in-ter-line
in-ter-lined
in-ter-lin-ing
in-ter-link
in-ter-lo-cal
in-ter-lock
in-ter-lo-cu-tion
in-ter-loc-u-tor
in-ter-loc-u-to-ry
in-ter-lope
in-ter-loped
in-ter-loped
in-ter-lop-ing
in-ter-lop-er
in-ter-lude
in-ter-lu-nar

in-ter-mar-ry
in-ter-mar-ried
in-ter-mar-ry-ing
in-ter-mar-riage
in-ter-med-dle
in-ter-me-di-a-cy
in-ter-me-di-ary
in-ter-me-di-ate
intermediate host
intermediate school
in-ter-me-di-a-tion
in-ter-ment
in-ter-me-tal-lic
in-ter-mez-zo
in-ter-mi-na-ble
in-ter-mi-na-ble-ness
in-ter-mi-na-bly
in-ter-min-gle
in-ter-min-gledd
in-ter-min-gling
in-ter-mis-sion
in-ter-mis-sive
in-ter-mit
in-ter-mit-tent
intermittent current
in-ter-mix
in-ter-mix-ture
in-ter-mo-lec-u-lar
in-tern
in-ter-ship
in-ter-nal
in-ter-nal-ly
internal--combustion engine
in-ter-nal-ize
in-ter-nal-ized
in-ter-nal-iz-ing
in-ter-nal-i-za-tion
internal medicine
internal respiration
internal rhyme
internal secretion
in-ter-na-tion-al
in-ter-na-tion-al-i-ty
in-ter-na-tion-al-ize
in-ter-na-tion-al-ized
in-ter-na-tion-al-ism
in-ter-na-tion-al-ize
international law

international pitch
international relations
international unit
international volt
in-ter-ne-cine
in-tern-ee
in-ter-neu-ron
in-tern-ist
in-tern-ment
in-ter-node
in-ter-nu-cle-ar
in-ter-nun-ci-al
in-ter-nun-cio
in-tero-cep-tive
in-tero-cep-tor
in-ter-of-fice
in-ter-pel-late
in-ter-pen-e-trate
in-ter-pen-e-tra-tion
in-ter-per-son-al
in-ter-phase
in-ter-plan-e-tary
in-ter-plant
in-ter-play
in-ter-plead
in-ter-plead-er
in-ter-po-late
in-ter-pose
in-ter-posed
in-ter-pos-ing
in-ter-pos-er
in-ter-po-si-tion
in-ter-pret
in-ter-pret-a-ble
in-ter-pret-er
in-ter-pre-tive
in-ter-pre-ta-tion
in-ter-pre-ta-tion-al
in-ter-pre-ta-tive
in-ter-pu-pil-lary
in-ter-ra-cial
interred
in-ter-reg-num
in-ter-re-late
in-ter-re-lat-ed
in-ter-re-alt-ing
in-ter-re-li-gious
interring

in-ter-ro-bang
in-ter-ro-gate
in-ter-ro-gat-ed
in-ter-ro-gat-ing
in-ter-ro-ga-tion
in-ter-ro-ga-tion-al
interrogation point
in-ter-rog-a-tive
in-ter-ro-ga-tor
in-ter-rupt
in-ter-rup-tion
in-ter-rup-tive
in-ter-rupt-er
in-ter-rupt-or
in-terr-scho-las-tic
in-ter se
in-ter-sect
in-ter-sec-tion
in-ter-ser-vice
in-ter-ses-sion
in-ter-sex
in-ter-sex-u-al
in-ter-space
in-ter-spaced
in-ter-spac-ing
in-ter-spe-cif-ic
in-ter-sperse
in-ter-spersed
in-ter-spers-ing
in-ter-sper-sion
in-ter-sta-di-al
in-ter-state
in-ter-stel-lar
in-ter-ster-ile
in-ter-stice
in-ter-sti-tial
in-ter-sub-jec-tive
in-ter-tes-ta-men-tal
in-ter-tid-al
in-ter-tie
in-ter-till
in-ter-trop-i-cal
in-ter-twine
in-ter-twined
in-ter-twin-ing
in-ter-twist
in-ter-ur-ban
in-ter-val

in-ter-vale
in-ter-val-om-e-ter
in-ter-vence
in-ter-vene
in-ter-ve-nor
in-ter-ven-tion-ism
in-ter-ver-te-bral
intervertebral disk
in-ter-view
in-ter-view-er
in-ter vi-vos
in-ter-vo-cal-ic
in-ter-war
in-ter-weave
in-ter-wove
in-ter-weav-ing
in-ter-wo-ven
in-ter-zon-al
in-tes-ta-cy
in-tes-tate
in-tes-ti-nal
intestinal fortitude
in-tes-tine
in-tes-ti-nal
in-ti-ma-cy
in-ti-mate
in-ti-mat-ed
in-ti-mat-ing
in-ti-mate-ly
in-ti-ma-tion
in-tim-i-date
in-tim-i-dat-ed
in-tim-i-dat-ing
in-tim-i-da-tion
in-tim-i-da-tor
in-tim-i-da-to-ry
in-tinc-tion
in-tine
in-ti-tled
in-ti-ling
in-to
in-tol-er-a-ble
in-tol-er-a-bly
in-tol-er-ance
in-tol-er-ant
in-tomb
in-to-nate
in-to-nat-ed

in-to-nat-ing
in-to-na-tion
intonation pattern
in-tone
in-toned
in-ton-ing
in-ton-er
in-tox-i-cant
in-tox-i-cate
in-tox-i-cat-ed
in-tox-i-cat-ing
in-tox-i-ca-tion
in-tra-ar-te-ri-al
in-tra-car-di-ac
in-tra-cel-lu-lar
in-tra-cra-ni-al
in-trac-ta-ble
in-trac-ta-bil-i-ty
in-tra-der-mal
intradermal test
in-tra-dos
in-tra-ga-lac-tic
in-tra-mo-lec-u-lar
in-tra-mu-ral
in-tra-mu-ral-ly
in-tra-mus-cu-lar
in-tran-si-geance
in-tran-si-gent
in-tran-si-gence
in-tran-si-tive
in-trant
in-tra-per-i-to-ne-al
in-tra-per-son-al
in-tra-pop-u-la-tion
in-tra-psy-chic
in-tra-spe-cies
in-tra-spe-cif-ic
in-tra-state
in-tra-uter-ine
intrauterine device
in-tra-ve-nous
in-trench
in-trep-id
in-tre-pid-i-ty
in-tri-cate
in-tri-ca-cy
in-tri-ca-cies
in-tri-cate-ness

in-trique
in-tri-quing
in-trin-sic
in-trin-si-cal
in-trin-si-cal-ly
in-tro-duce
in-tro-duced
in-tro-duc-ing
in-tro-duc-er
in-tro-duc-tion
in-tro-duc-to-ry
in-tro-gres-sion
in-trogres-sant
in-tro-gres-sive
in-troit
in-tro-mect
in-tro-jec-tion
in-tro-mis-sion
in-tro-mit
in-tro-mit-ted
in-tro-mit-tent
in-tro-mit-ting
in-trorse
in-trorse-ly
in-tro-spect
in-tro-spec-tion
in-tro-spec-tion-al
in-tro-spec-tion-ism
in-tro-spec-tive
in-tro-spec-tive-ly
in-tro-spec-tive-ness
in-tro-ver-sion
in-tro-ver-sive
in-tro-ver-sive-ly
in-tro-vert
in-tro-vert-ed
in-trude
in-trud-ed
in-trud-er
in-trud-ing
in-tru-sion
in-tru-sive
in-tru-sive-ly
in-tru-sive-ness
in-trust
in-tu-ba-tion
in-tu-it
in-tu-i-tion

in-tu-i-tion-al
in-tu-ition-ism
in-tu-i-tive
in-tu-mesce
  in-tu-mes-cence
  in-tu-mes-cent
in-tus-sus-cept
in-tus-sus-cep-tion
  in-tus-sus-cep-tive
in-u-lin
in-unc-tion
in-un-date
  in-un-dat-ed
  in-un-dat-ing
  in-un-da-tion
  in-un-da-to-ry
in-ure
  in-ured
  in-ur-ing
  in-ure-ment
in-urn
in-utile
  in-util-i-ty
in vac-uo
in-vade
in-vag-i-nate
in-vag-i-na-tion
in-val-id
  in-va-lid-i-ty
in-val-i-date
  in-val-i-dat-ed
  in-val-i-dat-ing
  in-val-i-da-tion
  in-val-i-da-tor
in-va-lid-ism
in-val-u-a-ble
in-vari-able
in-vari-ance
in-var-i-ant
in-va-sion
in-va-sive
  in-va-sive-ness
in-vec-tive
in-veigh
in-vei-gle
  in-vei-gled
  in-vei-gle-ment
  in-vei-gling

in-vent
  in-ven-tor
  in-ven-tress
in-ven-tion
in-ven-tive
  in-ven-tive-ness
in-ven-to-ry
  in-ven-to-ries
  in-ven-to-ried
  in-ven-to-ry-ing
in-ver-ness
in-verse
inverse function
in-ver-sion
in-ver-sive
in-vert
in-ver-tase
in-ver-te-brate
in-vert-ed
inverted comma
in-vert-er
in-vert-ible
invert sugar
in-vest
  in-ves-tor
in-ves-ti-gate
  in-ves-ti-gat-ed
  in-ves-ti-gat-ing
  in-ves-ti-ga-tion
  in-ves-ti-ga-tor
in-ves-ti-ture
in-vest-ment
investment company
in-vet-er-a-cy
in-vet-er-ate
in-vi-a-ble
in-vid-i-ous
in-vig-or-ate
in-vin-ci-ble
  in-vin-ci-bil-i-ty
  in-vin-ci-bly
in-vi-o-la-ble
in-vi-o-la-cy
in-vi-o-late
in-vis-cid
in-vis-i-ble
in-vi-ta-tion
in-vi-ta-tion-al

in-vi-ta-to-ry
in-vite
in-vi-tee
in-vi-ting
in vi-tro
in vi-vo
in-vo-cate
in-vo-ca-tion
in-voice
  in-voiced
  in-voic-ing
in-voke
  in-voked
  in-vok-er
  in-vok-ing
in-vo-lu-cre
in-vo-lu-crum
in-vol-un-tary
  in-vol-un-tar-i-ly
in-vo-lute
  in-vo-lut-ed
  in-vo-lut-ing
in-vo-lu-tion
  in-vo-lu-tion-al
  in-vo-lu-tion-ary
in-volve
  in-volved
  in-volv-ing
  in-volve-ment
  in-volv-er
in-vul-ner-a-ble
in-ward
  in-wards
  in-ward-ly
  in-ward-ness
in-weave
in-wrought
io-date
iod-ic
iodic acid
io-dide
io-din-ate
io-dine
io-dize
io-do-form
io-do-phor
io-dop-sin
io-dous

io moth
ion
ion engine
ion exchange
ion-ic
ionic bond
io-ni-um
ionization chamber
ion-ize
ion-o-sphere
iota
io-ta-cism
ip-e-cac
ip-se dix-it
ip-si-lat-er-al
ip-sis-si-ma ver-ba
ip-so fac-to
iras-ci-ble
iras-ci-ble-ness
irate
ire
ire-nic
ir-i-des-cent
 ir-i-des-cence
irid-ici
irid-i-um
ir-id-os-mine
iris
iris diaphragm
Irish
Irish bull
Irish coffee
Irish confetti
Irish-ism
Irish mail
Irish moss
irk-some
iron
 iron-er
iron-bound
iron-clad
iron curtain
iron-fisted
iron gray
iron hand
iron-heart-ed
iron-horse
iron-ic

iron-i-cal
iron-ing
ironing board
iro-nist
iron lung
iron-mas-ter
iron-mon-ger
iron out
iron oxide
iron pyrtes
iron ration
iron-side
iron-smith
iron-stone
ironstone chine
iron-ware
iron-weed
iron-wood
iron-work
 iron-work-er
iro-ny
ir-ra-di-ance
ir-ra-di-ate
ir-ra-di-a-tion
ir-rad-i-ca-ble
ir-ra-tion-al
 ir-ra-tion-al-i-ty
ir-ra-tio-nal-ism
irrational number
ir-re-al
ir-re-al-i-ty
ir-re-claim-a-ble
ir-rec-on-cil-a-ble
 ir-rec-on-cil-a-bil-i-ty
ir-re-cov-er-a-ble
ir-re-cu-sa-ble
irred
ir-re-deem-able
ir-re-den-ta
ir-re-den-tism
ir-re-duc-i-ble
ir-re-flex-ive
ir-re-form-able
ir-re-fra-ga-ble
ir-re-fran-gi-ble
ir-ref-u-ta-ble
ir-re-gard-less
ir-reg-u-lar

ir-reg-u-lar-i-ty
ir-rel-a-tive
ir-rel-e-vance
ir-rel-e-van-cy
ir-rel-e-vant
 ir-rel-e-vance
ir-re-li-gion
ir-re-li-gious
ir-re-me-albe
ir-re-me-di-a-ble
ir-re-me-di-a-ble-n ess
ir-rep-a-ra-bly
ir-re-mov-a-ble
ir-rep-a-ra-ble
ir-re-peal-able
ir-re-plac-a-ble
ir-re-press-i-ble
 ir-re-press-i-bil-i-ty
ir-re-press-i-bly
ir-re-proach-a-ble
ir-re-pro-duc-ible
ir-re-sist-i-ble
 ir-re-sist-i-bil-i-ty
ir-res-o-lute
 ir-res-o-lu-tion
ir-re-solv-able
ir-re-spec-tive
ir-re-spon-si-ble
ir-re-triev-a-ble
 ir-re-triev-a-bil-i-ty
 ir-re-trieev-a-bly
ir-rev-er-ence
ir-rev-er-ent
ir-re-vers-ible
ir-rev-o-ca-ble
 ir-rev-o-ca-bil-i-ty
irridenta
ir-ri-gate
ir-ri-ta-bil-i-ty
ir-ri-ta-ble
ir-ri-tant
ir-ri-tate
 ir-ri-tat-ed
 ir-ri-tat-ing
 ir-ri-tat-ing-ly
ir-ri-ta-tion
ir-ri-ta-tive
ir-ro-ta-tion-al

ir-rupt
ir-rup-tive
is-al-lo-bar
isch-emia
is-chi-um
is-en-tro-pic
isin-glass
is-lam
is-land
island universe
isle
is-let
isn't
iso-ag-glu-ti-na-tion
iso-an-ti-gen
iso-bar
iso-bu-tyl-ene
iso-chro-mat-ic
iso-chron
iso-chro-nal
iso-chro-nous
iso-cli-nal
iso-cline
iso-clin-ic
isoclinic line
iso-cy-a-nate
iso-cy-clic
iso-di-a-met-ric
iso-dose
iso-dy-nam-ic
iso-elec-tric
iso-elec-tron-ic
iso-en-zyme
iso-ga-mete
isog-a-mous
iso-ge-ne-ic
iso-gen-ic
iso-gloss
iso-gon-ic
isogonic line
iso-gram
iso-hel
iso-he-mol-y-sis
iso-hy-et
iso-la-ble
iso-late
  iso-lat-ed
iso-la-tion

iso-la-tion-ism
iso-leu-cine
iso-line
isoln
isol-o-gous
iso-mag-net-ic
iso0mer
isom-er-ase
iso-mer-ic
isom-er-ism
isom-er-ize
isom-er-ous
iso-met-ric
isometric drawing
isometric line
isometric projection
iso-met-rics
isom-e-try
iso-morph
iso-mor-phic
iso-mor-phism
iso-ni-a-zid
ison-o-my
iso-oc-tane
iso-phote
iso-pi-es-tic
iso-pleth
iso-pod
iso-pren-a-line
iso-prene
iso-pren-oid
iso-pro-pyl
isopropyl alcohol
iso-pro-ter-e-nol
isos-ce-les triangle
iso-seis-mal
is-os-mot-ic
iso-spin
iso-spon-dy-lous
iso-spo-rous
isos-ta-sy
iso-tach
iso-therm
iso-ther-mal
iso-ton-ic
iso-tope
iso-tro-pic
iso-zyme

is-su-able
is-su-ance
is-su-ant
issue
  is-sued
  is-su-er
  is-su-ing
isthmian
isth-mic
isth-mus
is-tle
ital-ian-ate
ital-ian-ize
ital-ic
ital-i-cize
itch
ite
item
item-iza-tion
item-ize
it-er-ance
it-er-ant
it-er-ate
it-er-a-tive
ithy-phal-lic
itin-er-a-cy
itin-er-an-cy
itin-er-ant
itin-er-ary
itin-er-ate
  itin-er-at-ed
  itin-er-at-ing
  itin-er-a-tion
its
it's
it-self
ivied
ivo-ry
ivo-ry-bill
ivo-ry-billed woodpecker
ivory black
ivory nut
ivory tower
ivo-ry--tow-ered
ivy
iwis
ix-o-did
iz-zard

jab
jabbed
jab-bing
jab-ber
jab-ber-er
jac-a-mar
jac-a-ram-da
jack-al
jack-ass
jack-ass-ery
jack bean
jack-boot
jack crevalle
jack-daw
jack-et
jack-et-ed
Jack Frost
jack-fruit
jack-ham-mer
jack--in--the--box
jack--in--the--box-es
jack-knife
jack-kives
jack-knifed
jack-knif-ing
jack-leg
jack-light
jack mackerel
jack--of--all--trades
jack off
jack--o'--lan-tern
jack pine
jack-pot
jack rab-bit
jack salmon
jack-screw
jack-smelt
jack-snipe
Jack-son Day
jack-stay
jack-straw
jack-tar
Ja-cob
jac-o-net
jac-quard
jac-que-rie
jac-ti-ta-tion
jade

jad-ed
jad-ing
jade green
jade plant
jae-ger
Jaf-fa
jag
jag-ged
jag-ging
jag-uar
jail-bird
jail-break
jail-er
ja-lopy
ja-lop-ies
jal-ou-sie
jam
jammed
jam-ming
jam-mer
jamb
jam-bo-ree
jam session
jan-gle
jan-gled
jan-gling
jan-gler
jan-gly
jan-i-tor
jan-i-to-ri-al
jar
jar-ful
jarred
jar-ring
jar-di-niere
jar-gon
jar-gon-ize
jar-goon
jarl
jar-rah
jar-red
jas-mine
jas-per
jas-per-ware
jas-sid
Jat
jaunce
jaun-dice

jaun-diced
jaun-dic-ing
jaunt
jaun-ty
jaun-ti-er
jaun-ti-est
jaun-ti-ly
jaun-ti-ness
jav-e-lin
ja-ve-li-na
jaw
jaw-bone
jaw-break-er
jawed
jaw-less fish
jaw-line
jay
jay-bird
jay-gee
jay-hawk-er
jay-walk
jay-walk-er
jazz
jazz-ist
jazz-man
jazzy
jazz-i-er
jazz-i-est
jazz-i-ly
jazz-i-ness
jeal-ous
jeal-ous-ies
jeal-ou-sy
jean
jeep
jeer
jeer-er
jehad
je-hu
je-ju-nal
je-june
je-ju-num
jell
jellied gasoling
jel-li-fy
jel-li-fies
jel-li-fy-ing
jel-ly

jel-lied
jel-lies
jel-ly-ing
jel-ly-like
jel-ly bean
jel-ly-fish
jelly roll
jel-u-tong
je ne sais quoi
jen-net
jen-ny
jen-nies
jeop-ard
jeop-ar-dize
jeop-ar-dy
jeop-ar-dize
jeop-ar-dized
jeop-ar-diz-ing
je-quir-i-ty bean
jer-boa
jerboa mouse
jer-e-mi-ad
jerk
jerk-er
jerk-i-ly
jerk-i-ness
jerk-y
jerk-i-er
jerk-i-est
jer-kin
jerk off
jerk-wa-ter
jerky
jer-o-bo-am
jer-ri-can
jer-ry--build
jer-ry--built
jer-ry--build-ing
jer-ry--build-er
jer-sey
jess
jes-sa-mine
jest-er
jest-ing
Je-sus
jet
jet-ted
jet-ting

jet airplane
jet-bead
jet engine
jet lag
jet-lin-er
jet-port
jet-pro-polled
jet propulsion
jet-sam
jet set
jet stream
jet-ti-son
jet-ty
jet-ties
jeu d'es-prit
jeu-nesse do-ree
jew-el
jew-eled
jew-el-ing
jew-el-er
jew-el-ry
jew-el-weed
jew-fish
Jew-ish
Jewish calendar
jib
jibbed
jib-bing
jib-boom
jibe
jibed
jib-ing
jiff
jif-fy
jif-fies
jig
jigged
jig-ging
jig-ger
jig-gle
jig-gled
jig-gling
jig-gly
jig-saw
jigsaw puzzle
ji-hal
jil-lion
jilt

jilt-er
jim crow
jim-dan-dy
jim-jams
jim-my
jim-mies
jim-mied
jim-my-ing
jim-son-weed
jin-gle
jin-gled
jin-gling
jin-go
jin-go-ism
jink
jinn
jin-rik-i-sha
jinx
ji-pi-ja-pa
jit-ney
jit-neys
jit-ter
jit-ters
jit-tery
jit-ter-bug
jit-ter-bugged
jive
job
jobbed
job-bing
job actiion
job-ber
job-bery
job-hold-er
job--hop-ping
job-less
job lot
jock
jock-ey
jock-eys
jock-eyed
jock-ey-ing
jockey club
jock itch
jock-strap
jo-cose
jo-cos-i-ty
joc-u-lar

jo-cund
  jo-cun-di-ty
jodh-pur
joe--pye weed
jo-ey
jog
  jogged
  jog-ging
  jog-ger
jog-gle
  jog-gled
  jog-gling
jo-han-nes
john
john-boat
John Bull
John Doe
John Do-ry
Joh-ne's disease
John Han-cock
John Mark
john-ny
john-ny-cake
John-ny--jump--up
John-ny--on--the--spot
Johnny Reb
John-son-ese
John-son grass
joie de vi-vre
join
  join-able
  join-er
join-der
join-ing
joint
  joint-ed
  joint-ly
joint grass
joint resolution
join-tress
joint-stock company
join-ture
joint-worm
joist
jo-jo-ba
joke
  joked
  jok-ing

joke-ster
jok-ing-ly
jok-er
jol-li-fi-ca-tion
jol-li-ty
jol-ly
  jol-li-er
  jol-li-est
  jol-lied
  jol-ly-ing
jol-ly boat
Jol-ly Rog-er
jolt
jolt-er
jolt-ing-ly
jolty
jolt--wagon
Jo-nah
Jo-nas
Joh-a-than
jon-gleur
jon-quil
Jor-dan almond
Jor-dan curve
Jordan curve theorem
jo-rum
jo-seph
Jo-seph-ite
josh
Josh-ua
Joshua tree
joss
joss house
joss stick
jos-tle
  jos-tled
  jos-tling
  jos-tler
Jos-ue
jot
  jott-ed
  jot-ting
Jo-tun
joule
jounce
jouncy
jour
jour-nal

journal box
jour-nal-ese
jour-nal-ism
jour-nal-ist
  jour-na-lis-tic
jour-nal-ize
jour-ney
  jour-ney-man
  jour-ney-men
jour-ney-work
joust
Jove
jo-vi-al
  jo-vi-al-i-ty
jow
jowl
  jowled
  jowy
jowly
joy
joy-ance
joy-ful
joy-less
joy-ous
joy-pop
joy-ride
joy-stick
ju-ba
Ju-bal
ju-bi-lant
  ju-bi-lance
  ju-bi-lan-cy
ju-bi-lar-i-an
ju-bi-late
ju-bi-la-tion
  ju-bi-late
  ju-bi-lat-ed
  ju-bi-lat-ing
ju-bi-lee
Ju-dah
Ju-da-ic
Ju-da-ism
Ju-da-ist
Ju-da-ize
Ju-das
Judas tree
Jud-der
Jude

judge
 judged
 judg-ing
judge advocate
judge advocate general
Judg-es
judg-mat-ic
 judg-ma-ti-cal
 judg-mat-i-cal-ly
judge-ment
 judge-men-tal
judgment day
ju-di-ca-to-ry
ju-di-ca-ture
ju-di-cial
judicial review
ju-di-cia-ry
ju-di-cious
Ju-dith
ju-do
jug
 jugged
 jug-gin
 jug-ful
 jug-gler
ju-gate
jug band
jug-ful
jug-ger-naut
jug-gle
jug-gler
jug-glery
jug-u-lar
jugular vein
jug-u-lum
ju-gum
juice
 juic-i-er
 juic-i-est
 juic-i-ly
 juic-i-ness
juiced
juice-head
juice up
juicy
ju-jit-su
ju-ju
ju-jube

juke
juke-box
juke joint
ju-lep
Ju-lian calender
ju-li-enne
Ju-liet
Ju-lius
Ju-ly
Ju-ma-da
jum-ble
 jum-bled
 jum-bling
jumble sale
jum-bo
 jum-bos
jump
 jump-ing
 jump-i-ness
 jumpy
jump ball
jump boot
jump cut
jump-er
jumping bean
jumping jack
jumping mouse
jumping--off place
jumping plant house
jumping spider
jump--off
jump pass
jump rope
jump seat
jump shot
jump suit
jumpy
 jump-i-er
 jump-i-est
jun-co
junc-tion
junc-tur-al
junc-ture
June
june beetle
June-ber-ry
jun-gle
jungle fowl

jungle gym
jun-ior
ju-ni-per
junk
 junk-man
 junky
jun-ket
junk-ie
jun-ta
Ju-pi-ter
ju-ris-dic-tion
 ju-ris-dic-tion-al
ju-ris-pru-dence
 ju-ris-pru-den-tial
ju-ris-pru-dent
ju-rist
ju-ris-tic
ju-ror
ju-ry
 ju-ries
 ju-ry-man
just
 just-ly
 just-ness
jus-tice
jus-tice-less
jus-tice-like
jus-ti-fi-ca-tion
jus-ti-fy
 jus-ti-fied
 jus-ti-fy-ing
jus-ti-fi-a-ble
jus-tif-i-ca-tory
jut
 jut-ted
 jut-ting
jute
ju-ve-nes-cence
ju-ve-nes-cent
ju-ve-nile
 ju-ve-nil-i-ty
juvenile court
juvenile delinquency
juvenile hormone
juvenile officer
ju-ve-nil-i-ty
jux-ta-pose
 jux-ta-posed

ka-bob
kai-ser
kale
ka-lei-do-scope
  ka-lei-do-scop-ic
ka-lim-ba
kal-li-din
kal-li-krein
kal-pa
kalsomine
Ka-ma
kame
ka-mi-ka-ze
kan-ga-roo
kangaroo court
kangaroo rat
Kan-na-da
kan-te-le
ka-olin
  ka-oline
ka-pok
ka-put
ka-ra-te
kar-ma
  kar-mic
ka-ty-did
kay-ak
kay-o
ka-zoo
kedge
  kedged
  kedg-ing
keek
keel
  keeled
  keel-less
keel-boat
keel-haul
keel-son
keen
  keen-ly
  keen-ness
keep-ing
keep-sake
keep up
kees-hont
keet
kef

ke-fir
keg
keg-ler
kelp
kelp bass
kel-pie
Kelt
kel-vin
kemp
ken
  kenned
  ken-ning
ken-nel
  ken-neled
  ken-nel-ing
ke-no
ken-speck-le
kent-ledge
ker-a-tin
ker-chief
ker-mis
ker-nel
ker-o-sene
kes-trel
ketch-up
ke-tone
ket-tle
ket-tle-drum
key
  keyed
key-board
key-hole
keyhole saw
keying sequence
key light
key-note
keynote address
keynote speaker
key-punch
key-set
key signature
key-stone
key-stroke
key-way
key word
kha-ki
  khak-is
kha-lif

khan
kib-butz
  kib-but-zim
ki-bitz-er
ki-bosh
kick
kick around
kick-back
kick-er
kick in
kick-off
kick out
kick over
kick-shaw
kick-stant
kick turn
kick-up
kid
  kid-ded
  kid-ding
  kid-dish
kid-die
kid-dush
kiddush ha-shem
kid glove
kid leather
kid-nap
kid-ney
  kid-neys
kidney bean
kidney stone
kid-skip
kid stuff
kiel-ba-sa
kie-ser-ite
kif
kike
kill
kill-deer
kill-er
killer whale
kil-lick
kil-li-fish
kill-ing
kill-joy
kill-off
kiln
kilo

kil-os
ki-lo-bar
ki-lo-bit
ki-lo-cal-o-rie
ki-lo-cu-rie
kilo-cy-cle
ki-lo-gram
kilogram calorie
kilogram--meter
kilo-li-ter
ki-lo-me-ter
ki-lo-oer-sted
ki-lo-par-sec
ki-lo-rad
ki-lo-ton
ki-lo-volt
kil-o-watt
kilowatt--hour
kilt
kil-ter
ki-mo-no
kin
ki-nase
kind
kin-der-gar-ten
kind-heart-ed
kin-dle
kin-dled
kin-dling
kind-less
kind-li-ness
kind-ly
kind-li-er
kind-li-est
kin-dred
kin-e-mat-ic
kin-e-scope
ki-ne-si-ol-o-gy
ki-ne-sis
kin-es-the-sia
ki-net-ic
ki-net-ics
kinetic art
kinetic energy
ki-net-i-cist
kinetic potential
kinetic theory
ki-ne-tin

ki-net-o-chore
ki-neto-nu-cle-us
ki-neto-plast
ki-neto-scope
ki-neto-some
kin-folk
king
king-bird
king-bolt
king-cobra
king crab
king-cratf
king-cup
king-dom
king-fish
king-fish-er
king-let
king-ly
king mackerel
king-mak-er
king of arms
king-pin
king post
king's evil
king-ship
king-side
king--size
king--sized
king snake
king's yellow
ki-nin
ki-nin-o-gen
kink
kink-y
kink-i-er
kink-i-est
kins-folk
kin-ship
kins-man
kins-men
kins-wom-an
ki-osk
kip
kip-per
kirk
kir-mess
kirsch
kir-tle

kish-ke
kis-met
kiss
kiss-a-ble
kiss-er
kissing bug
kissing cousin
kissing disease
kiss of death
kiss of peace
kist
kit bag
kitch-en
kitchen cabinet
kitch-en-ette
kitchen garden
kitchen midden
kitchen police
kitch-en-ware
kite
kit-ed
kit-ing
kit fox
kith
kithe
kitsch
kit-ten
kit-ten-ish
kit-ten-ish-ly
kit-ti-wake
kit-tle
kit-ty
kit-ties
kit-ty--cor-ner
ki-wi
klatch
klatsch
klep-to-ma-nia
klep-to-ma-ni-ac
klieg eyes
klieg light
kloof
kludge
klutz
kly-stron
knack
knack-er
knap

knap-sack
knap-weed
knave
knav-ery
knav-ish
 knav-ish-ly
knead
knee
 kneed
 knee-ing
knee action
knee-cap
knee--deep
knee-high
knee-hole
knee jerk
kneel
 knelt
 kneel-ing
 kneel-er
knee-pan
knell
knew
knick-er-bock-er
knick-ers
knick-knack
knife
 knives
 knifed
 knif-ing
 knife-like
knife--edge
knight
 knight-hood
 knight-ly
knight bachelor
knight-er-rant
 knights-er-rant
 knight-er-rant-ry
knight--hood
kinight-ly
knish
knit
 knit-ted
 knit-ting
 knit-ter
knit stitch
knit-ting

knit-wear
knob
 knobbed
 knob-by
 knob-bi-er
 knob-bi-est
knock
knock-a-bout
knock back
knock-down
knock-er
knock--knee
 knock--kneed
knock off
knock-out
knockout drops
knock over
knock up
knock-wurst
knoll
knop
knot
 knot-ted
 knot-ting
 knot-less
 knot-like
 knot-ty
knot-grass
knot-hole
knot-ty
knotty pine
knot-weed
knout
know
 knew
 known
 know-ing
 know-a-ble
 know-er
know--how
know-ing-ly
know--it--all
knowl-edge
knowl-edge-able
know--noth-ing
known--noth-ing-ism
knuck-le
 knuck-led

knuck-ling
knuck-le-ball
knuck-le-ball-er
knuck-le-bone
knuckle down
knuck-le--dus-ter
knuck-le-head
knuckle joint
knuckle under
knur
knurl
 knurled
 knurly
koa
ko-ala
ko-an
ko-bo
ko-bold
ko-el
ko-gas-in
kohl-ra-bi
 kohl-ra-bies
ko-la
ko-la nut
ko-lin-sky
 ko-lin-skies
kook
 kooky
 kook-i-er
 kook-i-est
kook-a-bur-ra
ko-peck
ko-ru-na
ko-sher
kou-mis
kow-tow
kra-ter
krem-lin
krem-lin-ol-o-gy
krill
krim-mer
kris
kro-na
kro-ne
kryp-ton
ku-dos
ku-miss
kum-quat

lab
lab-a-rum
lab-a-num
la-bel
  la-beled
  la-bel-ing
  la-bel-er
la-bel-lum
  la-bel-la
  la-bel-late
la-bi-al
  la-bi-al-ly
la-bia ma-jo-ra
labia mi-no-ra
la-bi-ate
la-bi-o-den-tal
la-bi-um
  la-bia
la-bor
  la-bor-er
lab-o-ra-to-ry
labor camp
la-bored
la-bo-ri-ous
  la-bo-ri-ous-ly
  la-bo-ri-ous-ness
la-bor-ite
la-bor-sav-ing
labor union
la-bour
lab-ra-dor-ite
la-bret
la-brum
la-bur-num
lab-y-rinth
  lab-y-rin-thine
  lab-y-rin-thi-an
lace
lace--curtain
lac-er-ate
  lac-er-at-ed
  lac-er-at-ing
  lac-er-a-tion
lace-wing
lace-work
lac-ey
la-ches
lach-ry-mal

lach-ry-mose
  lach-ry-mose-ly
lac-ing
la-cin-i-ate
lack
lack-a-dai-si-cal
  lack-a-dai-si-cal-ly
lack-ey
lack-lus-ter
la-ci-nia
la-con-ic
  la-con-i-cal-ly
lac-quer
  lac-quer-er
lac-ri-ma-tion
lac-ri-ma-tor
la-crosse
lac-tate
  lac-tat-ed
  lac-tat-ing
  lac-ta-tion
lac-te-al
lac-tic
lactic acid
lac-tif-er-ous
lac-to-ba-cil-lus
lac-to-gen-ic
lac-to-glob-u-lin
lac-tone
lac-tose
la-cu-na
  la-cu-nas
  la-cu-nae
la-cu-nar
la-cus-trine
lacy
lad
lad-a-num
lad-der
lad-der--back
ladder truck
lad-die
lade
  lad-ed
  lad-en
  lad-ing
la-di-da
ladies' man

ladies' room
ladies' tresses
lad-ing
la-di-no
la-dle
  la-dled
  la-dling
la-dy
  la-dy-bug
lady beetle
la-dy-bird
la-dy-bug
lady chapel
Lady Day
la-dy-fin-ger
la-dy-fish
la-dy--in--wait-ing
la-dy-like
la-dy-love
lady of the house
la-dy-ship
lady's slipper
la-dy's smock
lady's thumb
lag
  lagged
  lag-ging
la-ger
lag-gard
la-gniappe
lago-morph
la-goon
la-gu-na
la-ic
  la-i-cal
  la-i-cal-ly
la-icize
laid
laid paper
laigh
lain
lair
laird
lais-ser-faire
lai-tance
la-i-ty
  la-i-ties
lake

laked
lak-ing
laky
lake dweller
lake dwelling
lake-front
lake hearing
lake-shore
lake-side
lake trout
lakh
lal-la-tion
la-lop-a-thy
lam
lammed
lam-ming
la-ma
la-ma-sery
la-ma-ser-ies
lamb
lam-baste
lam-bast-ed
lam-bast-ing
lam-ben-cy
lam-bent
lam-bent-ly
lam-bert
lamb-kill
lam-bre-quin
lamb-skin
lame
lame-brain
lame duck
la-mel-la
la-mel-late
lam-el-la-tion
la-mel-li-branch
la-mel-li-form
la-ment
lam-en-ta-ble
lam-en-ta-bly
lam-en-ta-tion
lam-i-na
lam-i-nae
lam-i-nas
lamina pro-pria
lam-i-nar
laminar flow

lam-i-nar-ia
lam-i-nar-i-am
lam-i-nar-in
lam-i-nate
lam-i-nat-ed
lam-i-nat-ing
lam-i-na-tion
lamp
lamp-black
lamp brush
chromosome
lam-per eel
lamp-light
lam-poon
lam-prey
lam-preys
lamp-shell
lam-ster
la-nai
lance
lanced
lanc-ing
lance corporal
lance-let
len-ceo-late
lan-cet
lancet arch
lancet window
lance-wood
lan-dau
land-ed
land-ing
land-la-dy
land-la-dies
land-locked
land-lord
land-lub-ber
land-own-er
land-own-ing
land-own-er-ship
land-slide
land-ward
land-wards
lang syne
lan-gauge
lan-quid
lan-quid-ly
lan-quish

lan-quish-ing
lan-quish-ing-ly
lan-quor
lan-guor-ous
lan-guor-ous-ly
lank-ness
lanky
lank-i-er
lank-i-est
lank-i-ness
lan-o-lin
lan-tern
lan-tha-num
lan-yard
lap
la-pel
lap-ful
lap-fuls
laps-ful
lap-i-dary
lap-i-dar-ies
lap-in
lap-pet
lapse
lapsed
laps-ing
lar-board
lar-ce-ny
lar-ce-nies
lar-ce-nous
larch
lar-der
large
larg-er
larg-est
large-ly
lar-gess
lar-ghet-to
lar-ghet-tos
larg-ish
lar-go
lar-gos
lar-i-at
lar-rup
lar-va
lar-vae
lar-val
lar-yn-gi-tis

lar-ynx
  lar-ynx-es
  lar-ynx-ges
  la-ryn-ge-al
las-civ-i-ous
  las-ci-v-i-ous-ly
la-ser
lash
  lash-ing
  lash-er
las-sie
las-si-tude
las-so
  las-sos
  las-soes
  las-so-er
last-ing
  last-ing-ly
last-ly
latch-key
late
  lat-er
  lat-est
  late-ness
late-ly
la-tent
  la-ten-cy
  la-tent-ly
lat-er-al
  lat-er-al-ly
la-tex
  la-tex-es
lathe
lath-er
  lath-er-er
  lath-ery
lath-ing
lat-i-tude
  lat-i-tu-di-nal
lat-i-tu-di-nar-i-an
la-trine
lat-ter
lat-tice
  lat-tied
  lat-tic-ing
lat-tice-work
laud-able
  laud-ably

lau-da-num
lau-da-to-ry
  lau-da-tive
laugh
  laugh-ter
launch
  launch-er
laun-der
  laun-der-er
  laun-dress
laun-der-ette
laun-dry
  laun-dries
lau-re-ate
lau-rel
la-va
la-a-liere
lav-a-to-ry
  lav-a-to-ries
lave
  laved
  lav-ing
lav-en-der
lav-ish
  lav-ish-ly
  la-vish-ness
law-abid-ing
law-break-er
  law-break-ing
law-ful
  law-ful-ly
  law-ful-ness
law-less
  law-less-ly
  law-less-ness
law-mak-er
  law-mak-ing
lawn
law-ren-ci-um
law-suit
law-yer
lax
  lax-i-ty
  lax-ly
  lax-ness
lax-a-tive
lay-er
lay-ette

lay-man
  lay-men
lay-off
lay-out
lay-over
laze
  lazed
  laz-ing
la-zy
  la-zi-er
  la-zi-est
  la-zi-ly
la-zy-bones
lea
leach
lead
  lead-ing
lead-en
  lead-en-ly
lead-er
  lead-er-less
  lead-er-ship
leaf-age
leafy
  leaf-i-er
  leaf-i-est
leaque
  leaqued
  leaqu-ing
leak
  leak-age
  leak-i-ness
  leaky
  leak-i-er
  leak-i-est
lean
  lean-ly
  lean-ness
lean-ing
lean--to
  lean--tos
leap
  leaped
  leapt
  leap-ing
  leap-er
leap-frog
learn

learn-ed
learnt
learn-ing
learn-er
learn-ed-ly
learn-ed-ness
lease
leased
leas-ing
leash
least-wise
least-ways
leath-er
leath-er-neck
leath-ery
leave
left
leav-ing
lev-er
leav-en
leaves
leave-talk-ing
lech-er
lech-er-ous
lech-er-ous-ly
lech-ery
lech-er-ies
lec-tern
lec-ture
lec-tured
lec-tur-ing
lec-tur-er
ledge
ledg-er
leech
leek
leer-ing-ly
leery
lee-ward
lee-way
left--hand-ed
left--hand-ed-ly
left--hand-ed-ness
left-ist
left-over
left--wing
left--wing-er
leg

legged
leg-ging
leg-a-cy
leg-a-cies
le-gal
le-gal-ly
le-gal-ist
le-gal-is-tic
le-gal-i-ty
le-gal-i-ties
le-gal-ize
le-gal-ized
le-gal-iz-ing
le-gal-i-za-tion
leg-ate
leg-a-tee
le-ga-tion
le-ga-to
leg-end
leg-end-ary
leg-er-de-main
leg-gy
leg-gi-er
leg-gi-est
leg-horn
leg-i-ble
leg-i-bil-i-ty
leg-i-bly
le-gion
le-gion-ary
le-gion-ar-ies
le-gion-naire
leg-is-late
leg-is-lat-ed
leg-is-la-tive
leg-is-la-tor
leg-is-la-tion
leg-is-la-ture
le-git
le-git-i-mate
le-git-i-mat-ed
le-git-i-mat-ing
le-git-i-ma-cy
le-git-i-mate-ly
le-git-i-mist
le-git-i-mize
le-git-i-mized
le-git-i-miz-ing

le-gume
le-gu-mi-nous
lei
leis
lei-sure
lei-sure-ly
lei-sure-li-ness
leit-mo-tif
lem-ming
lem-on
lem-on-ade
le-mur
lend
lent
lend-ing
lend-er
length
length-en
length-wise
lengthy
length-i-er
length-i-est
length-i-ly
length-i-ness
le-nient
le-ni-ence
le-ni-en-cy
le-ni-ent-ly
len-i-tive
len-i-ty
lens
len-til
len-to
le-o-nine
leop-ard
leop-ard-ess
le-o-tard
lep-er
lep-i-dop-ter-ous
lep-re-chaun
lep-ro-sy
lep-rous
les-bi-an
les-bi-an-ism
le-sion
les-see
less-en
les-sor

least
let-down
le-thal
  le-thal-ly
leth-ar-gy
  leth-ar-gies
  le-thar-gic
  le-thar-gi-cal
let-ter
  let-ter-ed
let-ter-head
let-ter-ing
let-ter--per-fect
let-ter-press
let-tuce
let-up
leu-ke-mia
leu-ko-cyte
lev-ee
lev-el
  lev-eled
  lev-el-ing
  lev-el-er
  lev-el-ly
  lev-el-ness
lev-el-head-ed
  lev-el-head-ed-ness
lev-er
lev-er-age
le-vi-a-than
lev-i-tate
  lev-i-tat-ed
  lev-i-tat-ing
  lev-i-ta-tion
lev-i-ty
levy
  lev-ies
  lev-ied
  lev-y-ing
lewd
  lewd-ly
  lewd-ness
lex-i-cog-ra-phy
  lex-i-cog-ra-pher
  lex-i-co-graph-ic
  lex-i-co-graph-i-cal
lex-i-con
li-a-bil-i-ty

li-a-bil-i-ties
li-a-ble
li-ai-son
li-ar
li-ba-tion
li-bel
  li-beled
  li-bel-ing
  li-bel-er
li-bel-ous
  li-bel-ous-ly
lib-er-al
  lib-er-al-ly
  lib-er-al-ness
lib-er-al-ism
lib-er-al-i-ty
  lib-er-al-i-ties
lib-er-al-ize
  lib-er-al-ized
  lib-er-al-iz-ing
  lib-er-al-i-za-tion
lib-er-ate
  lib-er-at-ed
  lib-er-at-ing
  lib-er-a-tion
  lib-er-a-tor
lib-er-tar-i-an
lib-er-tine
  lib-er-tin-ism
lib-er-ty
  lib-er-ties
li-bid-i-nous
  li-bid-i-nous-ly
  li-bid-i-nous-ness
li-bi-do
  li-bid-in-al
li-brar-i-an
li-brary
  li-brar-ies
li-bret-to
  li-bret-tos
  li-bret-ist
li-cense
  li-censed
  li-cens-ing
  li-cens-see
  li-cens-er
li-cen-ti-ate

li-cen-tious
  li-cen-tious-ly
  li-cen-tious-ness
li-chee
li-chen
lic-it
lick-e-ty--split
lick-spit-tle
lic-o-rice
lid-ded
lief
liege
lien
lieu
lieu-ten-an-cy
lieu-ten-ant
life-blood
life-boat
life-guard
life-less
  life-less-ly
  life-less-ness
life-like
life-line
lif-er
life-sav-er
life--size
life--style
life-time
life-work
lift-off
lig-a-ment
lig-a-ture
  lig-tured
  lig-a-tur-ing
light-en
light-er
light-fin-gered
light-foot-ed
  light-foot-ed-ly
light-head-ed
  light-head-ed-ly
  light-head-ed-ness
light-heart-ed
  light-heart-ed-ly
  light-heart-ed-ness
light-house
light-ing

light-ly
light--mind-ed
  light--mind-ed-ly
  light--mind-ed-ness
light-ning
light-weight
light--year
lig-nite
like
  liked
  lik-ing
  lik-a-ble
  lik-a-ble-ness
  lik-a-ble-ness
like-li-hood
like-ly
  like-li-er
  like-li-est
like--mind-ed
lik-en
like-ness
like-wise
lik-ing
li-lac
lilt-ing
lily
  lil-lies
lil-y--liv-ered
li-ma
limb
limb-er
  lim-ber-ness
lim-bo
lime
  limed
  lim-ing
  limy
  lim-i-er
  lim-i-est
  lime-like
lime-light
  lime-light-cr
lim-er-ick
lime-stone
lim-it
lim-it-a-ble
lim-i-ta-tive
lim-i-ter

lim-it-less
lim-i-ta-tion
lim-it-ed
  lim-it-ed-ly
  lim-it-ed-ness
lim-ou-sine
limp
  limp-er
  limp-ing-ly
  limp-ly
  limp-ness
lim-pet
lim-pid
  lim-pid-i-ty
  lim-pid-ly
  lim-pid-ness
lin-age
lin-den
line
  lined
  lin-ing
lin-e-age
lin-eal
lin-ea-ment
lin-ear
  lin-ear-ly
line-back-er
  line-back-ing
line-man
  line-men
lin-en
lin-er
line-up
lin-ger
  lin-ger-er
  lin-ger-ing-ly
lin-ge-rie
lin-go
  lin-goes
lin-gua fran-ca
lin-qual
  lin-qual-ly
lin-quist
lin-quis-tic
  lin-quis-tics
  lin-quis-ti-cal
  lin-quis-ti-cal-ly
lin-i-ment

lin-ing
link
  linked
  link-er
link-age
lin-net
li-no-leum
lin-seed
lint
  linty
  lint-i-er
  lint-i-est
lin-tel
li-on
  li-on-ess
  li-on-like
li-on-heart-ed
li-on-ize
  li-on-ized
  li-on-iz-ing
  li-on-i-za-tion
  li-on-iz-er
lip-py
  lip-pi-er
  lip-pi-est
lip-stick
liq-ue-fy
  liq-ue-fied
  liq-ue-fy-ing
  liq-ue-fac-tion
  liq-ue-fi-able
  liq-ue-fi-er
li-queur
liq-uid
  li-quid-i-ty
  li-quid-ness
  li-quid-ly
liq-ui-date
  liq-ui-dat-ed
  liq-ui-dat-ing
  liq-ui-da-tion
  liq-ui-da-tor
liq-uor
lisle
lisp
  lisp-ing-ly
lis-some
  lis-some-ly

lis-some-ness
list
  list-ed
  list-er
  list-ing
lis-ten
  lis-ten-er
list-less
  list-less-ly
  list-less-ness
lit-a-ny
  lit-a-nies
li-tchi
  li-tchis
li-ter
lit-er-a-cy
lit-er-al
  lit-er-al-i-ty
  lit-er-al-ness
  lit-er-al-ly
lit-er-ary
  lit-er-ar-i-ly
  lit-er-ar-i-ness
lit-er-ate
  lit-er-ate-ly
lit-e-ra-ti
lit-er-a-ture
lithe
  lithe-some
  lithe-ly
  lithe-ness
lith-i-um
lith-o-graph
  lith-o-gra-pher
  lith-o-graph-ic
  lith-o-graph-i-cal-ly
li-thog-ra-phy
lit-i-gate
  lit-i-gat-ed
  lit-i-gat-ing
  lit-i-ga-tion
  lit-i-ga-tor
lit-ter
lit-ter-bug
lit-tle
  lit-tler
  lit-tlest
lit-to-ral

lit-ur-gy
  lit-ur-gies
  lit-ur-gist
  lit-ur-gic
  li-tur-gi-cal
liv-able
  live-able
  liv-able-ness
  live-able-ness
live-li-hood
live-long
live-ly
  live-li-er
  live-li-est
  live-li-ness
liv-en
  liv-en-er
liv-er
liv-er-wurst
liv-ery
  liv-er-ies
  liv-er-ied
  liv-er-y-man
  liv-er-y-men
live-stock
liv-id
  li-vid-i-ty
  liv-id-ness
  liv-id-ly
liv-ing
  liv-ing-ly
  liv-ing-ness
liz-ard
lla-ma
lla-no
  lla-mos
load
  load-ed
  load-er
loaf
  loaves
  loaf-er
loamy
loath
  loath-ness
loathe
  loathed
  loath-ing

loath-ing-ly
loath-some
  loath-some-ly
  loath-some-ness
lob
  lobbed
  lob-bing
lob-by
  lob-bies
  lob-by-ist
lobe
  lo-bar
  lo-bate
  lobed
lob-ster
lo-cal
  lo-cal-ly
lo-cale
lo-cal-i-ty
  lo-cal-i-ties
lo-cal-i-ties
lo-cal-ize
  lo-cal-ized
  lo-cal-iz-ing
  lo-cal-i-za-tion
lo-cate
  lo-cat-ed
  lo-cat-ing
  lo-ca-tor
lo-ca-tion
loch
lock-able
lock-er
lock-et
lock-jaw
lock-out
lock-smith
lock-up
lo-co
lo-co-mo-tion
lo-co-mo-tive
lo-co-weed
lo-cus
  lo-ci
lo-cust
lo-cu-tion
lode-stone
lodge

lodged
lodg-ing
lodg-er
lofty
loft-i-er
loft-i-est
loft-i-ly
lo-gan-ber-ry
lo-gan-ber-ries
log-a-rithm
log-a-rith-mic
log-a-rith-mi-cal
log-a-rith-mi-cal-ly
log-book
loge
log-ger
log-ger-hed
log-ic
lo-gi-cian
log-i-cal
log-i-cal-i-ty
log-i-cal-ly
lo-gis-tic
lo-gis-tics
lo-gis-ti-cal
log-jam
lo-gy
lo-gi-er
lo-gi-est
loin-cloth
loi-ter
loi-ter-er
lol-li-pop
lone-ly
lone-li-er
lone-li-est
lone-li-ly
lon-er
lone-some
lone-some-ly
lone-some-ness
lon-gev-i-ty
long-ing
long-ing-ly
lon-gi-tude
lon-gi-tu-di-nal
lon-gi-tu-di-nal-ly
long-lived

long--play-ing
long-shore-man
long-shore-men
long--suf-fer-ing
long--term
long--wind-ed
long--wind-ed-ly
long-wise
look-out
loony
loon-i-er
loon-i-est
loon-ies
loose
loos-er
loos-est
loosed
loos-ing
loose-ly
loose-ness
loos-en
loot-er
lop
looped
lop-ping
lope
loped
lop-ing
lop-er
lop-sid-ed
lo-qua-cious
lo-qua-cious-ly
lo-quac-i-ty
lo-quac-i-ties
lord-ly
lord-li-er
lord-li-est
lord-ship
lor-gnette
lor-ry
lor-ries
lose
lost
los-ing
los-a-ble
los-er
lot
lo-tion

lot-tery
lot-ter-ies
lot-to
lo-tus
lo-tus-es
loud
loud-ly
loud-ness
loud-mouthed
loud-speak-er
lounge
lounged
loung-ing
loung-er
louse
lice
lousy
lous-i-er
lous-i-est
lous-i-ly
lou-ver
lou-vered
love
loved
lov-ing
lov-able
love-lorn
love-ly
love-li-er
love-li-est
lov-er
lov-ing
loving-ly
low-er
low-er-case
low-er-ing
low-er-ing-ly
low-ery
low--key
low--keyed
low-land
low-land-er
low-ly
low-li-er
low-li-est
loy-al
loy-al-ist
loy-al-ly

loy-al-ties
loz-enge
lu-au
lub-ber
lub-ber-li-ness
lub-ber-ly
lu-beak
lu-bri-cate
lu-bri-cat-ed
lu-bri-cat-ing
lu-bri-ca-tion
lu-cid
lu-cid-i-ty
lu-cid-ness
lu-cid-ly
luck
luck-i-er
luck-i-est
lu-cra-tive
lu-cra-tive-ly
lu-cra-tive-ness
lu-cre
lu-cu-brate
lu-cu-brat-ed
lu-cu-brat-ing
lu-cu-bra-tion
lu-cu-bra-tor
lu-di-crous
lu-di-crous-ly
lu-di-crous-ness
lug
lugged
lug-ging
lug-gage
lug-ger
lug-sail
lu-gu-bri-ous
lu-gu-bri-ous-ly
luke-warm
luke-warm-ly
lull-a-by
lull-a-bies
lum-ba-go
lum-bar
lum-ber
lum-ber-ing-ly
lum-ber-er
lum-ber-ing

lum-ber-jack
lum-ber-man
lum-ber-men
lu-men
lu-mi-nary
lu-mi-nar-ies
lu-mi-nes-cence
lu-mi-nes-cent
lu-mi-nous
lu-mi-nos-i-ty
lu-mi-nous-ly
lum-mox
lumpy
lu-na-cy
lu-na-cies
lu-nar
lu-nate
lu-na-tic
lunch
lunch-er
lun-cheon
lunge
lunged
lung-ing
lu-pine
lurch
lure
lured
lur-ing
lu-rid
lu-rid-ly
lu-rid-ness
lurk
lurk-er
lurk-ing-ly
lus-cious
lus-cious-ly
lush
lush-ly
lust
lust-ful
lust-ful-ly
lust-er
lus-ter-less
lus-ter-ware
lust-i-hood
lus-tral
lus-trate

lus-tring
lus-trous
lus-trous-ly
lus-trous-ness
lus-trum
lusty
lu-sus na-tu-rae
lute
lut-ed
lut-ing
lu-tein
lu-tein-ize
lu-te-nist
lu-teo-tro-phic
lu-te-ous
lute-string
lu-te-tium
lut-ist
lux
lux-ate
luxe
lux-u-ri-ant
lux-u-ri-ance
lux-u-ri-an-cy
lux-u-ri-ant-ly
lux-u-ri-ate
lux-u-ri-at-ed
lux-u-ri-at-ing
lux-u-ri-a-tion
lux-u-ri-ous
lux-u-ri-ous-ly
lux-u-ry
lux-u-ries
ly-am--hound
ly-art
ly-ast
ly-can-thrope
ly-cee
ly-ce-um
ly-ing
ly-ing--in
lymph
lym-phoid
lym-phat-ic
lynch
lynch-er
lynch-in
lvre

ma-ca-bre
  ma-ca-bre-ly
mac-ad-am
mac-ad-am-ize
  mac-ad-am ised
  mac-ad-am-iz-ing
  mac-ad-am-i-za-tion
ma-caque
mac-a-ro-ni
mac-a-roon
ma-caw
mace
  maced
  mac-ing
ma-ce-doine
ma-ce-do-nian
mac-er-ate
  mac-er-at-ed
  mac-er-at-ing
  mac-er-a-tion
  mac-er-a-tor
ma-chete
ma-chic-o-late
ma-chic-o-la-tion
mach-i-nate
mach-i-na-tion
ma-chine
  ma-chin-able
  ma-chin-abil-i-ty
  ma-chined
  ma-chin-ing
machine gun
machine language
ma-chine-like
machine--readable
ma-chin-ery
machine shop
machine tool
ma-chis-mo
ma-chin-ery
  ma-chin-er-ies
ma-chin-ist
mack-er-el
mackerel shark
mackerel sky
mack-i-naw
mack-in-tosh
  mac-in-tosh

mack-le
mac-le
mac-ra-me
macrame knot
mac-ro-ag-gre-gate
mac-ro-bi-ot-ic
mac-ro-cosm
  mac-ro-cos-mic
  mac-ro-cos-mi-cal-ly
mac-ro-cyte
mac-ro-cy-to-sis
mac-ro-eco-nom-ics
mac-ro-evo-lu-tion
mac-ro-fos-sil
mac-ro-ga-mete
mac-ro-glob-u-lin
mac-ro-in-struc-tion
mac-ro-lep-i-dop-tera
mac-ro-mere
mac-ro-mol-e-cule
ma-cron
mac-ro-nu-cle-us
mac-ro-nu-tri-ent
mac-ro-phage
mac-ro-phyte
mac-ro-scop-ic
mac-ro-struc-ture
mac-u-la
macula lu-tea
mac-u-la-tion
mac-ule
mad
  mad-der
  mad-ly
  mad-ness
mad-am
  mes-dames
mad-brained
mad-cap
mad-den
  mad-den-ing
  mad-den-ing-ly
mad-e-moi-selle
  mes-de-moi-selles
made-up
mad-house
mad-man
  mad-men

ma-dras
mad-re-pore
mad-re-por-ite
mad-ri-gal
  mad-ri-gal-ist
ma-dri-lene
ma-dro-na
ma-du-ro
mad-wom-an
mad-wort
mael-strom
mae-stro-so
maf-fick
maf-ic
ma-fi-o-so
mag
mag-a-zine
mag-a-zin-ist
mag-da-len
ma-gen-ta
mag-got
  mag-goty
mag-ic
  mag-i-cal
  mag-i-cal-ly
ma-gi-cian
magic lantern
magic realism
mag-is-te-ri-al
  mag-is-te-ri-al-ly
  mag-is-te-ri-al-ness
mag-is-tra-cy
  mag-is-tra-cies
ma-gis-tral
mag-is-trate
magistrate's court
mag-is-tra-ture
mag-ma
  mag-mas
  mag-ma-ta
  mag-mat-ic
mag-na cum laude
mag-na-nim-i-ty
mag-nan-i-mous
  mag-nan-i-mous-ly
  mag-na-nim-i-ty
  mag-na-nim-i-ties
mag-nate

mag-ne-sia
mag-ne-sian
mag-ne-site
mag-ne-sium
magnesium carbonate
magnesium chloride
magnesium hydroxide
magnesium oxide
magnesium sulfate
mag-net
mag-net-ic
mag-net-i-cal-ly
magnetic core
magnetice equator
magnetic field
magnetic flux
magnetic head
magnetic moment
magnetic needle
magnetic north
magnetic pole
magnetic recording
magnetic resonance
magnetic storm
magnetic tape
magnetic wire
mag-net-ism
mag-net-ize
mag-net-ized
mag-net-iz-ing
mag-net-iz-a-ble
mag-net-i-za-tion
mag-net-iz-er
mag-ne-to
mag-ne-tos
mag-ne-to-elec-tric
mag-ne-tom-e-ter
mag-ne-to-met-ric
mag-ne-tom-e-try
mag-ne-ton
mag-ne-to--op-tic
mag-ne-to-pause
mag-ne-to-sphere
mag-ne-to-stat-ic
mag-ne-to-stric-tion
mag-ne-tron
mag-nif-ic
mag-nif-i-cent

mag-nif-i-cence
mag-nif-i-cent-ly
mag-ni-fy
mag-ni-fied
mag-ni-fy-ing
maf-ni-fi-a-ble
mag-ni-fi-ca-tion
mag-ni-fi-er
mag-nil-o-quent
mag-ni-tude
mag-no-lia
mag-num
mag-num opus
mag-pie
mag-uey
ma-ha-ra-jah
ma-ha-ra-ni
ma-hat-ma
ma-hat-ma-ism
ma-hoe
ma-hog-a-ny
ma-hog-a-nies
ma-hout
maid-en
mail-a-ble
mail-box
mail-man
mail-men
maim
maim-er
main-land
main-land-er
main-ly
main-mast
main-sail
main-tain
main-tain-a-ble
main-te-nance
maize
maj-es-ty
maj-es-ties
ma-jes-tic
ma-jes-ti-cal
ma-jol-i-ca
ma-jor
ma-jor-do-mo
ma-jor-do-mos
ma-jor-i-ty

ma-jor-i-ties
make
mak-a-ble
mak-er
mak-ing
make-shift
make-up
mal-a-dapt-ed
mal-ad-just-ment
mal-ad-just-ed
mal-ad-min-is-ter
mal-adroit
mal-adroit-ly
mal-adroit-ness
mal-a-dy
mal-a-dies
mal-aise
mal-a-prop
mal-a-prop-ism
ma-lar-ia
ma-lar-i-al
ma-lar-i-an
ma-lar-i-ous
ma-lar-key
mal-con-tent
male-dict
male-dic-tion
male-dic-to-ry
male-frac-tion
male-frac-tor
ma-lev-o-lent
ma-lev-o-lence
ma-lev-o-lent-ly
mal-fea-sance
mal-fea-sant
mal-for-ma-tion
mal-formed
mal-func-tion
mal-ice
ma-li-cious
ma-li-cious-ly
ma-lign
ma-lign-er
ma-lign-ly
ma-lig-nant
ma-lig-nan-cy
ma-lig-nan-cies
ma-lig-nant-ly

ma-lin-ger
  ma-lin-ger-er
mal-lard
mal-lea-ble
  mal-lea-bil-i-ty
mal-let
ma-low
mal-nour-ished
mal-nu-tri-tion
mal-oc-clu-sion
mal-odor
  mal-odor-ous
  mal-odor-ous-ly
mal-prac-tice
  mal-prac-ti-tion-er
malt
  malty
  malt-i-er
mal-treat
  mal-treat-ment
mam-ma
  ma-ma
mam-mal
  mam-ma-li-an
mam-mam-ries
mam-mon
mam-moth
mam-my
  mam-mies
man
  manned
  man-ning
man-a-cle
  man-a-cled
  man-a-cling
man-age
  man-aged
  man-a-ging
  man-age-a-ble
  man-age-a-bil-i-ty
  man-age-a-bly
man-age-ment
man-ag-er
  man-ag-er-ship
man-a-ge-ri-al
  man-a-ge-ri-al-ly
man-a-tee
man-da-la

man-da-rin
man-date
  man-dat-ed
  man-dat-ing
man-da-to-ry
  man-da-to-ries
  man-da-to-ri-ty
man-di-ble
  man-dib-u-lar
  man-dib-u-lary
  man-dib-u-late
man-do-lin
  man-do-lin-ist
man-drakes
man-drill
man-eat-er
  man-eat-ing
ma-neu-ver
  ma-neu-ver-a-nil-i-ty
  ma-neu-ver-a-ble
  ma-neu-ver-er
man-ga-nese
mange
man-ger
man-gle
  man-gled
  man-gling
man-go
  man-goes
  man-gos
man-grove
man-gy
  man-gi-er
  man-gi-est
  man-gi-ly
man-han-dle
  man-han-dled
  man-han-dling
man-hole
man-hood
man--hour
man-hunt
  man-hunt-er
ma-nia
  man-ic
ma-ni-ac
  ma-ni-a-cal
  ma-ni-a-cal-ly

man-ic-de-pres-sive
man-i-cure
  man-i-cur-eed
  man-i-cur-ing
  man-i-cur-ist
man-i-fest
  man-i-fest-er
  man-i-fest-ly
man-i-fes-ta-tion
man-i-fes-to
  man-i-fes-tos
  man-i-fes-toes
man-i-fold
man-i-kin
  man-a-kin
  man-ni-kin
ma-nila
  ma-nil-la
ma-nip-u-late
man-kind
man-ly
  man-li-er
  man-li-est
man--made
man-na
man-ne-quin
man-ner
man-nered
man-ner-ism
man-ner-ly
  man-ner-li-ness
man-nish
man--of--war
  men--of--war
ma-nom-e-ter
man-or
  ma-no-ri-al
man pow-er
man-sard
man-ser-vant
man-sion
man-sized
man-slaugh-ter
man-slay-er
man-til-la
man-tle
  man-tled
  man-tling

man-trap
man-u-al
  man-u-al-ly
man-u-fac-ture
  man-u-fac-tured
  man-u-fac-tur-ing
  man-u-fac-tur-a-ble
  man-u-fac-tur-al
  man-u-fac-tur-er
ma-nure
manu-script
many
man-y-sid-ed
map
mapped
  map-ping
  map-per
ma-ple
mar
  marred
  mar-ring
ma-ra-ca
mar-a-schi-no
mar-a-thon
ma-raud
  ma-raud-er
mar-ble
  mar-bled
  mar-bling
  mar-ble-ize
  mar-ble-ized
  mar-ble-iz-ing
  mar-bly
mar-cel
  mar-celled
  mar-cel-ling
march-er
mar-chio-ness
mare's tail
mar-ga-rine
mar-gin
mar-gi-nal
  mar-gi-na-lia
  mar-gin-al-i-ty
  mar-gin-al-ly
mar-gin-ate
  mar-gin-ated
  mar-gin-at-ing

mar-gin-a-tion
mar-gue-rite
mar-i-cul-ture
mari-gold
mar-i-jua-na
ma-rim-ba
ma-ri-na
mar-i-nade
  mar-i-nad-ed
  mar-i-nad-ing
  mar-i-na-tion
mar-i-nate
  mar-i-nat-ed
  mar-i-nat-ing
  mar-i-na-tion
ma-rine
mar-i-ner
mar-i-o-nette
mar-i-tal
mar-i-time
mar-jo-ram
marked
  mark-ed-ly
mark-er
mar-ket
  mar-ket-er
mar-ket-able
  mar-ket-abil-i-ty
mar-ket-ing
mar-ket-place
mark-ing
marks-man
  marks-men
  marks-man-ship
mar-lin
mar-ma-lade
mar-mo-set
mar-mot
ma-roon
mar-quee
mar-quis
  mar-quis-es
  mar-quess
mar-quise
  mar-quis-es
mar-riage
  mar-riage-able
  mar-riage-abil-i-ty

mar-ried
mar-row
  mar-rowy
mar-row-bone
mar-ry
  mar-ried
  mar-ry-ing
mar-shall
  mar-shaled
  mar-shal-ing
marsh-mal-low
marshy
  marsh-i-er
  marsh-i-est
  marsh-i-ness
mar-su-pi-al
mar-tial
mar-tin
mar-ti-ni
  mar-ti-nis
mar-tyr
  mar-tyr-ize
  mar-tyr-ized
  mar-tyr-iz-ing
  mar-tyr-dom
mar-vel
  mar-veled
  mar-vel-ing
mar-vel-ous
  mar-vel-ous-ly
mar-zi-pan
mas-cara
mas-cu-line
  mas-cu-line-ness
  mas-cu-lin-i-ty
mas-cu-lin-ize
  mas-cu-lin-ized
  mas-cu-lin-iz-ing
mash-er
mask
  mask-like
masked
mas-och-ism
  mas-och-ist
  mas-och-is-tic
ma-son
  ma-son-ic
ma-son-ary

ma-son-ries
masque
mas-quer-ade
  mas-quer-ad-ed
  mas-quer-ad-ing
  mas-quer-ad-er
mas-sa-cre
  mas-sa-cred
  mas-sa-cring
  mas-sa-cre
mas-sage
  mas-saged
  mas-sag-ing
  mas-sag-er
  mas-sag-ist
mas-seur
mas-sause
  mas-seus-es
mas-sive
mass-pro-duce
  mass-pro-duced
  mass-pro-duc-ing
  mass-pro-duc-er
  mass-pro-duc-tion
massy
  masss-i-er
  mass-i-est
  mass-i-ness
mas-tec-to-my
  mas-tec-to-mies
mas-ter
mas-ter-ful
mas-ter-mind
mas-ter-piece
mas-tery
  mas-ter-ics
mast-head
mas-tic
mas-ti-cate
  mas-ti-ca-ted
  mas-ti-ca-ting
  mas-ti-ca-ble
  mas-ti-ca-tion
  mas-ti-ca-tor
mas-tiff
mast-odon
mas-toid
mas-tur-bate

mas-tur-bat-ed
mas-tur-bat-ing
mas-tur-ba-tion
mat
  mat-ted
  mat-ting
mat-a-dor
match-book
match-mak-er
  match-mak-ing
mate
  mat-ed
  mat-ing
  mate-less
ma-te-ri-al
  ma-te-ri-al-ly
ma-te-ri-al-ism
  ma-te-ri-al-ist
  ma-te-ri-al-is-tic
  ma-te-ri-al-is-ti-cal-ly
ma-te-ri-al-ize
  ma-te-ri-al-ized
  ma-te-ri-al-iz-ing
ma-te-ri-el
ma-ter-nal
  ma-ter-nal-ism
  ma-ter-nal-is-tic
  ma-ter-nal-ly
ma-ter-ni-ty
  ma-ter-ni-ties
math-e-mat-i-cal
  math-e-mat-ic
  math-e-mat-i-cal-ly
math-e-ma-ti-cian
math-e-mat-ics
ma-tin
  mat-in-al
mat-i-nee
ma-tri-arch
  ma-tri-ar-chal-ism
  ma-tri-ar-chy
  ma-tri-ar-chies
ma-tri-cide
ma-tric-u-lant
ma-tric-u-late
  ma-tric-u-lat-ed
  ma-tric-u-lat-ing
  ma-tric-u-la-tion

ma-tri-lin-eal
mat-ri-mo-ny
  mat-ri-mo-nies
  mat-ri-mo-ni-al
ma-trix
  ma-tri-ces
  ma-trix-es
ma-tron
  ma-tron-ly
mat-ter
mat-ter-of-course
mat-ter--of--fact
  mat-ter--of--fact-ly
  mat-ter--of--fact-ness
mat-ting
mat-tress
mat-u-rate
  mat-u-rat-ed
  mat-u-rat-ing
  mat-u-ra-tion
ma-ture
ma-tur-i-ty
mat-zo
  mat-zoth
  mat-zos
maud-lin
mau-so-le-um
  mau-so-le-ums
  mau-so-lea
mauve
mav-er-ick
mawk-ish
max-im
max-i-mal
  max-i-mal-ly
max-i-mize
  max-i-mized
  max-i-miz-ing
max-i-mum
  max-i-mums
  max-i-ma
may-be
may-flow-er
may-fly
  may-flies
may-hem
may-on-naise
may-or

may-or-al
may-or-al-ty
may-or-al-ties
maze
  mazed
  maz-ing
ma-zy
  ma-zi-er
  ma-zi-est
  ma-zi-ly
  ma-zi-ness
mead-ow
mead-ow-lark
mea-ger
  mea-ger-ly
  mea-ger-ness
meal-time
meal-worm
mealy
  meal-i-er
  meal-i-est
  meal-i-ness
meal-y-mouthed
mean
  mean-ing
  mean-ly
  mean-ness
me-an-der
mean-ing-ful
  mean-ing-ful-ly
mean-ing-less
  mean-ing-less-ly
  mean-ing-less-ness
meant
mean-time
mean-while
mea-sles
mea-sly
  mea-sli-er
  mea-sli-est
meas-ur-a-ble
  meas-ur-a-bil-i-ty
  meas-ur-a-bly
meas-ure
  meas-ur-er
mea-sured
mea-sure-ment
meaty

meat-i-er
meat-i-est
meat-i-ness
mec-ca
me-chan-ic
mech-a-nism
mech-a-nis-tic
  mech-a-nis-ti-cal-ly
mech-a-nize
  mech-a-nized
  mech-a-niz-ing
  mech-a-ni-za-tion
  mech-a-niz-er
med-al
  med-aled
  med-al-ing
  me-dal-ic
me-dal-lion
med-dle
  med-dled
  med-dling
  med-dler
med-dle-some
me-dia
me-di-al
me-di-an
  me-di-an-ly
me-di-ate
  me-di-at-ed
  me-di-at-ing
me-di-a-tion
  me-di-a-tive
  me-di-a-to-ry
me-di-a-tor
med-ic
med-i-ca-ble
  med-i-ca-bly
med-i-cal
  med-i-cal-ly
me-di-ca-ment
med-i-cate
  med-i-cat-ed
  med-i-cat-ing
med-i-ca-tion
me-dic-i-nal
  me-dic-i-nal-ly
med-i-cine
  med-i-cined

med-i-cin-ing
med-i-co
me-di-e-val
  me-di-e-val-ism
me-di-o-cre
me-di-oc-ri-ty
  me-di-oc-ri-ties
med-i-tate
  med-i-tat-ed
  med-i-tat-ing
  med-i-tat-ing-ly
  med-i-ta-tor
med-i-ta-tion
  med-i-ta-tive
Med-i-ter-ra-ne-an
me-di-um
  me-dia
  me-di-ums
med-ley
  med-leys
meet-ing
meet-ing-house
meg-a-city
  meg-a-cit-ies
mega-cy-cle
meg-a-lo-ma-nia
  meg-a-lo-ma-ni-ac
  meg-a-lo-ma-ni-a-cal
meg-a-lop-o-lis
  meg-a-lo-pol-i-tan
mega-phone
  mega-phoned
  mega-phon-ing
mega-ton
mega-watt
mei-o-sis
  mei-ot-ic
mel-a-mine
mel-an-cho-lia
  mel-an-cho-li-ac
mel-an-choly
  mel-an-chol-ies
  mel-an-chol-ic
  mel-an-chol-i-cal-ly
  mel-an-chol-i-ty
  mel-an-chol-i-ness
mel-a-nin
mel-a-no-ma

mel-a-no-mas
mel-a-no-ma-ta
me-lee
me-lio-rate
me-lio-rat-ed
me-lio-rat-ing
me-lio-ra-ble
me-lio-ra-tion
me-lio-ra-tor
mel-lif-lu-ous
mel-lif-lu-nt
mel-lif-lu-ous-ly
mel-low
me-lo-de-on
melo-dra-ma
melo-dra-mat-ic
melo-dra-mat-i-cal-ly
melo-dra-mat-ics
mel-o-dy
mel-o-dies
me-lod-ic
me-lod-i-cal-ly
me-lo-di-ous
me-lo-di-ous-ness
mel-on
melt
melt-ed
melt-ing
melt-a-bil-i-ty
melt-a-ble
melt-er
mem-ber
mem-bered
mem-ber-less
mem-ber-ship
mem-brane
mem-bra-nous
me-men-to
me-men-tos
me-men-toes
memo
mem-oir
mem-o-ra-bil-ia
mem-o-ra-ble
mem-o-ra-bly
mem-o-ran-dum
mem-o-ran-dums
mem-o-ran-da

me-mo-ri-al
me-mo-ri-al-ly
me-mo-ri-al-ize
me-mo-ri-al-ized
me-mo-ri-al-iz-ing
me-mo-ri-al-i-za-tion
me-mo-ri-al-iz-er
me-mo-ri-al-ly
mem-o-rize
mem-o-rized
mem-o-riz-ing
mem-o-riz-a-ble
mem-o-ri-za-tion
mem-o-ry
mem-o-ries
men-ace
men-aced
men-ac-ing
me-nag-er-ie
mend
mend-able
men-da-cious
men-da-cious-ly
men-da-cious-ness
men-dac-i-ty
men-de-le-vi-um
men-di-cant
me-ni-al
me-ni-al-ly
me-nin-ges
men-in-gi-tis
me-nis-cus
me-nis-cus-es
me-nis-ci
men-o-pause
men-o-pau-sal
me-nor-ah
men-sal
men-ses
men-stru-al
men-stru-a-tion
men-stru-ate
men-stru-at-ed
men-stru-at-ing
men-sur-a-ble
men-tal
men-tal-ly
men-tal-i-ty

men-tal-i-ties
men-thol
men-tho-lat-ed
men-tion
men-tion-a-ble
men-tion-er
men-tor
menu
me-ow
mep-ro-bam-ate
mer-can-tile
mer-can-til-ism
mer-can-til-ist
mer-ce-nary
mer-ce-nar-ies
mer-ce-nar-ily
mer-cer-ize
mer-cer-ized
mer-cer-iz-ing
mer-chan-dise
mer-chan-dised
mer-chan-dis-ing
mer-chan-dis-er
mer-chant
mer-chant-man
mer-chant-men
mer-cu-ri-al
mer-cu-ry
mer-cu-ries
mer-cy
mer-cies
mer-ci-ful
mer-ci-ful-ly
mer-ci-less
mere-ly
mer-e-tri-cious
mer-e-tri-cious-ly
mer-e-tri-cious-ness
merge
merged
merg-ing
mer-gence
merg-er
me-rid-i-an
me-rid-i-o-nal
me-ringue
mer-it
mer-i-ted

mer-it-ed-ly
mer-it-less
mer-i-to-ri-ous
mer-maid
mer-man
mer-men
mer-ri-ment
mer-ry
mer-ri-er
mer-ri-est
mer-ri-ness
mer-ry--go--round
mer-ry-mak-er
mer-ry-mak-ing
me-sa
mes-cal
mes-dames
mes-de-moi-selles
mesh-work
me-si-al
mes-mer-ism
mes-mer-ic
mes-mer-i-cal-ly
mes-mer-ist
mes-mer-ize
mes-mer-ized
mes-mer-iz-ing
mes-mer-i-za-tion
mes-mer-iz-er
mes-o-morph
mes-o-mor-phic
mes-o-mor-phism
mes-o-mor-phy
me-son
mes-o-sphere
mes-quite
mess
mess-i-ly
mess-i-ness
messy
mess-i-er
mess-i-est
mes-sage
mes-sen-ger
mes-ti-zo
me-tab-o-lism
met-a-bol-ic
met-a-bol-i-cal

me-tab-o-lize
me-tab-o-lized
me-tab-o-liz-ing
met-al
met-aled
met-al-ing
met-al-ize
met-al-ized
met-al-iz-ing
me-tal-lic
me-tal-li-cal-ly
met-al-loid
met-al-lur-gy
met-al-lur-gic
met-al-lur-gi-cal
met-al-lur-gi-cal-ly
met-al-lur-gist
met-al-work
met-al-work-er
met-al-work-ing
meta-mor-phism
meta-mor-phic
meta-mor-phose
meta-mor-phosed
meta-mor-phos-ing
meta-mor-pho-sis
meta-mor-pho-ses
met-a-phor
met-a-phor-ic
met-a-phor-i-cal
meta-phys-ic
meta-phys-ics
meta-phys-i-cal
meta-tar-sus
meta-tar-si
meta-tar-sal
meta-zo-an
meta-zo-al
meta-zo-ic
mete
met-ed
met-ing
me-te-or
me-te-or-ic
me-te-or-ite
me-te-or-it-ic
me-te-or-oid
me-te-o-rol-o-gy

me-te-o-ro-log-i-cal
me-te-o-rol-o-gist
me-ter
met-es-trus
meth-a-done
meth-ane
meth-a-nol
meth-od
me-thodi-cal
me-thodi-cal-ly
meth-od-ize
meth-od-ized
meth-od-iz-ing
meth-od-iz-er
meth-od-ol-o-gy
meth-od-ol-o-gies
meth-od-o-log-i-cal
meth-od-ol-o-gist
me-tic-u-lous
me-tic-u-los-i-ty
me-tic-u-lous-ly
met-ric
met-ri-cal
met-ri-cal-ly
met-ri-fi-ca-tion
met-ro
met-ro-nome
met-ro-nom-ic
me-trop-o-lis
met-ro-pol-i-tan
met-ro-pol-i-tan-ism
met-tle
met-tle-some
mez-za-nine
mez-zo
mi-as-ma
mi-as-mas
mi-as-ma-ta
mi-as-mat-ic
mi-as-mic
mi-ca
mi-crobe
mi-cro-bi-al
mi-cro-bi-an
mi-cro-bic
mi-cro-bi-ol-o-gy
mi-cro-bi-o-log-i-cal
mi-cro-bi-ol-o-gist

mi-cro-copy
  mi-cro-cop-ies
mi-cro-cosm
  mi-cro-cos-mos
  mi-cro-cos-mic
  mi-cro-cos-mi-cal
mi-cro-film
mi-cro-gram
mi-cro-groove
mi-crom-e-ter
mi-crom-e-try
mi-cro-mi-cron
mi-cro-min-ia-ture
mi-cro-mil-li-me-ter
mi-cron
  mi-crons
  mi-cra
mi-cro-or-gan-ism
mi-cro-phone
  mi-cro-phon-ic
mi-cro-pho-to-graph
mi-cro-read-er
mi-cro-scope
  mi-cro-scop-i-cal
  mi-cro-scop-i-cal-ly
mi-cros-co-py
  mi-cros-co-pist
mi-cro-sec-ond
mi-cro-wave
mid-day
mid-dle
  mid-dles
  mid-dling
mid-dle--aged
mid-dle-man
  mid-dle-men
mid-dle-most
mid-dle-weight
mid-dy
  mid-dies
midg-et
mid-land
mid-night
mid-sec-tion
mid-ship
mid-ship-man
  mid-ship-men
midst

mid-sum-mer
mid-term
mid-way
mid-wife
  mid-wives
mid-wife-ry
mid-year
mien
mighty
  might-i-er
  might-i-est
  might-i-ly
  might-i-ness
mi-graine
mi-grant
mi-grate
  mi-grat-ed
  mi-grat-ing
  mi-gra-tion
  mi-gra-tor
  mi-gra-to-ry
mi-la-dy
  mi-la-dies
mild
  mild-ly
  mild-ness
mil-dew
  mil-dewy
mile-age
mil-er
mile-stone
mi-lieu
  mi-lieus
mil-i-tant
  mil-i-tan-cy
  mil-i-tant-ness
mil-i-ta-rism
  mil-i-ta-ris-tic
  mil-i-ta-ris-ti-cal-ly
  mil-i-ta-rize
  mil-i-ta-rized
  mil-i-ta-riz-ing
  mil-i-ta-ri-za-tion
mil-i-tary
  mil-i-tar-i-ly
mi-li-tia
milk
  milk-er

milky
milk-i-er
milk-i-est
milk-maid
milk-man
  milk-men
milk-weed
mill-board
mil-len-ni-um
  mil-len-nia
  mil-len-ni-al
mil-ler
mil-let
mil-li-am-pere
mil-li-bar
mil-li-gram
mil-li-li-ter
mil-li-me-ter
mil-li-mi-cron
mil-li-ner
  mil-li-nery
mill-ing
mil-lion
  mil-lionth
mill-lion-aire
mil-li-sec-ond
mill-pond
mill-run
mill-stone
mill-stream
mi-lord
milt
mime
  mimed
  mim-ing
  mim-er
mim-e-o-graph
mim-ic
  mim-icked
  mim-ick-ing
  mim-i-cal
  mim-i-cal
  mim-ick-r
mim-ic-ry
  mim-ic-ries
min-able
  mine-able
min-e-ret

mince
minced
minc-ing
minc-er
minc-ing-ly
mince-meat
mind-ed
mind-less
mind-less-ly
mind-less-ness
min-er
mine-field
min-er-al
min-er-al-ize
min-er-al-ized
min-er-al-iz-ing
min-er-al-i-za-tion
min-er-al-o-gy
min-er-al-og-ical
min-er-al-o-gist
min-e-stro-ne
mine-sweep-er
mine-sweep-ing
min-gle
min-gled
min-gling
min-i-a-ture
min-i-a-tur-ize
min-i-a-tur-ized
min-i-a-tur-iz-ing
min-i-a-tur-i-za-tion
min-im
min-i-mal
min-i-mal-ly
min-i-mize
min-i-mized
min-i-miz-ing
min-i-mi-za-tion
min-i-miz-er
min-i-mum
min-i-mums
min-i-ma
min-ing
min-ion
min-is-ter
min-is-te-ri-al
min-is-trant
min-is-tra-tion

min-is-tries
min-now
mi-nor
mi-nor-i-ty
mi-nor-i-ties
min-strel
mint-age
mint-er
min-u-end
mi-nus
mi-nus-cule
min-ute
min-ut-ed
min-ut-ing
mi-nut-er
mi-nut-est
min-ute-man
min-ute-men
mi-nu-tia
mi-nu-ti-ae
minx
mir-a-cle
mi-rac-u-lous
mi-rage
mire
mired
mir-ing
mir-ror
mirth
mirth-ful
mirth-ful-ly
mirth-ful-ness
mirth-less
mis-ad-ven-tage
mis-ad-vise
mis-ad-vised
mis-ad-vis-ing
mis-al-li-ance
mis-an-thrope
mis-an-tho-pist
mis-an-throp-ic
mis-an-throp-i-cal
mis-an-thro-py
mis-ap-ply
mis-ap-plied
mis-ap-ply-ing
mis-ap-pli-ca-tion
mis-ap-pre-hend

mis-ap-pre-hen-sion
mis-ap-pro-pri-ate
mis-ap-pro-pri-at-ed
mis-ap-pro-pri-at-ing
mis-ap-pro-pri-a-tion
mis-be-have
mis-be-haved
mis-be-hav-ing
mis-be-hav-er
mis-be-ha-vior
mis-cal-cu-late
mis-cal-cu-lat-ed
mis-cal-cu-lat-ing
mis-cal-cu-la-tion
mis-cal-cu-la-tor
mis-call
mis-car-riage
mis-car-ry
mis-car-ried
mis-car-ry-ing
mis-ce-ge-na-tion
mis-ce-ge-net-ic
mis-cel-la-neous
mis-cel-la-ny
mis-cel-la-nies
mis-chance
mis-chief
mis-chie-vous
mis-che-vous-ly
mis-che-vous-ness
mis-ci-ble
mis-ci-bil-i-ty
mis-con-ceive
mis-con-ceived
mis-con-ceiv-ing
mis-con-ceiv-er
mis-con-cep-tion
mis-con-duct
mis-con-strue
mis-con-strued
mis-con-stru-ing
mis-con-struc-tion
mis-count
mis-cre-ant
mis-cue
mis-cued
mis-cu-ing
mis-deal

mis-dealt
mis-deal-ing
mis-deed
mis-de-mean-or
mis-di-rect
mis-di-rec-tion
mis-do
mis-did
mis-done
mis-do-ing
mis-em-ploy
mis-em-ploy-ment
mi-ser
mi-ser-li-ness
mi-ser-ly
mis-er-a-ble
mis-er-a-ble-ness
mis-er-a-bly
mis-ery
mis-er-ies
mis-fea-sance
mis-fire
mis-fired
mis-fir-ing
mis-fit
mis-fit-ted
mis-fit-ting
mis-for-tune
mis-giv-ing
mis-gov-ern
mis-gov-ern-ment
mis-guide
mis-guid-ed
mis-guid-ing
mis-guid-ance
mis-han-dle
mis-han-dled
mis-han-dling
mis-hap
mish-mash
mis-in-form
mis-in-form-ant
mis-in-form-er
mis-in-for-ma-tion
mis-in-ter-pret
mis-in-ter-pre-ta-tion
mis-in-ter-pret-er
mis-judge

mis-judged
mis-judg-ing
mis-judg-ment
mis-lay
mis-laid
mis-lay-ing
mis-lead
mis-led
mis-lead-ing
mis-lead-er
mis-man-age
mis-man-aged
mis-man-ag-ing
mis-man-age-ment
mis-match
mis-mate
mis-mat-ed
mis-mat-ing
mis-name
mis-named
mis-nam-ing
mis-no-mer
mi-sog-a-my
mi-sog-y-ny
mi-sog-y-nist
mi-sog-y-nous
mis-place
mis-placed
mis-plac-ing
mis-place-ment
mis-play
mis-print
mis-pri-sion
mis-prize
mis-prized
mis-priz-ing
mis-pro-nounce
mis-pro-nounced
mis-pro-nouc-ing
mis-pro-nun-ci-a-tion
mis-quote
mis-quoted
mis-quot-ing
mis-quo-ta-tion
mis-read
mis-read-ing
mis-rep-re-sent
mis-rep-re-sen-ta-tion

mis-rep-re-sen-ta-tive
mis-rule
mis-ruled
mis-rul-ing
mis-sal
mis-shape
mis-shaped
mis-shap-ing
mis-shap-en
mis-sile
miss-ing
mis-sion
mis-sion-ary
mis-sion-ar-ies
mis-sive
mis-spell
mis-spelled
mis-spel-ling
mis-spend
mis-spent
mis-spend-ing
mis-state
mis-stat-ed
mis-stat-ing
mis-state-ment
mis-step
mist
mist-i-ly
mist-i-ness
mis-ta-a-ble
mis-take
mis-took
mis-tak-en
mis-tak-ing
mis-tak-en-ly
mis-tak-er
mis-tle-toe
mis-tral
mis-treat
mis-treat-ment
mis-tress
mis-tri-al
mis-trust
mis-trust-ful
mis-trust-ful-ly
mis-trust-ing-ly
misty
mist-i-er

mist-i-est
mis-un-der-stand
  mis-un-der-stood
  mis-un-der-stand-ing
mis-us-age
mis-use
  mis-used
  mis-us-ing
  mis-us-er
mis-val-ue
  mis-val-ued
  mis-val-u-ing
mi-ter
  mi-tre
mi-ti-cide
  mi-ti-cid-al
mit-i-gate
  mit-i-gat-ed
  mit-i-gat-ing
  mit-i-ga-tion
  mit-i-ga-tive
  mit-i-ga-tor
  mit-i-ga-to-ry
mi-to-sis
mi-tral
mit-ten
mix
  mixed
  mix-ing
mix-er
mix-ture
mix-up
miz-pah
miz-zen
mne-mon-ic
mne-mon-ics
moa
mob
  mobbed
  mob-bing
  mob-bish
mo-bile
  mo-bil-i-ty
mo-bi-lize
  mo-bi-lized
  mo-bi-liz-ing
  mo-bi-li-za-tion
mob-ster

moc-ca-sin
mo-cha
mock
  mock-er
  mock-ing-ly
mock-ery
  mock-er-ies
mock-ing-bird
mock-up
mod-al
  mo-dal-i-ty
  mod-al-ly
mod-el
  mod-eled
  mod-el-ing
  mod-el-er
mod-er-ate
  mod-er-at-ed
  mod-er-at-ing
  mod-er-ate-ly
  mod-er-ate-ness
mod-er-a-tion
mod-er-a-tor
  mod-er-a-tor-ship
mod-ern
mod-ern-ism
  mod-er-ist
  mod-er-ist-ic
mod-ern-ize
  mod-ern-ized
  mod-ern-iz-ing
  mod-ern-iz-er
  mod-ern-i-za-tion
mod-est
  mod-est-ly
  mod-est-ty
  mod-es-ties
mod-i-cum
mod-i-fi-ca-tion
mod-i-fy
  mod-i-fied
  mod-i-fy-ing
  mod-i-fi-a-ble
  mod-i-fi-er
mod-ish
  mod-ish-ly
  mod-ish-ness
mo-diste

mod-u-late
  mod-u-lat-ed
  mod-u-lat-ing
mod-u-la-tion
  mod-u-la-tor
  mod-u-la-to-ry
mod-ule
mod-u-lar
mo-gulmo-hair
moi-ety
  moi-eties
moil
  moil-er
  moil-ing-ly
mois-ten
  moist-en-er
mois-ture
  mois-tur-ize
  mois-tur-ized
  mois-tur-iz-ing
  mois-tur-iz-er
mo-lar
mo-las-ses
mold
  mold-able
  mold-er
mold-board
mold-ing
moldy
  mold-i-er
  mold-i-est
  mold-i-ness
mol-e-cule
mole-hill
mole-skin
mo-lest
  mo-les-ta-tion
  mo-lest-er
mol-li-fy
  mol-li-fied
  mol-li-fy-ing
  mol-i-fi-ca-tion
  mol-li-fi-er
  mol-li-fy-ing-ly
mol-lusk
mol-ly-cod-dle
  mol-ly-cod-dled
  mol-ly-cod-dling

molt
  moult
  molt-er
mol-ten
  mol-ten-ly
mo-lyb-de-num
mo-ment
me-men-tary
  mo-men-tar-i-ly
  mo-men-tar-i-ness
mo-men-tous
  mo-men-tous-ly
  mo-men-tous-ness
mo-men-tum
mo-nad
  mo-nad-ic
  mo-nad-i-cal
  mo-nad-al
  mo-nad-i-cal-ly
mon-arch
  mo-nar-chal
  mo-nar-chal-ly
mo-nar-chi-cal
  mo-nar-chic
  mo-nar-chi-cal-ly
mon-ar-chism
  mon-ar-chist
  mon-ar-chis-tic
mon-ar-chy
  mon-ar-chies
  mon-as-tery
  mon-as-ter-ies
  mon-as-te-ri-al
mo-nas-tic
mo-nas-ti-cal
  mo-nas-ti-cal-ly
mo-nas-ti-cism
mon-au-ral
  mon-au-ral-ly
mon-e-tary
  mon-e-tar-i-ly
mon-e-tize
  mon-e-tized
  mon-e-tiz-ing
  mon-e-ti-za-tion
mon-ey
mon-ey-chang-er
mon-eyed

mon-ied
mon-ey--mak-er
  mon-ey--mak-ing
mon-ger
mon-goose
  mon-gooses
mon-grel
mon-i-ker
mon-ism
  mon-ist
  mo-nis-tic
  mo-nis-ti-cal
  mo-nis-ti-cal-ly
mo-ni-tion
mon-i-tor
  mon-i-to-ri-al
monk
  monk-ish
  monk-ish-ly
mon-key
  mon-keys
  mon-keyed
  mon-key-ing
mon-key-shine
mon-chro-mat-ic
mon-o-chrome
  mon-o-chro-mic
  mon-o-chro-mi-cal
  mon-o-chro-mi-cal-ly
  mon-o-chrom-ist
mon-o-cle
  mon-o-cled
mon-o-cli-nal
mon-o-cline
  mon-o-cli-nal-ly
mon-o-cli-nous
mon-o-dist
mon-o-dy
  mon-o-dies
  mo-nod-ic
mo-noe-cious
  mo-noe-cious-ly
mo-nog-a-my
  mo-nog-a-mist
  mo-nog-a-mous
mon-o-gram
  mon-o-grammed
  mon-o-gram-ming

mon-o-gram-mat-ic
mon-o-graph
  mo-nog-ra-pher
  mon-o-graph-ic
mon-o-lith
mon-o-logue
  mon-o-log
  mon-o-logu-ist
  mon-o-log-ist
mon-o-ma-nia
  mon-o-ma-ni-ac
  mon-o-ma-ni-a-cal
mon-o-met-al-lism
  mon-o-me-tal-lic
mo-no-mi-al
mon-nu-cle-o-sis
mon-o-pho-nic
mono-plane
mo-nop-o-lize
  mo-nop-o-lized
  mo-nop-o-liz-ing
  mo-nop-o-li-za-tion
  mo-nop-o-liz-er
mo-nop-o-ly
  mo-nop-o-lies
mono-rail
mon-o-syl-lab-ic
  mon-o-syl-lab-i-cal-ly
mon-o-syl-la-ble
mon-o-the-ism
  mon-o-the-ist
  mon-o-the-is-tic
  mon-o-the-is-ti-cal-ly
mon-o-tone
mo-not-o-nous
  mo-not-o-nous-ly
  mo-not-o-nous-ness
mo-not-o-ny
mone-treme
mono-type
  mon-o-typ-er
  mon-o-typ-ic
mon-o-va-lent
  mon-o-va-lence
  mon-o-va-len-cy
mon-ox-ide
mon-sei-gneur
  mes-sei-gneurs

mon-sieur
mon-soon
mon-ster
mon-stros-i-ty
  mon-stro-i-ties
mon-strous
  mon-strous-i-ties
mon-tage
month-ly
  month-lies
mon-u-ment
mon-u-men-tal
  mon-u-men-tal-ly
mooch
  mooch-er
moody
  mood-i-er
  mood-i-est
  mood-i-ly
  mood-i-ness
moon-beam
moon-light
moon-light-er
  moon-light-ing
moon-scape
moon-shine
  moon-shiner
moon-stone
moon-struck
moony
  moon-i-er
  moon-i-est
moor-ing
moot-ness
mop
  mopped
  mop-ping
mope
  moped
  mop-ing
  mop-er
  mop-ish
mop-pet
mo-raine
  mo-rain-al
  mo-rain-ic
mor-al
  mor-al-ly

mo-rale
mor-al-ist
  mor-al-is-tic
mo-ral-i-ty
  mo-ral-i-ties
mor-al-ize
  mor-al-ized
  mor-al-iz-ing
  mor-al-i-za-tion
  mor-al-iz-er
mo-rass
mor-a-to-ri-um
  mor-a-to-ri-ums
  mor-a-to-ria
mo-ray
mor-bid
  mor-bid-ly
  mor-bid-i-ty
  mor-bid-ness
mor-dant
  mor-dan-cy
  mor-dant-ly
more-over
mo-res
mor-ga-nat-ic
  mor-ga-nat-i-cal-ly
morque
mor-i-bund
mo-ri-on
morn-ing
morn-ing glo-ry
  morn-ing glo-ries
mo-roc-co
mo-ron
  mo-ron-ic
  mo-ron-i-cal-ly
mo-rose
  mo-rose-ly
  mo-rose-ness
mor-pheme
mor-phine
mor-phol-o-gy
  mor-pho-log-ic
  mor-pho-log-i-cal
  mor-phol-o-gist
mor-row
mor-sel
mor-tal

mor-tal-ly
mor-tal-i-ty
  mor-tal-i-ties
mor-tar
mort-gage
  mort-gaged
  mort-gag-ing
  mort-gag-ee
  mort-gag-er
mor-ti-cian
mor-ti-fy
  mor-ti-fied
  mor-ti-fy-ing
  mor-ti-fi-ca-tion
mor-tise
  mor-tised
  mor-tising
mort-main
mor-tu-ary
  mor-tu-ar-ies
mo-sa-ic
Mo-ses
mo-sey
  mo-seyd
  mo-sey-ing
mosque
mos-qui-to
  mos-qui-toes
  mos-qui-tos
moss
most-ly
mo-tel
mo-tet
moth-ball
moth-eat-en
moth-er
moth-er-hood
moth-er-in-law
moth-er-ly
mo-tif
mo-tile
  mo-til-i-ty
mo-tion
  mo-tion-less
mo-ti-vate
  mo-ti-vat-ed
  mo-ti-vat-ing
  mo-ti-va-tion

mo-tive
mot-ley
mo-tor
mo-tor-bike
mo-tor-boat
mo-tor-bus
mo-tor-cade
mo-tor-cy-cle
  mo-tor-cy-cling
  mo-tor-cy-clist
mo-tor-ist
mo-tor-ize
  mo-tor-ized
  mo-tor-iz-ing
  mo-tor-i-za-tion
mo-tor-man
  mo-tor-men
mot-tle
  mot-tled
  mot-tling
  mot-tler
mound
mount
  mount-able
  mount-er
moun-tain
moun-tain-eer
moun-tain-ous
moun-te-bank
mount-ing
mourn
  mourn-er
mourn-ful
  mourn-ful-ly
  mourn-ful-ness
mourn-ing
  mourn-ing-ly
mouse
  moused
  mous-ing
mous-er
mous-tache
mousy
  mous-i-er
  mous-i-est
mouth
  mouthed
  mouth-er

mouth-ful
  mouth-fuls
mouth-piece
mouthy
  mouth-i-er
  mouth-i-est
mou-ton
mov-able
  mov-a-bil-i-ty
  mov-a-bly
move
  moved
  mov-ing
move-ment
mov-ie
mow
mox-ie
mu-ci-lage
  mu-ci-lag-i-nous
muck
  mucky
mu-cous
  mu-cos-i-ty
mu-cus
mud
  mud-ded
  mud-ding
mud-dle
  mud-dled
  mud-dling
  mud-dler
mud-dy
  mud-di-er
  mud-di-est
mu-ez-zin
muf-fin
muf-ti
mug
  mugged
  mug-ging
  mug-ger
mug-gy
  mug-gi-er
  mug-gi-est
mu-lat-to
  mu-lat-toes
mul-ber-ry
  mul-ber-ries

mulch
mu-le-teer
mul-ish
  mul-ish-ly
mul-let
mul-li-gan
mul-li-ga-taw-ny
mul-lion
  mul-lioned
mul-ti-far-i-ous
  mul-ti-far-i-ous-ly
mul-ti-lat-er-al
mul-ti-mil-lion-aire
mul-ti-ple
mul-ti-ple scle-ro-sis
mul-ti-i-cand
mul-ti-pli-ca-tion
mul-ti-plic-i-ty
mul-ti-pli-er
mul-ti-ply
  mul-ti-plied
  mul-ti-ply-ing
  mul-ti-pli-a-ble
mul-ti-tude
mul-ti-tu-di-nous
  mul-ti-tu-di-nous-ly
mum-ble
mum-mer
mum-mery
mum-mi-fy
  mum-mi-fied
  mum-mi-fy-ing
  mum-mi-fi-ca-tion
mum-my
  mum-mies
  mum-mied
  mum-my-ing
munch
  munch-er
mun-dane
  mun-dane-ly
mu-nic-i-pal
  mu-nic-i-pal-ly
mu-nic-i-pal-i-ty
mu-nif-i-cent
  mu-nif-i-cence
  mu-nif-i-cent-ly
mu-ni-tion

mu-ral
  mu-ral-ist
mur-der
  mur-der-er
  mur-der-ess
mur-der-ous
  mur-der-ous-ly
mu-ri-at-ic ac-id
murky
  murk-i-er
  murk-i-est
  murk-i-ly
mur-mur
mur-rain
mus-cat
  mus-ca-tel
mus-cle
  mus-cled
  mus-cling
mus-cle--bound
mus-cu-lar
  mus-cu-lar-i-ty
  mus-cu-lar-ly
mus-cu-lar dys-tro-phy
mus-cu-la-ture
muse
  mused
  mus-ing
  mus-ing-ly
mu-se-um
mush
  mushy
  mush-i-er
  mush-i-est
mush-room
mu-sic
mu-si-cal
  mu-si-cal-ly
mu-si-cale
mu-si-cian
musk
  musky
  musk-i-er
  misk-i-est
mus-ket
mus-ke-teer
mus-ket-ry
musk-mel-on

musk-rat
mus-lin
muss
  mussy
  muss-i-er
mus-sel
mus-tache
mus-tang
mus-tard
mus-ter
mus-ty
  mus-ti-er
  mus-ti-est
  mus-ti-ly
mu-ta-ble
  mu-ta-bil-i-ty
  mu-ta-bly
mu-tant
mu-ta-tion
  mu-tate
  mu-tat-ed
  mu-tat-ing
  mu-ta-tion-al
mute
  mut-ed
  mut-ing
  mute-ly
  mute-ness
mu-ti-late
mu-ti-neer
mu-ti-ny
  mu-ti-nies
  mu-ti-nied
  mu-ti-ny-ing
  mu-ti-nous
mut-ter
  mut-ter-er
mut-ton
mu-tu-al
  mu-tu-al-i-ty
  mu-tu-al-ly
muz-zle
my
my-al-gia
my-as-the-nia
my-ce-li-um
my-ce-to-ma
my-ce-toph-a-gous

my-ce-to-zo-an
my-cin
my-co-flo-ra
my-col-o-gy
  my-col-o-gist
my-na
  my-nah
my-o-pia
  my-op-ic
myr-i-ad
myr-ia-me-ter
myr-mi-don
myrrh
myr-tle
mys-te-ri-ous
  mys-te-ri-ous-ly
mys-tery
  mys-ter-ies
mystery play
mys-tic
mys-ti-cal
  mys-ti-cal-ly
mys-ti-cism
mys-ti-fy
  mys-ti-fied
  mys-ti-fy-ing
  mys-ti-fi-ca-tion
mys-tique
myth
  myth-ic
  myth-i-cal
  myth-i-cal-ly
  myth-i-cist
  myth-i-cize
my-thol-o-gy
  my-thol-o-gies
  myth-o-log-ic
  myth-o-log-i-cal
  my-thol-o-gist
my-tho-ma-nia
my-tho-poe-ia
my-thos
my word
myx-ede-ma
myx-o-ma
myx-o-ma-to-sis
myxo-my-cete
myxo-vi-rus

nab
nabbed
nab-bing
na-bob
na-celle
na-cre
na-cre-ous
na-dir
nag
nagged
nag-ging
nag-ger
nail
nail-brush
nail down
nail file
nail-er
nain-sook
nai-ra
na-ive
na-ive-ly
na-ive-te
na-ked
na-ked-ly
na-ked-ness
na-li-dix-ic acid
na-lor-phine
nal-ox-one
nam-by-pam-by
name
named
nam-ing
name-less
name-ly
name--call-ing
name day
name-less
name of the game
name-plate
name-sake
nan-keen
nan-kin
nan-ny
nan-nies
nan-ny goat
nano-gram
nano-me-ter
nano-sec-ond

nap
napped
nap-ping
nap-per
na-palm
nape
naph-tha
naph-tha-lene
nap-kin
na-po-leon
nar-cis-sism
nar-cism
nar-cis-sist
nar-co-sis
nar-cot-ic
nar-co-tize
nar-co-tized
nar-is
nar-es
nark
nar-rate
nar-ra-ted
nar-ra-ting
nar-ra-tor
nar-ra-tion
nar-ra-tive
nar-ra-tive-ly
nar-row
nar-row-ly
nar-row--mind-ed
nary
na-sal
na-scent
na-scence
na-scen-cy
na-so-pha-ryn-geal
na-so-phar-ynx
nas-tic
na-stur-tium
nas-ty
nas-ti-er
nas-ti-est
na-tal
na-tion
na-tion-hood
na-tion-al
na-tion-al-ly
na-tion-al-ism

na-tion-al-ist
na-tion-al-is-tic
na-tion-al-i-ty
na-tion-al-i-ties
na-tion-al-ize
na-tion-al-ized
na-tion-al-iz-ing
na-tion-al-i-za-tion
na-tion-wide
na-tive
na-tive-ly
na-tiv-i-ty
na-tiv-i-ties
nat-ty
nat-ti-er
nat-u-ral
nat-u-ral-ly
nat-u-ral-ness
nat-u-ral-ism
nat-u-ral-ist
nat-u-ral-is-tic
nat-u-ral-ized
nat-u-ral-iz-ing
nat-u-ral-i-za-tion
na-ture
naught
naugh-ty
naugh-ti-er
naugh-ti-est
nau-sea
nau-se-ate
nau-se-at-ed
nau-se-at-ing
nau-seous
nau-seous-ly
nau-ti-cal
nau-ti-cal-ly
nau-ti-lus
nau-ti-lus-es
nau-ti-li
na-val
na-vel
nav-i-ga-ble
nav-i-gate
nav-i-gat-ed
nav-i-gat-ing
nav-i-ga-tion
nav-i-ga-tion-al

nav-i-ga-tor
na-vy
  na-vies
near
  near-ly
  near-ness
near-by
neat
  neat-ly
  neat-ness
neb-bish
neb-u-la
nec-es-sary
  nec-es-sar-ies
  nec-es-sar-i-ly
  ne-ces-si-tate
  ne-ces-si-ta-ting
ne-ces-si-ty
  ne-ces-si-ties
neck-er-chief
neck-ing
neck-lace
neck-tie
ne-crol-o-gy
  ne-crol-o-gies
nec-ro-man-cy
  nec-ro-man-cer
ne-cro-sis
  ne-crot-ic
nec-tar
  nec-tar-ine
need-ful
  need-ful-ly
  need-ful-ness
nee-dle
  nee-dled
  nee-dling
  nee-dle-like
  nee-dler
nee-dle-point
need-less
  need-less-ly
nee-dle-work
  nee-dle-work-er
needy
  need-i-er
  need-i-est
  need-i-ness

ne'er--do--well
ne-far-i-ous
  ne-far-i-ous-ly
  ne-far-i-ous-ness
ne-gate
  ne-ga-ted
  ne-ta-ting
ne-ga-tion
neg-a-tive
  neg-a-tive-ly
  neg-a-tive-ness
  neg-a-tive-i-ty
  neg-a-tiv-ism
ne-glect
  ne-glec-ter
  ne-glec-tor
  ne-glect-ful-ness
  ne-glect-ful
  ne-glect-ful-ly
neg-li-gee
neg-li-gent
  neg-li-gence
  neg-li-gent-ly
neg-li-gi-ble
  neg-li-gi-bly
  neg-li-gi-bil-i-ty
ne-go-tia-ble
  ne-go-tia-bil-i-ty
ne-go-ti-ate
  ne-go-ti-at-ed
  ne-go-ti-at-ing
  ne-go-ti-a-tion
  ne-go-ti-a-tor
neigh-bor
  neigh-bor-ing
  neigh-bor-ly
  neigh-bor-li-ness
  neigh-bor-hood
nei-ther
nem-e-sis
  nem-e-ses
neo-clas-sic
  neo-clas-si-cism
neo-lith-ic
ne-ol-o-gism
ne-ol-o-gy
ne-on
ne-o-phyte

ne-pen-the
  ne-pen-the-an
neph-ew
ne-phri-tis
  ne-phrit-ic
nep-o-tism
  nep-o-tist
nep-tu-ni-um
nerve
  nerved
  nerv-ing
  nerve-less
nerve--rack-ing
  nerve--wrack-ing
ner-vous
  ner-vous-ly
  ner-vous-ness
nervy
  nerv-i-er
  nerv-i-est
  nerv-i-ness
net
  net-ted
  net-ting
neth-er
neth-er-most
net-tle
  net-tled
  net-tling
net-work
neu-ral
  neu-ral-ly
  neu-ral-gia
  neu-ral-gic
neu-ras-the-nia
  neu-ra-then-ic
neu-ri-tis
  neu-rit-ic
neu-rol-o-gy
  neu-ro-log-i-cal
  neu-rol-o-gist
neu-ron
  neu-ron-ic
neu-ro-sis

neu-ro-ses
neu-rot-ic
neu-rot-i-cal-ly
neu-ter
neu-tral
neu-tral-i-ty
neu-tral-ly
neu-tral-ism
neu-tral-ist
neu-tral-ize
neu-tral-ized
neu-tral-iz-ing
neu-tral-i-za-tion
neu-tral-iz-er
neu-tri-no
neu-tron
nev-er
nev-er-more
nev-er-the-less
new
new-ish
new-ness
new-born
new-com-er
new-el
new-fan-gled
new-ly
new-ly-wed
news-boy
news-cast
news-cast-er
news-pa-per
news-pa-per-man
news-print
news-reel
news-stand
newsy
news-i-er
news-i-est
newt
nex-us
ni-a-cin
nib-ble
nib-bled
nib-bling
nib-bler
nib-lick
nice

nic-er
nic-est
nice-ly
nice-ness
nice-ty
nice-ties
niche
nick-el
nick-el-ode-on
nick-name
nick-named
nick-nam-ing
nic-o-tine
nic-o-tin-ic
niece
nif-ty
nif-ti-er
nif-ti-est
nig-gard
nig-gard-li-ness
nig-gard-ly
nigh
nigh-er
nigh-est
night-cap
night-dress
night-fall
night-gown
night-hawk
night-in-gale
night-ly
night-mare
night-mar-ish
night-shade
night-shirt
night-time
ni-hil-ism
ni-hil-ist
ni-hil-is-tic
nim-ble
nim-bler
nim-blest
nim-ble-ness
nim-bly
nim-bus
nin-com-poop
nine-pin
nine-teen

nine-teenth
nine-ty
nine-ties
nine-ti-eth
nin-ny
nin-nines
ninth
nip
nipped
nip-ping
nip-per
nip-ple
nip-py
nip-pi-er
nip-pi-est
nir-va-na
nit
nit-ty
nit-ti-er
nit-ti-est
ni-ter
nit-pick
ni-trate
ni-trat-ed
ni-trat-ing
ni-tra-tion
ni-tra-tor
ni-tric
ni-tro-gen
ni-trog-e-nous
ni-tro-glyc-er-in
ni-trous ox-ide
nit-ty-grit-ty
nit-wit
no-be-li-um
no-bil-i-ty
no-bil-i-ties
no-ble
no-body
noc-tur-nal
noc-turne
nod
nod-ded
nod-ding
nod-der
node
nod-al
nod-ule

nod-u-lar
no-el
nog-gin
noise
noised
nois-ing
noise-less
noi-some
noi-some-ly
noisy
nois-i-er
nois-i-est
nois-i-ly
no-mad
no-mad-ic
no-mad-i-cal-ly
no-mad-ism
nom de plume
noms de plume
no-men-cla-ture
nom-i-nal
nom-i-nal-ly
nom-i-nate
nom-i-nat-ed
nom-i-nat-ing
nom-i-na-tion
nom-i-na-tor
nom-i-na-tive
nom-i-nee
non-age
nonce
non-cha-lant
non-cha-lance
non-cha-lant-ly
non-com
non-com-bat-ant
non-com-mit-tal
non-com-mit-tal-ly
non-con-duc-tor
non-con-duc-ing
non-con-form-ist
non-con-form-i-ty
non-de-script
non-en-ti-ty
non-en-ti-ties
none-the-less
non-in-ter-ven-tion
non-met-al

non-me-tal-lic
non-pa-reil
non-par-ti-san
non-par-ti-san-ship
non-plus
non-plused
non-plus-ing
non-prof-it
non-res-i-dent
non-res-i-dence
non-res-i-den-cy
non-res-i-den-cies
non-re-stric-tive
non-sec-tar-i-an
non-sense
non-sen-si-cal
non-sen-si-cal-ly
non se-qui-tur
non-stop
non-union
non-union-ism
non-union-ist
non-vi-o-lence
non-vi-o-lent
non-vi-o-lent-ly
noo-dle
noon
noon-day
noon-time
noose
noosed
noos-ing
nor-mal
nor-mal-cy
nor-mal-i-ty
nor-mal-ly
nor-mal-ize
nor-mal-ized
nor-mal-iz-ing
nor-mal-i-za-tion
north-east
north-east-ern
north-east-er
north-er
north-ern
north-ern-most
north-ern-er
north-ward

north-wards
north-ward-ly
north-west
nose
nosed
nos-ing
nose-gay
nos-tal-gia
nos-tal-gic
nos-tril
nos-trum
nosy
nos-i-er
nos-i-est
nos-i-ly
nos-i-ness
no-ta-ble
no-ta-rize
no-ta-rized
no-ta-riz-ing
no-ta-ri-za-tion
no-ta-ry
no-ta-ries
no-ta-tion
no-ta-tion-al
notch
notched
note
not-ed
not-ed
not-ed-ly
note-wor-thy
note-wor-thi-ness
noth-ing
noth-ing-ness
no-tice
no-ticed
no-tic-ing
no-tice-a-ble
no-tice-a-bly
no-ti-fy
no-ti-fied
no-ti-fy-ing
no-ti-fi-ca-tion
no-ti-fi-er
no-tion
no-to-ri-ous
no-to-ri-ous-ly

no-to-ri-e-ty
no-trump
nought
nour-ish
  nour-ish-er
  nour-ish-ing
  nour-ish-ment
no-va
  no-vas
nov-el
  nov-el-ist
  nov-el-is-tic
  nov-el-ette
nov-el-ty
  nov-el-ties
no-ve-na
  no-ve-nae
nov-ice
no-vi-tiate
no-where
no-wise
nox-ious
  nox-ious-ly
noz-zle
nu-ance
nub-bin
nu-bile
nu-cle-ar
nu-cle-us
  nu-cle-us-es
  nu-clei
nude
  nude-ly
  nude-ness
  nu-di-ty
nudge
  nudged
  nudg-ing
  nudg-er
nud-ism
  nud-ist
nug-get
nui-sance
null
  nul-li-ty
  nul-li-ties
nul-li-fy
  nul-li-fied

nul-li-fy-ing
nul-li-fi-ca-tion
nul-li-fi-er
numb
  numb-ly
  numb-ness
  numb-ing
num-ber
  num-ber-er
  num-ber-less
numb-skull
nu-mer-al
  num-er-al-ly
nu-mer-ate
  nu-mer-at-ed
  nu-mer-at-ing
  nu-mer-a-tion
nu-mer-a-tor
nu-mer-i-cal
  nu-mer-i-cal-ly
nu-mer-ous
  nu-mer-ous-ly
nu-mis-mat-ics
  nu-mis-mat-ic
  nu-mis-mat-i-cal
  nu-mis-ma-tist
num-skull
nun
nun-ci-a-ture
nun-cio
  nun-ci-os
nun-cle
nun-cu-pa-tive
nun-nery
  nun-ner-ies
Nu-pe
nup-tial
  nup-tial-ly
nurse
  nursed
  nurs-ing
  nurs-er
nurse-maid
nurs-ery
  nurs-er-ies
nurs-ery-maid
nurs-ery-man
nursery rhyme

nursery school
nurse's aid
nurse shark
nurs bottle
nursing home
nurs-ling
nur-tur-ance
nur-ture
  nur-tured
  nur-tur-ing
  nur-tur-er
nut
  nut-ted
  nut-ting
nut-crack-er
nut-gall
nut grass
nut-hatch
nut-house
nut-let
nut-meg
nut-pick
nu-tria
nu-tri-ent
  nu-tri-ment
nu-tri-tion
  nu-tri-tion-al
  nu-tri-tion-al-ly
  nu-tri-tion-ist
nu-tri-tious
  nu-tri-tious-ly
nu-tri-tive
  nu-tri-tive-ly
nut-shell
nut-ty
  nut-ti-er
  nut-ti-est
nuz-zle
  nuz-zled
  nuz-zling
ny-lon
nymph
  nym-phal
nym-pha-lid
nym-pho-ma-nia
  nym-pho-ma-ni-ac
Ny-norsk
nys-tag-mus

oaf
  oaf-ish
  oaf-ish-ly
oak
oak apple
oak-en
oak--leaf cluster
oak-moss
oa-kum
oak wilt
oar
  oared
  oars-man
  oars-men
oar-fish
oar-lock
oars-man
oa-sis
  oa-ses
oat
oat-cake
oat-en
oat-er
oat-grass
oath
oat-meal
ob-bli-ga-to
  ob-bli-ga-tos
ob-cor-date
ob-du-ra-cy
ob-du-rate
  ob-du-ra-cy
  ob-du-rate-ly
obe-di-ence
  obe-di-ent
  obe-di-ent-ly
obei-sance
  obei-sant
obe-lia
obe-lisk
obe-lize
obe-lus
obese
  obese-ness
  obes-i-ty
obey
  obey-er
ob-fus-cate

ob-fus-ca-ted
ob-fus-ca-ting
ob-fus-ca-tion
obit
obi-ter dic-tum
obit-u-ary
  obit-u-ar-ies
ob-ject
  ob-ject-less
  ob-ject-or
object ball
ob-jec-ti-fy
ob-jec-tion
  ob-jec-tion-a-ble
  ob-jec-tion-a-bly
ob-jec-tive
  ob-jec-tive-ly
  ob-jec-tive-ness
  ob-jec-tiv-i-ty
objective complement
objective correlative
objective test
ob-jec-tiv-ism
ob-jec language
object lesson
ob-jet d' art
ob-jet-trou-ve
ob-jur-gate
  ob-jur-gat-ed
  ob-jur-gat-ing
  ob-jur-ga-tion
  ob-jur-ga-to-ry
ob-lan-ceo-late
ob-last
ob-late
  ob-late-ly
  ob-late-ness
ob-la-tion
ob-li-gate
  ob-li-gat-ed
  ob-li-gat-ing
  ob-li-ga-tion
  ob-lig-a-to-ry
oblige
  obliged
  oblig-ing
  oblig-er
ob-li-gee

ob-li-gor
ob-lique
  ob-liqued
  ob-liqu-ing
  ob-lique-ly
oblique angle
oblique case
obliq-ui-ty
oblit-er-ate
  oblit-er-at-ed
  oblit-er-at-ing
  oblit-er-a-tion
  oblit-er-a-tive
obliv-i-on
  obliv-i-ous
  obliv-i-ous-ly
ob-long
ob-lo-quy
  ob-lo-quies
ob-nox-ious
  ob-nox-ious-ly
ob-nu-bi-late
oboe
obo-ist
obol
ob-ovate
ob-ovoid
ob-scene
  ob-scene-ly
  ob-scen-ity
  ob-scen-i-ties
ob-scur-ant
ob-scu-ran-tism
ob-scure
  ob-scur-er
  ob-scur-est
  ob-scured
  ob-scur-ing
  ob-scure-ly
ob-scu-ri-ty
ob-se-qui-ous
  ob-se-qui-ous-ly
ob-se-quy
  ob-se-quies
ob-serv-able
  ob-serv-ably
ob-ser-vance
ob-ser-vant

ob-ser-vant-ly
ob-ser-va-tion
ob-ser-va-tion-al
ob-ser-va-to-ry
ob-ser-va-to-ries
ob-serve
ob-served
ob-serv-ing
ob-serv-ed-ly
ob-serv-er
ob-serv-ing-ly
ob-sess
ob-ses-sive
ob-ses-sive-ly
ob-ses-sion
ob-sid-i-an
ob-ses-sive
ob-sid-i-an
ob-so-lesce
ob-so-les-cence
ob-so-les-cent
ob-so-les-cence
ob-so-les-cent-ly
ob-so-lete
ob-sta-cle
obstacle
obstacle course
obstet
ob-stet-ric
ob-ste-tri-cian
ob-stet-rics
ob-stet-ric
ob-stet-ri-cal
ob-sti-na-cy
ob-sti-nate
ob-sti-na-cy
ob-sti-na-cies
ob-sti-nat-ly
ob-strep-er-ous
ob-strep-er-ous-ly
ob-struct
ob-struc-tive
ob-struc-tor
ob-struc-tion
ob-struc-tion-ism
ob-struc-tion-ist
ob-tain
ob-tain-a-ble
ob-tain-er

ob-tain-ment
ob-tect
ob-test
ob-trude
ob-trud-ed
ob-trud-ing
ob-trud-er
ob-tru-sion
ob-tru-sive
ob-tund
ob-tu-rate
ob-tu-ra-tor
ob-tuse
ob-tuse-ly
ob-verse
ob-verse-ly
ob-vert
ob-vi-ate
ob-vi-ated
ob-vi-at-ing
ob-vi-a-tion
ob-vi-a-tor
ob-vi-ous
ob-vi-ous-ly
oc-a-ri-na
oc-ca-sion
oc-ca-sion-al
oc-ca-sion-al-ly
oc-ci-dent
oc-ci-den-tal
oc-ci-den-tal-ize
oc-cip-i-tal
occipital bone
occipital condyle
occipital lobe
oc-ci-put
oc-clude
oc-clud-ed
oc-clud-ing
oc-clu-sive
occluded front
oc-clu-sal
oc-clu-sion
oc-cult
oc-cul-ta-tion
oc-cult-ism
oc-cult-ist
oc-cu-pan-cy

oc-cu-pan-cies
oc-cu-pant
oc-cu-pa-tion
oc-cu-pa-tion-al
oc-cu-pa-tion-al-ly
occupational therapy
oc-cu-py
oc-cu-pied
oc-cu-py-ing
oc-cu-pi-er
oc-cur
oc-curred
oc-cur-ring
oc-cur-rence
oc-cur-rent
ocean
oce-an-ic
ocean-ar-i-um
ocean-front
ocean-go-ing
oce-an-ic
oceanog
ocean-og-ra-phy
ocean-og-ra-pher
ocean-o-graph-ic
ocean-ol-o-gy
ocean sunfish
ocel-lat-ed
ocel-lus
oce-lot
ocher
ocher-ous
ochery
och-loc-ra-cy
o'clock
oco-ti-llo
oc-ta-gon
oc-tag-o-nal
oc-tag-o-nal-ly
oc-ta-he-dral
oc-ta-he-dron
oc-ta-he-drons
oc-ta-he-dra
oc-ta-he-dral
oc-tal
oc-tam-e-ter
oct-an-dri-ous
oc-tane

octane number
oc-tant
oc-ta-pep-tide
oc-tave
oc-ta-vo
oc-tet
oc-til-lion
Oc-to-ber
oc-to-de-cil-lion
oc-to-dec-i-mo
oc-to-ge-nar-i-an
  oc-tog-e-nary
oc-to-ploid
oc-to-pod
oc-to-pus
oc-to-ron
oc-to-syl-lab-ic
oc-to-syl-la-ble
oc-troi
oc-u-lar
  oc-u-lar-ly
oc-u-list
oda-lisque
odd
  odd-ly
  odd-ness
odd-ball
Odd Fellow
odd function
odd-i-ty
  odd-i-ties
odd lot
odd-ly
odd man out
odd-ment
odd permutation
odd--pin-nate
odds
odds and ends
odds--on
odd trick
ode
ode-um
od-ic
odi-ous
  odi-ous-ly
odo-graph
odom-e-ter

odo-nate
odon-to-blast
odon-to-glos-sum
odon-toid process
odon-tol-o-gy
odor
  odored
  odor-less
  odor-ous
  odor-ous-ly
odorant
odor-if-er-ous
  odor-if-er-ous-ly
odor-ize
  odor-less
  odor-ous
od-ys-sey
oe-di-pal
oeil--de--boeuf
oeil-lade
oe-nol-o-gy
oe-no-mel
oer-sted
oe-soph-a-gus
oeu-vre
ofay
off
of-fal
off-beat
off Broadway
off-cast
off--col-or
of-fend
  of-fend-er
of-fense
  of-fense-less
of-fen-sive
  of-fen-sive-ly
  of-fen-sive-ness
of-fer
  of-fer-er
  of-fer-ing
of-fer-to-ry
  of-fer-to-ri-al
  of-fer-to-ries
off-hand
  off-hand-ed-ly
  off-hand-ed-ness

of-fice
office boy
of-fice-hold-er
of-fi-cer
officer of arms
of-fi-cial
  of-fi-cial-dom
  of-fi-cial-ism
  of-fi-cial-ly
official family
of-fi-cial-ism
of-fi-ci-ant
of-fi-ci-ary
of-fi-ci-ate
  of-fi-ci-at-ed
  of-fi-ci-at-ing
  of-fi-ci-a-tion
  of-fi-ci-a-tor
of-fi-cious
  of-fi-cious-ly
  of-fi-cious-ness
off-ing
off-ish
off--key
off limist
off--ling
off--load
off-print
off-scour-ing
off-screen
off--sea-son
off-set
  off-set-ting
off-shoot
off-shore
off-side
off--speed
off-spring
off-stage
off--the--cuff
off--the--record
off--the--shelf
off--white
off year
of-ten
of-ten-times
ogle
  ogled

ogler
ogling
ogre
ogre-ish
ohm
ohm-ic
ohm-age
ohm-me-ter
oil-cloth
oil-er
oil-skin
oily
oil-i-er
oil-i-est
oil-i-ness
oint-ment
okra
old
old-en
old-er
old-est
old-ish
old-ness
old--fash-ioned
old-ster
old--time
old--tim-er
old--world
ole-ag-i-nous
ole-ag-i-nous-ly
ole-ag-i-nous-ness
oleo
oleo-mar-ga-rine
ol-fac-tion
ol-fac-to-ry
ol-fac-to-ries
oli-garch
oli-gar-chic
oli-gar-chi-cal
oli-gar-chy
oli-gar-chies
oli-gop-oly
ol-ive
om-buds-man
om-buds-men
om-elet
omen
om-i-nous

om-i-nous-ly
om-i-nous-ness
omis-sion
omit
omit-ted
omit-ting
om-ni-bus
om-ni-bus-es
om-nip-o-tence
om-nip-o-tent-ly
om-ni-pres-ence
om-ni-pres-ent
om-ni-pres-ent-ly
om-ni-science
om-ni-scient
om-ni-scient-ly
om-ni-vore
om-niv-o-rous
om-niv-o-rous-ly
om-niv-o-rous-ness
onan-ism
onan-ist
onan-is-tic
once--over
on-com-ing
oner-ous
oner-ous-ly
oner-ous-ness
one-self
one--sid-ed
one--sid-ed-ly
one--sid-ed-ness
one-time
one--track
one--way
on-go-ing
on-ion
on-ion-like
on-iony
on-ion-skin
on--line
on-look-er
on-look-ing
on-ly
on-o-mato-poe-ia
on-o-mato-poe-ic
on-o-mato-po-et-ic
on-rush

on-rush-ing
on-set
on-shore
on-slaught
onto-
onus
on-ward
on-yx
oo-dles
ooze
oozed
oo-zi-er
oo-zi-est
oo-zi-ness
ooz-ing
oo-zy
opac-i-ty
opac-i-ties
opal
opal-es-cence
opal-es-cent
opaque
opaque-ly
opaque-ness
open
open-er
open-ly
open-ness
open--air
open door
open--end
open--eyed
open-hand-ed
open-hand-ed-ly
open house
open-ing
open--mind-ed
open--mind-ed-ly
open-mouthed
open ses-a-me
open-work
opera
op-er-at-ic
op-er-at-i-cal-ly
op-er-a-ble
op-er-a-bil-i-ty
op-er-a-bly
opera glass

opera house
op-er-ate
 op-er-at-ed
 op-er-at-ing
op-er-a-tion
 op-er-a-tive
 op-er-a-tive-ly
op-er-a-tor
op-er-et-ta
oph-thal-mic
 oph-thal-mo-log-ic
 oph-thal-mol-o-gist
 oph-thal-mol-o-gy
opi-ate
opine
 opined
 opin-ing
opin-ion
 opin-ion-at-ed
 opin-ion-at-ed-ly
opi-um
opos-sum
op-po-nent
op-por-tune
 op-por-tune-ly
 op-por-tune-ness
op-por-tun-ism
 op-por-tun-ist
 op-por-tun-is-tic
op-por-tu-ni-ty
 op-por-tu-ni-ties
op-pos-able
 op-pos-a-bil-i-ty
op-pose
 op-posed
 op-pos-er
 op-pos-ing
 op-pos-ing-ly
op-po-site
 op-po-site-ly
op-po-si-tion
 op-po-si-tion-al
op-press
 op-pres-si-ble
 op-pres-sor
op-pres-sion
op-pres-sive
 op-pres-sive-ly

op-pres-sive-ness
op-pro-bri-ous
 op-pro-bri-ous-ly
op-pro-bri-um
op-tic
 op-ti-cal
 op-ti-cal-ly
op-ti-cian
op-tics
op-ti-mal
op-ti-mism
 op-ti-mist
 op-ti-mis-tic
 op-ti-mis-ti-cal-ly
op-ti-mize
 op-ti-mi-za-tion
 op-ti-mized
 op-ti-miz-ing
op-ti-mum
 op-ti-ma
op-tion
 op-tion-al
 op-tion-al-ly
op-tom-e-trist
op-tom-e-try
 op-to-met-ric
 op-to-met-ri-cal
op-u-lence
op-u-lent
 op-u-lent-ly
opus
 opus-es
or-a-cle
 orac-u-lar
 orac-u-lar-i-ty
 orac-u-lar-ly
oral
 oral-ly
or-ange
or-ange-ade
orang-utan
orate
 orat-ed
 orat-ing
ora-tion
or-a-tor
 or-a-tor-i-cal
 or-a-tor-i-cal-ly

or-a-to-rio
 or-a-to-ri-os
or-a-to-ry
or-bic-u-lar
 or-bic-u-lar-i-ty
 or-bic-u-lar-ly
or-bic-u-late
or-bit
 or-bit-al
 or-bit-er
or-chard
or-ches-tra
 or-ches-tral
 or-ches-tral-ly
or-ches-trate
 or-ches-trat-ed
 or-ches-trat-ing
 or-ches-tra-tion
or-chid
or-dain
 or-dain-er
 or-dain-ment
or-deal
or-der
 or-dered
 or-der-li-ness
 or-der-ly
or-di-nal
or-di-nance
or-di-nari-ly
or-di-nary
 or-di-nari-ness
or-di-na-tion
ord-nance
or-dure
oreg-a-no
or-gan
or-gan-dy
or-gan-ic
 or-gan-i-cal-ly
or-gan-ism
 or-gan-is-mal
 or-gan-is-mic
or-gan-ist
or-ga-ni-za-tion
 or-gan-i-za-tion-al
or-ga-nize
 or-ga-niz-able

or-ga-nized
or-ga-niz-er
or-ga-niz-ing
or-ga-niz-a-ble
or-gasm
or-gas-mic
or-gi-as-tic
or-gi-as-ti-cal-ly
or-gy
or-gies
ori-ent
Ori-en-tal
ori-en-tal-ism
ori-en-tal-ist
ori-en-tal-ly
ori-en-tate
ori-en-tat-ed
ori-en-tat-ing
ori-en-ta-tion
or-i-fice
ori-ga-mi
orig-i-nal
orig-i-nal-i-ty
orig-i-nal-ly
orig-i-nate
orig-i-nat-ed
orig-i-nat-ing
orig-i-na-tion
orig-i-na-tive
orig-i-na-tive-ly
orig-i-na-tor
or-i-son
or-na-ment
or-na-men-tal
or-na-men-ta-tion
or-nate
or-nate-ly
or-nate-ness
or-nery
or-ner-i-ness
or-ni-thol-o-gy
or-ni-tho-log-ic
or-ni-tho-log-i-cal
or-ni-tho-log-i-cal-ly
or-ni-thol-o-gist
oro-tund
oro-tun-di-ty
or-phan

or-phan-hood
or-phan-age
orth-odon-tics
orth-odon-tic
orth-odon-tist
or-tho-dox
or-tho-dox-ly
or-tho-dox-ness
or-tho-doxy
or-tho-dox-ies
or-tho-gen-ic
or-thog-o-nal
or-thog-o-nal-ly
or-thog-ra-phy
or-tho-graph-ic
or-tho-graph-i-cal
or-tho-graph-i-cal-ly
or-thog-ra-phies
or-thog-ra-pher
or-tho-pe-dic
or-tho-pe-dics
or-tho-pe-dist
os-cil-late
os-cil-lat-ed
os-cil-lat-ing
os-cil-la-tion
os-cil-la-tor
os-cil-la-to-ry
os-cil-lo-scope
os-cu-late
os-cu-lat-ed
os-cu-lat-ing
os-cu-la-tion
os-cu-la-to-ry
os-mi-um
os-mose
os-mosed
os-mos-ing
os-mo-sis
os-mot-ic
os-mot-i-cal-ly
os-prey
os-si-fy
os-si-fied
os-si-fi-er
os-si-fy-ing
os-ten-si-ble
os-ten-si-bly

os-ten-sive
os-ten-sive-ly
os-ten-ta-tion
os-ten-ta-tious
os-ten-ta-tious-ly
os-te-op-a-thy
os-teo-path
os-teo-path-ic
os-teo-path-i-cal-ly
os-tra-cism
os-tra-cize
os-tra-cized
os-tra-ciz-ing
os-trich
oth-er
oth-er-ness
oth-er-wise
oth-er-world
oth-er-world-ly
oti-ose
oti-ose-ly
oti-os-i-ty
ot-ter
ot-to-man
ought
ounce
our-self
our-selves
oust-er
out-bid
out-bid-den
out-bid-ding
out-bid-der
out-board
out-bound
out-brave
out-braved
out-brav-ing
out-break
out-build-ing
out-burst
out-cast
out-come
out-cry
out-cries
out-dat-ed
out-dis-tance
out-dis-tanced

out-dis-tanc-ing
out-do
  out-did
  out-do-ing
  out-done
out-door
out-er
out-er-most
outer space
out-face
  out-faced
  out-fac-ing
out-field
  out-field-er
out-fit
  out-fit-ted
  out-fit-ter
  out-fit-ting
out-flank
out-fox
out-grow
  out-grew
  out-grow-ing
  out-grown
out-growth
out-guess
out-ing
out-land-ish
  out-land-ish-ly
out-last
out-law
  out-law-ry
out-lay
  out-laid
  out-lay-ing
out-let
out-line
  out-lined
  out-lin-ing
out-live
  out-lived
  out-liv-ing
out-look
out-ly-ing
out-mod-ed
out-num-ber
out--of--date
out-post

out-put
out-rage
  out-raged
  out-rag-ing
out-ra-geous
  out-ra-geous-ly
out-range
  out-ranged
  out-rang-ing
out-rank
out-rig-ger
out-right
out-run
  out-ran
  out-run-ning
out-sell
  out-sell-ing
  out-sold
out-set
out-shine
  out-shin-ing
  out-shone
out-side
  out-sid-er
out-smart
out-spo-ken
  out-spo-ken-ly
out-stand-ing
  out-stand-ing-ly
out-strip
  out-stripped
  out-strip-ping
out-ward
  out-ward-ly
  out-wards
out-wear
  out-wear-ing
  out-wore
  out-worn
out-weigh
out-wit
  out-wit-ted
  out-wit-ting
ova
oval
  oval-ly
ova-ry
  ovar-i-an

ova-ries
ovate
ova-tion
ov-en
over
over-act
over-age
over-all
over-awe
  over-awed
  over-aw-ing
over-bear-ing
  over-bear-ing-ly
over-blown
over-board
over-build
  over-build-ing
  over-built
over-cast
over-charge
  over-charged
  over-charg-ing
over-coat
over-come
  over-came
over-com-pen-sa-tion
  over-com-pen-sate
  over-com-pen-sat-ed
  over-com-pen-sat-ing
over-con-fi-dence
  over-con-fi-dent
over-do
  over-did
  over-do-ing
  over-done
over-dose
  over-dos-age
over-draft
over-draw
  over-draw-ing
  over-drawn
  over-drew
over-drive
over-due
over-em-pha-sis
  over-em-pha-size
  over-em-pha-sized
  over-em-pha-sizing

over-es-ti-mate
over-es-ti-mat-ed
over-es-ti-mat-ing
over-es-ti-ma-tion
over-flow
over-flowed
over-flowing
over-flown
over-gen-er-ous
over-grow
over-grew
over-grow-ing
over-grown
over-growth
over-hand
over-hand-ed
over-hang
over-hang-ing
over-hung
over-haul
over-haul-ing
over-head
over-hear
over-heard
over-hear-ing
over-joy
over-joyed
over-kill
over-land
over-lap
over-lapped
over-lap-ping
over-lay
over-laid
over-lay-ing
over-look
over-lord
over-ly
over-much
over-night
over-pass
over-play
over-pow-er
over-pow-er-ing
over-rate
over-rat-ed
over-rat-ing
over-reach

over-ride
over-rid-den
over-rid-ing
over-rode
over-rule
over-ruled
over-rul-ing
over-run
over-seas
over-see
over-saw
over-see-ing
over-seen
over-seer
over-shad-ow
over-shoe
over-shoot
over-shoot-ing
over-shot
over-sight
over-sim-pli-fy
over-sim-pli-fi-ca-tion
over-sim-pli-fied
over-sim-pli-fy-ing
over-size
over-sleep
over-sleep-ing
over-slept
over-spread
over-spread-ing
over-state
over-stat-ed
over-state-ment
over-stat-ing
over-stay
over-step
over-stepped
over-step-ping
over-strung
over-stuff
overt
overt-ly
over-take
over-tak-en
over-tak-ing
over-took
over-tax
over--the--coun-ter

over-throw
over-threw
over-thrown
over-throw-ing
over-time
over-tone
over-ture
over-turn
over-view
over-ween-ing
over-ween-ing-ly
over-weight
over-whelm
over-whelm-ing
over-work
over-worked
over-work-ing
over-wrought
ovi-duct
ovip-a-rous
ovip-ar-ous-ly
ovoid
ovoi-dal
ovu-late
ovu-lat-ed
ovu-lat-ing
ovu-la-tion
ovule
ovu-lar
ovum
ova
owe
owed
ow-ing
owl-ish
own-er
ox-al-ic ac-id
ox-bow
ox-en
ox-ford
ox-i-da-tion
ox-ide
ox-i-dize
ox-y-a-cet-y-lene
ox-y-gen
ox-y-gen-ate
oys-ter
ozone

pab-u-lum
pace
  paced
  pac-ing
  pac-er
pace car
pace lap
pace-mak-er
pa-cif-ic
pa-cif-i-ca-tion
  pa-cif-i-ca-tor
  pa-cif-i-ca-to-ry
pac-i-fi-er
pac-i-fism
  pac-i-fist
pac-i-fy
  pac-i-fied
  pac-i-fy-ing
pack
pack-age
  pack-ag-er
package deal
package store
pack animal
pack-board
pack-er
pack-et
pack-horse
pack ice
pack-ing
pack-ing-house
pack-man
pack rat
pack-sack
pack-sad-dle
pack-thread
pact
pad
  pad-ded
  pad-ding
pad-dle
pad-dle-ball
pad-dle-board
pad-dle-boat
pad-dle-fish
paddle tennis
paddle wheel
pad-dock

pad-dy
  pad-dies
pad-dy wagon
pad-lock
pa-dre
pa-dro-ne
pad-u-a-soy
pae-an
  pe-an
pae-do-gen-e-sis
pae-do-mor-phic
pa-el-la
pae-on
pa-gan
  pa-gan-ism
page
  paged
  pag-ing
pag-eant
  pag-ent-ry
page boy
pag-i-nal
pag-i-nate
  pag-i-nat-ed
  pag-i-nat-ing
pa-go-da
paid
pail
pail-lette
pain
  pain-ful
  pain-less
pain-kil-ler
pains-tak-ing
  pains-tak-ing-ly
paint
paint-brush
painted bunting
painted cup
painted lady
painted trillium
paint-er
pair
paired--associate
learning
pair of compassed
pair of virginals
pair production

pai-sa
pais-ley
pa-ja-mas
pal-ace
pal-a-din
pa-laes-tra
pal-at-a-ble
  pal-at-a-bil-i-ty
  pal-at-a-bly
pal-ate
pa-la-tial
  pa-la-tial-ly
pal-a-tiner
  pa-lat-i-nate
pa-lav-er
pale
pa-le-on-tol-o-gy
  pa-le-on-to-log-ic
  pa-le-on-to-log-i-cal
pal-ette
pal-imp-sest
pal-in-drome
pal-ing
pal-i-sade
  pal-i-sad-ed
  pal-i-sad-ing
pal-la-di-um
pall-bear-er
pal-let
pal-li-ate
  pal-li-at-ed
  pal-li-at-ing
  pal-li-a-tion
pal-lid
pal-lor
palm
  pal-ma-ceous
pal-mar
pal-mate
  pal-mate-ly
palm-er
palm-er-worm
pal-met-to
palm-ist
palm-is-try
  palm-ist
pal-mi-tate
pal-mit-ic-acid

palm off
palm oil
palmy
  palm-i-er
  palm-i-est
pal-o-mi-no
  pal-o-mi-nos
palp
pal-pa-ble
  pal-pa-bil-i-ty
  pal-pa-bly
pal-pal
pal-pate
  pal-pat-ed
  pal-pat-ing
pal-sy
  pal-sied
  pal-sy-ing
pal-ter
  pal-ter-er
pal-try
  pal-tri-er
  pal-tri-est
pam-pas
  pam-pe-an
pam-per
  pam-per-er
pam-phlet
pan
  panned
  pan-ning
pan-a-ce-a
  pan-a-ce-an
pa-nache
pan-cake
pan-cre-as
  pan-cre-at-ic
pan-dem-ic
pan-de-mo-ni-um
pan-der
pan-el
  pan-eled
  pan-el-ing
pan-el-ist
pang
pan-ic
  pan-icked
  pan-ick-ing

pan-nier
  pan-ier
pan-o-ply
  pan-o-plies
  pan-o-plied
pan-ora-ma
  pan-oram-ic
  pan-oram-i-cal-ly
pan-sy
  pan-sies
pan-ta-loon
pan-the-ism
  pan-the-is-tic
pan-the-on
pan-ther
pan-ties
pan-to-mime
  pan-to-mimed
pan-try
  pan-tries
pant-suit
pant-y-hose
pa-pa
pa-pa-cy
  pa-pa-cies
pa-pal
pa-per
  pa-per-er
  pa-pery
  pa-per-back
pa-pil-la
  pa-pil-pae
pa-poose
pap-ri-ka
pa-py-rus
par-a-ble
para-chute
  para-chut-ed
  para-chut-ing
  para-chut-ist
pa-rade
  pa-rad-ed
  pa-rad-ing
par-a-digm
  par-a-dig-mat-ic
par-a-dise
  par-a-di-si-a-cal
par-a-dox

par-a-dox-i-cal
par-af-fin
par-a-gon
par-a-graph
  par-a-graph-er
par-a-keet
par-al-lax
  par-al-al-lac-tic
par-al-lel
  par-al-leled
  par-al-lel-ing
  par-al-lel-o-gram
pa-ral-y-sis
  pa-ral-y-ses
par-a-lyt-ic
par-a-lyze
  par-a-lyzed
  par-a-lyz-ing
par-a-me-cium
par-a-med-ic
pa-ram-e-ter
par-a-mount
  par-a-mount-cy
  par-a-mount-ly
par-amour
para-noia
  para-noid
par-a-pet
par-a-pher-nal-ia
para-phrase
  para-phrased
  para-phras-ing
para-ple-gia
  para-ple-gic
para-psy-chol-o-gy
par-a-site
  par-a-sit-ic
para-sol
par-a-sym-pa-thet-ic
para-thi-on
para-troop-er
para-ty-phoid
par-boil
par-cel
  par-celed
  par-cel-ing
parch-ment
par-don

par-don-a-ble
par-don-a-bly
pare
  pared
  par-ing
par-e-gor-ic
par-ent
  pa-ren-tal
par-ent-age
pa-ren-the-sis
pa-re-sis
  pa-ret-ic
par-fait
pa-ri-ah
par-i-mu-tu-el
par-ish
  pa-rish-ion-er
par-i-ty
par-ka
par-lance
par-lay
  par-lay-ed
  par-lay-ing
par-ley
  par-leyed
  par-ley-ing
par-lia-ment
par-lia-men-tar-ian
par-lia-men-ta-ry
par-lor
pa-ro-chi-al
par-o-dy
  par-o-dies
  par-o-died
pa-role
  pa-roled
par-ot-id
par-ox-ysm
  par-ox-ys-mal
par-quet
  par-queted
  par-quet-ing
par-quet-ry
par-rot
  par-rot-like
  par-roty
par-ry
  par-ried

par-ry-ing
parse
par-si-mo-ny
  par-si-mo-ni-ous
  par-si-mo-ni-ous-ly
pars-ley
pars-nip
par-son-age
par-take
  par-took
  par-tak-en
part-ed
par-the-no-gen-e-sis
par-tial
  par-tial-ly
par-tial-i-ty
  par-tial-i-ties
par-tic-i-pant
par-tic-i-pate
  par-tic-i-pat-ed
  par-tic-i-pat-ing
par-ti-cip-i-al
par-ti-ci-ple
par-ti-cle
par-ti--col-ored
par-tic-u-lar
  par-tic-u-lar-ly
  par-tic-u-lar-i-ties
  par-tic-u-lar-ize
  par-tic-u-lar-ized
  par-tic-u-lar-iz-ing
par-tic-u-late
  part-ing
par-ti-san
  par-ti-san-ship
par-tite
par-ti-tion
par-ti-tive
part-ly
part-ner
  part-ner-ship
par-tridge
  par-tridg-es
part--time
par-tu-ri-ent
par-tu-ri-tion
par-ty
  par-ties

par-ve-nu
pas-chal
pa-sha
pass-able
pass-ably
pas-sen-ger
pass-er-by
  pass-ers-by
pass-ing
pas-sion
  pas-sion-ies
pas-sion-ate
  pas-sion-ate-ly
pas-sive
pas-ta
paste
  pas-ted
  pas-ting
paste-board
pas-tel
pas-teur-ize
  pas-teur-ized
  pas-teur-iz-ing
  pas-teur-i-za-tion
pas-tille
pas-time
pas-tor
pas-to-ral
  pas-to-ral-ly
pas-tor-ate
pas-tra-mi
past-ry
  pas-tries
pas-ture
pas-ty
  past-i-er
  past-i-est
patch-work
patchy
  patch-i-er
  patch-i-est
pat-ent
  pa-ten-cy
  pat-ent-ly
pat-en-tee
pat-er-nal
  pat-er-nal-ly
pa-ter-nal-ism

pa-ter-ni-ty
pa-thet-ic
path-find-er
pa-thol-o-gy
pa-thos
pa-tience
pa-tient
  pa-tient-ly
pat-i-na
pa-tio
  pa-tios
pa-tri-arch
pa-tri-ar-chy
  pa-tri-ar-chies
pa-tri-cian
pat-ri-mo-ny
  pat-ri-mo-nies
pa-tri-ot
  pa-tri-ot-ic
  pa-tri-ot-ism
pa-trol
  pa-trolled
  pa-trol-ling
pa-trol-man
  pa-trol-men
pa-tron
  pa-tron-ess
pa-tron-age
pa-tron-ize
  pa-tron-ized
  pa-tron-iz-ing
  pa-tron-iz-ing-ly
pat-ro-nym-ic
pat-sy
  pat-sies
pat-ter
pat-tern
  pat-terned
pat-ty
  pat-ties
pau-ci-ty
paunch
pau-per
  pau-per-ism
pause
  paused
  paus-ing
pa-vil-ion

pawn
  pawn-er
pawn-bro-ker
pay-a-ble
pay-ment
pay-off
peace
peace-able
  peace-ably
peace-ful
  peace-ful-ly
peach
pea-cock
peak-ed
pea-nut
pearl
  pear-ly
peas-ant
  peas-ant-ly
peaty
peb-ble
pe-can
pec-ca-dil-lo
  pec-ca-dil-loes
pec-ca-dil-los
peck-er
pec-tin
pec-to-ral
pec-u-late
  pec-u-lat-ed
  pec-u-lat-ing
pe-cu-liar
  pe-cu-liar-ly
  pe-cu-li-ar-i-ty
  pe-cu-li-ar-i-ties
pe-cu-ni-ary
ped-a-go-gue
ped-a-go-gy
ped-al
  ped-aled
  ped-al-ing
ped-ant
  pe-dan-tic
  pe-dan-ti-cal-ly
  ped-ant-ry
ped-dle
ped-es-tal
pe-des-tri-an

pe-des-tri-an-ism
pe-di-at-ric
  pe-di-at-rics
pe-di-a-tri-cian
  pe-di-at-rist
ped-i-cure
  ped-i-cur-ist
ped-i-gree
  ped-i-greed
ped-i-ment
  ped-i-men-tal
  ped-i-ment-ed
pe-dom-e-ter
peep-hole
peer
peer-less
  peer-less-ly
peeve
  peeved
peev-ing
pee-vish
  pee-vish-ly
pee-wee
pe-jo-ra-tive
  pe-jo-ra-tive-ly
pe-koe
pel-let
pell--mell
pel-lu-cid
  pel-lu-cid-i-ty
  pel-lu-cid-ly
pelt-er
  pelt-ry
pel-vis
  pel-vis-es
  pel-ves
  pel-vic
pem-mi-can
  pem-i-can
pe-nal
pe-nal-ize
  pe-nal-ized
  pe-nal-iz-ing
pen-al-ty
  pen-al-ties
pen-ance
pen-chant
pen-cil

pend-ant
pend-ent
  pend-en-cy
  pend-ent-ly
pend-ing
pen-du-lous
  pen-du-lous-ly
pen-du-lum
pen-a-tra-ble
  pen-a-tra-bil-i-ty
  pen-a-tra-bly
pen-e-trate
  pen-e-trat-ed
  pen-e-trat-ing
pen-e-tra-tion
pen-i-cil-lin
pen-in-su-la
  pen-in-su-lar
pe-nis
pen-i-tent
  pen-i-tence
  pen-i-ten-tial
pen-i-ten-tia-ry
  pen-i-ten-tia-ries
pen-knife
  pen-knives
pen-man-ship
pen-nant
pen-ni-less
pen-non
pen-ny
  pen-nies
pen-ny an-te
pe-nol-o-gy
  pe-no-log-i-cal
  pe-nol-o-gist
pen-sion
pen-sive
  pen-sive-ly
pen-ta-gon
  pen-tag-o-nal
  pen-tag-o-nal-ly
pen-tam-e-ter
pen-tath-lon
pent-up
pe-nult
  pe-nul-ti-ma
  pe-nul-ti-mate

pe-num-bra
  pe-num-bras
  pe-num-brae
  pe-num-bral
pe-nu-ri-ous
  pe-nu-ri-ous-ly
pen-u-ry
pe-on
  pe-on-age
pe-o-ny
  pe-on-ies
peo-ple
pep
  pepped
  pep-ping
pep-per
pep-pery
pep-py
  pep-pi-er
  pep-pi-est
pep-sin
pep-tic
per-am-bu-late
per-am-bu-la-tor
per an-num
per-cale
per cap-i-ta
per-ceive
  per-ceived
  per-ceiv-ing
  per-ceiv-a-ble
per-cent
  per-cent-age
per-cen-tile
per-cep-ti-ble
  per-cep-ti-bil-i-ty
  per-cep-ti-bly
per-cep-tion
  per-cep-tion-al
  per-cep-tu-al
  per-cep-tu-al-ly
perch
per-co-late
  per-co-lat-ed
  per-co-lat-ing
  per-co-la-tion
per-co-la-tor
per-cus-sion

per-cus-sion-ist
per di-em
per-di-tion
per-e-gri-nate
pe-remp-to-ry
  pe-remp-to-ri-ly
pe-ren-ni-al
  pe-ren-ni-al-ly
per-fec-tion
  per-fec-tion-ist
per-fect-ly
per-fi-dy
  per-fid-i-ous
  per-fid-i-ous-ly
per-fo-rate
  per-fo-rat-ed
per-force
per-form
  per-form-a-ble
  per-form-er
per-for-mance
per-fume
  per-fumed
per-func-to-ry
  per-func-to-ri-ly
per-haps
per-i-gee
  per-i-ge-al
  per-i-ge-an
peri-he-li-on
  peri-he-lia
per-il
  per-il-ous
  per-il-ous-ly
pe-rim-e-ter
  per-i-met-ic
  per-i-met-ri-cal
pe-ri-od
pe-ri-od-ic
  pe-ri-o-dic-i-ty
pe-ri-od-i-cal
  pe-ri-od-i-cal-ly
pe-riph-ery
  pe-riph-er-ies
  pe-riph-er-al
  pe-riph-er-al-ly
per-i-phrase
peri-scope

peri-scopic
peri-scop-i-cal
per-ish
per-ish-able
  per-ish-abil-i-ty
  per-ish-ably
peri-stal-sis
  peri-stal-ses
  peri-style
peri-to-ne-um
  peri-to-ne-ums
  peri-to-nea
  peri-to-ne-al
peri-to-ni-tis
peri-wig
peri-win-kle
per-jure
  per-jured
  per-jur-ing
  per-jur-er
per-ju-ry
  per-ju-ries
perky
  perk-i-er
  perk-i-est
per-ma-nent
per-me-able
  per-me-abil-i-ty
  per-me-ably
per-me-ate
  per-me-at-ed
  per-me-at-ing
  per-me-a-tion
  per-me-a-tive
per-mis-si-ble
  per-mis-si-bil-i-ty
  per-mis-si-bly
per-mis-sion
per-mis-sive
  per-mis-sive-ly
per-mit
  per-mit-ted
  per-mit-ting
  per-mit-ter
per-mu-ta-tion
per-ni-cious
  per-ni-cious-ly
per-ora-tion

per-ox-ide
  per-ox-id-ed
  per-ox-id-ing
per-pen-dic-u-lar
  per-pen-dic-u-lar-i-ty
  per-pen-dic-u-lar-ly
per-pe-trate
  per-pe-trat-ed
  per-pe-trat-ing
  per-pe-tra-tion
  per-pe-tra-tor
per-pet-u-al
  per-pet-u-al-ly
per-pet-u-ate
  per-pet-u-at-ed
  per-pet-u-at-ing
  per-pet-u-a-tion
  per-pet-ua-tor
per-pe-tu-ity
  per-pe-tu-ities
per-plex
  per-plexed
  per-plex-ing
  per-plex-ing-ly
  per-plex-ed-ly
  per-plex-i-ty
  per-plex-i-ties
per-qui-site
per-se-cute
  per-se-cut-ed
  per-se-cut-ing
  per-se-cu-tive
  per-se-cu-tor
  per-se-cu-tion
per-se-vere
  per-se-vered
  per-se-ver-ing
  per-sse-ver-ance
  per-se-ver-ing-ly
per-si-flage
per-sim-mon
per-sist
  per-sist-ence
  per-sis-ten-cy
per-sist-ent
  per-sist-ent-ly
per-snick-e-ty
per-son

per-son-able
per-son-age
per-son-al-i-ty
  per-son-al-i-ties
per-son-al-ize
  per-son-al-ized
  per-son-al-iz-ing
per-son-al-ly
per-so-na non gra-ta
per-son-ate
  per-son-at-ed
  per-son-at-ing
  per-son-a-tion
  per-son-a-tor
per-son-i-fy
  per-son-i-fied
  per-son-i-fy-ing
  per-son-i-fi-ca-tion
  per-son-i-fi-er
per-son-nel
per-spec-tive
  per-spec-tive-ly
per-spi-ca-cious
  per-spi-ca-cious-ly
  per-spi-cac-i-ty
per-spi-cu-i-ty
  per-spic-u-ous
  per-spic-u-ous-ly
per-spi-ra-tion
per-spire
  per-spired
  per-spiring
per-suade
  per-suad-ed
  per-suad-ing
  per-suad-a-ble
  per-suad-er
per-sua-sion
per-sua-sive
  per-sua-sive-ly
  per-sua-sive-ness
pert
  pert-ly
  pert-ness
per-tain
per-ti-na-cious
  per-ti-na-cious-ly
  per-ti-nac-i-ty

per-ti-nent
per-ti-nence
per-ti-nen-cy
per-ti-nent-ly
per-turb
per-turb-a-ble
per-tur-ba-tion
pe-ruke
pe-ruse
pe-rused
pe-rus-ing
pe-rus-al
pe-rus-er
per-vade
per-vad-ed
per-vad-ing
per-vad-er
per-va-sion
per-va-sive
per-va-sive-ly
per-verse
per-verse-ly
per-verse-ness
per-ver-si-ty
per-ver-sion
per-vert
per-vert-ed
per-vert-ed-ly
per-vert-er
per-vert-i-ble
per-vi-ous
per-vi-ous-ness
pes-ky
pes-ki-er
pes-ki-est
pesk-i-ly
pes-si-mism
pes-si-mist
pes-si-mist
pes-si-mis-tic
pes-si-mis-ti-cal-ly
pes-ter
pest-hole
pest-i-cide
pes-tif-er-ous
pes-tif-er-ous-ly
per-ti-lence
pes-ti-len-tial

pes-ti-lent
pes-ti-lent-ly
pes-tle
pes-tled
pes-tling
pet
pet-ted
pet-ting
pet-ter
pet-al
pet-aled
pet-cock
pe-ter
pet-i-ole
pe-tite
pe-tite-ness
pet-it four
pe-ti-tion
pe-ti-tion-ary
pe-ti-tion-er
pe-trel
pet-ri-fy
pet-ri-fied
pet-ri-fy-ing
pe-tri-fac-tion
pe-tro-chem-is-try
pe-tro-chem-i-cal
pet-rol
pet-ro-la-tum
pe-trol-eum
pet-ti-coat
pet-ti-fog
pet-ti-fogged
pet-ti-fog-ging
pet-ti-fog-ger
pet-ti-fog-gery
pet-tish
pet-tish-ly
pet-tish-ness
pet-ty
pet-ti-er
pet-ti-est
pet-ti-ly
pet-ti-ness
pet-u-lant
pet-u-lance
pet-u-lan-cy
pet-u-lant-ly

pe-tu-nia
pew-ter
pey-o-te
pey-o-tes
pha-lanx
pha-lanx-es
pha-lang-es
pal-lus
pal-li
pahl-lus-es
phal-lic
phan-tasm
phan-tas-ma
phan-tas-mal
phan-tas-mic
phan-tas-ma-go-ria
phan-tas-ma-go-ri-al
phan-tas-ma-gor-ic
phan-ta-sy
phan-ta-sies
phan-tom
phar-aoh
phar-ma-ceu-ti-cal
phar-ma-cue-tic
phar-ma-ceu-ti-cal-ly
phar-ma-cue-tics
phar-ma-cist
phar-ma-col-o-gy
phar-ma-co-log-ic
phar-ma-co-log-i-ca
phar-ma-col-o-gist
phar-ma-co-poe-ia
phar-ma-co-poe-ial
phar-ma-cy
phar-ma-cies
phar-ynx
pha-ryn-ges
pha-ryn-ge-al
pha-ryn-gal
phase
phased
phas-ing
pha-sic
pheas-ant
phe-no-bar-bi-tal
phe-nol
phe-nol-ic
phe-nom-e-non

phe-nom-e-na
phe-nom-e-nons
phe-nom-e-nal
phe-nom-e-nal-ly
phi-al
phi-lan-der
phi-lan-der-er
phi-lan-thro-py
phi-lan-thro-pies
phil-an-throp-ic
phil-an-throp-i-cal
phi-lan-thro-pist
phi-late-ly
phil-a-tel-ic
phil-a-tel-i-cal
phi-lat-e-list
phil-har-mon-ic
phil-o-den-dron
phil-o-den-drons
phil-o-den-dra
phi-log-o-gy
phi-lol-o-gist
phi-lol-o-ger
phil-o-lo-gi-an
phil-o-log-i-cal
phil-o-log-ic
phil-o-log-i-cal-ly
phi-los-o-pher
phil-o-soph-i-cal
phil-o-soph-ic
phil-o-soph-i-cal-ly
phi-los-o-phize
phi-los-o-phized
phi-los-o-phiz-ing
phi-los-o-phiz-er
phi-los-o-phy
phi-los-o-phies
phil-ter
phil-tered
phil-ter-ing
phle-bi-tis
phle-bit-ic
phle-bot-o-my
phle-bot-o-mist
phlegm
phleg-mat-ic
phleg-mat-i-cal
phleg-mat-i-cal-ly

phlox
pho-bia
pho-bic
phoe-be
phoe-nix
phone
phoned
phon-ing
pho-neme
pho-ne-mic
pho-net-ic
pho-net-ics
pho-net-i-cal
pho-net-i-cal-ly
phon-ic
phon-ics
pho-no-graph
pho-no-graph-ic
pho-no-graph-i-cal-ly
pho-nol-o-gy
pho-nol-o-gies
pho-no-log-ic
pho-no-log-i-cal
pho-no-log-i-cal-ly
pho-nol-o-gist
pho-ny
pho-ni-er
pho-ni-est
pho-nies
pho-ni-ness
phos-phate
phos-pho-res-cence
phos-pho-resce
phos-pho-resced
phos-pho-resc-ing
phos-pho-res-cent
phos-pho-res-cent-ly
phos-pho-rus
pho-to
pho-tos
pho-to-copy
pho-to-cop-ies
pho-to-cop-ied
pho-to-cop-y-ing
pho-to-e-lec-tric
pho-to-en-grav-ing
pho-to-en-grave
pho-to-en-graved

pho-to-en-grav-er
pho-to-flash
pho-to-gen-ic
pho-to-graph
pho-to-graph-er
pho-tog-ra-phy
pho-to-graph-ic
pho-to-graph-i-cal
pho-to-graph-i-cal-ly
pho-to-gra-vure
pho-to--off-set
pho-to-stat
pho-to-stat-ed
pho-to-stat-ing
pho-to-stat-ic
pho-to-syn-the-sis
phrase
phrased
phras-ing
phras-al
phrase-ol-o-gy
phre-net-ic
phre-nol-o-gy
phre-nol-o-gist
phy-lac-tery
phy-lac-ter-ies
phy-log-e-ny
phy-lo-gen-e-sis
phy-lo-ge-net-ic
phy-lo-gen-ic
phy-log-e-nist
phy-lu
phys-ic
phys-icked
phys-ick-ing
phys-i-cal
phys-i-cal-ly
phy-si-cian
phys-ics
phys-i-cist
phys-i-og-no-my
phys-i-og-no-mies
phys-i-og-nom-ic
phys-i-og-nom-i-cal
phys-i-og-no-mist
phys-i-og-ra-phy
phys-i-o-graph-ic
phys-i-o-graph-i-cal

phys-i-ol-o-gy
  phys-i-o-log-ic
  phys-i-o-log-i-cal
  phys-i-o-log-i-cal-ly
  phys-i-ol-o-gist
phys-i-o-ther-a-py
phy-sique
pi-a-nis-si-mo
pi-an-ist
pi-ano
  pia-nos
pi-ano-forte
pi-az-za
pi-ca
pic-a-dor
pic-a-resque
pic-a-yune
  pic-a-yun-ish
pic-ca-lil-li
pic-co-lo
  pic-co-los
  pic-co-lo-list
pick-ax
picked
pick-er-el
pick-et
  pick-et-er
pick-ing
pick-le
  pick-led
  pick-ling
pick-pock-et
pick-up
picky
  pick-i-er
  pick-i-est
pic-nic
  pic-nicked
  pic-nick-ing
  pic-nick-er
pic-to-ri-al
  pic-to-ri-al-ly
pic-ture
  pic-tured
  pic-tur-ing
pic-tur-esque
  pic-tur-esque-ly
pid-dle

pid-dled
pid-dling
pid-gin
pie-bald
piece
  piec-er
piece-meal
piece-work
  piece-worker
pied
pier
pierce
  pierc-ed
  pierc-ing
pierc-ing-ly
pi-etism
  pi-etis-tic
  pi-etis-ti-cal
pi-ety
  pi-eties
pif-fle
pig
  pigged
  pig-ging
pi-geon
pe-geon-hole
  pi-geon-holed
  pi-geon-hol-ing
pi-geon--toed
pig-gish
  pig-ish-ly
  pig-gis-ness
pig-head-ed
  pig-head-ed-ly
  pig-head-ed-ness
pig-ment
  pig-men-tary
  pig-men-ta-tion
pig-pen
pig-skin
pig-sty
  pig-sties
pig-tail
pike
  piked
  pik-ing
pik-er
pi-las-ter

pil-chard
pile
  piled
  pil-ing
pil-fer
  pil-fer-age
  pil-fer-er
pil-grim
pil-grim-age
  pil-grim-aged
  pil-grim-ag-ing
pil-lage
  pil-laged
  pil-lag-ing
  pil-lag-er
pil-lar
pill-box
pil-lion
pil-lo-ry
  pil-lo-ries
  pil-lo-ry-ing
pil-low
pil-low-case
pi-lot
  pi-lot-age
  pi-lot-less
pi-lot-house
pi-men-to
  pi-men-tos
pim-ple
  pim-pled
  pim-ply
pin
  pinned
  pin-ning
pin-afore
pince-nez
pin-cers
pinch
  pinch-er
pinch-beck
pin-cush-ion
pin-dling
pine
  pine-like
  piney
  pin-ing
pi-ne-al

pine-ap-ple
pin-feath-er
  pin-feath-ered
  pin-feath-ery
pin-fold
pin-head
  pin-head-ed
pin-hole
pin-ion
pink-eye
pink-ie
pinko
  pink-os
  pink-oes
pin-na
  pin-nas
  pin-nae
  pin-nal
pin-na-cle
  pin-na-cled
  pin-na-cling
pi-nate
  pin-nate-ly
  pin-na-tion
pi-noch-le
  pi-noc-le
pin-point
pin-prick
pin-set-ter
pin-tail
  pin-tailed
pin-tle
pin-to
  pin-tos
pin-up
pin-wheel
pin-worm
pi-o-neer
pi-ous
  pi-ous-ly
  pi-ous-ness
pip
  pipped
  pip-ping
pipe-line
  pipe-lined
  pipe-lin-ing
pip-er

pip-ing
pip-it
pip-pin
pip-squek
pi-quant
  pi-quan-cy
  pi-quant-ly
pique
  piqued
  pi-quing
pi-ra-cy
  pi-ra-cies
pi-ra-nha
pi-rate
  pi-rat-ed
  pi-rat-ing
  pi-rat-i-cal
  pi-rat-i-cal-ly
pi-roque
pir-ou-ette
  pir-ou-et-ted
  pir-ou-et-ting
pi-sci-cul-ture
pis-ta-chio
  pis-ta-chi-os
pis-til
pis-til-late
pis-tol
  pis-toled
  pis-tol-ing
pis-ton
pit
  pit-ted
  pit-ting
pitch--blake
pitch-blend
pitch-er
pitch-fork
pitchy
  pitch-i-er
  pitch-i-est
pit-e-ous
  pit-e-ous-ly
pit-fall
pith
  pith-i-er
  pith-i-est
  pith-i-ly

piti-a-ble
  piti-anle-ness
  piti-a-bly
piti-ful
  piti-ful-ly
  piti-ful-ness
piti-less
  piti-less-ly
pit-man
  pit-men
pit-tance
pi-tu--tar-ies
pity
  pit-ies
  pit-ied
  pit-y-ing
  pit-y-ing-ly
piv-ot
  piv-ot-al
  piv-ot-al-ly
pix-i-lat-ed
pixy
  pix-ie
  pix-ies
piz-za
piz-ze-ria
piz-zi-ca-to
place-a-ble
  plac-a-bil-i-ty
  plac-a-bly
plac-ard
pla-cate
  pla-cat-ed
  pla-cat-ing
  pla-ca-tion
  pla-ca-tive
  pla-ca-to-ry
place
  placed
  plac-ing
pla-ce-bo
  pla-ce-bos
  pla-ce-boes
place-ment
pla-cen-ta
  pla-cen-tas
  pla-cen-tae
  pla-cen-tal

plac-er
plac-id
  pla-cid-i-ty
  plac-id-ness
pla-gal
pla-gia-rism
  pla-gia-rized
  pla-gia-riz-ing
  pla-gia-riz-er
pla-gia-ry
  pla-gia-ries
plaque
  plaqued
  pla-quing
  pla-quer
pla-guy
  pla-guey
  pla-gui-ly
plaid
plain
  plain-ly
  plain-ness
plain-song
plain-spo-ken
plain-tiff
plain-tive
  plain-tive-ly
plait
  plait-ing
plan
  planned
  plan-ning
  plan-less
  plan-ner
plane
  planed
  plan-ing
plan-er
plan-et
plan-e-tar-i-um
  plan-e-tar-i-ums
  plan-e-tar-ia
plan-e-tary
plan-e-toid
plan-ish
  plan-ish-er
plank-ing
plank-ton

plank-ton-ic
plant
  plant-able
  plant-like
plan-tain
plan-ta-tion
plant-er
plaque
plasm
plas-ma
  plas-mic
  plas-mat-ic
plas-ter
  plas-ter-er
  plas-ter-ing
  plas-ter-work
plas-ter-board
plas-tered
plas-tic
  plas-ti-cal-ly
  plas-tic-i-ty
  plas-ti-ciz-er
plat
  plat-ted
  plat-ting
plate
  plat-ed
  plat-ing
  plat-er
pla-teau
  pla-teaus
  pla-teaux
plate-ful
  plate-fuls
plate-let
plat-form
plat-i-num
plat-i-tude
  plat-i-tu-di-nal
  plat-i-tu-di-nous
plat-i-tu-di-nize
  plat-i-tu-di-nized
  plat-i-tu-di-niz-ing
pla-ton-ic
  pla-ton-i-cal-ly
pla-toon
plat-ter
platy-pus

platy-pus-es
platy-pi
plau-dut
plau-si-ble
  plau-si-bil-i-ty
  plau-si-bly
play-act
  play-act-ing
play-back
play-bill
play-boy
play-er
play-ful
  play-ful-ly
  play-ful-ness
play-go-er
play-ground
play-house
  play-hous-es
play-let
play-mate
play--off
play-pen
play-thing
play-time
play-wright
pla-za
plea
plead
  plead-ed
  plead-ing
  plead-a-ble
  plead-er
pleas-ant
  pleas-ant-ly
  pleas-ant-ness
pleas-ant-ry
  pleas-an-trioes
please
  pleased
  pleas-ing
  pleas-ing-ly
  pleas-ing-ness
plea-sur-a-ble
  plea-sur-able-ness
  plea-sur-ably
pleas-ure
pleat

pleat-ed
pleat-er
plebe
ple-be-ian
pleb-i-scite
pledge
  pledged
  pledg-ing
  pledg-ee
  pledg-er
ple-na-ry
pleni-po-ten-tia-ry
  pleni-po-ten-tia-ries
plen-i-tude
plen-te-ous
  plen-te-ous-ly
plen-ti-ful
  plen-ti-ful-ly
plen-ty
pleth-o-ra
  ple-thor-ic
pleu-ra
  pleu-rae
  pleu-ral
pleu-ri-sy
  pleu-rit-ic
plex-us
  plex-us-es
pli-able
  pli-a-bil-i-ty
  pli-a-ble-ness
  pli-a-bly
pli-ant
  pli-an-cy
  pli-ant-ness
  pli-ant-ly
pli-ca-tion
pli-ers
plight
plink
plod
  plod-ded
  plod-ding
  plod-der
plop
  plopped
  plop-ping
plot

plot-ted
plot-ting
plot-ter
plow
plow-a-ble
plow-er
plow-man
plow-share
pluck
pluck-er
plucky
pluck-i-er
pluck-i-est
pluck-i-ly
pluck-i-ness
plug
plugged
plug-ging
plug-ger
plum-age
plumb-er
plumb-ing
plume
plumed
plum-ing
plume-like
plumy
plum-i-er
plum-i-est
plum-met
plump
plump-er
plump-ly
plump-ness
plun-der
plun-der-er
plun-der-ous
plunge
plunged
plung-ing
plung-er
plunk-er
plu-ral
plu-ral-ly
plu-ral-ize
plu-ral-ized
plu-ral-iz-ing
plu-ral-ism

plu-ral-ist
plu-ral-is-tic
plu-ral-i-ty
plu-ral-i-ties
plush
plush-i-ness
plushy
plush-i-er
plush-i-est
plu-toc-ra-cy
plu-tac-ra-cies
plu-ta-crat
plu-to-cart-ic
plu-to-ni-um
plu-vi-al
ply
plied
ply-ing
ply-wood
pneu-mat-ic
pneu-mat-i-cal-ly
pneu-mat-ics
pneu-mo-nia
pneu-mon-ic
poach
poach-er
pock-et
pock-et-book
pock-et-ful
pock-et-knife
pock-et-knives
pock-mark
pock-marked
pod
pod-ded
pod-ding
pod-like
podgy
podg-i-er
podg-i-est
po-di-trist
po-di-a-try
po-di-um
po-dia
po-di-ums
po-esy
po-esies
po-et

po-et-ess
po-et-ize
  po-et-ized
  po-et-iz-ing
  po-et-iz-er
po-et lau-re-ate
  po-ets lau-re-ate
po-et-ry
po-go
po-grom
poi-gnant
  poi-gnan-cy
  poi-gnant-ly
poin-set-tia
point--blank
point-ed
  point-ed-ly
  point-ed-ness
point-er
poin-til-lism
  poin-til-list
point-less
poise
  poised
  pois-ing
poi-son
  poi-son-er
  poi-son-ing
  poi-son-ous
poi-son--pen
poke
  poked
  pok-ing
pok-er
poky
  pok-i-er
  pok-i-est
  pok-i-ly
  pok-i-ness
po-lar
po-lar-i-ty
  po-lar-i-ties
po-lar-i-za-tion
po-lar-ize
  po-lar-ized
  po-lar-iz-ing
  po-lar-iz-a-ble
  po-lar-iz-er

pole
  poled
  pol-ing
  pole-less
pole-cat
po-lem-ic
  po-lem-i-cal
  po-lem-i-cal-ry
  po-lem-i-cist
po-lem-ics
pole-star
po-lice
  po-liced
  po-lic-ing
pol-i-cy
  pol-i-cies
pol-i-o-my-e-li-tis
pol-ish
  pol-ish-er
po-lite
  po-lite-ly
  po-lite-ness
pol-i-tic
po-lit-i-cal
  po-lit-i-cal-ly
po-lit-i-ti-cian
po-lit-i-cize
  po-lit-i-cized
  po-lit-i-ciz-ing
pol-i-tick
  pol-i-tick-er
pol-i-tics
pol-i-ty
  pol-i-ties
pol-ka
  pol-kaed
  pol-ka-ing
poll
  poll-ee
  poll-er
pol-len
pol-li-nate
  pol-li-nat-ed
  pol-li-nat-ing
  pol-li-na-tion
  pol-li-na-tor
pol-li-wog
poll-ster

pol-lu-tant
pol-lute
  pol-lut-ed
  pol-lut-ing
  pol-lu-ter
  pol-lu-tion
po-lo
  po-lo-ist
pol-o-naise
po-lo-ni-um
pol-ter-geist
poly-an-dry
  poly-an-drous
poly-chro-mat-ic
poly-chrome
poly-es-ter
poly-eth-yl-ene
polyg-a-mist
polyg-a-my
  polyg-a-mous
poly-glot
poly-gon
  polyg-o-nal
  polyg-o-nal-ly
poly-graph
  poly-graph-ic
po-lyg-y-ny
  po-lyg-y-nous
poly-he-dron
  poly-he-drons
  poly-he-dra
  poly-he-dral
poly-mer
po-ly-mer-ize
  po-ly-mer-ized
  po-ly-mer-iz-ing
  po-lym-er-ism
  po-lym-er-i-za-tion
pol-y-mor-phism
  pol-y-mor-phic
  pol-y-mor-phous
poly-no-mi-al
pol-yp
poly-phon-ic
  po-lyph-ony
poly-sty-rene
poly-syl-lab-ic
  poly-syl-lab-i-cal-ly

poly-syl-la-ble
poly-tech-nic
poly-the-ism
  poly-the-ist
  poly-the-is-tic
  poly-the-is-ti-cal
poly-un-sat-u-rat-ed
pom-ace
po-made
  po-mad-ed
  po-mad-ing
pome-gran-ate
pom-mel
  pom-meled
  pom-mel-ing
pom-pa-dour
pom-pon
pomp-ous
  pom-pos-i-ty
  pom-pous-ly
pon-cho
pon-der
  pon-der-a-ble
  pon-der-er
pon-der-ous
  pon-der-ous-ly
  pon-der-ou-ness
pon-iard
pon-tiff
pon-tif-i-cal
  pon-tif-i-cal-ly
pon-tif-i-cate
  pon-tif-i-cat-ed
  pon-tif-i-cat-ing
pon-toon
po-ny
  po-nies
  po-nied
  po-ny-ing
po-ny-tail
poo-dle
pool-room
poor
  poor-ish
  poor-ly
pop-corn
pop-ery
  pop-ish

pop-eyed
pop-gun
pop-in-jay
pop-lar
pop-lin
pop-per
pop-py
  pop-pies
  pop-pied
pop-py-cock
pop-u-lace
pop-u-lar
  pop-u-lar-ly
pop-u-lar-i-ty
pop-u-lar-ize
  pop-u-lar-ized
  pop-u-lar-iz-ing
  pop-u-lar-i-za-tion
  pop-u-lar-iz-er
pop-u-late
  pop-u-lat-ed
  pop-u-lat-ing
pop-u-la-tion
pop-u-lism
  pop-u-list
pop-u-lous
  pop-u-lous-ly
por-ce-lain
por-cine
por-cu-pine
pore
  pored
  por-ing
pork-er
por-nog-ra-phy
  por-nog-ra-pher
  por-no-graph-ic
  por-no-graph-i-cal-ly
po-rous
  po-rous-i-ty
  po-rous-ly
  po-rous-ness
por-poise
  por-pios-es
por-ridge
port-a-ble
  port-a-bil-i-ty
  port-a-bly

por-tage
  por-taged
  por-tag-ing
por-tal
por-tend
por-tent
  por-ten-tous
por-ter
por-ter-house
port-fo-lio
  port-fo-lios
port-hole
por-ti-co
  por-ti-coes
  por-ti-cos
por-tion
  por-tion-less
port-ly
  port-li-er
  port-li-est
por-trait
  por-trat-ist
  por-trai-ture
por-tray
  por-tray-er
por-tray-al
pose
  posed
  pos-ing
pos-er
po-suer
pos-it
po-si-tion
  po-si-tion-al
  po-si-tion-er
pos-i-tive
  pos-i-tive-ly
  pos-i-tive-ness
pos-i-tiv-ism
pos-i-tron
pos-se
pos-sess
  pos-ses-sor
pos-sessed
pos-ses-sion
pos-ses-sive
  pos-ses-sive-ly
  pos-ses-sive-ness

pos-si-bil-i-ty
pos-si-ble
pos-si-bly
pos-sum
post-age
post-box
post-date
  post-dat-ed
  post-dat-ing
post-er
pos-te-ri-or
  pos-te-ri-or-i-ty
pos-ter-i-ty
post-grad-u-ate
post-haste
post-hu-mous
  post-hu-mous-ly
post-lude
post-man
  post-men
post-mark
post-mas-ter
  post-mis-tress
post me-ri-di-em
post-mor-tem
post-na-sal
post-na-tal
  post-na-tal-ly
post-paid
post-par-tum
post-pone
  post-poned
  post-pon-ing
  post-pon-a-ble
  post-pone-ment
  post-pon-er
post-scipt
pos-tu-lant
pos-tu-late
  pos-tu-lat-ed
  pos-tu-lat-ing
  pos-tu-la-tion
  pos-tu-la-tor
pos-ture
  pos-tured
  pos-tur-ing
  pos-tur-al
  pos-tur-er

post-war
po-sy
  po-sies
pot
  pot-ted
  pot-ting
po-ta-ble
pot-ash
po-tas-si-um
po-ta-to
  po-ta-toes
pot-bel-ly
  pot-bel-lied
pot-boil-er
po-tent
  po-ten-cy
  po-tent-ly
po-ten-tate
po-ten-tial
  po-ten-ti-al-i-ty
  po-ten-tial-ly
pot-hole
po-tion
pot-luck
pot-pour-ri
pot-sherd
pot-tage
pot-ter
pot-tery
  pot-ter-ies
pot-ty
  pot-ties
pot-ty--chair
pouch
  pouched
  pouchy
  pouch-i-er
  pouch-i-est
poul-tice
  poul-ticed
  poul-tic-ing
poul-try
pounce
  pounced
  pounc-ing
pound-age
pound--fool-ish
pour

pour-a-ble
pour-er
pout
pov-er-ty
pov-er-ty--strick-en
pow-der
  pow-dery
pow-er
pow-er-boat
pow-er-ful
  pow-er-ful-ly
  pow-er-ful-ness
pow-er-house
pow-er-less
Pow-ha-tan
pow-wow
prac-ti-ca-ble
  prac-ti-ca-bil-i-ty
  prac-ti-ca-bly
prac-ti-cal
  prac-ti-cal-i-ty
  prac-ti-cal-ly
prac-tice
prac-ti-tio-ner
prae-di-al
pre-di-al
prag-mat-ic
  prag-mat-i-cal
  prag-mat-i-cal-ly
prag-ma-tism
  prag-ma-tist
  prag-ma-tis-tic
prai-rie
praise
  praised
  prais-ing
  prais-er
praise-wor-thy
  praise-wor-thi-ly
  praise-wor-thi-ness
pra-line
prance
  pranced
  pranc-ing
  pranc-er
prank
  prank-ish
  prank-ster

prate
  prat-ed
  prat-ing
  prat-er
  prat-ing-ly
prat-fall
prat-tle
  prat-tled
  prat-tling
  prat-tler
  prat-tling-ly
prawn
  prawn-er
pray-er
  pray-er-ful
preach
  prach-er
preach-ify
  preach-ified
  preach-ify-ing
preach-ment
preachy
  preach-i-er
  preach-i-est
pre-ad-o-les-cence
  pre-ad-o-les-cent
pre-am-ble
pre-ar-range
  pre-ar-ranged
  pre-ar-rang-ing
  pre-ar-range-ment
pre-as-signed
pre-can-cel
  pre-can-celed
  pre-can-cel-ing
  pre-can-cel-la-tion
pre-car-i-ous
  pre-car-i-ous-ly
  pre-car-i-ous-ness
pre-cau-tion
  pre-cau-tion-ary
pre-cede
  pre-ced-ed
  pre-ced-ing
prec-e-dence
prec-e-dent
pre-cept
pre-cep-tive

pre-cep-tor
  pre-cep-to-ri-al
pre-ces-sion
  pre-ces-sion-al
pre-cinct
pre-cious
  pre-ci-os-i-ty
  pre-cious-ness
prec-i-pice
  pre-cip-i-tous
pre-cip-i-tant
  pre-cip-i-tant-ly
pre-cip-i-tate
  pre-cip-i-tat-ed
  pre-cip-i-tat-ing
  pre-cip-i-ta-tive
  pre-cip-i-ta-tor
pre-cip-i-ta-tion
pre-cip-i-tous
  pre-cip-i-tous-ly
pre-cise
  pre-cise-ness
pre-ci-sion
  pre-ci-sion-ist
pre-clude
  pre-clud-ed
  pre-clud-ing
  pre-clu-sion
  pre-clu-sive
pre-co-cious
  pre-coc-cious-ly
  pre-coc-cious-ness
  pre-coc-i-ty
pre-cog-ni-tion
  pre-cog-ni-tive
pre-con-ceive
  pre-con-ciev-ed
  pre-con-ceiv-ing
  pre-con-cep-tion
pre-cook
pre-cur-sor
  pre-cur-so-ry
pre-date
pred-a-tor
pred-a-to-ry
  pred-a-to-ri-ly
pre-dawn
pre-de-ces-sor

pre-des-ti-nate
  pre-des-ti-nat-ed
  pre-des-ti-nat-ing
pre-des-ti-na-tion
pre-des-tine
  pre-des-tined
  pre-des-tin-ing
pre-de-ter-mine
  pre-de-ter-mined
  pre-de-ter-min-ing
  pre-de-ter-mi-na-tion
pred-i-ca-ble
  pred-i-ca-bil-i-ty
pre-dic-a-ment
pred-i-cate
  pred-i-cat-ed
  pred-i-cat-ing
  pred-i-ca-tion
  pred-i-ca-tive
pre-dict
  pre-dict-a-ble
  pre-dict-a-bly
  pre-dict-a-bil-i-ty
pre-dic-tion
  pre-dic-tive
pre-di-lec-tion
pre-dis-po-si-tion
  pre-dis-pose
  pre-dis-posed
  pre-dis-pos-ing
pre-dom-i-nant
  pre-dom-i-nance
  pre-dom-i-nan-cy
pre-dom-i-nate
  pre-dom-i-nat-ed
  pre-dom-i-nat-ing
  pre-dom-i-na-tion
pre-em-i-nent
  pre-em-i-nence
pre-empt
  pre-emp-tor
pre-emp-tion
  pre-emp-tive
preen-er
pre-ex-ist
  pre-ex-ist-ence
  pre-ex-ist-ent
pre-fab-ri-cate

pre-fab-ri-cat-ed
pre-fab-ri-cat-ing
pre-fab-ri-a-tion
pref-ace
pref-aced
pref-ac-ing
pref-a-to-ry
pre-fer
pre-ferred
pre-fer-ring
pre-fer-rer
pref-er-a-ble
pre-fer-a-bil-i-ty
pref-er-a-bly
pref-er-ence
pref-er-en-tial
pref-er-en-tial-ly
pre-fer-ment
pre-fix
pre-flight
pre-form
preg-n-able
preg-na-bil-i-ty
preg-nan-cy
preg-nan-cies
preg-nant
pre-heat
pre-hen-sile
pre-hen-sil-i-ty
pre-his-tor-ic
pre-his-to-ry
pre-judge
pre-judged
pre-judg-ing
pre-judg-er
pre-judge-ment
prej-u-dice
prej-u-diced
prej-u-dic-ing
prej-u-di-cial
prej-u-di-cial-ly
prel-ate
prel-ate-ship
prel-a-ture
pre-lim-i-nar-y
pre-lim-i-nar-ies
pre-lim-i-nar-i-ly
prel-ude

prel-uded
prel-ud-ing
pre-ma-ture
pre-na-tu-ri-ty
pre-med-i-cal
pre-med-i-tate
pre-med-i-tat-ed
pre-med-i-tat-ing
pre-med-i-tat-tor
pre-med-i-tat-ed-ly
pre-med-i-ta-tive
pre-med-i-ta-tion
pre-men-stru-al
pre-mier
pre-mier-ship
pre-miere
prem-ise
prem-ised
prem-is-ing
pre-mi-um
pre-mo-ni-tion
pre-mon-i-to-ry
pre-mon-i-to-ri-ly
pre-name
pre-na-tal
pre-na-tal-ly
pre-nom-i-nate
pre-no-tion
pren-tice
pre-oc-cu-pan-cy
pre-oc-cu-pa-tion
pre-oc-cu-py
pre-oc-cu-pied
pre-oc-cu-py-ing
pre-op-er-a-tive
pre-or-bit-al
pre-or-dain
pre-ovi-po-si-tion
pre-ovu-la-to-ry
prep
pre-pack-age
prep-a-ra-tion
pre-par-a-to-ry
pre-par-a-to-ri-ly
pre-pare
pre-pared
pre-par-ing
pre-par-er

pre-par-ed-ness
pre-pay
pre-paid
pre-pay-ing
pre-pay-ment
pre-plan
pre-planned
pre-plan-ning
pre-plant
prepn
pre-pon-der-ance
pre-pon-der-ant
pre-pon-der-ance
pre-pon-der-an-cy
pre-pon-der-ant-ly
pre-pon-der-ate
pre-pon-der-at-ed
pre-pon-der-at-ing
pre-pon-der-at-ing-ly
pre-pon-der-a-tion
prep-o-si-tion
prep-o-si-tion-al
pre-pos-i-tive
pre-pos-sess
pre-pos-sess-ing
pre-pos-sess-ing-ly
pre-pos-ter-ous
pre-po-ten-cy
pre-po-tent
prep-pie
pre-pran-di-al
pre-print
pre-pro-cess
pre-pro-fes-sion-al
pre-pro-gram
prep school
pre-pu-ber-al
pre-pu-ber-tal
pre-pu-bes-cence
pre-pub-li-ca-tion
pre-puce
pre-pu-tial
pre-punch
pre-re-cord
pre-reg-is-tra-tion
pre-reg-is-ter
pre-re-ui-site
pre-rog-a-tive

pres
presa
pres-age
  pres-aged
  pres-ag-ing
  pres-ag-er
pre-sanc-ti-fied
pres-by-ope
pres-by-ter
pres-by-ter-i-al
pres-by-ter-y
  pres-by-ter-ies
pre-school
pre-science
pre-scind
pre-score
pre-scribe
  pre-scribed
  pre-scrib-ing
  pre-scrib-er
pre-script
pre-scrip-tion
  pre-scrip-tive
prescription drug
pre-scrip-tive
pre-scrip-tive drug
pre-se-lect
pre-sell
pres-ence
presence chamber
presence of mind
pre-sent
  pre-sent-er
pres-ent
pre-sent-a-ble
  pre-sent-a-bil-i-ty
  pre-sent-a-ble-ness
  pre-sent-a-bly
pres-en-ta-tion
pres-ent-day
pres-ent-ly
pre-serv-a-tive
per-serve
  pre-served
  pre-serv-ing
  pre-serv-a-ble
  pres-er-va-tion
  pre-serv-er

pre-side
  pre-sid-ed
  pre-sid-ing
  pre-sid-er
pres-i-den-cy
  pres-i-den-cies
pres-i-dent
  pres-i-den-tial
press-board
press-ing
pres-sure
  pres-sured
  pres-sur-ing
pre-su-rize
  pres-su-rized
  pres-su-riz-ing
  pres-su-riz-er
  pres-sur-i-za-tion
press-work
pres-ti-dig-i-ta-tion
  pres-ti-dig-i-ta-tor
pres-tige
pres-tig-ious
pres-to
pe-sum-a-ble
  pre-sum-a-bly
pre-sume
  pre-sumed
  pre-sum-ing
  pre-sum-er
pre-sump-tion
pre-sump-tive
pre-sum-tu-ous
pre-sup-pose
  pre-sup-posed
  pre-sup-pos-ing
  pre-sup-po-si-tion
pre-tend
  pre-tend-ed
pre-tend-er
pre-tense
pre-ten-sion
pre-ten-tious
  pre-ten-tious-ness
pre-test
pre-text
pret-ti-fy
  pret-ti-fied

pret-ti-fy-ing
pret-ti-fi-ca-tion
pret-ty
  pret-ties
  pret-tied
  pret-ty-ing
  pret-ti-ly
  pret-ti-ness
  pret-ty-ish
pret-zel
pre-vail
pre-vail-ing
prev-a-lent
  prev-a-lence
pre-vent
  pre-vent-a-ble
  pre-vent-a-bil-i-ty
  pre-vent-er
pre-ven-tion
pre-view
pre-vi-ous
pre-war
prey
  prey-er
price-less
prick-er
prick-le
prick-ly
  prick-li-er
  prick-li-est
  prick-li-ness
pride
  prid-ed
  prid-ing
pride-ful
pri-er
priest
  priest-ess
  priest-hood
priest-ly
  priest-li-er
  priest-li-est
priest-li-ness
prig
  prig-gish
prim
  prim-mer
  prim-mest

primmed
prim-ming
prim-ness
pri-ma-cy
  pri-ma-cies
pri-ma don-na
  pri-ma don-nas
pri-mal
pri-ma-ri-ly
pri-ma-ry
  pri-mar-ies
pri-mate
prime
  primed
  prim-ing
prime me-rid-i-an
prim-er
pr-me-val
prim-i-tive
pri-mo-gen-i-tor
pri-mo-gen-i-ture
pri-mor-di-al
  pri-mor-di-al-ly
primp
prim-rose
prince-ly
  prince-li-er
  prince-li-est
prin-cess
prin-ci-pal
  prin-ci-pal-ly
prin-ci-pal-i-ty
  prin-ci-pal-i-ties
prin-ci-ple
prin-ci-pled
print-a-ble
print-ing
print-out
pri-or
  pri-or-ate
pri-or-ess
pri-or-i-ty
  pri-or-i-ties
pri-or-y
  pri-or-ies
prism
  pris-mat-ic
  pris-mat-i-cal-ly

pris-on
pris-on-er
pris-sy
  pris-si-er
  pris-si-est
  pris-si-ly
pris-tine
pri-va-cy
pri-vate
pri-va-tion
priv-et
priv-i-ledge *wrong!*
  priv-i-ledged
  priv-i-leg-ing
priv-y
  priv-ies
  priv-i-ly
prize
  prized
prize-fight
prob-a-bil-i-ty
  prob-a-bil-i-ties
prob-a-ble
  prob-a-bly
pro-bate
  pro-bat-ed
  pro-bat-ing
pro-ba-tion
  pro-ba-tion-al
  pro-ba-tion-ary
pro-na-tion-er
pro-ba-tive
probe
  probed
  prob-ing
  prob-er
prob-lem
prob-lem-at-ic
  pro-lem-at-i-cal
pro-bos-cis
  pro-bos-cis-es
  pro-bos-ci-des
pro-ce-dure
  pro-ce-dur-al
  pro-ce-dur-al-ly
pro-ceed
pro-ceed-ing
pro-ceeds

pro-ces-sion
pro-ces-sion-al
pro-claim
  pro-claim-er
proc-la-ma-tion
pro-cliv-i-ty
  pro-cliv-i-ties
pro-cras-ti-nate
  pro-cras-ti-nat-ed
  pro-cras-ti-nat-ing
  pro-cras-ti-na-tion
  pro-cras-ti-na-tor
pro-cre-ate
  pro-cre-at-ed
  pro-cre-at-ing
  pro-cre-a-tion
proc-tor
  proc-to-ri-al
proc-u-ra-tor
  proc-u-ra-to-ri-al
  proc-u-ra-tor-ship
pro-cure
  pro-cured
  pro-cur-ing
  pro-cure-ment
prod
  prod-ded
  prod-ding
  prod-dler
prod-i-gal
  prod-i-gal-i-ty
  prod-i-gal-ly
pro-di-gious
  pro-di-gious-ness
prod-i-gy
  prod-i-gies
pro-duce
  pro-duced
  pro-duc-ing
pro-duc-er
prod-uct
pro-duc-tion
pro-duc-tive
  pro-duc-tive-ness
  pro-duc-tiv-i-ty
pro-fane
  pro-faned
pro-fan-i-ty

pro-fess
  pro-fessed
  pro-fess-ed-ly
pro-fes-sion
pro-fes-sion-al
  pro-fes-sion-al-ism
pro-fes-sion-al-ize
  pro-fes-sion-al-ized
  pro-fes-sion-al-iz-ing
pro-fes-sor
  pro-fes-so-ri-al
  pro-fes-sor-ship
prof-fer
  prof-fer-er
pro-fi-cien-cy
pro-fi-cient
pro-file
  pro-filed
  pro-fil-ing
prof-it
  prof-it-less
prof-it-able
  prof-it-a-bil-i-ty
  prof-it-ably
prof-i-teer
prof-li-gate
  prof-li-ga-cy
pro-found
pro-fun-di-ty
  pro-fun-di-ties
pro-fuse
pro-fu-sion
pro-gen-i-tor
prog-e-ny
  prog-e-nies
pro-ges-ter-one
prog-no-sis
  prog-no-ses
  prog-nos-tic
prog-nos-ti-cate
  prog-nos-ti-cat-ed
  prog-nos-ti-cat-ing
  prog-nos-ti-ca-tion
  prog-nos-ti-ca-tive
  prog-nos-ti-ca-tor
pro-gram
prog-ress
pro-gres-sion

pro-gres-sive
  pro-gres-siv-ism
pro-hib-it
pro-hi-bi-tion
pro-hi-bi-tion-ist
pro-hib-i-tive
pro-ject
pro-jec-tile
pro-jec-tion
pro-jec-tion-ist
pro-jec-tive
  pro-jec-tive-ly
  pro-jec-tiv-i-ty
pro-jec-tor
pro-le-tar-i-at
  pro-le-tar-i-an
pro-lif-er-ate
  pro-lif-er-at-ed
pro-lif-ic
  pro-lif-i-ca-cy
pro-lix
  pro-lix-i-ty
pro-logue
  pro-logued
  pro-logu-ing
pro-long
  pro-lon-ga-tion
  pro-long-er
prom-e-nade
  prom-e-nad-ed
  prom-e-nad-ing
  prom-e-nad-er
prom-i-nence
prom-i-nent
  prom-i-nent-ly
pro-mis-cu-ity
  pro-mis-cu-i-ties
pro-mis-cu-ous
  pro-mis-cu-ous-ly
prom-ise
  prom-ised
  prom-is-ing
prom-is-so-ry
prom-on-to-ry
  prom-on-to-ries
pro-mote
  pro-mot-ed
  pro-mot-ing

pro-mot-a-ble
pro-mot-er
pro-mo-tion
  pro-mo-tive
prompt
  prompt-er
  prompt-ly
pro-mul-gate
  pro-mul-gat-ed
  pro-mul-ga-tion
prone
prong
pro-noun
pro-nounce
  pro-nounced
pro-nounce-ment
pron-to
pro-nun-ci-a-tion
proof
proof-read
prop
pro-pa-gan-da
pro-pa-gate
pro-pa-ga-tion
  pro-pa-ga-tion-al
pro-pane
pro-pel
  pro-pelled
  pro-pel-ling
pro-pel-lant
pro-pel-ler
pro-pen-si-ty
  pro-pen-si-ties
prop-er
proph-e-cy
  proph-e-cies
proph-e-sy
  proph-e-sied
  proph-e-sy-ing
proph-et
pro-phet-ic
  pro-phet-i-cal-ly
pro-phy-lax-is
pro-pin-qui-ty
pro-pi-ti-ate
  pro-pi-ti-at-ed
  pro-pi-ti-a-tion
pro-pi-tious

pro-pi-tious-ly
pro-po-nent
pro-por-tion
  pro-por-tion-a-ble
  pro-por-tion-a-bly
pro-por-tion-al
  pro-por-tion-al-i-ty
pro-por-tion-ate
  pro-por-tion-at-ed
  pro-por-tion-at-ing
pro-pos-al
pro-pose
  pro-posed
prop-o-si-tion
  prop-o-si-tion-al
pro-pound
  pro-pound-er
pro-pri-e-tary
  pro-pri-e-tar-ies
pro-pri-etor
  pro-pri-e-tor-ship
pro-pri-ety
pro-pul-sion
pro-pul-sive
pro-rate
  pro-rat-ed
pro-sa-ic
  pro-sa-i-cal-ly
pro-scribe
  pro-scribed
  pro-scrib-ing
  pro-scrib-er
pro-scrip-tion
  pro-srip-tive
prose
pros-e-cute
  pros-e-cute-a-ble
pros-e-cu-tion
pros-e-cu-tor
pros-pect
  pros-pec-tor
pro-spec-tive
pro-spec-tus
pros-per-i-ty
pros-per-ous
pros-tate
pros-the-sis
  pros-the-ses

pros-thet-ic
pros-thet-ics
pros-the-tis
prosth-odon-tics
prosth-odon-tist
pros-ti-tute
pros-trate
  pros-trat-ing
  pros-tra-tor
  pros-tra-tive
prosy
  pros-i-er
  pros-i-est
pro-tag-o-nist
pro-te-an
pro-tect
  pro-tect-ing
  pro-tec-tive
  pro-tec-tor
pro-tec-tion
pro-tec-tion-ism
  pro-tec-tion-ist
pro-tec-tor-ate
pro-tein
pro-test
prot-es-ta-tion
pro-tist
  pro-tis-tan
  pro-to-col
pro-ton
pro-to-plasm
  pro-to-plas-mic
pro-to-type
pro-to-typ-i-cal
pro-to-typ-ic
pro-to-typ-i-cal-ly
pro-to-zo-an
  pro-to-zo-ic
pro-tract
  pro-trac-tion
  pro-trac-tive
pro-trac-tile
pro-trac-tor
pro-trude
  pro-trud-ed
  pro-trud-ing
pro-tru-sion
pro-tru-sive

pro-tu-ber-ance
pro-tu-ber-ant
proud
  proud-ly
prov-erb
pro-ver-bi-al
  pro-ver-bi-al-ly
pro-vide
  pro-vid-ed
  pro-vid-ing
prov-i-dence
  prov-i-den-tial
prov-i-dent
prov-ince
pro-vin-cial
pro-vin-cial-ism
pro-vi-sion
  pro-vi-sion-er
pro-vi-sion-al
  pro-vi-sion-ary
prov-o-ca-tion
pro-voc-a-tive
  pro-voc-a-tive-ly
  pro-voc-a-tive-ness
pro-voke
  pro-voked
  pro-vok-ing
pro-vost
prow-ess
prowl
  prowl-er
prowl car
prox
prox-e-mics
prox-i-mal
prox-i-mate
  prox-i-mate-ly
prox-im-i-ty
prox-i-mo
proxy
  prox-ies
proxy marriage
prude
pru-dence
  pru-dent
  pru-den-tial
prud-ery
  prud-er-ies

prud-ish
pru-inose
prune
  pruned
  prun-ing
pru-nel-la
pru-ri-ent
  pru-ri-ence
  pru-ri-en-cy
psalm-book
psalm-ist
pseu-do
pseud-onym
  pseud-on-y-mous
pseu-do-preg-nan-cy
  pseu-do-preg-nant
pseu-do-sci-ence
  pseu-do-sci-en-tif-ic
pshaw
psil-o-cy-bin
pso-ri-a-sis
  pso-ri-at-ic
psych
  psyched
  psych-ing
psy-che-del-ic
psy-chi-a-trist
psy-chi-a-try
  psy-chi-at-ric
  psy-chi-at-ri-cal-ly
psy-chic
  psy-chi-cal
  psy-chi-cal-ly
psy-cho
psy-cho-anal-y-sis
  psy-cho-an-a-lyt-ic
  psy-cho-an-a-lyt-i-cal
psy-cho-an-a-lyst
  psy-cho-an-a-lyze
  psy-cho-an-a-lyzed
  psy-cho-an-a-lyz-ing
psy-cho-bi-ol-o-gy
  psy-cho-bi-o-log-ic
  psy-cho-bi-o-log-i-cal
psy-cho-dra-ma
psy-cho-dy-nam-ic
  psy-cho-dy-nam-ics
psy-cho-gen-e-sis

psy-cho-ge-net-ic
psy-cho-gen-ic
  psy-cho-gen-i-cal-ly
psy-cho-log-i-cal
  psy-cho-log-ic
  psy-cho-log-i-cal-ly
psy-chol-o-gist
psy-chol-o-gy
psy-cho-mo-tor
psy-cho-neu-ro-sis
  psy-cho-neu-rot-ic
psy-cho-path
psy-cho-pa-thol-o-gy
  psy-cho-path-o-log-ic
psy-chop-a-thy
  psy-cho-path-ic
  psy-cho-path-i-cal-ly
psy-cho-sis
  psy-cho-ses
  psy-chot-ic
  psy-chot-i-cal-ly
psy-cho-ther-a-py
  psy-cho-ther-a-pist
pto-maine
pu-ber-ty
pu-bes-cence
  pu-bes-cen-cy
  pu-bes-cent
pu-bic
pub-lic
  pub-lic-ly
pub-li-ca-tion
pub-li-cist
pub-li-ci-ty
pub-li-cize
  pub-li-cized
  pub-li-ciz-ing
pub-lish
  pub-lish-a-ble
pub-lish-er
puce
puck-er
pud-ding
pud-dle
  pud-dled
  pud-dling
pudgy
  pudg-i-er

  pudg-i-est
pueb-lo
  pueb-los
pu-er-ile
  pu-er-il-i-ty
puff
  puffy
puff-er
pu-gi-lism
  pu-gi-list
  pu-gi-lis-tic
pug-na-cious
  pug-nac-i-ty
pulke
  puked
  puk-ing
pull-back
pul-let
pul-ley
pul-mo-nary
pulp
pul-pit
pulp-wood
pul-sate
  pul-sat-ed
  pul-sat-ing
pul-sa-tion
pul-sa-tor
  pul-sa-to-ry
pulse
  pulsed
  puls-ing
pul-ver-ize
pu-ma
  pu-mas
pum-ice
  pu-mi-ceous
pum-mel
pump
  pump-a-ble
  pump-er
pum-per-nick-el
pump-kin
pun
  punned
  pun-ning
punch
  punch-er

punch--drunk
punchy
  punch-i-er
  punch-i-est
punc-tu-al
punc-tu-ate
  punc-tu-at-ed
  punc-tu-at-ing
  punc-tu-a-tor
punc-tu-a-tion
punc-ture
  punc-tured
  punc-tur-ing
pun-dit
pun-gent
  pun-gen-cy
  pun-gent-ly
pun-ish
  pun-ish-able
pun-ish-ment
pu-ni-tive
pun-ster
punt-er
pu-ny
  pu-ni-er
  pu-ni-est
pup
  pupped
  pup-ping
pu-pa
  pu-pae
  pu-pas
  pu-pal
pu-pate
  pu-pat-ed
  pu-pat-ing
  pu-pa-tion
pu-pil
pup-pet
pup-pe-teer
pep-pet-ry
  pup-pet-ries
pup-py
  pup-pies
  pup-py-ish
pur-chase
  pur-chased
  pur-chas-ing

pure
  pure-ly
pur-ga-tive
pur-ga-to-ry
  pur-ga-to-ries
  pur-ga-to-ri-al
purge
  purged
pu-ri-fy
pur-ism
  pur-ist
  pu-ris-tic
pu-ri-tan
  pu-ri-tan-i-cal
  pu-ri-tan-i-cal-ly
pu-ri-ty
purl
pur-loin
  pur-loin-er
pur-port
  pur-port-ed
  pur-port-ed-ly
pur-pose
  pur-posed
  pur-pos-ing
pur-pose-ly
pur-pos-ive
purse
  pursed
  purs-ing
purs-er
pur-su-ant
pur-sue
  pur-sued
  pur-su-ing
pur-suit
pur-sy
pu-ru-lent
  pu-ru-lence
  pu-ru-len-cy
pur-vey
  pur-vey-or
pur-vey-ance
pur-view
pushy
pu-sil-lan-i-mous
  pu-sil-la-nim-i-ty
  pu-sal-lan-i-mous-ly

pus-sy
pussy-foot
pussy-wil-low
pus-tule
  pus-tu-lar
  pus-tu-late
put
  put-ing
pu-ta-tive
  pu-ta-tive-ly
put--on
pu-tre-fac-tion
pu-tre-fy
  pu-tre-fied
  pu-tre-fy-ing
pu-trid
  pu-trid-i-try
putt
  putt-ed
  putt-ing
putt-er
  put-ter-er
put-ty
  put-tied
  put-ty-ing
put--up
puz-zle
puz-zle-ment
py-lon
pyr-a-mid
  py-ra-mi-dal
pyre
py-ric
py-ro-ma-nia
  py-ro-ma-ni-ac
  py-ro-ma-ni-a-cal
py-rom-e-ter
  py-rom-e-try
py-ro-tech-nics
  py-ro-tech-nic
  py-ro-tech-ni-cal
py-thon
py-tho-ness
py-uria
pyx
pyx-id-i-um
pyx-ie
pyxie moss

quack
quack-ery
  quack-er-ies
quack grass
quack-sal-ver
quad
  quad-ded
  quad-ding
quad-ran-gle
  quad-ran-gu-lar
quad-rant
  quad-ran-tal
quad-ra-phon-ic
quad-rate
  quad-rat-ed
  quad-rat-ing
qua-drat-ic
  qua-drat-i-cal-ly
qua-drat-ics
quad-ra-ture
qua-dren-ni-al
qua-dren-ni-um
quad-ric
quad-ri-cen-ten-ni-al
quad-ri-ceps
quad-ri-cip-i-tal
qua-ri-fid
qua-dri-ga
quad-ri-lat-er-al
qua-drille
qua-dril-lion
  qua-dril-lionth
quad-ri-par-tite
quad-ri-ple-gic
quad-ri-va-lent
qua-driv-i-al
qua-driv-i-um
qua-droon
qua-dru-ma-na
quad-ru-ped
  quad-ru-pe-dal
qua-dru-ple
  qua-dru-pled
  qua-dru-pling
qua-dru-plet
qua-dru-pli-cate
  qua-dru-pli-cat-ed
  qua-dru-pli-cat-ing

quaff
  quaff-er
quag
quag-mire
  quag-mired
  quag-miry
qua-hog
quai
quainch
quail
quaint
quake
  quaked
  quak-ing
qual-i-fi-ca-tion
qual-i-fied
  qual-i-fied-ly
qual-i-fy
  qual-i-fy-ing
  qual-i-fi-a-ble
  qual-i-fier
qual-i-ta-tive
qual-i-ty
  qual-i-ties
quality control
quality point
quality point average
qualm
  qualm-ish
quan-da-ry
  quan-dar-ies
quant
quan-tal
quan-ta-some
quan-ti-fi-ca-tion
quan-ti-fi-er
quan-ti-fy
  quan-ti-fy-ing
  quan-ti-fi-ca-tion
quan-ti-tate
quan-ti-ta-tive
quantitative analysis
quan-ti-ty
  quan-ti-ties
quantity theory
quan-tize
quan-tum
  quan-ta

quantum jump
quantum mechanics
quantum number
quantum theory
quar-an-tin-able
quar-an-tine
  quar-an-tin-able
quare
quark
quar-rel
  quar-reled
  quar-rel-ing
  quar-rel-er
quar-rel-some
quar-ri-er
quar-ry
  quar-ries
  quar-ried
  quar-ry-ing
quart
quar-tan
quar-ter
quar-ter-age
quar-ter-back
quarterback sneak
quarter--bound
quarter crack
quarter day
quar-ter-deck
quar-ter-fi-nal
quarter horse
quarter hour
quar-ter-ing
quar-ter-ly
  quar-ter-lies
quar-ter-mas-ter
quar-tet
quartz
quash
qua-si
qua-si-ju-di-cial
qua-si-leg-is-la-tive
qua-si-par-ti-cle
qua-si-pub-lic
quasi--stellar object
quas-sia
qua-ter-cen-te-na-ry
qua-ter-na-ry

qua-ter-ni-on
qua-ter-ni-ty
qua-train
qua-tre-foil
quat-tro-cen-to
quat-tu-or-de-cil-lion
qua-ver
  quav-er-ing-ly
  qua-very
quay
quay-age
quay-side
quean
quea-sy
  quea-si-er
  quea-si-est
  quea-si-ly
queen
  queen-ly
queen consort
quen mother
queen post
queen regent
queen regnant
queen-ship
queen-side
queen--size
queen substance
queen truss
queer
quell
  quell-er
quench
  quench-able
  quench-er
quer-ce-tin
quer-cit-ron
que-rist
quern
quer-u-lous
que-ry
  que-ries
  que-ried
  que-ry-ing
quest
ques-tion
  ques-tion-er
ques-tion-able

ques-tion-ably
ques-tion-less
question mark
ques-tion-naire
question time
ques-tor
quet-zal
  quet-za-les
queue
  queued
  queu-ing
quib-ble
  quib-bled
  quib-bling
quicke
quick
quick assets
quick bread
quick-en
  quick-en-er
  quick--freeze
quick-is
quick kick
quick-lime
quick--lunch
quick-sand
quick-set
quick-sil-ver
quick-step
quick-tem-pered
quick time
quick--wit-ted
  quick--wit-ted-ly
  quick--wit-ted-ness
quid
quid-di-ty
quid-nunc
qui-es-cent
  qui-es-cence
qui-et
  qui-et-ly
  qui-et-ter
qui-e-tude
quill
quilt
quilt-er
quilt-ing
quince

quin-til-lion
quin-tu-ple
  quin-tu-pled
  quin-tu-pling
quin-tu-plet
quip
  quipped
  quip-ping
quirk
  quirky
quis-ling
quit
  quit-ed
  quit-ing
quit-claim
quitclaim deed
quite
quit-rent
quits
quit-tance
quit-er
quit-tor
quiv-er
  quiv-ered
  quiv-er-ing
quix-ot-ic
quiz
quiz-zi-cal
  quiz-zi-cal-ly
quoin
quoit
quon-dam
quo-rum
quot
quo-ta
quot-able
  quot-a-bil-i-ty
quo-ta-tion
quotation mark
quote
quoth
quotha
quo-tid-i-an
quo-tient
quotient group
quotient ring
quo war-ran-to
qursh

rab-bet
  rab-bet-ted
  rab-bet-ting
rabbet joint
rab-bi
  rab-bis
ra-bin-ate
rab-bin-i-cal
  rab-bin-i-al-ly
rab-bit
rabbit brush
rabbit ears
rab-bit-eye
rabbit fever
rabbit punch
rab-bit-ry
rab-ble
  rab-bled
  rab-bling
ra-bid
  ra-bid-ly
ra-bies
rac-coon
race
  raced
  rac-er
  rac-ing
race-course
race-horse
ra-ce-mate
ra-ceme
ra-ce-mic
ra-ce-mi-za-tion
ra-ce-mose
racemose gland
rac-er
race riot
ra-ce-ric
ra-ce-ri-za-tion
race runner
race-track
race-way
ra-chis
  ra-chis-es
  rach-i-des
ra-cial
  ra-cial-ism
  ra-cial-ly

rac-ing
racing form
rac-ism
  ra-cial-ism
  rac-ist
rack
rack-et
rack-e-teer
ra-con-teur
rack-ety
rack-le
rack railway
rack--rent
rack up
ra-clette
racy
  rac-i-ly
  rac-i-ness
ra-dar
radar astronomy
radar beacon
ra-dar-scope
radar telescope
raddle
  raddled
  raddling
ra-di-al
  ra-di-al-ly
radial engine
radial symmetry
ra-di-an
ra-di-ance
  ra-di-an-cy
ra-di-ant
radiant energy
radiant flux
radiant heet
ra-di-ate
  ra-di-at-ed
  ra-di-at-ing
ra-di-a-tion
radiation sickness
ra-di-a-tor
rad-i-cal
  rad-i-cal-ly
radical expression
rad-i-cal-ism
ra-dio

ra-dio-ac-tive
ra-dio-ac-tive-i-ty
radio astronomy
ra-dio-au-to-graph
radio beacon
ra-dio-bi-ol-o-gy
ra-dio-broad-cast
radio car
ra-dio-car-bon
ra-dio-chem-is-try
radio compass
ra-dio-ecol-o-gy
ra-dio-el-e-ment
ra-di-o fre-quen-cy
radio galaxy
ra-dio-gen-ic
ra-dio-gram
ra-dio-graph
  ra-diog-ra-phy
ra-dio-iso-tope
ra-dio-la-bel
ra-di-o-lar-i-an
ra-dio-lo-ca-tion
ra-dio-log-i-cal
ra-di-ol-o-gist
ra-di-ol-o-gy
  ra-di-ol-o-gist
ra-dio-lu-cen-cy
ra-di-ol-y-sis
ra-dio-man
ra-di-om-e-ter
ra-di-on-ics
ra-dio-nu-clide
ra-di-opaque
ra-dio-phone
ra-dio-pho-to
ra-dio-proc-tec-tive
radio range
ra-dio-sonde
radio spectrum
radio star
ra-dio-tron-tium
ra-dio-tele-graph
ra-dio-te-lem-e-try
ra-dio-tele-phone
radio telescope
ra-dio-ther-a-py
ra-dio-tho-ri-um

ra-dio-trac-er
ra-dio--ul-na
radio wave
rad-ish
ra-di-um
radium therapy
ra-di-us
  ra-dii
  ra-di-us-es
radium of curvature
radius vector
ra-dix
ra-dome
ra-don
rad-u-la
raf-fia
raffia palm
raf-fi-nose
raff-ish
raf-fle
  raf-fled
  raf-fling
raf-fle-sia
raft
raft-er
rafts-man
rag
ra-ga
rag-a-muf-fin
rag-bag
rag doll
rage
rag-ged
ragged robin
rag-gedy
rag-gle
ra-gi
ra-ging
rag-lan
raglan sleeve
rag-man
ra-gout
rag-pick-er
rag-tag
ragtag and bobtail
rag-time
rag-weed
rag-wort

rah
rah-rah
raid
raid-er
rail
rail-bird
rail fence
rail-head
rail-ing
rail-lery
  rail-ler-ies
rail-road
  rail-road-er
  rail-road-ing
railroad flat
railroad worm
rail--split-ter
rail-way
rai-ment
rain
rain-bird
rain-bow
rainbow fish
rainbow perch
rainbow runner
rainbow trout
rain-check
rain-coat
rain-drop
rain-fall
rain-forest
rain gauge
rain-mak-ing
rain out
rain-proof
rain-spout
rain-squall
rain-storm
rain tree
rain-wash
rain-wa-ter
rain-wear
rainy
rainy day
raise
  raised
rai-sin
rake

raked
rak-ing
rake-hell
rake--off
rake up
rak-ish
  rak-ish-ly
ral-li-form
ral-ly
  ral-lied
ral-ly-ing
ral-ly-ist
ral-ly-mas-ter
ram
  rammed
ra-mate
ram-ble
  ram-bled
  ram-bling
ram-bler
ram-bouil-let
ram-bunc-tious
ram-bu-tan
ram-e-kin
ra-men-tum
ra-met
ra-mie
ram-i-fi-ca-tion
ra-mi-form
ram-i-fy
  ram-i-fied
  ram-i-fy-ing
ra-mose
ra-mouse
ramp
ram-page
  ram-paged
  ram-pag-ing
ram-pan-cy
ram-pant
  ram-pant-ly
ram-part
ram-pike
ram-pi-on
ram-rod
ram-shack-le
rams-horn
ram-til

ra-mus
ranch
ranch-er
ranch house
ranch-man
ran-cho
ran-cid
ran-cid-i-ty
ran-cor
ran-cor-ous
ran-dom
ran-dom-ly
random--access
ran-dom-iza-tion
ran-dom-ize
randomized block
random variable
random walkrandy
range
ranged
rang-ing
range finder
range-lang
range paralysis
rang-er
rangy
rang-i-er
rang-i-est
ra-ni
ra-nid
rank
rank and file
rank correlation
rank-er
rank-ing
ran-kle
ran-kling
ran-sack
ran-som
rant
rant-er
ran-u-la
ra-nun-cu-lus
rap
rapped
rap-ping
ra-pa-cious
ra-pa-cious-ly

ra-pac-i-ty
rape
rap-ist
ra-phe
raph-ide
rap-id
rapid eye movement
ra-pid--fire
ra-pid-i-ty
rapid transit
ra-pi-er
rap-ine
rap-pel
rap-pa-ree
rap-pee
rap-pel
rap-pen
rap-per
rap-pi-ni
rap-port
rap-proche-ment
rap-scal-lion
rap-to-ri-al
rap-ture
rap-tur-ous
rare
rar-er
rar-est
rare-bit
rar-efy
rar-efied
rar-efy-ing
rare-ly
rar-i-ty
rar-i-ties
ras-cal
ras-cal-i-ty
ras-cal-ly
rash
ra-so-ri-al
rasp
rasp-ber-ry
rat
rat-ted
rat-ting
rat-able
ratch-et
rate

rat-ed
rat-ing
rath-er
rat-icide
rat-i-fy
rat-i-fi-ca-tion
ra-tio
ra-tios
ra-ti-o-ci-na-tion
ra-tion
ra-tio-nal
ra-tio-nal-i-ty
ra-tio-nal-ly
ra-tion-able
ra-tio-nal-ism
ra-tio-nal-ize
ra-tio-nal-iz-ing
ra-tio-nal-i-za-tion
rat-line
rat-tan
rat-tle
rat-tled
rat-tling
rat-tle-snake
rat-ty
rat-ti-er
rat-ti-est
rau-cous
rau-cous-ly
raun-chy
raun-chi-er
raun-chi-est
rav-age
rav-aged
rave
rav-el
ra-ven
rav-en-ous
rav-en-ous-ly
ra-vine
rav-i-o-li
rav-ish
rav-ish-ment
rav-ish-ing
raw
raw-hide
ray-on
raze

razed
raz-ing
ra-zor
raz-zle--daz-zle
re-act
  re-ac-tive
re-ac-tion
re-ac-tion-ary
  re-ac-tion-ar-ies
re-ac-ti-vate
  re-ac-ti-vat-ed
  re-ac-ti-vat-ing
re-ac-tor
read-able
read-er
read-ing
re-ad-just
  re-ad-just-ment
ready
  read-i-er
  read-i-est
  read-ied
  read-y-ing
  read-i-ly
  read-i-ness
ready--made
re-agent
re-al
re-al-ism
  re-al-ist
  re-al-is-tic
  re-al-is-ti-cal-ly
re-al-ize
  re-al-ized
  re-al-iz-ing
  re-al-iz-a-ble
  re-al-i-za-tion
re-al-ly
realm
Re-al-tor
re-al-ty
ream-er
re-an-i-mate
  re-an-i-mat-ed
  re-an-i-mat-ing
  re-an-i-ma-tion
reap-er
re-ap-pear

re-ap-pear-ance
re-ap-por-tion
re-ap-por-tion-ment
rear ad-mir-ral
re-arm
  re-ar-ma-ment
re-ar-range
  re-ar-ranged
  re-ar-rang-ing
  re-ar-range-ment
rear-ward
rea-son
  rea-son-er
rea-son-able
  rea-son-abil-i-ty
  rea-son-able-ness
  rea-son-ably
rea-son-ing
re-as-sem-ble
  re-as-sem-bled
  re-as-sem-bling
  re-as-sem-bly
re-as-sume
  re-as-sump-tion
re-as-sure
  re-as-sured
  re-as-sur-ing
  re-as-sur-ance
  re-as-sur-ing-ly
re-bate
  re-bat-ed
  re-bat-ing
  re-bat-er
reb-el
re-bel
  re-belled
  re-bel-ling
re-bel-lion
re-bel-lious
  re-bel-lious-ly
re-birth
re-born
re-bound
re-buff
re-build
  re-built
  re-build-ing
re-buke

re-bus
  re-bus-es
re-but
re-but-tal
re-cal-ci-trant
  re-cal-ci-trance
  re-cal-ci-tran-cy
re-call
re-cant
  re-can-ta-tion
re-ca-pit-u-late
re-cap-ture
  re-cap-tured
re-cede
  re-ced-ed
  re-ced-ing
re-ceipt
re-ceiv-able
re-ceive
  re-ceiv-ed
  re-ceiv-ing
re-ceiv-er
re-ceiv-er-ship
re-cent
  re-cent-ly
  re-cen-cy
re-cep-ta-cle
re-cep-tion
re-cep-tion-ist
re-cep-tive
re-cess
re-ces-sion
  re-ces-sion-ary
re-ces-sion-al
re-ces-sive
re-charge
  re-charg-ed
  re-charg-ing
rec-i-pe
re-cip-i-ent
  re-cip-i-ence
  re-cip-i-en-cy
re-cip-ro-cal
  re-cip-ro-cal-ly
re-cip-ro-cate
rec-i-proc-i-ty
re-cit-al
rec-i-ta-tion

rec-i-ta-tive
re-cite
  re-cited
  re-cit-ing
reck-less
  reck-less-ly
reck-on
re-claim
rec-la-ma-tion
re-cline
  re-clined
rec-luse
rec-og-ni-tion
re-cog-ni-zance
rec-og-nize
  rec-og-nized
  rec-og-niz-ing
  rec-og-niz-a-ble
re-coil
  re-coil-less
re-col-lect
re-col-lect
  re-col-lec-tion
rec-om-mend
  rec-om-mend-able
  rec-om-mend-er
rec-om-men-da-tion
rec-om-pense
  rec-om-pensed
  rec-om-pens-ing
rec-on-cile
  rec-on-ciled
rec-con-dite
re-con-di-tion
re-con-firm
re-con-nais-sance
re-con-noi-ter
  re-con-noi-tered
  re-con-noi-ter-ing
re-con-sid-er
  re-con-sid-er-a-tion
re-con-struct
re-con-struc-tion
re-cord
re-cord-er
re-count
re-coup
re-course

re-cov-er
re-cov-ery
  re-cov-er-ies
rec-re-ant
re-cre-ate
  re-cre-at-ed
  re-cre-at-ing
  re-cre-a-tion
rec-re-ation
  rec-re-ation-al
re-crim-i-nate
  re-crim-i-nat-ed
  re-crim-i-nat-ing
re-cruit
  re-cruit-er
  re-cruit-ment
rec-tal
rect-an-gle
rect-an-gu-lar
rec-ti-fi-er
rec-ti-fy
  rec-ti-fied
  rec-ti-fy-ing
  rec-ti-fi-ca-tion
rec-ti-lin-ear
rec-ti-tude
rec-tor
rec-to-ry
  rec-to-ries
rec-tum
  rec-tums
rec-ta
re-cum-bent
  re-cum-ben-cy
  re-cum-bent-ly
re-cu-per-ate
re-cur
  re-cur-ring
  re-cur-rence
re-cur-rent
red-bird
red--blood-ed
re-dec-o-rate
  re-dec-o-rat-ed
  re-dec-o-ra-tion
re-ded-i-cate
  re-ded-i-cat-ed
  re-ded-i-ca-tion

re-deem
  re-deem-able
re-deem-er
re-demp-tion
  re-demp-tive
red--hand-ed
red--hot
re-di-rect
  re-di-rec-tion
red--let-ter
red--neck
re-do
red-o-lence
red-o-len-cy
red-o-lent
re-dou-ble
  re-dou-bled
  re-dou-bling
re-doubt-able
  re-doubt-ably
re-dound
re-dress
red-start
re-duce
re-duc-tion
re-dun-dance
re-dun-dant
re-du-pli-cate
  re-du-pli-cat-ed
  re-du-pli-ca-tion
red-wood
re-echo
  re-ech-oed
reedy
  reed-i-er
reef-er
re-elect
  re-elec-tion
re-em-pha-sie
  re-em-pha-sized
  re-em-pha-siz-ing
re-en-force
  re-en-forced
  re-en-forc-ing
  re-en-force-ment
re-en-list
  re-en-list-ment
re-en-ter

re-en-trance
re-en-try
　re-en-tries
re-es-tab-lish
　re-es-tab-lish-ment
re-ex-am-ine
　re-ex-am-i-na-tion
re-fec-to-ry
　re-fec-to-ries
re-fer
　re-fer-ral
ref-er-ee
ref-er-ence
　ref-er-enced
　ref-er-enc-ing
ref-er-en-dum
　ref-er-en-dums
　ref-er-en-da
ref-er-ent
re-fill
　re-fill-able
re-fine
　re-fined
　re-fin-ing
re-fine-ment
re-fin-ery
　re-fin-er-ies
re-fin-ish
re-fit
　re-fit-ted
　re-fit-ting
re-flect
re-flec-tion
re-flec-tive
　re-flec-tive-ly
　re-flec-tive-ness
re-flec-tor
re-flex
re-flex-ive
re-for-est
　re-for-est-a-tion
re-form
re-form-a-tory
re-fract
　re-frac-tive
re-frac-tion
re-frac-to-ry
　re-frac-to-ri-ly

re-frain
re-fresh
　re-fresh-ing
re-fresh-ment
re-frig-er-ant
　re-frig-er-ate
　re-frig-er-at-ed
re-frig-er-a-tor
re-fu-el
ref-uge
ref-u-gee
re-ful-gence
re-ful-gent
re-fund
re-fur-bish
re-fus-al
re-fuse
　re-fused
　re-fus-ing
ref-use
re-fute
re-gain
re-gal
　re-gal-ly
re-gale
　re-galed
　re-gal-ing
re-ga-lia
re-gard
re-gard-ful
re-gard-ing
re-gard-less
　re-gard-less-ly
re-gat-ta
re-gen-cy
　re-gen-cies
re-gen-er-ate
　re-gen-er-at-ed
　re-gen-er-at-ing
　re-gen-er-a-vy
　re-gen-er-a-tion
　re-gen-er-a-tive
re-gent
re-grime
reg-i-men
reg-i-ment
　reg-i-men-tal
　reg-i-men-ta-tion

re-gion
re-gion-al
　re-gion-al-ly
reg-is-ter
　reg-is-tered
　reg-is-trant
reg-is-trar
reg-is-tra-tion
reg-is-try
　reg-is-tries
re-gress
　re-gres-sion
　re-gres-sor
re-gret
　re-gret-ted
　re-gret-ting
　re-gret-ta-ble
　re-gret-ta-bly
　re-gret-er
　re-gret-ful
　re-gret-ful-ly
reg-u-lar
　reg-u-lar-i-ty
reg-u-late
　reg-u-lat-ed
　reg-u-lat-ing
　reg-u-la-tive
　reg-u-la-tor
　reg-u-la-to-ry
reg-u-la-tion
re-gur-gi-tate
　re-gur-gi-tat-ed
　re-gur-gi-tat-ing
　re-gur-gi-ta-tion
re-ha-bil-i-tate
　re-ha-bil-i-tat-ed
　re-ha-bil-i-tat-ing
　re-ha-bil-i-ta-tion
　re-ha-bil-i-ta-tive
re-hash
re-hears-al
re-hearse
　re-hearsed
　re-hears-ing
　re-hears-er
reign
re-im-burse
　re-im-bursed

re-im-burs-ing
re-im-burse-meny
rein
re-in-car-na-tion
rein-deer
re-in-force
re-in-forced
re-in-forc-ing
re-in-force-ment
re-in-state
re-in-stat-ed
re-in-stat-ing
re-in-state-ment
re-it-er-ate
re-it-er-at-ed
re-it-er-at-ing
re-it-er-a-tion
re-ject
re-jec-tion
re-joice
re-joiced
re-joic-ing
re-joic-er
re-joic-ing-ly
re-join
re-join-der
re-ju-ve-nate
re-ju-ve-nat-ed
re-ju-ve-nat-ing
re-ju-ve-na-tion
re-ju-ve-na-tor
re-kin-dle
re-kin-dled
re-kin-dling
re-lapse
re-lapsed
re-laps-ing
re-laps-er
re-late
re-lat-ed
re-lat-ing
re-lat-er
re-lat-or
re-la-tion
re-la-tion-al
re-la-tion-ship
rel-a-tive
rel-a-tive-ly

rel-a-tiv-ism
rel-a-tiv-ist
rel-a-tiv-is-tic
rel-a-tiv-i-ty
rel-a-tiv-ize
re-la-tor
re-lax
re-lax-er
re-lax-ation
re-lay
re-laid
re-lay-ing
re-lay
re-layed
re-lay-ing
re-lease
re-leas-ed
re-leas-ing
re-leas-a-ble
re-leas-er
rel-e-gate
rel-e-gat-ed
rel-e-ga-tion
re-lent
re-lent-less
rel-e-vant
rel-e-vance
rel-e-van-cy
rel-e-vant-ly
re-li-able
re-li-abil-i-ty
re-li-able-ness
re-li-ably
re-li-ance
re-li-ant
rel-ic
re-lief
re-leive
re-liev-ed
re-liev-ing
re-liev-able
re-liev-er
re-li-gion
re-li-gi-os-i-ty
re-li-gious
re-lin-quish
rel-ish
re-live

re-lived
re-liv-ing
re-lo-cate
re-lo-ct-ed
re-lo-cat-ing
re-lo-ca-tion
re-luc-tance
re-luc-tant
re-ly
re-lied
re-ly-ing
re-main
re-main-der
re-mand
re-mark
re-mark-able
re-mark-able-ness
re-mark-ably
re-me-di-a-ble
re-me-di-al
rem-e-dy
rem-e-dies
rem-e-died
rem-e-dy-ing
re-mem-ber
re-mem-brance
re-mind
re-mind-er
re-mind-ful
rem-i-nisce
rem-i-nisced
rem-i-nisc-ing
rem-i-nis-cence
rem-i-nis-cent
re-miss
re-mis-sion
re-mit
re-mit-ted
re-mit-ting
re-mit-tance
rem-nant
re-mod-el
re-mon-strance
re-mon-strate
re-mon-strat-ed
re-mon-strat-ing
re-morse
re-morse-ful

re-morse-ful-ly
re-morse-less
re-mote
re-mot-er
re-mot-est
re-mount
re-mov-able
re-mov-al
re-move
re-moved
re-mov-ing
re-mu-ner-ate
re-mu-ner-at-ed
re-mu-ner-at-ing
re-mu-ner-a-tion
re-nais-sance
re-na-scence
re-na-scent
rend
rend-er
ren-dez-vous
ren-dez-voused
ren-dez-vous-ing
ren-di-tion
ren-e-gade
re-nege
re-neged
re-neg-ing
re-new
re-new-al
ren-net
re-nounce
re-nounced
re-nounc-ing
ren-o-vate
ren-o-vat-ed
ren-o-vat-ing
ren-o-va-tion
re-nown
re-nowned
rent-al
re-nun-ci-a-tion
re-or-ga-ni-za-tion
re-or-ga-nize
re-or-ga-niz-ed
re-or-gan-iz-ing
re-pair
re-pair-man

re-pair-men
rep-a-ra-ble
rep-a-ra-tion
rep-ar-tee
re-pa-tri-ate
re-pa-tri-at-ed
re-pay
re-paid
re-pay-ing
re-pay-ment
re-peal
re-peat
re-peat-able
re-peat-ed
re-peat-er
re-pel
re-pelled
re-pel-ling
re-pel-lent
re-pent
re-pent-ance
re-pen-tant
re-per-cus-sion
rep-er-toire
rep-er-to-ry
rep-er-to-ries
rep-e-ti-tion
rep-e-ti-tious
re-pet-i-tive
re-place
re-placed
re-plac-ing
re-plac-able
re-place-ment
re-plen-ish
re-plete
re-ple-tion
rep-li-ca
re-ply
re-plied
re-ply-ing
re-plies
re-port
re-port-ed-ly
re-port-er
rep-or-to-ri-al
re-pose
re-posed

re-pos-ing
re-pose-ful
re-pos-i-to-ry
re-pos-i-tor-ies
re-pos-sess
re-pos-ses-sion
rep-re-hend
rep-re-hen-si-ble
rep-re-sent
rep-re-sen-ta-tion
rep-re-sen-ta-tive
re-press
re-pres-sion
re-prieve
re-prieved
re-priev-ing
rep-ri-mand
re-print
re-pris-al
re-proach
re-proach-ful
rep-ro-bate
rep-ro-ba-tion
re-pro-duce
re-pro-duced
re-pro-duc-ing
re-pro-duc-tion
re-pro-duc-tive
re-proof
re-prove
re-proved
re-prov-ing
rep-tile
rep-til-ian
re-pub-lic
re-pub-li-can
re-pub-li-can-ism
re-pu-di-ate
re-pu-di-at-ed
re-pu-di-at-ing
re-pu-di-a-tion
re-pu-di-a-tion-ist
re-pugn
re-pug-nan-cy
re-pug-nant
re-pulse
re-pulsed
re-puls-ing

re-sid-ing
res-i-dence
res-i-den-cy
res-i-den-cies
res-i-dent
res-i-den-tial
re-sid-u-al
res-i-due
re-sign
res-ig-na-tion
re-signed
re-sil-ient
re-sil-ience
re-sil-ien-cy
res-in
res-in-ous
re-sist
re-sist-er
re-sist-ible
re-sist-ance
re-sis-tant
re-sist-less
re-sis-tor
res-o-lute
res-o-lu-tion
re-solve
re-solved
re-solv-ing
res-o-nance
res-o-nant
res-o-nate
res-o-nat-ed
res-o-nat-ing
res-o-na-tor
re-sort
re-sound
re-sound-ing
re-source
re-source-ful
re-spect
re-spect-ful
re-spect-ful-ly
re-spect-able
re-spect-a-bil-i-ty
re-spect-ing
re-spec-tive
re-spec-tive-ly
res-pi-ra-tion

res-pi-ra-to-ry
res-pi-ra-tor
re-spire
re-spired
re-spir-ing
re-spite
re-splend-ant
re-splend-ence
re-spond
re-spon-dent
re-sponse
re-spon-si-bil-i-ty
re-spon-si-bil-i-ties
re-spon-si-ble
re-spon-sive
res-tau-rant
rest-ful
res-ti-tu-tion
res-tive
rest-less
res-to-ra-tion
re-stor-a-tive
re-store
re-stored
re-stor-ing
re-strain
re-straint
re-strict
re-strict-ed
re-strict-ed-ly
re-stric-tion
re-stric-tive
re-sult
re-sul-tant
re-sume
re-sumed
re-sum-ing
re-sump-tion
re-sur-gence
re-sur-gent
res-ur-rect
res-ur-rec-tion
re-sus-ci-tate
re-sus-ci-tat-ed
re-sus-ci-tat-ing
re-sus-ci-ta-tion
re-sus-ci-ta-tor
re-tail

re-tail-er
re-tain
re-tainer
re-take
re-took
re-tak-en
re-tak-ing
re-tal-i-ate
re-tal-i-at-ed
re-tal-i-at-ing
re-tal-i-a-tion
re-tard
re-tard-ant
re-tar-da-tion
re-tard-ed
re-ten-tion
re-ten-tive
ret-i-cence
ret-i-cent
ret-i-na
ret-i-nas
ret-i-nae
ret-i-nal
ret-i-nue
re-tire
re-tired
re-tir-ing
re-tire-ment
re-tool
re-tort
re-touch
re-trace
re-traced
re-trac-ing
re-tract
re-trac-tion
re-trac-tor
re-trac-tile
re-tread
re-treat
re-trench
re-trench-ment
re-tri-al
ret-ri-bu-tion
re-trieve
re-trieved
re-triev-ing
re-triev-er

ret-ro-ac-tive
ret-ro-grade
  ret-ro-grad-ed
  ret-ro-grad-ing
ret-ro-gress
  ret-ro-gees-sion
  ret-ro-ges-sive
ret-ro--rock-et
ret-ro-spect
  ret-ro-spec-tion
  ret-ro-spec-tive
re-turn
re-turn-able
re-turn-ee
re-union
re-unite
  re-unit-ed
  re-unit-ing
rev
  rev-ved
  rev-ving
re-vamp
re-veal
rev-eil-le
rev-el
  rev-el-er
rev-e-la-tion
rev-el-ry
  rev-el-ries
re-venge
  re-venged
  re-veng-ing
re-venge-ful
rev-e-nue
rev-e-nu-er
re-ver-ber-ate
  re-ver-ber-at-ed
  re-ver-ber-at-ing
  re-ver-ber-a-tion
re-vere
  re-vered
  re-ver-ing
rev-er-ence
  rev-er-enced
  rev-er-enc-ing
rev-er-end
rev-er-ent
rev-er-en-tial

rev-er-ie
rev-er-sal
re-verse
  re-versed
  re-vers-ing
re-vers-i-ble
re-ver-sion
re-vert
re-view
re-view-er
re-vile
  re-viled
  re-vil-ing
re-vise
  re-vised
  re-vis-ing
re-vi-sion
re-vi-sion-ist
  re-vi-sion-ism
re-viv-al
re-viv-al-ist
re-vive
  re-vived
  re-viv-ing
rev-o-ca-ble
rev-o-ca-tion
re-voke
  re-voked
  re-vok-ing
re-volt
rev-o-lu-tion
rev-o-lu-tion-ary
  rev-o-lu-tion-ar-ies
rev-o-lu-tion-ist
rev-o-lu-tion-ize
  rev-o-lu-tion-ized
  rev-o-lu-tion-iz-ing
re-volve
  re-volved
  re-volv-ing
re-volv-er
re-vue
re-vul-sion
re-write
  re-wrote
  re-writ-ten
  re-writ-ting
rhap-sod-ic

rhap-sod-i-cal
  rhap-sod-i-cal-ly
rhap-so-dize
  rhap-so-dized
  rhap-so-diz-ing
rhap-so-dy
  rhap-so-dies
  rhap-so-dist
rhea
rhe-ni-um
rheo-stat
rhe-tor
rhet-o-ric
rhe-tor-i-cal
rhet-o-ri-cian
rheum
rheu-mat-ic
  rheu-mat-i-cal-ly
rheu-ma-tism
rhine-stone
rhi-no
rhi-noc-er-os
  rhi-noc-er-os-es
rhi-zome
rho-di-um
rho-do-den-dron
rhom-bic
rhom-boid
  rhom-boi-dal
rhom-bus
  rhom-bus-es
  rhom-bi
rhu-barb
rhyme
  rhymed
  rhym-ing
rhyme-ster
rhythm
  rhyth-mic
  rhyth-mi-cal
  rhyth-mi-cal-ly
rib
  ribbed
  rib-bing
rib-ald
  rib-ald-ry
  rib-ald-ries
rib-bon

ri-bo-fla-vin
rib-bo-nu-cle-ase
rice
  riced
  ric-ing
rich-es
rich-less
rick-ets
rick-ety
  rick-et-i-er
  rick-et-i-est
rick-sha
ric-o-ch
rid
  rid-ded
  rid-ding
rid-dance
rid-dle
  rid-dled
  rid-dling
ride
  rid-den
  rid-ding
ride-er
ridge
  ridged
  ridg-ing
ridge-pole
rid-i-cule
  rid-i-culed
  rid-i-cul-ing
ri-dic-u-lous
rif-fle
  rif-fled
  rif-fling
riff-raff
rig
  rigged
  rig-ging
rig-ger
righ-teous
right-ful
right-hand
right--hand-ed
right-ism
rig-id
  ri-gid-i-ty
rig-ma-role

rig-or
rig-or-ous
rile
  riled
  ril-ing
rim
rime
ring-er
ring-lead-er
ring-let
ring-mas-ter
ring-worm
rinse
  rinsed
  rins-ing
ri-ot-ous
rip
  ripped
  rip-ping
  rip-per
ri-par-i-an
rip-en
rip--off
rip-ple
  rip-pled
  rip-pling
rip-saw
rip-tide
rise
  rose
  ris-en
  ris-ing
ris-er
ris-i-ble
  ris-i-bil-i-ty
risky
  risk-i-er
  risk-i-est
rit-u-al
rit-u-al-ism
  rit-u-al-ist
  rit-u-al-is-tic
  rit-u-al-is-ti-cal-ly
ritzy
  ritz-i-er
  ritz-i-est
ri-val
ri-val-ry

ri-val-ries
riv-er
riv-er-side
riv-et
riv-et-er
riv-i-era
riv-u-let
roach
road-runner
road-ster
road-way
roast-er
rob
  robbed
  rob-bing
  rob-ber
rob-bery
  rob-ber-ies
robe
  robed
  rob-ing
rob-in
ro-bot
ro-bust
rock-er
rock-et
rock-et-ry
rocky
  rock-i-er
  rock-i-est
ro-co-co
ro-dent
ro-deo
  ro-de-os
roe-buck
roent-gen
rog-er
roque
ro-guish
ro-guish-ly
roqu-ery
  roqu-er-ies
roist-er
roll-er
roll-er bear-ing
roll-er coast-er
roll-er skate
rol-lick

rol-lick-ing
roll-ing pin
ro-ly--po-ly
ro-ly--po-lies
ro-maine
ro-mance
ro-manced
ro-manc-ing
ro-man-tic
ro-man-ti-cism
ro-man-ti-cize
ro-man-ti-ciz-ing
romp-er
roof-ing
rook-ery
rook-er-ies
rook-ie
room-er
room-ful
room-mate
roomy
room-i-er
room-i-est
room-i-ly
room-i-ness
roos-ter
root-stock
rope
roped
rop-ing
ropy
rop-i-er
rop-i-est
ro-sa-ry
ro-sa-ries
ro-se-ate
rose-bud
rose--col-ored
rose-mary
rose-mar-ies
ro-sette
ros-in
ros-ter
ros-trum
ros-tra
ros-trums
rosy
ros-i-er

ros-i-est
rot
rot-ted
rot-ting
ro-ta-ry
ro-tar-ies
ro-tate
ro-tat-ed
ro-tat-ing
ro-ta-tion
ro-tis-ser-ie
ro-tor
rot-ten
ro-tund
ro-tun-di-ty
ro-tun-di-ties
ro-tun-da
rouge
rouged
roug-ing
rough-age
rough--and--tumble
rough-en
rough-house
rough-neck
rough-shod
rou-lette
round-ed
round-er
round-ish
round-up
rouse
roused
rous-ing
rous-er
roust
roust-a-bout
rout
route
rout-ed
rout-ing
rout-er
rou-tine
rou-tin-ize
rou-tin-ized
rou-tin-iz-ing
rove
roved

rov-ing
rov-er
row-boat
row-dy
row-dies
row-di-er
row-di-est
row-lock
roy-al
roy-al-ly
roy-al-ist
roy-al-ty
roy-al-ties
rub
rubbed
rub-bing
rub-ber
rub-bery
rub-ber-ize
rub-ber-ized
rub-ber-iz-ing
rub-ber-neck
rub-bish
rub-bish-ly
rub-ble
rub-bly
rub-bli-er
rub-bli-est
rub-down
ru-bel-la
ru-be-o-la
ru-bi-cund
ru-bid-i-um
ru-bric
ru-by
ru-bies
ruck-sack
ruck-us
rud-der
rud-dy
rud-di-er
rud-di-est
rud-di-ly
rude
ru-di-ment
ru-di-ment-al
ru-di-men-ta-ry
rue

rued
ru-ing
rue-ful
rue-ful-ly
ruff
ruffed
ruf-fi-an
ruf-fle
ruf-fled
ruf-fling
rug-ged
rug-ged-ly
rug-ged-ness
ru-in
ru-in-ation
ru-in-ous
rule
ruled
rul-ing
rul-er
rum-ba
rum-baed
rum-ba-ing
rum-ble
rum-bled
rum-bling
rum-bler
rum-bly
ru-mi-nant
ru-mi-nate
ru-mi-nat-ed
ru-mi-nat-ing
ru-mi-na-tion
ru-mi-na-tor
rum-mage
rum-maged
rum-mag-ing
rum-mag-er
rum-my
rum-mies
ru-mor
ru-mor-mon-ger
rum-ple
rum-pled
rum-pling
rum-pus
run
run-ning

run-about
run-off
run--on
runt
runty
runt-i-er
runt-i-est
run--through
run-way
rup-ture
rup-tured
rup-tur-ing
ru-ral
ru-ral-ly
ru-ral-ize
ru-ral-ized
ru-ral-iz-ing
ru-ral-i-za-tion
rus-set
rus-tic
rus-ti-cate
rus-ti-cat-ed
rus-ti-cat-ing
rus-ti-ca-tion
rus-tle
rus-tled
rus-tling
rus-tler
rust-proof
rus-ty
rust-i-er
rust-i-est
rut
rut-ted
rut-ting
ru-ta-ba-ga
ruth
ru-the-nic
ru-the-ni-ous
ru-the-ni-um
ruth-ful
ruth-ful-ly
ruth-ful-ness
ruth-less
ru-ti-lant
ru-tile
rut-tish
rut-ty

sab-bat
sab-bat-i-cal
sa-ber
saber rattling
saber saw
sa-ber-toothed ti-ger
sa-bine
sa-ble
sab-o-tage
sab-o-taged
sab-o-tag-ing
sab-o-teur
sa-bra
sac
sa-ca-huis-te
sac-a-ton
sac-cade
sac-cate
sac-cha-rase
sac-cha-rate
sac-cha-ride
sac-char-i-fy
sac-cha-rim-e-ter
sac-cha-rin
sac-cha-roi-dal
sac-cha-rom-e-ter
sac-cha-rose
sa-chem
sa-chet
sack-ful
sack-fuls
sack-ing
sack out
sa-cral
sac-ra-ment
sac-ra-men-tal
sa-cred
sa-cred-ly
sa-cred-ness
sacred baboon
sacred cow
sacred mushroom
sac-ri-fice
sac-ri-ficed
sac-ri-fic-ing
sac-ri-fic-er
sac-ri-fi-cial
sacrifice fly

sacrifice hit
sac-ri-lege
sac-ri-le-gious
sc-ro-il-li-ac
sac-ro-sanct
  sac-ro-sanc-i-ty
sac-rum
  sac-rums
  sac-ra
  sa-cral
sad
  sad-der
  sad-dest
  sad-ly
  sad-ness
sad-den
sad-dle
  sad-dled
  sad-dling
sad-ism
  sad-ist
  sa-dis-tic
sad-o-mas-o-chism
  sad-o-mas-o-chist
sa-fa-ri
  sa-fa-ris
safe
  saf-er
  saf-est
safe--con-duct
safe-crack-er
  safe-crack-ing
safe--de-pos-it
safe-guard
safe-keep-ing
safe-ty
  safe-ties
saf-flow-er
sag
  sagged
  sag-ging
sa-ga
sa-ga-cious
  sa-gac-i-ty
sage
  sag-er
  sag-est
sage-brush

sail-boat
sail-cloth
sail-er
sail-fish
sail-ing
sail-or
saint
  saint-hood
saint-ed
saint-ly
  saint-li-er
  saint-li-est
sa-ke
sal-a-ble
  sal-a-ble
  sal-a-bil-i-ty
  sal-a-bly
sa-la-cious
sal-ad
sal-a-man-der
sa-la-mi
sal-a-ry
  sal-a-ries
sales-man
  sales-men
sales-man-ship
sales-per-son
  sales-peo-ple
sales-room
sa-li-ent
  sa-li-ence
  sa-li-en-cy
  sa-li-ent-ly
sa-line
  sa-lin-i-ty
sa-li-va
  sal-i-vary
sal-i-vate
  sal-i-vat-ed
  sal-i-vat-ing
  sal-i-va-tion
sal-low
  sal-low-ish
sal-ly
  sal-lies
  sal-lied
  sal-ly-ing
salm-on

sa-lon
sa-loon
salt-cel-lar
salt-ed
sal-tine
salt-shak-er
salt-wa-ter
salt-wort
salt-y
  salt-i-er
  salt-i-est
  salt-i-ness
sa-lu-bri-ous
sal-u-tar-y
sal-u-ta-tion
sa-lu-ta-to-ry
  sa-lu-ta-to-ries
sa-lute
  sa-luted
  sa-lut-ing
  sa-lut-er
sal-vage
  sal-vaged
  sal-vag-ing
  sal-vage-a-ble
  sal-vag-er
sal-va-tion
salve
  salved
  salv-ing
  salv-or
sal-vo
  sal-vos
  sal-voes
sam-ba
  sam-baed
  sam-ba-ing
same-ness
sam-o-var
sam-ple
  sam-pled
  sam-pling
sam-pler
san-a-to-ri-um
sanc-ti-fy
  sanc-ti-fied
  sanc-ti-fy-ing
  sanc-ti-fi-ca-tion

sanc-ti-fi-er
sanc-ti-mo-ny
sanc-ti-mo-ni-ous
sanc-tion
sanc-tion-a-ble
sanc-tion-er
sanc-ti-ty
sanc-ti-ties
sanc-tu-ary
sanc-tu-ar-ies
sanc-tum
sanc-ta
san-dal
san-dal-wood
sand-bag
sand-bagged
sand-bank
sand-blast
sand-box
sand-cast
sand-cast-ed
sand-cast-ing
sand-lot
sand-man
sand-men
sand-pa-per
sand-pi-per
sand-stone
sand-wich
sandy
sand-i-er
sand-i-est
sane
san-er
san-est
sane-ly
sang-froid
san-gui-nary
san-quine
san-quine-ly
san-i-tar-i-um
san-i-tar-i-ums
san-i-tar-ia
san-i-tary
san-i-tar-i-ly
san-i-ta-tion
san-i-tize
san-i-tized

san-i-tiz-ing
san-i-ty
sap
sapped
sap-ping
sap-head
sap-head-ed
sa-pi-ent
sa-pi-ence
sa-pi-en-cy
sap-less
sap-ling
sa-pon-i-fy
sa-pon-i-fied
sa-pon-i-fy-ing
sap-per
sap-phire
sap-phism
sap-py
sap-pi-er
sap-pi-est
sap-suck-er
sap-wood
sa-ran
sar-casm
sar-cas-tic
sar-cas-ti-cal-ly
sar-co-ma
sar-co-mas
sar-co-ma-ta
sar-coph-a-gus
sar-coph-a-gus-es
sar-dine
sar-don-ic
sar-don-i-cal-ly
sar-gas-sum
sa-ri
sa-ris
sa-rong
sar-sa-pa-ril-la
sar-to-ri-al
sa-shay
sas-sa-fras
sas-sy
sas-si-er
sas-si-est
sa-tan-ic
sa-tan-i-cal

sa-tan-ism
sa-tan-ist
satch-el
sate
sat-ed
sat-ing
sa-teen
sat-el-lite
sa-ti-a-ble
sa-ti-a-bly
sa-ti-a-bil-i-ty
sa-ti-ate
sa-ti-at-ed
sa-ti-at-ing
sa-ti-a-tion
sa-ti-e-ty
sat-in
sat-iny
sat-ire
sa-tir-i-cal
sa-tir-i-cal-ly
sat-i-rist
sat-i-rize
sat-i-rized
sat-i-riz-ing
sat-i-riz-er
sat-is-fac-tion
sat-is-fac-to-ry
sat-is-fa-to-ri-ly
sat-is-fy
sat-is-fied
sat-is-fy-ing
sat-is-fi-a-ble
sat-is-fi-er
sat-is-fy-ing-ly
sat-u-rate
sat-u-rat-ed
sat-u-rat-ing
sat-u-ra-tion
sat-ur-na-li-a
sat-ur-nine
sa-tyr
sa-tyr-ic
sauce
sauced
sauc-ing
sau-cer
sau-cy

sau-er-bra-ten
sau-er-kraut
sau-na
saun-ter
  saun-ter-er
sau-sage
  sau-sage-like
sav-age
  sav-age-ry
  sav-age-ries
sa-van-na
sa-vant
save
  saved
  sav-ing
  sav-er
sav-ior
sa-voir-faire
sa-vor
  sa-vor-er
sa-vory
  sa-vor-i-er
  sa-vor-i-est
sav-vy
saw-buck
saw-dust
sawed--off
saw-horse
saw-mill
saw-toothed
saw-yer
sax-o-phone
  sax-o-phon-ist
say
  said
  say-ing
  say-a-ble
  say-er
say-s-o
scab
  scabbed
  scab-bing
scab-bard
scab-by
  scab-bi-er
  scab-bi-est
sca-bies
scaf-fold

sac-fold-ing
sca-lar
scal-a-wag
scald
  scald-ing
scale
  scaled
  scal-ing
  scale-less
scamp
  scamp-er
scan
scan-dal
scan-dal-ize
  scan-dal-ized
  scan-dal-iz-ing
scan-dal-mon-ger
scan-dal-ous
scan-sion
scant
  scant-ness
  scan-ties
scanty
  scant-i-er
  scant-i-est
scape-goat
scape-grace
scap-u-la
  scap-u-las
  scap-u-lae
scar
  scarred
  scar-ring
scarce
  scar-ci-ty
scare
  scared
  scar-ing
  scar-er
scare-crow
scare-mon-ger
scarf
  scarfs
scarf-skin
scar-i-fy
  scar-i-fied
  scar-i-fy-ing
scar-let

scarp
scary
  scar-i-er
  scar-i-est
scat
  scat-ted
  scat-ting
scathe
scat-o-log-i-cal
scat-ter
  scat-ter-a-ble
  scat-ter-er
scav-enge
  scav-enged
  scav-eng-ing
scav-en-ger
sce-nar-i-o
  sce-nar-i-os
sce-nar-ist
scen-ery
  scen-er-ies
sce-nic
  sce-ni-cal
scent
  scent-ed
scep-ter
  scep-tered
  scep-ter-ing
sched-ule
  sched-ul-ed
  sched-ul-ing
sche-ma
  sche-ma-ta
  sche-mat-i-cal-ly
sche-ma-tize
  sche-ma-tized
  sche-ma-tiz-ing
scheme
  schem-er
  schem-ing
scher-zo
  scher-zos
  scher-zi
schism
schis-mat-ic
  schis-mat-i-cal
schist
schizo

schiz-os
schiz-oid
schiz-o-phre-ni-a
schiz-o-phren-ic
schle-miel
schmaltz
schmaltzy
schmo
schnapps
schnau-zer
schnit-zel
schnook
schnor-kel
schnoz-zle
schol-ar
schol-ar-ly
schol-ar-li-ness
schol-ar-ship
scho-las-tic
scho-las-ti-cal
scho-las-ti-cism
school board
school bus
school-child
school-chil-dern
school-ing
school-mas-ter
school-teach-er
school-teach-ing
school-work
schoon-er
schuss
schwa
sci-at-ic
sci-ence
sci-en-tif-ic
sci-en-tif-i-cal-ly
sci-en-tist
scim-i-tar
scin-tig-ra-phy
scin-til-la
scin-til-lant
scin-til-late
scin-til-lat-ed
scin-til-lat-ing
scin-til-la-tion
sci-on
scis-sor

scis-sors
scle-ra
scle-rot-i-ca
scle-ro-sis
scle-ro-ses
scle-rot-ic
scle-rous
scoff
scoff-er
scoff-ing-ly
scold
scold-er
scold-ing
scol-lop
sconce
scone
scoop
scoot-er
scope
scorch
scorched
scorch-ing
scorch-er
score
scored
scor-ing
score-less
scor-er
score-board
score-keep-er
scorn
scorn-er
scorn-ful
scot-free
scot-tie
scoun-drel
scoun-drel-ly
scour
scour-er
scourge
scourged
scourg-ing
scourg-er
scour-ing
scout-ing
scout-mas-ter
scowl
scowl-er

scrab-ble
scrab-bled
scrab-bling
scrab-bler
scrag
scragged
scrag-ging
scrag-gly
scrag-gli-er
scrag-gli-est
scrag-gy
scrag-gi-er
scrag-gi-est
scram
scrammed
scram-ming
scram-ble
scram-bled
scram-bling
scram-bler
scrap
scrapped
scrap-ping
scrap-book
scrape
scrap-per
scrap-py
scrap-pi-er
scrap-pi-est
scrap-pi-ly
scratch
scratch-a-ble
scratch-er
scratch-y
scratch-i-er
scratch-i-est
scratch-i-ly
scratch-i-ness
scrawl
scrawn-y
scrawn-i-er
scrawn-i-est
screamer
scream-ing-ly
screech
screech-er
screen
scrren-a-ble

screen-er
screen-play
screw
screw-driv-er
screw-y
  screw-i-er
  screw-i-est
scrib-ble
  scrib-bled
  scrib-bling
  scrib-bler
scribe
  scribed
  scrib-ing
  scrib-al
scrim
  scrim-mage
  scrim-mag-ing
scrimp-y
  scrimp-i-er
  scrimp-i-est
script
scrip-tur-al
scrip-ture
script-writ-er
scroll-work
scrooge
scro-tum
  scro-ta
scrounge
  scroung-er
scrub
  scrubbed
  scrub-bing
  scrub-ber
scrub-by
  scrub-bi-er
  scrub-bi-est
scrub-wom-an
  scrub-wom-en
scruffy
  scruff-i-er
  scruff-i-est
scrump-tious
scru-ple
  scru-bled
  scru-bling
scru-pu-lous

scru-pu-los-i-ty
scru-pu-lous-ly
scru-ta-ble
scru-ti-nize
  scru-ti-nized
scru-ti-ny
  scru-ti-nies
scu-ba
scud
  scud-ded
  scud-ding
scuf-fle
  scuf-fled
  scuf-fling
scul-ler-y
  scul-ler-ies
sculp-tor
sculp-ture
  sculp-tur-ed
  sculp-tur-ing
  sculp-tur-al
scum
  scummed
  scum-ming
scur-ri-lous
  scur-ril-i-ty
  scur-ril-i-ties
scur-ry
  scur-ri-ed
  scur-ry-ing
scur-vy
scut-tle
  scut-tled
  scut-tling
scut-tle-butt
scythe
  scythed
  scyth-ing
sea-bed
sea-coast
sea-drome
sea-far-ing
  sea-far-er
sea-food
sea gull
sea horse
seal
  seal-er

sea-lam-prey
sea legs
sea lev-el
seal-ing wax
sea li-on
seal-skin
seam
  seam-er
sea-maid
sea-man
  sea-men
sea-man-ship
seam-stree
seam-y
  seam-i-er
  seam-i-est
sea ot-ter
sea-plane
sea-port
search
search-a-ble
search-er
search-ing
search-light
search war-rant
sea-scape
sea ser-pent
sea-shell
sea-shore
sea-sick
  sea-sick-ness
sea-side
sea-son
  sea-son-er
sea-son-a-ble
sea-son-al
  sea-son-al-ly
sea-son-ing
seat-ing
sea ur-chin
sea-ward
sea-weed
sea-wor-thy
  sea-wor-thi-ness
se-ba-ceous
se-cant
se-cede
  se-ced-ed

se-ced-ing
se-ced-er
se-ces-sion
se-ces-sion-ist
se-clude
se-clud-ed
se-clud-ing
se-clu-sion
se-clu-sive
sec-ond
sec-ond-ar-y
sec-ond-ar-i-ly
sec-ond--best
sec-ond--class
sec-ond-quess
sec-ond-hand
sec-ond-rate
sec-ond--sto-ry man
se-cre-cy
se-cre-cies
se-cret
sec-re-tar-i-at
sec-re-tary
sec-re-tar-ies
sec-re-tar-i-al
se-crete
se-cret-ed
se-cret-ing
se-cre-tion
se-cre-tive
se-cre-to-ry
se-cre-to-ries
sec-tar-i-an
sec-tar-i-an-ism
sec-tion
sec-tion-al
sec-tor
sec-to-ri-al
sec-u-lar
sec-u-lar-ism
sec-u-lar-ize
sec-u-lar-ized
sec-u-lar-iz-ing
se-cure
se-cured
se-cur-ing
se-cu-ri-ty
se-cu-ri-ties

se-dan
se-date
se-dat-ed
se-dat-ing
se-da-tion
sed-a-tive
sed-en-tary
sed-en-tar-i-ness
sedge
sed-i-ment
sed-i-men-tal
sed-i-men-ta-ry
sed-i-men-ta-tion
se-di-tion
se-di-tion-ary
se-di-tious
se-duce
se-duced
se-duc-ing
se-duc-er
se-duc-tive
se-duc-tive-ness
sed-u-lous
se-du-li-ty
sed-u-lous-ness
seed-bed
seed-case
seed-ing
seed-pod
seedy
seed-i-er
seed-i-est
see-ing
seek
sought
seek-ing
seem-ing
seem-ing-ness
seem-ly
seep
seepy
seep-i-er
seep-i-est
seep-age
se-er
seer-ess
seer-suck-er
see-saw

seethe
seethed
seeth-ing
seg-ment
seg-men-tal
seg-men-tary
seg-men-ta-tion
seg-re-gate
seg-re-gat-ed
seg-re-gat-ing
seg-re-ga-tion
seg-re-ga-tion-sit
sei-gneur
seine
seined
sein-ing
seis-mic
seis-mal
seis-mi-cal
seis-mi-cal-ly
seis-mo-graph
seis-mog-ra-pher
seis-mo-graph-ic
seis-mog-ra-phy
seis-mol-o-gy
seis-mo-log-ic
seis-mo-log-i-cal
seis-mol-o-gist
seize
seized
seiz-ing
seiz-er
sei-zure
sel-dom
se-lect
se-lect-ed
se-lec-tor
se-lec-tion
se-lec-tive
se-lec-tiv-i-ty
se-le-ni-um
self-a-base-ment
self-ab-ne-ga-tion
self-a-buse
self--ad-dressed
self-ag-gran-dize-ment
self-ag-gran-diz-ing
self--as-sur-ance

self--as-sured
self--cen-tered
  self--cen-tered-ness
self--col-lect-ed
self--com-mand
self--com-posed
self--con-fessed
self--con-fi-dence
  self--con-fi-dent
self--con-scious
  self--con-scious-ness
self--con-tained
self--con-trol
  self--con-trolled
self--cor-rect-ing
self--crit-i-cal
self--crit-i-cism
self--de-cep-tion
  self--de-cep-tive
self--de-fense
self--de-ni-al
  self--de-ny-ing
self--de-ter-mi-na-tion
  self--de-ter-min-ing
self--dis-ci-pline
  self--dis-ci-plined
self--ed-u-cate-ed
  self--ed-u-ca-tion
self--ef-fac-ing
self--em-ployed
  self--em-ploy-ment
self--es-teem
self--ev-i-dent
  self--ev-i-dence
self--ex-plan-a-to-ry
self--ex-pres-sion
  self--ex-pres-sive
self--ful-fill-ing
self--ful-fill-ment
self--gov-ern-ment
  self--gov-erned
  self--gov-ern-ing
self--help
self--im-age
self--im-por-tance
self--im-por-tant
self--im-posed
self--im-prove-ment

self--in-duced
self--in-dul-gence
  self--in-dul-gent
self--in-flict-ed
self--in-ter-est
  self--in-ter-est-ed
self--ish
  self--ish-ness
self--kow-ledge
self--less
  self--less-ness
self--love
  self--lov-ing
self--made
self--per-pet-u-at-ing
  self--per-pet-u-a-tion
self--pity
  self--pit-y-ing
self--pol-li-na-tion
self--pos-sessed
  self--pos-sess-ed-ly
  self--pos-ses-sion
self--pres-er-va-tion
self--pro-pelled
  self--pro-pel-ling
self--re-al-i-za-tion
self--re-li-ance
  self--re-li-ant
self--re-spect
  self--re-spect-ing
self--re-straint
  self--re-strain-ing
self--right-eous
  self--right-eous-ness
self--sac-ri-fice
  self--sac-ri-fic-ing
self--same
self--sat-is-fied
  self--sat-is-fac-tion
  self--sat-is-fy-ing
self--ser-vice
  self--serv-ing
self--start-er
  self--start-ing
self--styled
self--suf-fi-cient
  self--suf-fic-ing
  self--suf-fi-cien-cy

self--sup-port
  self--sup-port-ing
self--taught
self--will
  self--willed
sell
  sell-ing
sell-er
sell-out
sel-vage
  sel-vaged
se-man-tics
  se-man-tic
  se-man-ti-cal
  se-man-ti-cal-ly
sem-a-phore
  sem-a-phor-ed
  sem-a-phor-ing
sem-blance
se-men
se-mes-ter
sem-i-an-nu-al
  sem-i-an-nu-al-ly
sem-i-ar-id
sem-i-au-to-mat-ic
sem-i-cir-cle
  sem-i-cir-cu-lar
sem-i-clas-si-cal
  sem-i-clas-sic
sem-i-co-lon
sem-i-con-duc-tor
  sem-i-con-duct-ing
sem-i-con-scious
  sem-i-con-sious-ness
sem-i-de-tached
sem-i-fi-nal
  sem-i-fi-nal-ist
sem-i-flu-id
sem-i-for-mal
sem-i-gloss
sem-i-liq-uid
sem-i-month-ly
sem-i-nal
  sem-i-nal-ly
sem-i-nar-y
  sem-i-nar-ies
  sem-i-nar-ian
sem-i-of-fi-cial

sem-i-of-fi-cial-ly
sem-i-per-ma-nent
sem-i-per-me-a-ble
sem-i-pre-cious
sem-i-pri-vate
sem-i-pro-fes-sion-al
sem-i-pro
sem-i-pub-lic
sem-i-skilled
sem-i-sol-id
sem-i-trail-er
sem-i-trop-ic
sem-i-trop-i-cal
sem-i-trop-ics
sem-i-vow-el
sem-i-week-ly
sem-i-week-lies
sem-i-year-ly
sen-a-ry
sen-ate
sen-a-tor
sen-a-tor-ship
sen-a-to-ri-al
sen-a-to-ri-al-ly
send--off
se-nile
se-nil-i-ty
sen-ior
sen-ior-i-ty
sen-na
sen-sate
san-sa-tion
san-sa-tion-al
sen-sa-tion-al-ly
sen-sa-tion-al-ism
sense
sensed
sens-ing
sense-less
sense-less-ness
sen-si-bil-i-ty
sen-si-ble-ness
sen-si-ble
sen-si-ble-ness
sen-si-bly
sen-si-tive
sen-si-tiv-i-ty
sen-si-tiv-i-ties

sen-si-tize
sen-si-tized
sen-si-tiz-ing
sen-si-ti-za-tion
sen-si-tizer
sen-sor
sen-so-ry
sen-so-ri-al
sen-su-al
sen-su-al-i-ty
sen-su-al-ly
sen-su-al-ism
sen-su-al-ist
sen-su-al-ize
sen-su-al-ized
sen-su-al-iz-ing
sen-su-al-i-za-tion
sen-su-ous
sen-tence
sen-tenced
sen-tenc-ing
sen-tient
sen-ti-ment
sen-ti-men-tal
sen-ti-men-tal-ly
sen-ti-men-til-i-ty
sen-ti-men-tal-i-ties
sen-ti-men-tal-ist
sen-ti-men-tal-ize
sen-ti-men-tal-ized
sen-ti-men-tal-iz-ing
sen-ti-nel
sen-ti-neled
sen-ti-nel-ing
sen-try
sen-tries
se-pal
se-paled
se-palled
sep-a-ra-ble
sep-a-ra-bil-i-ty
sep-e-ra-bly
sep-a-rate
sep-a-rat-ed
sep-a-rat-ing
sep-a-ra-tion
sep-a-ra-tist
sep-a-ra-tism

sep-a-ra-tive
sep-a-ra-tor
se-pi-a
sep-sis
sep-ses
sep-ten-ni-al
sep-tet
sep-tic
sep-ti-cal-ly
sep-tic-i-ty
sep-tu-a-ge-nar-i-an
sep-tum
sep-ta
sep-tu-ple
sep-tu-pled
sep-tu-pling
sep-ul-cher
sep-u-chered
sep-u-cher-ing
se-pul-chral
se-quel
se-quence
se-quent
se-quen-tial
se-quen-tial-ly
se-ques-ter
se-ques-tered
se-ques-tra-ble
se-ques-tra-tion
se-quin
se-quined
se-quoi-a
se-ra-pe
ser-aph
ser-aphs
ser-a-phim
se-raph-ic
ser-e-nade
ser-e-nad-ed
ser-e-nad-ing
ser-e-nad-er
ser-en-dip-i-ty
ser-en-dip-i-tous
se-rene
se-rene-ness
se-ren-i-ty
se-ren-i-ties
serf

serge
ser-geant
ser-geant at arms
ser-geant ma-jor
se-ri-al
  se-ri-al-ly
  se-ri-al-ist
  se-ri-al-i-za-tion
  se-ri-al-ize
  se-ri-al-ized
  se-ri-al-iz-ing
se-ries
se-ri-ous
  se-ri-ous-ly
  se-ri-ous-ness
se-ri-ous--mind-ed
  se-ri-us--mind-ed-ly
ser-mon
  ser-mon-ize
  ser-mon-ized
  ser-mon-iz-ing
se-rol-o-gy
  se-ro-log-ic
  se-ro-log-i-cal
  se-rol-o-gist
se-rous
ser-pent
ser-pen-tine
ser-rate
  ser-rat-ing
ser-ra-tion
se-rum
  se-rums
  se-ra
serv-ant
serve
  served
  serv-ing
serv-er
serv-ice
  serv-iced
  serv-ic-ing
serv-ice-a-ble
  serv-ice-a-bil-i-ty
  serv-ice-a-ble-ness
  serv-ice-a-bly
serv-ice-man
ser-vile

ser-vil-i-ty
ser-vile-ness
ser-vi-tude
ser-vo-mech-an-ism
ses-a-me
ses-qui-cen-ten-ni-al
ses-sion
set-back
set-in
set-off
set-ter
set-ting
set-tle
  set-tled
  set-tling
set-tle-ment
set-tler
set-to
set-up
sev-en
sev-enth
sev-en-teen
  sev-en-teenth
sev-en-ty
  sev-en-ti-eth
sev-er
  sev-er-a-bil-i-ty
  sev-er-a-ble
sev-er-al
  sev-er-al-ly
sev-er-al-fold
sev-er-ance
se-vere
  se-ver-er
  se-ver-est
  se-vere-ness
se-ver-i-ty
  se-ver-i-ties
sew
sew-age
sew-ing
sew-ing ma-chine
sex-less
sex-ol-o-gy
  sex-o-log-i-cal
  sex-ol-o-gist
sex-tant
sex-tet

sex-ton
sex-tu-ple
  sex-tu-pled
  sex-tu-pling
sex-tu-plet
sex-u-al
  sex-u-al-ly
  sex-u-al-i-ty
sex-y
  sex-i-er
  sex-i-est
shab-by
  shab-bi-er
  shab-bi-est
  shab-bi-ly
shack-le
  shack-led
  shack-ling
  shack-ler
shade
  shad-ed
  shad-ing
  shade-less
shad-ow
shad-ow-box
shad-owy
shad-y
  shad-i-er
  shad-i-est
  shad-i-ly
shaft-ing
shag
  shagged
  shag-ging
  shag-gi-ly
shake
  shak-en
  shak-ing
shake-down
shak-er
shake-up
shak-y
  shak-i-er
  shak-i-est
  shak-i-ly
shal-lot
shal-low
  shal-low-ness

sham
 shammed
 sham-ming
sha-man
 sha-man-ism
 sha-man-ist
sham-bles
shame
 shamed
 sham-ing
shame-faced
 shame-fac-ed-ly
shame-ful
 shame-ful-ly
 shame-ful-ness
sham-mer
sham-my
sham-poo
 sham-pooed
 sham-poo-ing
 sham-poo-er
sham-rock
shan-tey
 shan-ties
shan-ty-town
shape
 shaped
 shap-ing
 shap-a-ble
 shap-er
shape-less
shape-ly
 shape-li-ier
 shape-li-est
share
 shared
 shar-ing
 shar-er
share-crop-per
 share-crop
 share-cropped
 share-crop-ping
share-hold-er
shark-skin
sharp-en
 sharp-en-er
sharp-er
sharp-eyed

sharp-ie
sharp-shoot-er
 sharp-shoot-ing
sharp-tongued
sharp-wit-ted
 sharp-wit-ted-ly
 sharp-wit-ted-ness
shat-ter
shat-ter-proof
shave
 shaved
 shav-ing
shav-er
shawl
sheaf
 sheaves
shear
 sheared
 shear-ing
 shear-er
sheath
 sheath-less
sheathe
 sheathed
 sheath-ing
 sheath-er
shed
 shed-ding
sheen
 sheeny
 sheen-i-er
sheep-dog
sheep-herd-er
 sheep-herd-ing
sheep-ish
sheep-skin
sheer
 sheer-ly
sheet-ing
sheik
shelf
 shelves
shell
 shelled
shel-lac
 shel-lacked
 shel-lack-ing
shell-fire

shell-fish
shell shock
shel-ter
 shel-ter-er
shelve
 shelved
 shelv-ing
she-nan-i-gan
shep-herd
 shep-herd-ess
sher-bet
sher-iff
sher-ry
 sher-ries
shib-bo-leth
shield
 shield-er
shift
 shift-er
shift-less
shift-y
 shift-i-er
 shift-i-est
 shift-i-ly
shil-ly--shal-ly
 shil-ly-shal-lied
 shil-ly-shal-ly-ing
shim-mer
 shim-mery
 shim-mer-i-er
 shim-mer-i-est
shim-my
 shim-mies
 shim-mied
 shim-my-ing
shin
 shinned
 shin-ning
shin-bone
shin-dig
shine
 shined
 shone
 shin-ing
shin-er
shin-gle
 shin-gled
 shin-gling

shin-gler
shin-gles
shin-ing
shin-ing-ly
shin-ny
shin-nied
shin-ny-ing
shin-y
shin-i-er
shin-i-est
ship
shipped
ship-ping
ship-a-ble
ship-board
ship-build-er
ship-build-ing
ship-mate
ship-ment
ship-per
ship-yard
shirk
shirker
shirt-tail
shirt-waist
shish ke-bab
shiv-er
shiv-ery
shiv-er-i-er
shiv-er-i-est
shoal
shock-er
shock-ing
shod-dy
shod-di-er
shod-di-ly
shod-di-ness
shoe-horn
shoe-lace
shoe-mak-er
sho-er
shoe-string
shoo--in
shoot
shot
shoot-ing
shoot-er
shop

shopped
shop-ping
shop-keep-er
shop-lift-er
shop-lift-ing
shop-per
shop-talk
shop-worn
shore
shore-line
short
short-ly
short-ness
short-age
short--change
short--changed
short--chang-ing
short-com-ing
short-cut
short-cut-ting
short-en
short-en-er
short-en-ing
short-hand
short--hand-ed
short--lived
short--sight-ed
short--sight-ed-ly
short--sight-ed-ness
short--tem-pered
short--term
short-wave
short--wind-ed
shot-gun
shot-gunned
shot-gun-ning
shoul-der
shoul-der blade
shout-er
shout-ing
shove
shoved
shov-ing
shov-er
shov-el
shov-eled
shov-el-ing
shov-el-ful

show
showed
shown
show-ing
show-bill
show-boat
show-case
show-cased
show-cas-ing
show-down
show-er
show-ery
show-man
show-men
show-man-ship
show-off
show-piece
show-place
show-room
show-y
show-i-er
show-i-est
show-i-ly
shrap-nel
shred
shred-ded
shred-ding
shred-der
shrew
shrewd
shrewd-ly
shrewd-ness
shrew-ish
shriek
shrill
shirl-ly
shrimp
shrine
shrined
shrin-ing
shrink
shrunk-ed
shrink-a-ble
shrink-er
shrink-age
shriv-el
shriv-eled
shriv-el-ing

shroud
shrub-bery
  shrub-ber-ies
shrub-by
  shrub-bi-er
  shrub-bi-est
shrug
  shrugged
  shrug-ging
shuck-er
shud-der
  shud-dery
suf-fle
  shuf-fled
  shuf-fling
  shuf-fler
shuf-fle-board
shun
  shunned
  shun-ning
  shun-ner
shunt
  shunt-er
shut-down
shut-eye
shut-in
shut-off
shut-out
shut-ter
shut-tle
  shut-tled
  shut-tling
shut-tle-like
shy
  shi-er
  shy-est
  shy-ness
shy-ster
sib-i-lant
  sib-i-lance
sib-ling
sick
  sicked
  sick-ing
sick-bed
sick-en
  sick-en-ing
sick-ish

sick-le
sick-ly
  sick-li-er
  sick-li-est
sick-ness
sick-room
side-arm
side-board
sid-ed
side-kick
side-line
  side-lined
  side-lin-ing
side--long
side-show
side-split-ting
side-step
  side-step-ped
  side-step-ping
side-swipe
  side-swiped
  side-swip-ing
side-track
side-ways
sid-ing
si-dle
  si-dled
  si-dling
siege
si-en-na
si-er-ra
si-es-ta
sieve
  sieved
  siev-ing
sift-er
sift-ings
sigh-er
sight-ed
sight-less
sight-ly
sight-read
  sight-read-ing
sight-see-ing
  sight-see-er
sig-nal
  sig-naled
  sig-nal-ing

sig-nal-er
sig-nal-man
sig-nal-men
sig-na-to-ry
  sig-na-to-ries
sig-na-ture
sign-board
sig-net
sig-nif-i-cance
sig-nif-i-cant
sig-ni-fi-ca-tion
sig-ni-fy
  sig-ni-fied
  sig-ni-fy-ing
  sig-ni-fi-a-ble
  sig-ni-fi-er
sign-post
si-lage
si-lence
  si-lenced
  si-lenc-ing
  si-lenc-er
si-lent
si-lent part-ner
sil-hou-ette
  sil-hou-et-ted
  sil-hou-et-ting
sil-ic-a
sil-i-con
sil-i-cone
silk-en
silk-like
silk-weed
silk-worm
silk-y
  silk-i-er
  silk-i-est
  silk-i-ly
sil-ly
  sil-li-er
  sil-li-est
  sil-li-ness
si-lo
  si-los
  si-loed
  si-lo-ing
silt
  sil-ta-tion

silt-y
silt-i-er
silt-i-est
sil-ver
sil-ver-fish
sil-ver-fox
sil-ver-ware
sil-ver-y
sim-i-an
sim-i-lar
  sim-i-lar-i-ty
  sim-i-lar-i-ties
sim-i-le
si-mil-i-tude
sim-mer
si-mon-ize
  si-mon-ized
  si-mon-iz-ing
sim-pa-ti-co
sim-per
  sim-per-er
  sim-per-ing-ly
sim-ple
  sim-pler
  sim-plest
  sim-ple-ness
sim-ple--mind-ed
sim-ple sen-tence
sim-ple-ton
sim-plex
sim-plic-i-ty
  sim-plic-i-ties
sim-pli-fy
  sim-pli-fied
  sim-pli-fy-ing
  sim-pli-fi-ca-tion
  sim-pli-fi-er
sim-plism
  sim-plis-tic
  sim-plis-ti-cal-ly
sim-ply
sim-u-late
  sim-u-lat-ed
  sim-u-lat-ing
  sim-u-la-tion
  sim-u-la-tive
  sim-u-la-tor
si-mul-cast

si-mul-cast-ing
si-mul-ta-ne-ous
  si-mul-ta-ne-ous-ly
  si-mul-ta-ne-i-ty
sin
  sinned
  sin-ning
sin-cere
sin-cer-i-ty
si-ne-cure
si-ne qua non
sin-ew
sin-ew-y
sin-ful
  sin-ful-ly
  sin-ful-ness
sing
  sing-ing
  sing-a-ble
singe
  singed
  singe-ing
sing-er
sin-gle
  sin-gled
  sin-gling
  sin-gle-ness
sin-gle-brest-ed
sin-gle--hand-ed
  sin-gle-hand-ed-ly
sin-gle--mind-ed
  sin-gle--mind-ed-ly
sin-gle--space
  sin-gle--spaced
  sin-gle--spac-ing
sin-gle-ton
sin-gle--track
sin-gly
sing-song
sin-gu-lar
sin-gu-lar-i-ty
  sin-gu-lar-i-ties
sin-is-ter
  sin-is-ter-ness
sink-a-ble
sink-er
sink-hole
sin-less

sin-ner
sin-u-ate
  sin-u-at-ed
  sin-u-at-ing
sin-u-ous
  sin-u-os-i-ty
  sin-u-ous-ness
si-nus
si-nus-i-tis
sip
  sipped
  sip-ping
  sip-per
si-phon
sire
  sired
  sir-ing
si-ren
sir-loin
sis-sy
  sis-sies
  sis-si-fied
  sis-sy-ish
sis-ter
  sis-ter-li-ness
  sis-ter-ly
sis-ter-in-law
  sis-ters-in-law
si-tar
sit-in
sit-ter
sit-ting
sit-u-ate
  sit-u-at-ed
  sit-u-at-ing
sit-u-a-tion
six--pack
six--shoot-er
six-teen
  six-teenth
sixth
six-ty
  six-ti-eth
siz-a-ble
  siz-a-ble-ness
  siz-a-bly
size
  sized

siz-ing
siz-zle
  siz-zled
  siz-zling
  siz-zler
skate
  skat-ed
  skat-ing
  skat-er
ske-dad-dle
  ske-dad-dled
  ske-dad-dling
skein
skel-e-ton
  skel-e-tal
skep-tic
  skep-ti-cal
  skep-ti-cism
sketch
  sketch-er
sketch-book
sketch-y
  sketch-i-er
  sketch-i-est
  sketch-i-ly
skew-er
skew-ness
ski
  skied
  ski-ing
  ski-er
skid
  skid-ded
  skid-ding
  skid-der
skilled
skil-let
skill-ful
  skill-ful-ly
  skill-ful-ness
skim
  skimmed
  skim-ming
skim-mer
skimp
  skimp-i-ly
skimp-y
  skimp-i-er

skimp-i-est
skin
  skinned
  skin-ning
skin--deep
skin dive
  skin div-ing
  skin div-er
skin-flint
skin-less
skin-ner
skin-ny
  skin-ni-er
  skin-ni-est
skin-tight
skip-per
skir-mish
  skir-mish-er
skirt-er
  skirt-ing
skit-ter
skit-tish
skiv-vy
  skiv-vies
skoal
skul-dug-ger-y
skulk-er
skull-cap
skunk
sky
  skies
  skied
  sky-ing
sky-blue
sky-cap
sky-div-ing
sky-rock-et
sky-svap-er
sky-ward
sky-way
sky-writ-ing
  sky-writ-er
slab
  slabbed
  slab-bing
slack
  slack-ness
slack-en

slack-er
slack-jawed
slake
  slaked
  slak-ing
sla-lom
slam
  slammeed
  slam-ming
slam-bang
slan-der
  slan-der-er
  slan-der-ous
slang
  slang-i-er
  slang-i-est
slant
  slant-ways
  slant-wise
slap
  slapp-ed
  slap-ping
  slap-per
slap-dash
slap-hap-py
  slap-hap-pi-er
  slap-hap-pi-est
slap-stick
slash-er
slash-ing
slat
  slat-ted
  slat-ting
slate
  slat-ed
  slat-ing
slath-er
slat-tern
  slat-tern-ly
slaugh-ter
  slaugh-ter-er
slaugh-ter-house
slave
  slaved
  slav-ing
slav-er
slav-er-y
slav-ish

sla-vish-ly
slay
 slain
 slay-ing
 slay-er
slea-zy
 slea-zi-er
 slea-zi-est
sled
 sled-ded
 sled-ding
 sled-der
sledge
 sledged
 sledg-ing
sleek
 sleek-er
 sleek-ness
sleep-er
sleep-less
 sleep-less-ness
sleep-walk
 sleep-walk-er
 sleep-walk-ing
sleep-y
 sleep-i-er
 sleep-i-est
 sleep-i-ly
sleep-y-head
sleet
 sleet-y
 sleet-i-ness
sleeve
 sleeved
 sleev-ing
 sleeve-less
sleigh
 sleigh-er
sleight
slen-der
 slen-der-ness
slen-der-ize
 slen-der-ized
 slen-der-iz-ing
sleuth
slice
 sliced
 slic-ing

slic-er
slick-er
slick-ness
slide
slid
 slid-ing
 slid-er
slight
 slight-er
 slight-ing
slim
 slim-mer
 slim-mest
 slimmed
 slim-ming
 slim-ness
slime
 slimed
 slim-ing
slimy
 slim-i-er
 slim-i-est
 slim-i-ly
sling-er
sling-shoot
slink-y
 slink-i-er
 slink-i-est
slip
 slipped
 slip-ping
slip-cov-er
slip-knot
slip--on
slip-o-ver
slip-page
slip-per
slip-per-y
 slip-per-i-er
 slip-per-i-est
slip-py
slip-shod
slip-stick
slip-up
slit
 slit-ting
 slit-ter
slith-er

slith-ery
sliv-er
 sliv-er-er
 sliv-er-like
slob-ber
 slob-ber-er
 slob-ber-ing-ly
sloe--eyed
slo-gan
 slo-gan-eer
slop
 slopped
 slop-ping
slope
 sloped
 slop-ing
 slop-er
slop-py
 slop-pi-er
 slop-pi-est
 slo-pi-ly
 slop-pi-ness
slosh-y
 slosh-i-er
 slosh-i-est
slot
 slot-ted
 slot-ting
sloth
 sloth-ful
 sloth-ful-ly
slouch
 slouch-er
 slouch-i-ly
 slouch-i-ness
 slouch-y
 slouch-i-er
 slouch-i-est
slough
 slough-y
 slough-i-er
 slough-i-est
slov-en
slov-en-ly
 slov-en-li-ness
slow-down
slow--mo-tion
slow-poke

slow--wit-ted
sludge
  slug-y
  sludg-i-er
  sludg-i-est
slug
  slugged
  slug-ging
  slug-ger
slug-gard
  slug-gard-li-ness
slug-gish
  slug-gish-ness
sluice
  sluiced
  sluic-ing
slum
  slummed
  slum-ming
slum-ber
  slum-ber-er
slum-ber-ous
slur
  slurred
  slur-ring
slush
  slush-i-ness
  slush-y
  slush-i-er
  slush-i-est
slut
  slut-tish
sly
smack
smack-ing
small--mind-ed
  small--mind-ed-ness
small-pox
small--time
  small--tim-er
smart
  smart-ness
smart al-eck
  smart-al-eck-y
smash
smash-ing
smash--up

smat-ter
smat-ter-er
smat-ter-ing
smear
smear-er
smear-y
smear-i-er
smear-i-est
smell
smelled
smel-ling
smell-er
smell-y
smell-i-er
smell-i-est
smelt
smelt-er
smelt-ery
smid-gen
snile
smil-er
smil-ing-ly
smirch
smirk
smirk-er
smirk-ing-ly
smite
smote
smit-ten
smit-ting
smit-er
smith-er-eens
smit-ten
smock-ing
smog-gy
smog-gi-er
smog-gi-est
smoke
smoked
smok-ing
smoke-less
smoke-house
smok-er
smoke-stack
smok-ing jack-et
smok-y
smok-i-er
smok-i-est

smok-i-ly
smol-der
smooth
smooth-er
smooth-ness
smooth-en
smooth-ie
smoth-er
smoth-er-y
smoth-er-i-er
smoth-er-i-est
smudge
smudged
smudg-ing
smudg-i-ly
smug
smug-ger
smug-gest
smug-ly
smug-ness
smug-gle
smug-gled
smug-gling
smug-gler
smut
smut-ted
smut-ting
smut-ty
smut-ti-er
smut-ti-est
smut-ti-ly
sna-fu
sna-fued
sna-fu-ing
snag
snagged
snag-ging
snag-gy
snag-gle-tooth
snag-gle-teeth
snag-gle-toothed
snail
snail-like
snail-paced
snake
snake-bite
snake-skin
snak-y

snak-i-er
snak-i-est
snap
snapped
snap-ping
snap-back
snap-drag-on
snap-per
snap-pish
snap-pish-ness
snap-py
snap-pi-er
snap-pi-est
snap-pi-ly
snap-shot
snare
snared
snar-ing
snar-er
snarl
snarl-er
snarl-y
snarl-i-er
snarl-i-est
snatch
snatch-i-er
snatch-i-est
snatch-i-ly
snaz-zy
snaz-zi-er
snaz-zi-est
sneak-er
sneak-ing
sneak-y
sneak-i-er
sneak-i-est
sneak-i-ly
sneer
sneer-er
sneer-ing-ly
sneeze
sneezed
sneez-ing
sneez-er
sneez-y
sneez-i-er
sneez-i-est
snick-er

snif-fle
snif-fled
snif-fling
snif-fler
snif-fy
snif-fi-er
snif-fi-est
snif-fi-ly
snif-ter
snip
snipped
snip-ping
snip-per
snipe
sniped
snip-ing
snip-er
snip-py
snip-pi-er
snip-pi-est
snip-pi-ly
snitch-er
sniv-el
sniv-eled
sniv-el-ing
sniv-el-er
snob
snob-ber-y
snob-bish
snob-bish-ness
snoop
snoop-y
snoop-i-er
snoop-i-est
snoop-er
snoot-y
snoot-i-er
snoot-i-est
snoot-i-ly
snoot-i-ness
snooze
snoozed
snooz-ing
snooz-er
snore
snored
snor-ing
snor-er

snor-kel
snort
snort-er
snot-ty
snot-ti-er
snot-ti-est
snout
snout-ed
snout-y
snout-i-er
snout-i-est
snow-ball
snow-blow-er
snow-bound
snow-cap
snow-drift
snow-fall
snow-flake
snow-man
snow-men
snow-mo-bile
snow-plow
snow-shoe
snow-shoed
snow-shoe-ing
snow-suit
snow--white
snow-y
snow-i-er
snow-i-est
snub
snubbed
snub-bing
snub-ber
snub-by
snub-bi-er
snub-bi-est
snub-bi-ness
snub--nosed
snuf-fle
snuff-y
snuff-i-er
snuff-i-est
snug
snug-gle
snug-gled
snug-gling
soak

soak-age
soak-er
soak-ing-ly
so--and--so
soap-box
soap-suds
soap-y
soap-i-er
soap-i-est
soap-i-ly
soap-i-ness
soar-er
sob
sobbed
sob-bing
sob-ber
so-ber
so-ber-ing-ly
so-ber-ness
so-bri-e-ty
so-bri-quet
so--called
soc-cer
so-cia-ble
so-cia-bil-i-ty
so-cia-bly
so-cial
so-ci-al-i-ty
so-cial-ly
so-cial-ism
so-cial-ist
so-cial-is-tic
so-cial-is-ti-cal-ly
so-cial-ite
so-cial-ize
so-cial-ized
so-cial-iz-ing
so-cial-i-za-tion
so-cial-iz-er
so-ci-e-ty
so-ci-e-ties
so-ci-e-tal
so-ci-o-ec-o-nom-ic
so-ci-ol-o-gy
so-ci-o-log-i-cal
so-ci-ol-o-gist
so-ci-o-po-lit-i-cal
sock-et

sod
sod-ded
sod-ding
so-da
so-dal-i-ty
so-dal-i-ties
sod-den
sod-den-ness
so-di-um
sod-om-y
so-ev-er
so-fa
soft
soft-ness
soft-ball
soft--boiled
sof-ten
sof-ten-er
soft--head-ed
soft--heart-ed
soft--heart-ed-ness
soft ped-al
soft-ped-aled
soft-ped-al-ing
soft--shell
soft--shoe
soft--spok-en
soft-ware
soft-wood
soft-y
sof-ties
sog-gy
sog-gi-er
sog-gi-est
sog-gi-ly
sog-gi-ness
so-journ
so-journ-er
sol-ace
sol-aced
sol-ac-ing
sol-ac-er
so-lar
so-lar-i-um
so-lar-i-ums
so-lar-ia
so-lar-ize
so-lar-ized

so-lar-iz-ing
so-lar-i-za-tion
sol-der
sol-der-er
sol-dier
sol-dier-y
sol-e-cism
sole-ly
sol-emn
sol-emn-ly
sol-emn-less
so-lem-ni-ty
so-lem-ni-ties
sol-em-nize
sol-em-nized
sol-em-niz-ing
sol-em-ni-za-tion
sole-ness
so-lic-it
so-lic-i-ta-tion
so-lic-i-tor
so-lic-i-tous
so-lic-i-tous-ness
so-lic-i-tude
sol-id
sol-id-i-ty
sol-id-ness
sol-i-dar-i-ty
sol-i-dar-i-ties
so-lid-i-fy
so-lid-i-fied
so-lid-i-fy-ing
so-lid-i-fi-ca-tion
so-lil-o-quize
so-lil-o-quized
so-lil-o-quiz-ing
so-lil-o-quist
so-lil-o-quy
so-lil-o-quies
sol-i-taire
sol-i-tar-y
sol-i-tar-ies
sol-i-tar-i-ly
sol-i-tar-i-ness
sol-i-tude
so-lo
so-loed
so-lo-ing

so-lo-ist
sol-stice
sol-u-ble
  sol-u-bil-i-ty
  sol-u-bly
sol-ute
so-lu-tion
solve
  solved
  solv-ing
  solv-a-ble
  solv-a-bil-i-ty
  solv-er
sol-vent
  sol-ven-cy
so-mat-ic
so-ma-to-type
som-ber
  som-ber-ly
  som-ber-ness
som-bre-ro
  som-bre-ros
some-bod-y
  some-bod-ies
some-day
some-how
some-place
som-er-sault
some-thing
some-time
some-times
some-way
some-what
some-where
sosm-nam-bu-late
som-no-lent
  som-no-lence
  som-no-len-cy
so-nar
so-na-ta
song-bird
song-fest
song-ster
  song-stress
song-writ-er
son-ic
son--in--law
  sons--in--law

son-net
son-ny
  son-nies
so-no-rous
  so-nor-i-ty
  so-no-rous-ness
soon-er
soothe
  soothed
  sooth-ing
  sooth-er
sooth-say-er
  sooth-say-ing
soot-y
  soot-i-er
  soot-i-est
  soot-i-ly
sop
  sopped
  sop-ping
soph-ist
  soph-ism
so-phis-tic
  so-phis-ti-cal
so-phis-ti-cate
  so-phis-ti-cat-ed
  so-phis-ti-cat-ing
  so-phis-ti-ca-tion
  so-phis-ti-ca-tor
soph-ist-ry
  soph-ist-ries
soph-o-more
soph-o-mor-ic
  soph-o-mor-i-cal
  soph-o-mor-i-cal-ly
sop-o-rif-ic
sop-py
  sop-pi-er
  sop-pi-est
so-pran-o
  so-pran-os
sor-cer-er
  sor-cer-ess
sor-cer-y
  sor-cer-ies
  sor-cer-ous
sor-did
  sor-did-ness

sore
  sor-er
  sor-est
  sore-ly
  sore-ness
sore-head
  sore-head-ed
sor-ghum
so-ror-i-ty
  so-ror-i-ties
sor-rel
sor-row
  sor-row-er
  sor-row-ful
sor-ry
  sor-ri-er
  sor-ri-est
  sor-ri-ly
sort-a-ble
sort-er
sor-tie
so--so
sot
  sot-ted
  sot-tish
  sot-tish-ness
sot-vo vo-ce
sought
soul-ful
  soul-ful-ly
  soul-ful-ness
soul-less
soul-searching
sound
  sound-a-ble
  sound-ly
  sound-ness
sound-box
sound-er
sound-ing
sound-less
  sound-less-ly
sound-proof
soup-y
  soup-i-er
  soup-i-est
sour
  sour-ish

sour-ness
sour-ball
source
souse
soused
sous-ing
south-bound
south-east
south-east-er
south-east-er-ly
south-east-ern
south-east-ward
south-east-ward-ly
south-er
south-er-ly
south-ern
south-ern-most
south-ern-er
south-paw
south-ward
south-ward-ly
south-west
south-west-er
south-west-ern
south-west-ern-er
south-west-ward
south-west-ward-ly
sou-ve-nir
sov-er-eign
sov-er-eign-ty
sov-er-eign-ties
so-vi-et
sow-er
soy-bean
space
spaced
spac-ing
space-less
spac-er
space-craft
space-man
space-men
space-ship
space-walk
spa-cious
spa-cious-ness
spade
spad-ed

spad-ing
spade-ful
spad-er
spade-work
spa-ghet-ti
span
spanned
span-ning
span-gle
span-gled
span-gling
span-iel
spank-er
spank-ing
spar
sparred
spar-ring
spare
spared
spar-ing
spar-er
spar-est
spar-a-ble
spare-ness
spare-rib
spar-ing
spar-ing-ness
spark-er
spar-kle
spar-kled
spar-kling
spar-kler
spar-row
spar-row-grass
sparse
spars-er
spars-est
spasm
spas-mod-ic
spas-mod-i-cal
spas-mod-i-cal-ly
spas-tic
spas-ti-cal-ly
spat
spat-ted
spat-ting
spa-tial
spa-cial

spa-ti-al-i-ty
spa-tial-ly
spat-ter
spat-u-la
spawn
speak
spok-en
speak-ing
speak-a-ble
speak-eas-y
speak-eas-ies
speak-er
speak-er-ship
spear-er
spear-head
spear-mint
spe-cial
spe-cial-ly
spe-cial-ist
spe-cial-ize
spe-cial-ized
spe-cial-iz-ing
spe-cial-i-za-tion
spe-cial-ty
spe-cial-ties
spe-cie
spe-cies
spec-i-fia-ble
spe-cif-ic
spe-cif-i-cal-ly
spec-i-fic-i-ty
spec-i-fi-ca-tion
spec-i-fy
spec-i-fied
spec-i-fy-ing
spec-i-fi-er
spec-i-men
spe-cious
spe-ci-os-i-ty
spe-ci-os-i-ties
spe-cious-ness
speck-le
speck-led
speck-ling
spec-ta-cle
spec-ta-cled
spec-tac-u-lar
spec-tac-u-lar-ly

spec-ta-tor
spec-ter
spec-tral
spce-tro-scope
  spec-tro-scop-ic
  spec-tro-scop-i-cal
  spec-tros-co-py
spec-trum
  spec-tra
  spec-trums
spec-u-late
  spec-u-lat-ed
  spec-u-lat-ing
  spec-u-la-tion
  spec-u-la-tive
  spec-u-la-tor
speech-i-fy
  speech-i-fie
  speech-i-fy-ing
speech-less
  speech-less-ness
speed
  speed-ed
  speed-ing
  speed-er
  speed-ster
speed-boat
  speed-boat-ing
speed-om-e-ter
speed--up
speed-way
speed-y
  speed-i-er
  speed-i-est
  speed-i-ly
  speed-i-ness
spe-le-ol-o-gy
  spe-le-ol-o-gist
spell
  spelled
  spell-ing
spell-bind
  spell-bouns
  spell-bind-ing
  spell-bind-er
spell-er
spe-lun-ker
spend

spent
spend-ing
spend-a-ble
spend-er
spend-thrift
sper-ma-cet-i
sper-mat-ic
sper-ma-to-zo-on
sper-ma-to-zo-a
sper-ma-tozo-ic
spew-er
sphag-num
sphere
  sphered
  spher-ing
  spher-ic
  sphe-ric-i-ty
sphe-roid
  sphe-roi-dal
sphinc-ter
  sphin-ter-al
  sphin-ter-ic
sphinx
  sphinxes
  sphin-ges
spice
  spiced
  spic-ing
spi-cule
  spic-u-lar
  spic-u-late
spic-y
  spic-i-er
  spic-i-esst
  spic-i-ly
spi-der
spi-der-y
spiel
  spiel-er
spi-er
spiff-y
  spiff-i-er
  spiff-i-est
spig-ot
spike
  spiked
  spik-ing
spik-y

spik-i-er
spik-i-est
spill
  spilled
  spill-ing
spil-lage
spill-way
spin
  spun
  spin-ning
spin-ach
spi-nal
  spi-nal-ly
spin-dle
  spin-dled
  spin-dling
spin-dle-legs
  spin-dle-leg-ged
spin-dly
  spin-dli-er
  spin-dli-est
spine-less
spin-et
spin-na-ker
spin-ner
spin-ning wheel
spin--off
spi-nose
spi-nous
spin-ster
spin-y
  spin-i-ness
spi-ra-cle
spi-ral
  spi-raled
  spi-ral-ing
  spi-ral-ly
spire
  spired
  spir-ing
spir-it
spir-it-ed
spir-it-ism
  spir-ir-ist
spir-it-less
  spir-it-les-ness
spir-i-tous
spir-it-u-al

spir-it-u-al-ly
spir-it-u-al-ism
spir-it-u-al-ist
spir-it-u-al-is-tic
spir-it-u-al-i-ty
spir-it-u-al-i-ties
spir-it-u-al-ize
spir-it-u-al-ized
spir-it-u-al-iz-ing
spir-it-u-al-i-za-tion
spir-it-u-ous
spir-it-u-os-i-ty
spi-ro-chete
spit
spat
spit-ting
spit-ter
spite
spit-ed
spit-ing
spite-ful
spit-fire
spit-tle
spit-toon
splash
splash-er
splashy
splash-i-er
splash-i-est
splash-i-ly
splash-board
splash-down
splat-ter
splay-foot
splay-feet
splay-foot-ed
spleen
spleen-ful
splen-did
splen-dif-er-ous
sple-net-ic
splice
spliced
splic-ing
splic-er
splin-ter
splin-tery
split

split-ting
split-a-ble
split-ter
split--lev-el
split--sec-ond
splotch
spotch-y
splotch-i-er
splotch-i-est
splurge
splurged
splurg-ing
splut-ter
splut-ter-er
spoil
spoil-ed
spoil-ing
spoil-age
spoil-er
spoil-sport
spoke
spoked
spok-ing
spo-ken
spokes-man
spokes-men
spokes-wom-an
spokes-wom-en
sponge
sponged
spong-ing
spong-er
spon-gy
spon-gi-er
spon-gi-est
spon-gi-ness
spon-sor
spon-sor-ship
spon-ta-ne-i-ty
spon-ta-ne-i-ties
spon-ta-ne-ous
spon-ta-ne-ous-ly
spon-ta-ne-ous-ness
spook
spook-ish
spook-y
spook-i-er
spook-i-est

spook-i-ly
spoon-er-ism
spoon-er-is-tic
spoon--fed
spoon--feed
spoon--feed-ing
spoon-ful
spoon-fuls
spo-rad-ic
spo-rad-i-cal
spo-rad-i-cal-ly
spo-ran-gi-um
spo-ran-gia
spore
spored
spor-ing
sport
sport-ing
sport-ing-ly
spor-tive
sports-cast
sports-cast-er
sports-man
sports-wear
sports-writ-er
sport-y
sport-i-er
sport-i-est
sport-i-ly
spot
spot-ted
spot-ting
spot-less
spot-less-ly
spot-light
spot-ted
spot-ted fe-ver
spot-ter
spot-ty
spot-ti-er
spot-ti-est
spot-ti-ly
spouse
spout
spout-er
sprain
sprawl
spray

spray-er
spread
spread-ing
spread--ea-gle
spread--ea-gled
spread--ea-gling
spread-er
sprig
sprigged
sprig-ging
spright-ly
spright-li-er
spright-li-est
spring
spring-ing
spring-board
spring--clean-ing
spring-time
spring-y
spring-i-er
spring-i-est
spring-i-ly
sprin-kle
sprin-kled
sprin-kling
sprink-ler
sprint
sprint-er
sprock-et
spruce
spruc-er
spruc-est
spruced
spruc-ing
spry
spry-er
spry-est
spry-ly
spue
spued
spu-ing
spume
spumed
spum-ing
spum-ous
spunk-y
spunk-i-er
spunk-i-est

spunk-i-ly
spunk-i-ness
spur
spurred
spur-ring
spu-ri-ous
spu-ri-ous-ness
spurner
spurt
spurt-er
spur-tive
sput-nik
sput-ter
sput-ter-er
spu-tum
spu-ta
spy
spies
spied
spy-ing
spy-glass
squad-ron
squal-id
squal-id-ly
squal-id-ness
squall
squally
squall-i-er
squall-i-est
squal-or
squan-der
squan-der-er
square
squared
squar-ing
square-ly
square-ness
square-dance
square-danced
square-danc-ing
squar-ish
squar-ish-ly
squash
squash-er
squash-es
squash-y
squash-i-er
squash-i-est

squat
squat-ted
squat-ting
squat-ly
squat-ter
squat-ty
squat-ti-er
squat-ti-est
squawk
squawk-er
sqauwk-y
squawk-i-er
squawk-i-est
squeak
squeak-er
squeak-ing-ly
squeak-y
squeak-i-er
squeak-i-est
squeal
squeal-er
squeam-ish
squeam-ish-ly
squeam-ish-ness
squee-gee
squeeze
squeez-ed
squeez-ing
squeez-er
squelch
squelch-er
squib
squid
squig-gle
squig-gled
squig-gling
squint
squint-er
squint-ing-ly
squinty
squint-i-er
squint-i-est
squint--eyed
squire
squired
squir-ing
squirm
squirmy

squirm-i-er
squirm-i-est
squir-rel
squirt
squirt-er
squish
squish-y
squish-i-er
squish-i-est
stab
stabbed
stab-bing
stab-ber
sta-bil-i-ty
sta-bil-i-ties
sta-bi-lize
sta-bi-lized
sta-bi-liz-ing
sta-bi-li-za-tion
sta-bi-liz-er
sta-ble
sta-bled
sta-bling
stac-ca-to
stack-er
sta-di-um
staff-er
stag
stagged
stag-ging
stage-coach
stage-hand
stage--struck
stag-ger
stag-ger-er
stag-ger-ing
stag-nant
stag-nan-cy
stag-nate
stag-nat-ed
stag-nat-ing
stag-na-tion
stag-y
stag-i-er
stag-i-est
stag-i-ly
stag-i-ness
stain

stain-a-ble
stained
stain-er
stained glass
stain-less
stair-case
stair-way
stair-well
stake
staked
stak-ing
stake-hold-er
sta-lac-tite
sta-lag-mite
stale
stal-er
stal-est
staled
stal-ing
stale-ness
stale-mate
stale-mat-ed
stale-mat-ing
stalk
stalled
stal-lion
stal-wart
stal-wart-ness
sta-men
sta-mens
stam-i-na
stam-mer
stam-mer-ing-ly
stam-pede
stam-ped-ed
stam-ped-ing
stam-ped-er
stam-ped-ing-ly
stamp-er
stance
stand
stand-ing
stand-er
stand-ard
stand-ard-ize
stand-ard-ized
stand-ard-iz-ing
stand-ard-i-za-tion

stand-by
stnad-ee
stand--in
stand--off-ish
stand--off-ish-ness
stand-out
stand-pipe
stand-point
stand-still
sta-nine
stan-za
stan-za-ic
sta-pes
sta-pes
sta-ped-es
sta-pe-di-al
staph-y-lo-coc-cus
sta-ple
sta-pled
sta-pling
sta-pler
star
star-board
star-dom
stare
stared
star-ing
star-er
star-fish
star-gaze
star-gazed
star-gaz-ing
star-let
star-light
star-ling
star-ry
star-ri-er
star-ri-est
star-ri-ly
star-ry--eyed
star-span-gled
start-er
star-tle
star-tled
star-tling
star-tling-ly
star-va-tion
starve

starved
starv-ing
sta-sis
state
  stat-ed
  stat-ing
  stat-a-ble
state-craft
state-hood
state-less
  state-less-ness
state-ly
  state-li-er
  state-li-est
state-ment
state-room
state-side
states-man
  states-men
  states-man-like
  states-man-ship
stat-ic
stat-ics
sta-tion
sta-tion-ar-y
ssta-tion-er
sta-tion-er-y
stat-ism
  stat-ist
sta-tic-tic
  sta-tis-ti-cal
  sta-tic-ti-cal-ly
stat-is-ti-cian
sta-tis-tics
sta-tor
stat-u-ar-y
  stat-u-ar-ies
stat-ue
stat-u-esque
stat-u-ette
stat-ure
sta-tus
stat-ute
staunch
stave
  staved
  stav-ing
stay

stay-ed
stay-ing
stay-er
stead-fast
  stead-fast-ly
stead-y
steal
  stol-en
  steal-ing
  steal-er
stealth
  stealth-y
  stealth-i-er
  stealth-i-est
steam-boat
steam-er
steam-fit-ter
  steam-fit-ting
steam-roll-er
steam-ship
steam-y
  steam-i-er
  steam-i-est
  steam-i-ly
ste-a-tite
sted-fast
steel-head
steel-works
  steel-work-er
steel-y
  steel-i-er
steel-yard
steep
  steep-ly
steep-en
stee-ple
stee-ple-chase
  stee-ple-chas-er
stee-ple-jack
steer
  steer-a-ble
  steer-er
steer-age
stein
stel-lar
stem
  stemmed
stem-ware

stem-wind-er
  stem-wind-ing
stench
  stench-y
  stench-i-er
  stench-i-est
sten-cil
  sten-ciled
  sten-cil-ing
ste-nog-ra-pher
ste-nog-ra-phy
  sten-o-graph-ic
  sten-o-raph-i-cal-ly
sten-to-ri-an
step
  stepped
  step-ping
step-broth-er
step-child
  step-child-ren
step-daugh-ter
step-fa-ther
step-lad-der
step-moth-er
step-par-ent
stepped-up
step-sis-ter
step-son
ster-e-o
  ster-e-os
ster-e-o-phon-ic
  ster-e-o-phon-i-cal-ly
ster-e-o-scope
  ster-e-o-scop-ic
ster-e-o-type
  ster-e-o-typed
  ster-e-o-typ-ing
ster-ile
  ste-ril-i-ty
ster-i-lize
  ster-i-lized
  ster-i-liz-ing
  ster-i-li-za-tion
  ster-i-li-zer
ster-ling
stern
  stern-ly
  stern-ness

ster-num
  ster-na
  ster-nums
stern-wheel-er
ster-oid
steth-o-scope
  steth-o-scop-ic
ste-ve-dore
  ste-ve-dored
  ste-ve-dor-ing
ste-ward
stew-ard-ness
stick-er
stick-ing
stick-le-back
stick-ler
stick-pin
stick-up
stick-y
  stick-i-er
  stick-i-est
stiff
  stiff-ly
  stiff-ness
stiff-en
  stiff-en-er
stiff--necked
sti-fle
  sti-fled
  sti-fling
  sti-fler
  sti-fling-ly
stig-ma
  stig-mas
  stig-ma-ta
  stig-ma-tic
  stig-mat-i-cal-ly
stig-ma-tize
  stig-ma-tized
  stig-ma-tiz-ing
  stig-ma-ti-za-tion
sti-let-to
  sti-let-tos
  sti-let-toes
still-birth
  still-born
still life
still-ness

stilt-ed
  stilt-ed-ly
stim-u-lant
stim-u-late
  stim-u-lat-ed
  stim-u-lat-ing
  stim-u-la-tion
  stim-u-la-tive
stim-u-lus
  stim-u-li
sting
  sting-ing
  sting-er
  sting-ing-ly
stin-gy
  stin-gi-er
  stin-gi-est
  stin-gi-ly
  stin-gi-ness
stink
  stink-ing
  stink-er
  stink-y
  stink-i-er
  stink-i-est
stint-er
sti-pend
stip-ple
  stip-pled
  stip-pling
stip-u-late
  stip-u-lat-ed
  stip-u-lat-ing
  stip-u-la-tion
  stip-u-la-to-ry
stir
  stirred
  stir-ring
  stri-ring-ly
stir-rup
stitch
  stitch-er
stock-ade
  stock-ad-ed
  stock-ad-ing
stock-brok-er
stock-hold-er
Stock-holm

stock-ing
stock-pile
  stock-piled
  stock-pil-ing
stock-y
  stock-i-er
  stock-i-est
  stock-i-ly
  stock-i-ness
stock-yard
stodg-y
  stodg-i-er
  stodg-i-est
  stodg-i-ly
sto-ic
sto-i-cal
stoke
  stoked
  stok-ing
  stok-er
stol-id
  sto-lid-i-ty
  stol-id-ly
sto-ma
  sto-ma-ta
  sto-mas
stom-ach
stom-ach-er
stone
  stoned
  ston-ing
stone-deaf
stone-ma-son
  stone-ma-son-ry
stone-wall
ston-y
  ston-i-er
  ston-i-est
  ston-i-ly
stop
  stopped
  stop-ping
stop-gap
stop-light
stop-o-ver
stop-page
stop-per
stop-watch

stor-age
store
  stored
  stor-ing
store-house
store-keep-er
store-room
sto-ried
storm-y
  storm-i-er
  storm-i-est
  storm-i-ly
  storm-i-ness
sto-ry
  sto-ries
  sto-ry-ing
sto-ry-book
sto-ry-tell-er
  stor-y-tell-ing
stout
  stout-ly
  stout-ness
stout--heart-ed
stove
  stoved
  stov-ing
stove-pipe
stow-age
stow-a-way
stra-bis-mus
strad-dle
  strad-dled
  strad-dling
  strad-dler
strafe
  strafed
  straf-ing
strag-gle
  strag-gled
  strag-gling
  strag-gler
strag-gly
  strag-gli-er
  strag-gli-est
straight-en
  straight-en-er
straight-for-ward
  straight-for-ward-ly

straight-way
strain-er
strait-en
strait-jack-et
strait-laced
strange
  strang-er
  strang-est
  strang-ly
  strange-ness
stran-ger
stran-gle
  stran-gled
  stran-gling
  stran-gler
stran-gu-la-tion
  strn-gu-late
  stran-gu-lat-ed
  stran-gu-lat-ing
strap
  srapped
  strap-ping
  strap-less
stra-te-gic
  str-te-gi-cal-ly
strat-e-gy
  strat-e-gies
  strat-e-gist
strat-i-fi-ca-tion
strat-i-fy
  strat-i-fied
  strat-i-fy-ing
stra-to-cu-mu-lus
strat-o-sphere
  strat-o-spher-ic
stra-tum
  stra-ta
  stra-tums
stra-tus
  stra-ti
straw-ber-ry
  straw-ber-ries
stray-er
stray-ing
streak
  streaky
  streak-i-er
  streak-i-est

stream-er
stream-line
  stream-lined
  stream-lin-ing
street-car
street-walk-er
  street-walk-ing
strength-en
  strength-en-er
stren-u-ous
  stren-u-os-i-ty
  stren-u-ous-ly
strep-to-coc-cus
  strep-to-coc-ci
  strep-to-coc-cal
  strep-to-coc-cic
strep-to-my-cin
stress
  stress-ful
  stress-ful-ly
  stress-ful-ness
stretch
  stretch-a-bil-i-ty
  stretch-a-ble
stretch-er
strew
  strewed
  strew-ing
stri-a
  stri-ae
stri-ate
  stri-at-ed
  stri-at-ing
strick-en
strict
  strict-ly
  strict-ness
stric-ture
stride
  strid-den
  strid-ding
stri-dent
strid-u-la-tion
strife
  strife-ful
  strife-less
strike
  strick-en

strick-ing
string
strung
string-ing
strin-gent
strin-gen-cy
strin-gent-ly
string-y
string-i-er
string-i-est
strip
stripped
strip-ping
stripe
striped
strip-ing
strip-ling
strip-per
strip-tease
strip-teas-er
strive
strove
striv-en
striv-ing
stro-bo-scope
stro-bo-scop-ic
stro-bo-scop-i-cal-ly
stroke
stroked
strok-ing
stroll-er
strong
strong-ish
strong-ly
strong--arm
strong-box
strong-hold
strong-mind-ed
strong-mind-ed-ly
strong-mind-ed-ness
stron-ti-um
stron-tic
strop
stropped
strop-ping
struc-tur-al
struc-tur-al-ly
struc-ture

struc-tured
struc-tur-ing
struc-ture-less
strug-gle
strug-gled
strug-gling
strug-gler
strum
strum-mer
strum-pet
strut
strut-ted
strut-ting
strych-nine
strych-nia
strych-nic
stub
stubbed
stub-bing
stub-by
stub-bi-er
stub-bi-est
stub-ble
stub-bled
stub-bling
stub-by
stub-bi-er
stub-bi-est
stub-born
stub-born-ly
stub-born-ness
stuc-co
stuc-coes
stuc-cos
stuc-coed
stuc-co-ing
stuck--up
stud
stud-ded
stud-ding
stu-dent
stud-ied
stud-ied-ly
stud-ied-ness
stu-di-o
stu-di-os
stu-di-ous
stu-di-ous-ly

stu-di-ous-ness
stud-y
stud-ies
stud-ied
stud-y-ing
stuff-er
stuff-ing
stuff-y
stul-ti-fy
stul-ti-fied
stul-ti-fy-ing
stul-ti-fi-ca-tion
stul-ti-fi-er
stum-ble
stum-bled
stum-bling
stum-bler
stum-bling-ly
stump
stump-er
stumpy
stump-i-er
stump-i-est
stun-ning
stunt
stunt-ed
stunt-ed-ness
stu-pe-fy
stu-pe-fied
stu-pe-fy-ing
stu-pe-fac-tion
stu-pe-fi-er
stu-pe-fy-ing-ly
stu-pen-dous
stu-pen-dous-ly
stu-pen-dous-ness
stu-pid
stu-pid-i-ty
stu-pid-ly
stu-pid-ness
stu-por
stu-por-ous
stur-dy
stur-di-er
stur-di-est
stur-geon
stut-ter
stut-ter-er

stut-ter-ing-ly
style
styled
styl-ing
styl-er
styl-ish
styl-ish-ly
styl-ish-ness
styl-ist
sty-lis-tic
sty-lis-ti-cal
sty-lis-ti-cal-ly
styl-ize
styl-ized
styl-iz-ing
styl-i-za-tion
styl-iz-er
sty-lus
sty-lus-es
sty-li
sty-mie
sty-mies
sty-mied
sty-mie-ing
styp-tic
styp-ti-cal
styp-tic-i-ty
suave
suave-ly
suave-ness
suav-i-ty
sub
subbed
sub-bing
sub-al-tern
sub-arc-tic
sub-as-sem-bly
sub-as-sem-blies
sub-as-sem-bler
sub-base-ment
sub-chas-er
sub-class
sub-com-mit-tee
sub-con-scious
sub-con-scious-ly
sub-con-scious-ness
sub-con-ti-nent
sub-con-ti-nen-tal

sub-con-tract
sub-con-trac-tor
sub-cul-ture
sub-cul-tur-al
sub-cu-ta-ne-ous
sub-cu-ta-ne-ous-ly
sub-ded-u-tante
sub-di-vide
sub-di-vid-ed
sub-di-vid-ing
sub-di-vid-a-ble
sub-di-vid-er
sub-di-vi-sion
sub-di-vi-sion-al
sub-due
sub-dued
sub-du-ing
sub-du-a-ble
sub-du-al
sub-du-er
sub-en-try
sub-en-tries
sub-freez-ing
sub-group
sub-head
sub-hu-man
sub-ject
sub-jec-tion
sub-jec-tive
sub-jec-tive-ly
sub-jec-tive-ness
sub-jec-tiv-i-ty
sub-join
sub-ju-gate
sub-ju-gat-ed
sub-ju-gat-ing
sub-ju-ga-tion
sub-ju-ga-tor
sub-junc-tive
sub-lease
sub-leased
sub-leas-ing
sub-let
sub-let-ting
sub-li-mate
sub-li-mat-ed
sub-li-mat-ing
sub-li-ma-tion

sub-lime
sub-lim-i-nal
sub-lim-i-nal-ly
sub-lim-i-ty
sub-lim-i-ties
sub-ma-chine gun
sub-mar-gin-al
sub-ma-rine
sub-merge
sub-merged
sub-merg-ing
sub-mer-gence
sub-mer-gi-ble
sub-merse
sub-mersed
sub-mers-ing
sub-mer-sion
sub-mers-i-ble
sub-mi-cro-scop-ic
sub-mis-sion
sub-mis-sive
sub-mis-sive-ly
sub-mis-sive-ness
sub-mit
sub-mit-ted
sub-mit-ting
sub-nor-mal
sub-nor-mal-i-ty
sub-or-di-nate
sub-or-di-nat-ed
sub-or-di-nat-ing
sub-or-di-nate-ly
sub-or-di-nate-ness
sub-or-di-na-tion
sub-or-di-na-tive
sub-orn
sub-or-na-tion
sub-orn-er
sub-poe-na
sub-poe-naed
sub-poe-na-ing
sub-scribe
sub-scribed
sub-scrib-ing
sub-scrib-er
sub-scrip-tion
sub-se-quent
sub-se-quence

sub-se-quent-ly
sub-ser-vi-ent
sub-ser-vi-ence
sub-ser-vi-en-cy
sub-side
sub-sid-ed
sub-sid-ing
sub-sid-ence
sub-sid-i-ar-y
sub-sid-i-ar-ies
sub-si-dize
sub-si-dized
sub-si-diz-ing
sub-si-dy
sub-si-dies
sub-sist
sub-sist-ence
sub-soil
sub-son-ic
sub-stance
sub-stand-ard
sub-stan-tial
sub-stan-ti-al-i-ty
sub-stan-tial-ly
sub-stan-ti-ate
sub-stan-ti-at-ed
sub-stan-ti-at-ing
sub-stan-tive
sub-stan-ti-val
sub-stan-ti-val-ly
sub-stan-tive-ly
sub-sti-tute
sub-sti-tut-ed
sub-sti-tut-ing
sub-sti-tu-tion
sub-stra-tum
sub-stra-ta
sub-stra-tums
sub-struc-ture
sub-sume
sub-sumed
sub-sum-ing
sub-sum-a-ble
sub-sump-tive
sub-sump-tion
sub-teen
sub-tend
sub-ter-fuge

sub-ter-ra-ne-an
sub-ter-ra-ne-ous
sub-ter-ra-ne-an-ly
sub-ter-ra-ne-ous-ly
sub-ti-tle
sub-tle
sub-tle-ness
sub-tle-ty
sub-tle-ties
sub-tly
sub-tract
sub-tract-er
sub-trac-tion
sub-trac-tive
sub-tra-hend
sub-trop-i-cal
sub-trop-ic
sub-trop-ics
sub-urb
sub-ur-ban
sub-ur-ban-ite
sub-ur-bia
sub-ver-sion
sub-ver-sion-ary
sub-ver-sive
sub-ver-sive-ly
sub-ver-sive-ness
sub-vert
sub-vert-er
sub-way
suc-ceed
suc-ceed-er
suc-cess
suc-cess-ful-ly
suc-cess-ful-ness
suc-ces-sion
suc-ces-sion-al
suc-ces-sion-al-ly
suc-ces-sive
suc-ces-sive-ly
suc-ces-sive-ness
suc-ces-sor
suc-cinct
suc-cinct-ly
suc-cinct-ness
suc-cor
suc-cor-er
suc-co-tash

suc-co-bus
suc-cu-bi
suc-cu-lent
suc-cu-lence
suc-cu-len-cy
suc-cu-lent-ly
suc-cumb
suck-er
suck-le
suck-led
suck-ling
su-crose
suc-tion
sud-den-ly
sud-den-less
suds-y
suds-i-er
suds-i-est
sue
sued
su-ing
su-er
suede
su-et
su-ety
suf-fer
suf-fer-a-ble
suf-fer-a-bly
suf-fer-ing
suf-fer-ance
suf-fice
suf-ficed
suf-fic-ing
suf-fic-er
suf-fi-cien-cy
suf-fi-cien-cies
suf-fi-cient
suf-fi-cient-ly
suf-fix
suf-fo-cate
suf-fo-cat-ed
suf-fo-cat-ing
suf-frage
suf-fra-gette
suf-fuse
suf-fused
suf-fus-ing
sug-ar

sug-ary
sug-ar-i-er
sug-ar-i-est
sug-ar-coat
sug-gest
sug-gest-er
sug-gest-i-ble
sug-ges-tion
sug-ges-tive
sug-ges-tive-ly
sug-ges-tive-ness
su-i-cide
su-i-cid-ed
su-i-cid-ing
su-i-cid-al
suit-a-ble
suit-a-bil-i-ty
suit-case
suite
suit-ing
suit-or
sul-fa
sul-fa-nil-a-mide
sul-fate
sul-fide
sul-fur
sul-fu-ric
sul-fur-ous
sul-fur-ous-ly
sulk-y
sul-ly
sul-lied
sul-ly-ing
sul-tan
sul-tan-ic
sul-tan-a
sul-tan-ess
sul-tan-ate
sul-try
sul-tri-er
sul-tri-est
sum
su-mac
sum-ma-rize
sum-ma-rized
sum-ma-riz-ing
sum-ma-ri-za-tion
sum-ma-ry

sum-ma-ries
sum-mar-i-ly
sum-ma-tion
sum-ma-tion-al
sum-mer
sum-mery
sum-mer-house
sum-mit
sum-mon
sum-mon-er
sum-mons
sum-mons-es
sump-tu-ar-y
sump-tu-ous
sump-tu-ous-ly
sun
sunned
sun-ning
sun-bathe
sun-beam
sun-bon-net
sun-burn
sun-burned
sun-burnt
sun-dae
sun-der
sun-der-ance
sun-di-al
sun-down
sun-dries
sun-dry
sun-dries
sun-fish
sun-flow-er
sun-glass-es
sunk-en
sun-light
sun-lit
sun-ny
sun-rise
sun-set
sun-shine
sun-shiny
sun-spot
sun-stroke
sun-up
sup
supped

su-per
su-per-a-bun-dant
su-per-a-bun-dance
su-per-an-nu-ate
su-perb
su-perb-ly
su-per-car-go
su-per-car-goes
su-per-charge
su-per-charg-er
su-per-cil-i-ous
su-per-cil-i-ous-ly
su-per-e-go
su-per-e-rog-a-to-ry
su-per-fi-cial
su-per-fi-ci-al-i-ty
su-per-fi-ci-al-i-ties
su-per-high-way
su-per-hu-man
su-per-hu-man-i-ty
su-per-hu-man-ly
su-per-im-pose
su-per-im-posed
su-per-im-pos-ing
su-per-in-tend
su-per-in-tend-en-cy
su-per-in-tend-ent
su-pe-ri-or
su-pe-ri-or-i-ty
su-pe-ri-or-ly
su-per-la-tive
su-per-la-tive-ly
su-per-man
su-per-mar-ket
su-per-nal
su-per-nal-ly
su-per-nat-u-ral
su-per-nu-mer-ar-y
su-per-nu-mer-ar-ies
su-per-pow-er
su-per-scribe
su-per-scib-ing
su-per-scrip-tion
su-per-script
su-per-sede
su-per-sed-ed
su-per-sed-ing
su-per-son-ic

su-per-son-i-cal-ly
su-per-star
su-per-sti-tion
su-per-sti-tious
su-per-sti-tious-ly
su-per-struc-ture
su-per-vene
su-per-vened
su-per-ven-ing
su-per-ven-tion
su-per-vise
su-per-vised
su-per-vis-ing
su-per-vi-sion
su-pine
su-pine-ly
sup-per
sup-plant
sup-plan-ta-tion
sup-plant-er
sup-ple
sup-pler
sup-plest
sup-ple-ment
sup-ple-men-tal
sup-pli-ant
sup-pli-ant-ly
sup-pli-cant
sup-ply
sup-port
sup-port-a-ble
sup-port-er
sup-por-tive
sup-pose
sup-po-si-tion
sup-po-si-tion-al
sup-pos-i-to-ry
sup-press
sup-pres-sion
sup-pres-sor
sup-pu-rate
sup-pu-rat-ed
sup-pu-ra-tion
sup-pu-ra-tive
su-pra-re-nal gland
su-prem-a-cy
su-prem-a-cies
su-prem-a-cist

su-preme
su-preme-ly
sur-cease
sur-charge
sur-charged
sur-charg-ing
sur-cin-gle
sure
sur-er
sur-est
sure-ly
sure--fire
sure--foot-ed
sure--foot-ed-ly
sure-ty
sure-ties
sure-ty-ship
surf
surfy
surf-i-er
sur-face
sur-faced
sur-fac-ing
surf-board
surf-board-er
sur-feit
sur-feit-er
surge
surged
surg-ing
sur-geon
sur-ger-y
sur-ger-ies
sur-gi-cal
sur-ly
sur-mise
sur-mised
sur-mis-ing
sur-mount
sur-mount-a-ble
sur-name
sur-pass
sur-pass-a-ble
sur-pass-ing
sur-plice
sur-plus
sur-plus-age
sur-prise

sur-prised
sur-pris-ing
sur-re-al-ism
sur-re-al-ist
sur-re-al-is-tic
sur-ren-der
sur-rep-ti-tious
sur-rep-ti-tious-ly
sur-rey
sur-reys
sur-ro-gate
sur-ro-gat-ed
sur-ro-gat-ing
sur-round
sur-round-er
sur-round-ing
sur-tax
sur-veil-lance
sur-veil-lant
sur-vey
sur-vey-ing
sur-vey-or
sur-viv-al
sur-vive
sur-vived
sur-viv-ing
sur-vi-vor
sus-cep-ti-ble
sus-cep-ti-bil-i-ty
sus-cep-ti-bly
sus-pect
sus-pend
sus-pend-er
sus-pense
sus-pense-ful
sus-pen-sion
sus-pi-cious
sus-pi-cious-ly
sus-tain
sus-tain-a-ble
sus-tain-er
sus-tain-ment
sus-te-nance
su-ture
su-ze-rain
su-ze-rain-ly
svelte
svelte-ly

swab
  swabbed
  swab-bing
  swab-ber
swad-dle
  swad-dled
  swad-dling
swag-ger
  swag-ger-er
  swag-ger-ing
swain
  swain-ish
swal-low
  swal-low-er
swal-low-tail
swa-mi
  swa-mis
swamp
  swampy
swank
  swank-i-ly
swan's--down
swap
  swapped
  swap-ping
sward
swarth-y
  swarth-i-er
  swarth-i-est
swas-ti-ka
swat
swathe
  swathed
  swath-ing
swat
  sway-a-ble
  sway-er
sway-back
  sway-backed
swear
  swore
  swear-ing
  swear-er
swear-word
sweat
sweat-er
sweat-shop
sweep

swept
sweep-ing
sweep-er
sweep-stakes
sweet
  sweet-ish
  sweet-ly
sweet-bread
  sweet-bri-er
sweet-en
  sweet-en-er
  sweet-en-ing
sweet-heart
sweet-meat
sweet-talk
swell
  swelled
  swoll-en
  swell-ing
swell-head
swel-ter
  swel-ter-ing
swerve
  swerved
  swerv-ing
swift
  swift-ly
swim-ming
  swim-ming-ly
swin-dle
  swin-dled
  swin-dling
  swin-dler
swipe
  swiped
  swip-ing
swirl
swish
  swish-er
switch
  switch-er
switch-blade
switch-board
switch--hit-ter
swiv-el
  swiv-eled
  swiv-el-ing
swiz-zle

swoon
  swoon-er
  swoon-ing-ly
swoop-er
swop
  swopped
  swop-ping
sword
sword-fish
sword-play
  sword-play-er
swords-man
  swords-man
  swords-man-ship
syc-a-more
syc-o-phant
  syc-o-phan-cy
  syc-o-phan-tic
syl-lab-bic
syl-lab-i-cate
  syl-lab-i-cat-ed
  syl-lab-i-cat-ing
  syl-lab-i-ca-tion
syl-la-ble
  syl-la-bled
  syl-la-bling
syl-la-bus
  syl-la-bus-es
  syl-la-bi
syl-lo-gism
  sul-lo-gis-tic
sylph-like
syl-van
sym-bi-o-sis
  sym-bi-ot-ic
  sym-bi-ot-i-cal-ly
sym-bol
  sym-bol-ic
  sym-bol-i-cal
sym-bol-ism
  sym-bol-ist
sym-bol-ize
  sym-bol-ized
  sym-bol-iz-ing
  sym-bol-i-za-tion
  sym-bol-iz-er
sym-me-try
  sym-me-tries

sym-pa-thize
  sym-pa-thized
  sym-pa-thiz-ing
  sym-pa-thiz-er
sym-pa-thy
  sym-pa-thies
sym-pho-ny
  sym-pho-nies
  sym-phon-ic
sym-po-si-um
  sym-po-sia
sym-po-si-ums
symp-tom
symp-to-mat-ic
  symp-to-mat-i-cal
  symp-to-mat-i-cal-ly
syn-a-gogue
  syn-gog-al
  syn-gog-i-cal
syn-apse
sync
  synced
  sync-ing
syn-chro-nism
  syn-chro-nis-tic
  syn-chro-nis-ti-cal
  syn-chro-nis-ti-cal-ly
syn-chro-nize
  syn-chro-nized
  syn-chro-niz-ing
  syn-chro-ni-za-tion
syn-chro-nous
  syn-chro-nous-ly
syn-co-pate
  syn-co-pat-ed
  syn-co-pat-ing
  syn-co-pa-tion
  syn-co-pa-tor
syn-di-cate
  syn-di-cat-ed
  syn-di-cat-ing
syn-drome
  syn-drom-ic
syn-od
  syn-od-al
syn-o-nym
  syn-no-nym-ic
  syn-no-nym-i-cal

syn-no-nym-i-ty
syn-on-y-mous
  syn-on-y-mous-ly
syn-on-y-my
  syn-on-y-mies
syn-op-sis
  syn-op-ses
  syn-op-ti-cal
syn-tac-tic
  syn-tac-ti-cal
  syn-tac-ti-cal-ly
syn-tax
syn-the-sis
  syn-the-ses
  syn-the-sist
syn-the-size
  syn-the-sized
  syn-the-siz-ing
syn-the-ic
  syn-thet-i-cal
  syn-thet-i-cal-ly
syph-i-lis
syph-i-lit-ic
sy-rin-ga
sy-ringe
  sy-ringed
  sy-ring-ing
surom-go-my-elia
syr-inx
syr-phid
syr-up
  syr-upy
  syr-up-i-er
  syr-up-i-est
sys-tem
sys-tem-at-ic
  sys-tem-at-i-cal
sys-tem-a-tize
  sys-tem-a-tized
  sys-tem-a-tiz-ing
  sys-tem-a-ti-za-tion
  sys-tem-a-tiz-er
sys-tem-ic
  sys-tem-i-cal-ly
sys-to-le
  sys-tol-ic
sy-zy-gial
syz-y-gy

tab
  tabbed
  tab-bing
ta-ba-nid
tab-ard
tab-by
tab-er-na-cle
ta-ble
ta-ble-cloth
ta-ble-ful
ta-ble--hop
ta-ble-land
table linen
table of organization
table salt
ta-ble-spoon
  ta-ble-spoon-ful
table sugar
tab-let
table talk
table tennis
ta-ble-top
ta-ble-ware
table wine
tab-loid
ta-boo
ta-bor
  ta-bor-er
  tab-o-ret
tab-u-lar
  tab-u-lar-ly
tab-u-late
tab-u-la-tor
tac-a-ma-hac
tace
tacet
tach
tach-i-na fly
tach-i-nid
tach-ism
ta-chis-to-scope
ta-chom-e-ter
tachy-car-dia
ta-chyg-ra-phy
tachy-lyte
ta-chym-e-ter
tac-it
  tac-it-ly

tac-i-turn
tack
  tack-er
tack claw
tack-i-fy
tack-i-ly
tacki-ness
tack-le
  tack-led
  tack-ler
  tack-ling
tacky
ta-co
tac-o-nite
tact
  tact-ful
  tact-less
tac-tic
  tac-tic-al
  tac-tic-ian
tac-tile
tactile corpuscle
tac-tion
tact-less
  tact-less-ness
tac-tu-al
tad
tad-pole
taf-fe-ta
  taf-fet-ized
taff-rail
tag
  tag-ger
tag along
tag-board
tag day
tag end
tag line
tag sale
tag team
tag up
tail
tail-back
tail-board
tail-bone
tail-coat
tail covert
tailed sonnet

tail end
tail fin
tail-gate
tail lamp
tail-light
tai-lor
tai-lor-bird
tai-lor--made
tailor's chalk
tail-piece
tail pipe
tail plane
tail-race
tail rhyme
tail-spin
tail-wa-ter
tail wind
taint
tai-pan
take
  tak-en
  tak-er
  tak-ing
take back
take-down
take--home pay
take in
take-off
take-out
take-over
take up
ta-kin
ta-la
talc
tal-cum powder
tale
tale-bear-er
tal-ent
  tal-ent-ed
tal-ent scout
talk
  talk-er
  talk-a-tive
tall
  tall-ish
tal-low
  tal-low
tal-ly

tal-on
  tal-on-ed
tam-bou-rine
tame
  tame-ly
tam-per
tan
tan-dem
tang
  tangy
tan-gent
  tan-gen-cy
  tan-gen-tial
tan-ger-ine
tan-gi-ble
  tan-gi-bil-ity
tan-gle
  tanglement
tan-go
tank
  tank-ful
tan-kard
tan-ta-lize
  tan-ta-lizer
  tan-ta-liz-ingly
tan-ta-lum
tan-trum
tap
tape
ta-per
tap-es-try
tap-i-o-ca
taps
tar-dy
  tar-di-ness
tar-get
tar-iff
tar-nish
  tar-nish-able
tar-ot
tar-pau-lin
tar-ry
tart
  tart-ly
  tart-ness
tar-tan
tar-tar
  tar-tar-ic

task
tas-sel
taste
  taste-ful
  taste-less
tat-ter
tat-tle
  tat-tler
tattle-tale
tat-too
  tat-too
  tat-too-er
taught
taut
  taut-ly
  taut-ness
tau-tol-o-gy
tav-ern
  tav-ern-er
tax
  tax-able
  tax-a-tion
tax--ex-empt
tax shel-ter
tax-i
taxi-cab
tax-i-der-my
  tax-i-derm-ist
tea
teach
  teach-ing
  teach-able
teach-er
team
team-ster
tear
  teary
tease
  teaser
tech-ne-tium
tech-ni-cal
  tech-ni-cal-ly
tech-nique
tech-nol-o-gy
te-dious
  te-dious-ly
tee
teem

teens
teeth
tele-cast
tele-graph
  tele-graph-er
  tele-graph-ic
te-lep-a-thy
  te-lep-a-thic
  te-lep-a-thist
tele-phone
  tele-phoner
tele-pho-to
  tele-pho-to-graph
tele-scope
  tele-scopic
tele-thon
tele-vi-sion
tel-ex
tell
  tell-able
  tell-ing
  tell-er
tel-lu-ri-um
tem-per
  tem-per-able
  tem-per-a-ment
  tem-per-a-ment-al
  tem-per-ance
  tem-per-ate
  tem-per-ate-ly
tem-per-a-ture
tem-pest
tem-ple
tem-po
tem-po-rary
tempt
  tempt-er
ten
te-na-cious
  te-na-cious-ly
ten-ant
tend
ten-den-cy
ten-der
  ten-der-ly
  ten-der-ness
ten-der-loin
ten-don

ten-dril
  ten-dril-ed
ten-nis
ten-or
tense
ten-sion
  ten-sion-al
tent
ten-ta-cle
ten-ta-tive
  ten-ta-tive-ly
ten-ure
te-pee
tep-id
  tep-id-ly
ter-bi-um
ter-cen-ten-a-ry
term
ter-mi-nal
ter-mi-nate
  ter-mi-nation
ter-mite
ter-race
ter-rain
ter-ra-pin
ter-res-tri-al
ter-ri-ble
  ter-ri-bly
ter-ri-er
ter-rif-ic
  ter-rif-ical-ly
ter-ri-fy
  ter-ri-fied
  ter-ri-fying
ter-ri-to-ry
  ter-ri-to-rial
  ter-ri-to-rial-ly
ter-ror
ter-ror-ism
terse
test
  test-er
tes-ta-ment
  tes-ta-ment-ary
tes-tate
tes-ti-fy
  tes-ti-fier
tes-ti-mo-ni-al

tes-ti-mo-ny
tes-tis
test tube
test--tube baby
tet-a-nus
teth-er
text
text-book
tex-tile
tex-ture
  tex-tural
  tex-tural-ly
thal-li-um
than
thank
thank-ful
  thank-ful-ly
  thank-ful-ness
  thank-less
thanks
that
thatch
thaw
the
the-atre
the-at-ri-cal
  the-at-ri-cals
theft
their
the-ism
them
theme
  the-matic
them-selves
then
thence
  thence-forth
  thence-for-ward
the-oc-ra-cy
  the-oc-rat
the-ol-o-gy
  the-ol-o-gian
the-o-rize
  the-o-re-ti-cian
  the-o-ri-za-tion
  the-o-rist
the-o-ry
  ther-a-peu-tics

ther-a-peu-tist
ther-a-py
  ther-a-pist
there
  there-abouts
  there-after
  there-by
  there-fore
  there-from
  there-in
ther-mal
ther-mom-e-ter
  ther-mom-e-tric
ther-mo-plas-tic
ther-mo-stat
  ther-mo-stat-ic
the-sau-rus
these
the-sis
they
they'd
they'll
they're
they've
thick
  thick-ly
  thick-ness
  thick-en
thief
thieve
thigh
thim-ble
  thim-ble-ful
thin
  thin-ly
  thin-ness
thing
think
  think-able
  think-er
third
thirst
  thirst-y
thir-teen
this
this-tle
thith-er
thong

tho-rax
  tho-racic
tho-ri-um
thorn
  thorn-y
thor-ough
  thor-ough-ness
  thor-ough-ly
thor-ough-bred
thor-ough-fare
those
though
thought
  thought-ful
  thought-less
thou-sand
thrash
  thrash-er
thread
  thread-y
thread-bare
threat
  threat-en
three
thresh
thresh-old
threw
thrice
thrift
  thrift-i-ly
  thrift-i-ness
  thrift-y
thrill
  thrill-ing
  thrill-ing-ly
thrive
throat
throb
throm-bo-sis
throng
throt-tle
through
through-out
throw
thru
thrush
thrust
thru-way

thud
thug
  thug-gish
thumb
thump
thun-der
thun-der-bolt
thun-der-cloud
thun-der-show-er
thus
thwack
thwart
thy
thyme
thy-roid
thy-rox-ine
ti-ara
tick
tick-et
tick-le
  tick-ler
tidal wave
tid-bit
tide
tid-ings
ti-dy
  ti-di-ly
  ti-di-ness
tie
tier
  tier-ed
ti-ger
tiger-eye
tight
tight-en
  tight-en-er
tight-rope
tights
tile
till
  till-er
tilt
tim-ber
time
time--shar-ing
time tri-al
tim-id
tin

tinc-ture
tin-der
tin-der-box
tine
tinge
tin-gle
  tin-gly
tink-er
tin-kle
tin-ny
tin-sel
tint
ti-ny
tip
tip-ple
tip-sy
  tip-si-ness
ti-rade
tire
tire-less
  tire-less-ly
tis-sue
ti-ta-ni-um
tithe
  tither
tit-il-late
  tit-il-lat-ing
  tit-il-la-tive
  tit-il-lat-ing-ly
  tit-il-lat-ion
ti-tle
to
toad
  toad-stool
toast
  toast-y
  toast-er
to-bac-co
to-bog-gan
  to-bog-gan-ist
to-day
tod-dle
  tod-dler
tod-dy
toe
tof-fee
to-geth-er
  to-geth-er-ness

toil
  toil-some
toi-let
toi-lette
to-ken
tol-er-ate
  tol-er-a-tion
  tol-er-ance
  tol-er-ant
toll
tom-a-hawk
to-ma-to
tomb
tom-boy
  tom-boy-ish
tomb-stone
tom-cat
to-mor-row
ton
tone
tongs
tongue
ton-ic
to-night
ton-sil
ton-sil-lec-to-my
too
tool
tooth
  tooth-ed
  tooth-less
top
to-paz
top-coat
top-ic
top-most
to-pog-ra-phy
top-ple
top-sy--tur-vy
torch
tor-ment
  tor-ment-ing-ly
  tor-ment-or
tor-na-do
tor-pe-do
tor-pid
  tor-pid-ity
  tor-pid-ly

tor-rent
  tor-rent-ial
tor-rid
  tor-rid-ly
tor-sion
  tor-sion-al
tor-so
tort
tor-toise
tor-tu-ous
  tor-tu-ous-ness
toss
tot
to-tal
  to-tal-ly
to-tal-i-tar-i-an
  to-tal-i-tar-i-an
tote
to-tem
tot-ter
tou-can
touch
  touch-able
tough
  tough-ly
  tough-ness
tou-pee
tour
  tour-ism
  tour-ist
tour-na-ment
tour-ni-quet
tou-sle
tout
  tout-er
tow
to-ward
tow-el
tow-er
  tow-er-ing
town
town-ship
tox-e-mi-a
tox-ic
tox-in
toy
trace
  trace-able

trace-ably
trac-er
track
  track-able
  track-er
tract
trac-tion
trac-tor
trade
  trade-able
trade-mark
trade--off
tra-di-tion
  tra-di-tion-al
  tra-di-tion-al-ly
tra-duce
  tra-duce-ment
  tra-ducer
traf-fic
trag-e-dy
trail
  trail-er
train
  train-able
  train-er
  train-ing
trait
trai-tor
tra-jec-to-ry
tram-mel
  tram-mel-er
tramp
tram-ple
  tram-pler
tram-po-line
  tram-po-lin-ist
trance
tran-quil
  tran-quil-lity
  tran-quil-ly
  tran-quil-ize
trans-act
  trans-action
  trans-actor
tran-scend
  tran-scend-ent
  tran-scend-ence
tran-scribe

tran-script
tran-scrip-tion
trans-fer
  trans-fer-able
  trans-fer-ence
  trans-fer-er
trans-fig-ure
  trans-fig-ura-tion
trans-fix
  trans-fix-ion
trans-form
  trans-for-mable
  trans-for-ma-tion
  trans-for-mer
trans-fuse
  trans-fus-ion
  trans-fus-er
trans-gress
  trans-gress-ion
  trans-gress-or
  trans-gres-sive
tran-sient
  tran-sient-ly
tran-sit
trans-late
  trans-la-tion
  trans-la-tor
trans-lu-cent
trans-mis-sion
trans-mit
  trans-miss-ible,
  trans-mitt-able
  trans-mitt-er
trans-mute
  trans-mu-ta-tion
tran-som
trans-par-ent
  trans-par-ency
  trans-par-ent-ly
tran-spire
trans-plant
  trans-plant-able
trans-port
  trans-port-able
  trans-por-ta-tion
  trans-port-er
trans-pose
trans-sex-u-al

trap
tra-peze
trap-shoot-ing
trau-ma
tra-vail
trav-el
  trav-el-er
tra-verse
  tra-vers-able
  tra-ver-sal
  tra-ver-ser
trawl
tray
treach-er-ous
  treach-er-ous-ly
  treach-ery
tread
trea-son
  trea-son-able
  trea-son-ous
treas-ure
treas-ur-er
treas-ur-y
treat
  treat-able
  treat-er
treat-ment
treb-le
tree
  tree-less
tre-foil
trek
trel-lis
trem-ble
  trem-bler
  trem-bly
tre-men-dous
trem-or
trench
  trench-er
trend
  trend-set-ter
tres-pass
tres-tle
tri-al
tri-an-gle
  tri-an-gu-lar-i-ty
tribe

trib-u-la-tion
trib-un-al
trib-ute
tri-ceps
trick
  trick-y
trick-er-y
trick-le
tri-col-or
  tri-col-or-ed
tri-cy-cle
tri-dent
tried
tri-en-ni-al
  tri-en-ni-al-ly
tri-fle
trig-ger
trill
tril-lion
trim
tri-ni-tro-tol-u-ene
trin-ket
tri-o
trip
tripe
trip-le
trip-let
trip-li-cate
tri-pod
trite
tri-umph
  tri-umph-ant
  tri-umph-ant-ly
triv-i-al
Tro-jan
troll
trol-ley
trom-bone
troop
  troop-er
tro-phy
trop-ic
trop-i-cal
  trop-i-cal-ly
tro-pism
tro-po-sphere
trot
troth

trou-ble
  trou-bler
  trou-bling-ly
trough
trounce
troupe
trou-sers
trous-seau
trout
trow-el
  trow-el-er
tru-ant
truce
truck
  truck-er
trudge
true
  true-ness
trump
trum-pet
trunk
truss
trust
  trust-er
  trust-less
truth
  truth-ful
  truth-ful-ly
  truth-ful-ness
try
  try-ing
tryst
tsu-na-mi
tub
tu-ba
tube
tu-ber
tu-ber-cu-lo-sis
tuck
tuft
tug
tu-i-tion
tu-lip
tum-ble
  tum-bler
tum-ble-down
tum-brel
tu-mor

tu-mult
tu-mul-tu-ous
tu-na
tun-dra
tune
tune-ful
tung-sten
tu-nic
tun-nel
tur-ban
tur-bine
tur-bu-lent
  tur-bu-lent-ly
tu-reen
turf
tur-key
tur-moil
turn
  turn-er
turn-buck-le
turn-down
tur-nip
turn-key
turn-off
turn-over
tur-pen-tine
tur-quoise
tur-ret
tur-tle
tur-tle-neck
tusk
tus-sle
tu-tor
tut-ti-frut-ti
tu-tu
tux-e-do
twain
twang
tweak
tweed
twee-zers
twelve
twen-ty
twice
twid-dle
twig
twi-light
twill

twin
twine
twinge
  twing-ed
twin-kle
twirl
twist
  twist-er
twit
twitch
twit-ter
  twit-ter-y
two-fold
two--sid-ed
two-some
two-spot-ted
two--step
two--suit-er
two--tailed test
two--time
two--tone
two--way
two--way streed
two--winged fly
ty-coon
tying
tyke
tym-bal
tym-pan
tym-pan-ic
tympanic boes
tympanic membrane
tym-pa-num
type
type-face
type-set-ter
type-writ-er
ty-phoid
ty-phoon
typ-i-cal
  typ-i-cal-ly
typ-i-fy
  typ-i-fy-ing
typ-ist
ty-po
ty-ran-no-sau-rus
tyr-an-ny
ty-ro-sine

ubiq-ui-tous
  ubiq-ui-tary
  ubig-ui-tous-ly
  ubiq-ui-ty
ud-der
ug-ly
  ug-li-er
  ug-li-est
ugly duckling
ug-some
uh-lan
uin-ta-ite
ukase
uke
uki-yo-e
uku-le-le
ula-ma
u-lar
ul-cer
  ul-cer-ous
ul-cer-ate
  ul-cer-at-ed
  ul-cer-at-ing
  ul-cer-at-ion
ul-cero-gen-ic
ule
u-lent
ulex-ite
ul-lage
ul-na
  ul-nae
u-lose
ulot-ri-chous
u-lous
ul-ster
ul-te-ri-or
  ul-te-ri-or-ly
ul-ti-mate
  ul-ti-mate-ly
ul-ti-ma-tum
  ul-ti-ma-tums
  ul-ti-ma-ta
ul-ti-mo
ul-ti-mo-gen-i-ture
ul-tra
ul-tra-con-serv-a-tive
ul-tra-fash-ion-able
ul-tra-fiche

ul-tra-fil-tra-tion
ul-tra-high
ultrahigh frequency
ul-tra-ism
ul-tra-lib-er-al
ul-tra-maf-ic
ul-tra-ma-rine
ul-tra-mi-cro
ul-tra-mi-cro-scope
ul-tra-mi-cro-tome
ul-tra-min-ia-ture
ul-tra-mod-ern
ul-tra-mon-tane
ul-tra-son-ic
ul-tra-so-phis-ti-cat-ed
ul-tra-sound
ul-tra-struc-ture
ul-tra-vi-o-let
ul-u-late
  ul-u-lat-ed
  ul-u-lat-ing
um-bel
  um-bel-lar
  um-bel-late
  um-bel-lat-ed
um-ber
  un-bered
  un-ber-ing
um-bil-i-cal
ambilical cord
um-bil-i-cate
um-bi-li-cus
um-bo
  um-bo-nal
  un-bo-nate
  um-bo-nes
um-bra
  um-bras
  um-brae
um-brage
  um-bra-geous
um-brel-la
umi-ak
um-laut
um-pire
  um-pired
  um-pir-ing
ump-teen

ump-teenth
un-a-bashed
  un-a-bash-ed-ly
un-a-ble
un-a-bridged
un-ac-cep-t-able
  un-ac-cept-ed
un-ac-com-pa-nied
un-ac-count-able
  un-ac-count-a-bly
un-ac-cus-tomed
un-ac-quaint-ed
un-a-dorned
un-a-dul-ter-at-ed
  un-a-dul-ter-at-ed-ly
un-ad-vised
  un-ad-vis-ed-ly
un-af-fect-ed
  un-af-fect-ed-ly
un-a-fraid
un--Amer-i-can
unan-i-mous
  una-nim-i-ty
  unan-i-mous-ly
un-an-swer-able
  un-an-swered
un-ap-pe-tiz-ing
un-ap-pre-ci-at-ed
  un-ap-pre-ci-a-tive
un-ap-proach-able
  un-ap-proach-ably
  un-ap-proached
un-armed
un-a-shamed
un-asked
un-a-spir-ing
un-as-sail-able
  un-as-sail-ably
  un-as-sailed
un-at-tached
un-at-tain-able
  un-at-tained
un-at-tend-ed
un-au-thor-ized
un-a-vail-a-ble
  un-a-vail-a-bil-i-ty
  un-a-vail-a-bly
un-a-void-a-ble

un-a-void-a-bil-i-ty
un-a-void-ably
un-a-ware
  un-a-ware-ness
un-a-wares
un-backed
un-bal-anced
un-bar
  un-barred
  un-bar-ring
un-bear-able
  un-bear-ably
un-beat-en
  un-beat-able
un-be-com-ing
  un-be-com-ing-ly
un-be-lief
  un-be-liev-able
  un-be-liev-ably
un-be-liev-er
  un-be-liev-ing
  un-be-liev-ing-ly
un-bend
  un-bend-ed
  un-bend-ing
un-bi-ased
  un-bi-ased-ly
un-bid-den
un-bind
  un-bound
  un-bind-ing
un-blem-ished
un-bolt
  un-bolt-ed
un-born
un-bos-om
un-bound
  un-bound-ed-ly
un-bowed
un-bread-able
un-bri-dle
  un-bri-dled
  un-bri-dling
un-bro-ken
  un-bro-ken-ly
un-buck-le
  un-buck-led
  un-buck-ling

un-bur-den
un-but-ton
  un-but-toned
un--called--for
un-can-ny
  un-can-ni-er
  un-can-ni-est
  un-can-ni-ly
un-cap
  un-capped
  un-cap-ping
un-ceas-ing
  un-ceas-ing-ly
un-cer-e-mo-ni-ous
  un-cer-e-mo-ni-ous-ly
un-cer-tain
  un-cer-tain-ly
  un-cer-tain-ty
  un-cer-tain-ties
un-chal-lenged
un-change-able
  un-change-ably
  un-changed
  un-chang-ing
un-char-i-ta-ble
  un-char-i-ta-bly
un-chart-ed
un-chris-tian
un-cir-cum-cised
un-civ-il
  un-civ-il-ly
  un-civ-i-lized
un-class-i-fi-able
  un-clas-si-fied
un-cle
un-clean
  un-clean-ly
un-clear
un-cloak
un-clothe
un-clut-tered
un-coil
un-com-fort-able
  un-com-fort-ably
un-com-mit-ted
un-com-mon
  un-com-mon-ly
un-com-mu-ni-ca-tive

un-com-pre-hend-ing
un-com-pro-mis-ing
  un-com-pro-mised
un-con-cern
  un-con-cerned
un-con-di-tion-al
  un-con-di-tion-al-ly
un-con-firmed
un-con-nect-ed
  un-con-nect-ed-ly
un-con-quer-a-ble
  un-con-quered
un-con-scion-able
  un-con-scion-ably
un-con-scious
  un-con-scious-ly
  un-con-scious-ness
un-con-sti-tui-tion-al
un-con-strained
un-con-test-ed
un-con-trol-la-ble
  un-con-trol-la-bly
  un-con-trolled
un-con-ven-tion-al
  un-con-ven-tion-al-ly
un-count-ed
un-cou-ple
  un-cou-pled
  un-cou-pling
un-couth
  un-couth-ly
  un-couth-ness
un-cov-er
  un-cov-ered
unc-tion
unc-tu-ous
  unc-tu-os-i-ty
  unc-tu-ous-ly
un-curl
un-cut
un-daunt-ed
  un-daunt-ed-ly
un-de-ceive
  un-de-ceived
  un-de-ceiv-ing
  un-de-ceiv-a-ble
un-de-cid-ed
  un-de-cid-ed-ly

un-de-cid-ed-ness
un-de-fined
un-de-fin-a-ble
un-de-mon-stra-tive
un-de-ni-a-ble
  un-de-ni-a-bly
  un-de-nied
un-de-pend-able
  un-de-pend-a-bil-i-ty
un-der
un-der-a-chiev-er
  un-der-a-chiev-ment
un-der-act
un-der-age
un-der-arm
un-der-bel-ly
un-der-car-riage
un-der-charge
  un-der-charged
  un-der-charg-ing
un-der-class-man
  un-der-class-men
un-der-clothes
un-der-coast
un-der-cov-er
un-der-cur-rent
un-der-cut
  un-der-cut-ting
un-der-de-vel-oped
  un-der-de-vel-op-ing
un-der-dog
un-der-done
un-der-es-ti-mate
  un-der-es-ti-mat-ed
  un-der-es-ti-mat-ing
  un-der-es-ti-ma-tion
un-der-foot
un-der-gar-ment
un-der-go
  un-der-went
  un-der-gone
un-der-grad-u-ate
un-der-ground
un-der-growth
un-der-hand
un-der-lie
  un-der-lay
  un-der-lain

un-der-ly-ing
un-der-line
un-der-lined
un-der-lin-ing
un-der-ling
un-der-mine
un-der-mined
un-der-min-ing
un-der-min-er
un-der-most
un-der-neath
un-der-pants
un-der-pass
un-der-pin-ning
un-der-priv-i-leged
un-der-rate
un-der-rat-ed
un-der-rat-ing
un-der-score
un-der-scored
un-der-scor-ing
un-der-sea
un-der-sec-re-tary
un-der-sec-re-tar-ies
un-der-sell
un-der-sold
un-der-ell-ing
un-der-sell-er
un-der-shirt
un-der-shot
un-der-side
un-der-signed
un-der-stand
un-der-stood
un-der-stand-ing
un-der-stand-a-ble
un-der-stand-a-bly
un-der-stand-ing-ly
un-der-state
un-der-stat-ed
un-der-stat-ing
un-der-state-ment
un-der-stood
un-der-study
un-der-stud-ied
un-der-stud-y-ing
un-der-stud-ies
un-der-take

un-der-took
un-der-tak-en
un-der-tak-ing
un-der-tak-er
un-der-the-coun-ter
un-der-tone
un-der-tow
un-der-wa-ter
un-der-wear
un-der-weight
un-der-world
un-der-write
un-der-wrote
un-der-writ-ten
un-der-writ-ing
un-der-writ-er
un-de-sir-a-ble
un-de-sir-a-bil-i-ty
un-de-sir-a-bly
un-de-ter-mined
un-dies
un-dip-lo-mat-ic
un-dip-lo-mat-i-cal-ly
un-dis-ci-plined
un-dis-closed
un-dis-posed
un-dis-tin-guished
un-di-vid-ed
un-do
un-did
un-done
un-do-ing
un-do-er
un-doubt-ed
un-doubt-ed-ly
un-doubt-ing
un-dress
un-dress-ed
un-dress-ing
un-due
un-du-lant
un-du-late
un-du-lat-ed
un-du-lat-ing
un-du-la-tion
un-du-ly
un-dy-ing
un-earth

un-earth-ly
un-easy
un-eas-i-er
un-eas-i-est
un-ease
un-eas-i-ly
un-eas-i-ness
un-em-ployed
un-em-ploy-ment
un-e-qual
un-e-qual-ly
un-e-qual-ed
un-e-quiv-o-cal
un-e-quiv-o-cal-ly
un-err-ing
un-err-ing-ly
un-eth-i-cal
un-eth-i-cal-ly
un-e-ven
un-e-ven-ly
un-e-ven-ness
un-ex-cep-tion-able
un-ex-pect-ed
un-ex-pect-ed-ly
un-fail-ing
un-fail-ing-ly
un-faith-ful
un-faith-ful-ly
un-faith-ful-ness
un-fa-mil-iar
un-fa-mil-i-ar-i-ty
un-fa-mil-iar-ly
un-fast-en
un-fas-ten-a-ble
un-fas-ten-er
un-fath-om-a-ble
un-fa-vor-a-ble
un-fa-vor-a-bly
un-feel-ing
un-feel-ing-ly
un-feigned
un-feign-ed-ly
un-fet-ter
un-fet-tered
un-fin-ished
un-fit
un-fit-ly
un-fit-ness

un-fit-ting
un-flat-ter-ing
un-flinch-ing
un-flinch-ing-ly
un-fold
un-for-get-ta-ble
un-for-get-ta-bly
un-for-giv-a-ble
un-for-tu-nate
un-for-tu-nate-ly
un-found-ed
un-found-ed-ness
un-friend-ly
un-friend-li-er
un-friend-li-est
un-friend-li-ness
un-frock
un-furl
un-gain-ly
un-gain-li-ness
un-gird
un-gird-ed
un-gird-ing
un-glazed
un-god-ly
un-god-li-er
un-god-li-est
un-god-li-ness
un-gov-ern-able
un-gov-ern-ably
un-gra-cious
un-gra-cious-ly
un-gra-cious-ness
un-gram-mat-i-cal
un-gram-mat-i-cal-ly
un-grate-ful
un-grate-ful-ly
un-grate-ful-ness
un-guard-ed
un-guard-ed-ly
un-guent
un-gu-late
un-ham-pered
un-hand
un-handy
un-hand-i-er
un-hand-i-est
un-hap-py

un-hap-pi-er
un-hap-pi-est
un-hap-pi-ly
un-hap-pi-ness
un-harmed
un-healthy
un-health-i-er
un-health-i-ly
un-heard
un-heed-ed
un-heed-ful
un-heed-ing
un-hinge
un-hinged
un-hing-ing
un-hitch
un-ho-ly
un-ho-li-er
un-ho-li-est
un-hol-li-ly
un-ho-li-ness
un-hook
un-horse
un-horsed
un-hors-ing
un-hur-ried
un-hurt
uni-cam-er-al
uni-cam-er-al-ly
uni-cel-lu-lar
uni-corn
uni-fi-ca-tion
uni-form
uni-formed
uni-form-i-ty
uni-form-ly
uni-fy
uni-fied
uni-fy-ing
uni-fi-er
uni-lat-er-al
uni-lat-er-al-ism
uni-lat-er-al-ly
un-imag-in-able
un-im-pair-ed
un-im-peach-able
un-im-peach-a-bly
un-im-por-tance

un-im-por-tant
un-im-proved
un-in-hib-it-ed
un-in-hib-it-ed-ly
un-in-ter-est-ed
un-in-ter-est-ing
un-ion
un-ion-ism
un-ion-ist
un-ion-ize
un-ion-ized
un-ion-iz-ing
un-ion-i-za-tion
unique
unique-ly
unique-ness
uni-son
unit
unite
unit-ed
unit-ing
unit-er
uni-ty
uni-ties
uni-valve
uni-valved
uni-val-vu-lar
uni-ver-sal
uni-ver-sal-i-ty
uni-ver-sal-ly
uni-ver-sal-ness
uni-ver-sal-ize
uni-ver-sal-ized
uni-ver-sal-iz-ing
uni-verse
uni-ver-si-ty
uni-ver-si-ties
un-just
un-just-ly
un-kempt
un-kind
un-kind-ness
un-kind-ly
un-known
un-law-ful
un-law-ful-ly
un-law-ful-ness
un-learn

un-learned
un-learn-ing
un-learn-ed
un-learn-ed-ly
un-leash
un-less
un-let-ter-ed
un-like
un-like-ness
un-like-ly
un-like-li-er
un-like-li-est
un-like-li-ness
un-lim-ber
un-lim-it-ed
un-load
un-load-er
un-lock
un-looked--for
un-loose
un-loosed
un-loos-ing
un-loos-en
un-lucky
un-luck-i-er
un-luck-i-est
un-luck-i-ly
un-make
un-made
un-mak-ing
un-mak-er
un-man
un-manned
un-man-ning
un-mask
un-mean-ing
un-mean-ing-ly
un-men-tion-able
un-mer-ci-ful
un-mer-ci-ful-ly
un-mis-tak-able
un-mis-tak-a-bly
un-mit-i-gat-ed
un-mit-i-gat-ed-ly
un-nat-u-ral
un-nat-u-ral-ly
un-nat-u-ral-ness
un-nec-es-sary

un-nec-es-sar-i-ly
un-nerve
un-nerved
un-nerv-ing
un-num-bered
un-ob-jec-tion-able
un-or-gan-ized
un-pack
un-par-al-leled
un-par-don-able
un-pleas-ant
un-pleas-ant-ly
un-pleas-ant-ness
un-plumbed
un-pop-u-lar
un-pop-u-lar-i-ty
un-pop-u-lar-ly
un-prec-e-dent-ed
un-prec-e-dent-ed-ly
un-prin-ci-pled
un-print-able
un-pro-fes-sion-al
un-pro-fes-sion-al-ly
un-qual-i-fied
un-qual-i-fied-ly
un-ques-tion-able
un-ques-tion-ably
un-ques-tioned
un-quote
un-quot-ed
un-quot-ing
un-rav-el
un-rav-eled
un-rav-el-ing
un-rav-el-ment
un-read
un-re-al
un-rea-son-able
un-rea-son-ably
un-rea-son-ing
un-re-fined
un-re-gen-er-ate
un-re-lat-ed
un-re-lent-ing
un-re-lent-ing-ly
un-remit-ting
un-re-serve
un-re-served

un-re-serv-ed-ly
un-rest
un-ri-valed
un-roll
un-ruf-fled
un-ru-ly
un-ruy-li-er
un-ru-li-est
un-sad-dle
un-sad-dled
un-sad-dling
un-said
un-sa-vory
un-say
un-say-ing
un-scathed
un-schooled
un-scram-ble
un-scram-bled
un-scram-bling
un-screw
un-scru-pu-lous
un-scru-pu-lous-ly
un-seal
un-sea-son-able
un-sea-son-ably
un-seat
un-seem-ly
un-set-tle
un-set-tled
un-set-tling
un-sheathe
un-sheathed
un-sheath-ing
un-shod
un-sight-ly
un-sight-li-er
un-sight-li-est
un-skilled
un-skill-ful
un-skill-ful-ly
un-snap
un-snapped
un-snap-ping
un-snarl
un-so-phis-ti-cat-ed
un-so-phis-ti-cat-ed-ly
un-so-phis-ti-ca-tion

un-sound
un-sound-ly
un-spar-ing
un-spar-ing-ly
un-speak-a-ble
un-speak-a-bly
un-sta-ble
un-sta-bly
un-steady
un-stead-i-er
un-stead-i-est
un-stead-i-ly
un-stop
un-stopped
un-stop-ping
un-strung
un-stud-ied
un-sung
un-tan-gle
un-tan-gled
un-tan-gling
un-taught
un-think-able
un-think-ing
un-think-ing-ly
un-ti-dy
un-tie
un-tied
un-ty-ing
un-til
un-time-ly
un-time-li-ness
un-to
un-told
un-touch-a-ble
un-touch-a-bly
un-to-ward
un-to-ward-ly
un-truth
un-tu-tored
un-used
un-u-su-al
un-u-su-al-ly
un-u-su-al-ness
un-ut-ter-able
un-ut-ter-ably
un-var-nished
un-veil

un-wary
un-war-i-ly
un-well
un-whole-some
un-whole-some-ly
un-wieldy
un-wield-i-ness
un-will-ing
un-will-ing-ly
un-will-ing-ness
un-wind
un-wound
un-wind-ing
un-wise
un-wise-ly
un-wit-ting
un-wit-ting-ly
un-wont-ed
un-wont-ed-ly
un-wor-thy
un-wor-thi-ly
un-wor-thi-ness
un-wrap
un-wrapped
un-wrap-ping
un-yield-ing
up-beat
up-braid
up-braid-er
up-braid-ing
up-com-ing
up-coun-try
up-date
up-dat-ed
up-dat-ing
up-end
up-grade
up-grad-ed
up-grad-ing
up-heav-al
up-heave
up-heaved
up-heav-ing
up-hill
up-hold
up-held
up-hold-ing
up-hol-ster

up-hol-ster-er
up-hol-stery
up-keep
up-land
up-lift
up-most
up-on
up-per
up-per--class
up-per-cut
up-per-cut-ting
up-per-most
up-pish
up-pish-ly
up-pi-ty
up-raise
up-raised
up-rais-ing
up-rear
up-right
up-right-ly
up-right-ness
up-ris-ing
up-roar
up-roar-i-ous
up-root
up-root-er
up-set
up-set-ting
up-shot
up-side
up-stage
up-staged
up-stag-ing
up-stairs
up-stand-ing
up-start
up-state
up-stream
up-swing
up-take
up-to-date
up-town
up-trend
up-turn
up-ward
up-ward-ly
up-ward-ness

ura-ni-um
ur-ban
ur-bane
ur-bane-ly
ur-ban-i-ty
ur-ban-ize
ur-ban-ized
ur-ban-iz-ing
ur-ban-i-za-tion
ur-chin
urea
ure-al
ure-ter
ure-thra
ure-thrae
ure-thras
ure-thral
uge
urged
urg-ing
urg-er
urg-ing-ly
ur-gent
ur-gen-cy
ur-gen-cies
ur-gent-ly
uric
uri-nal
uri-nal-y-sis
uri-nal-y-ses
uri-nary
uri-nar-ies
uri-nate
urine
urol-o-gy
uro-log-ic
uro-log-i-cal
urol-o-gist
us-able
us-ably
us-abil-i-ty
us-age
use
used
us-ing
us-er
use-ful
use-ful-ly

use-ful-ness
use-less
use-less-ly
use-less-ness
ush-er
usu-al
usu-al-ly
usurp
usur-pa-tion
usurp-er
usu-ry
usu-ries
usu-rer
usu-ri-ous
uten-sil
uter-us
ut-eri
util-i-tar-ian
util-i-ty
util-i-ties
uti-lize
uti-lized
uti-liz-ing
uti-li-za-tion
ut-most
uto-pia
uto-pi-an
uto-pi-an-ism
utri-cle
atric-u-lar
utric-u-lus
ut-ter
ut-ter-a-ble
ut-ter-er
ut-ter-ance
ut-ter-most
uva-rov-ite
uvea
uve-itis
uvu-la
uvu-las
uvu-lae
ux-o-ri-al
ux-or-i-cide
ux-o-ri-ous
ux-o-ri-ous-ly
ux-o-ri-ous-ness
Uz-bek

va-can-cy
va-can-cies
va-cant
va-cant-ly
va-cate
va-cat-ed
va-cat-ing
va-ca-tion
vac-ci-nate
vac-ci-nat-ed
vac-ci-nat-ing
vac-ci-na-tion
vac-cine
vac-il-late
vac-il-lat-ed
vac-il-lat-ing
vac-il-la-tion
vac-il-la-tor
va-cu-i-ty
va-cu-i-ties
vac-u-o-late
vac-u-ole
vac-u-ous
vac-u-ous-ly
vac-u-um
vac-u-ums
vac-ua
vacuum bottle
vacuum cleaner
vacuum guage
vac-u-um-ize
vac-u-um--packed
vacuum pan
vacuum pump
vacuum tube
va-de me-cum
va-dose
vag-a-bond
vag-a-bond-age
vag-a-bond-ish
vag-a-bond-ism
va-gary
va-gar-ies
va-gar-i-ous
va-gar-i-ous-ly
va-gal
va-gile
va-gi-na

va-gi-nas
va-gi-nae
vag-i-nal
vag-i-nis-mus
vag-i-ni-tis
va-got-a-my
va-go-to-nia
va-go-tro-pic
va-grant
va-gran-cy
va-gran-cies
va-grant-ly
vague
vague-ly
vague-ness
vain
vain-ly
vain-ness
vain-glo-ry
vain-glo-ries
vain-glo-ri-ous
vair
val-ance
val-anced
vale
val-e-dic-tion
val-e-dic-to-ri-an
val-e-dic-to-ry
val-e-dic-to-ries
va-lence
va-len-cy
val-en-tine
val-er-ate
va-le-ric acid
va-let
val-e-tu-di-nar-i-an
val0gus
val-iance
val-iant
val-iant-ly
val-id
val-id-ly
val-id-ness
val-i-date
val-i-dat-ed
val-i-dat-ig
val-i-da-tion
va-lid-i-ty

va-lid-i-ties
va-line
va-lise
val-late
val-lec-u-la
val-ley
val-leys
valley fever
val-or
val-or-ous
val-or-ous-ly
val-u-able
val-u-ably
valuable consideration
val-u-ate
val-u-a-tion
val-u-a-tion-al
val-ue
val-ued
val-u-ing
val-ue-less
valve
valve-less
val-vu-lar
va-moose
vamp
vam-pire
vam-pir-ic
vam-pir-ism
va-na-di-um
vanadium pentoxide
va-na-dous
va-nas-pa-ti
van-da
van-dal
van-dal-ism
van-dal-ize
van-dal-ized
van-dal-iz-ing
vane
vaned
vane-less
van-guard
va-nil-la
van-ish
van-ish-er
van-i-ty
van-i-ties

van-quish
van-quish-a-ble
van-quish-er
van-tage
vap-id
va-pid-i-ty
vap-id-ly
va-por
va-por-er
va-por-ish
va-por-ize
va-por-ized
va-por-iz-ing
va-por-i-za-tion
va-por-iz-er
va-por-ous
va-por-opus-ly
va-que-ro
va-que-ros
var-i-able
var-i-abil-i-ty
var-i-ably
var-i-ance
var-i-ant
var-i-a-tion
var-i-a-tion-al
var-i-a-tion-al-ly
var-i-col-ored
var-i-cose
var-ied
var-ied-ness
var-ie-gate
var-ie-gat-ed
var-ie-gat-ing
var-ie-ga-tion
var-ie-ga-tor
va-ri-etal
va-ri-etal-ly
va-ri-ety
va-ri-e-ties
var-i-ous
var-i-ous-ly
var-nish
var-nish-er
var-si-ty
var-si-ties
vary
var-ied

vary-ing
var-i-er
vary-ing-ly
vas-cu-lar
vas-cu-lar-i-ty
va-sec-to-my
va-sec-to-mies
vas-o-mo-tor
vas-sal
vas-sal-age
vast-ness
vat
vat-ted
vat-ting
vaude-ville
vault
vault-ed
vault-er
vault-ing
vaunt
vaunt-er
vaunt-ing-ly
vec-tor
vec-to-ri-al
veer-ing
veg-e-ta-ble
veg-e-tal
veg-e-tar-i-an
veg-e-tar-i-an-ism
veg-e-tate
veg-e-tat-ed
veg-e-tat-ing
veg-e-ta-tion
veg-e-ta-tion-al
veg-e-ta-tive
ve-he-ment
ve-he-mence
ve-he-men-cy
ve-hi-cle
ve-hic-u-lar
veil
veiled
veil-ing
vein
veiny
vein-i-er
vein-i-est
vein-ing

vel-lum
ve-loc-i-ty
ve-loc-i-ties
vel-our
ve-lum
ve-la
vel-vet
vel-vet-ed
vel-ve-teen
vel-vety
vel-vet-i-er
vel-vet-i-est
ve-nal
ve-nal-i-ty
ve-nal-ly
ve-na-tion
ve-na-tion-al
vend-er
vend-or
ven-det-ta
vend-i-ble
vend-i-bil-i-ty
ve-neer
ve-neer-er
ve-neer-ig
ven-er-able
ven-er-abil-i-ty
ven-er-ably
ven-er-ate
ven-er-a-tion
ven-er-a-tor
ve-ne-re-al
venge-ance
venge-ful
venge-ful-ness
ve-ni-al
ve-ni-al-i-ty
ve-ni-al-ness
ve-ni-al-ly
ven-i-son
ven-om
ven-om-ous
ve-nous
ve-nous-ly
vent
vent-ed
vent-ing
ven-ti-late

ven-ti-lat-ed
ven-ti-lat-ing
ven-ti-la-tion
ven-ti-la-tor
ven-tral
ven-tral-ly
ven-tri-cle
ven-tril-o-quism
ven-tri-lo-qui-al
ven-tril-o-quist
ven-tril-o-quize
ven-tril-o-quized
ven-tril-o-quiz-ing
ven-ture
ven-ture-some
ven-tur-ous
ve-ra-cious
ve-rac-i-ty
ve-rac-i-ties
ve-ran-da
ver-bal
ver-bal-ly
ver-bal-ize
ver-bal-ized
ver-bal-iz-ing
ver-bal-i-za-tion
ver-bal-iz-er
ver-ba-tim
ver-bi-age
ver-bose
ver-bose-ness
ver-bos-i-ty
ver-bo-ten
ver-dant
ver-dan-cy
ver-dict
ver-di-gris
ver-dure
ver-dured
ver-dur-ous
verge
verged
verg-ing
ver-i-fi-ca-tion
ver-i-fy
ver-i-fied
ver-i-fy-ing
ver-i-fi-abil-i-ty

ver-i-fi-able
ver-i-fi-er
veri-si-mil-i-tude
veri-ta-ble
veri-ta-bly
ver-i-ty
ver-i-ties
ver-meil
ver-mic-u-lar
ver-mic-u-late
ver-mic-u-lat-ed
ver-mi-fuge
ver-mil-ion
ver-min
ver-min-ous
ver-mouth
ver-nac-u-lar
ver-nac-u-lar-ism
ver-nal
ver-nal-ly
ver-sa-tile
ver-sa-til-i-ty
versed
ver-si-fy
ver-si-fied
ver-si-fy-ing
ver-si-fi-er
ver-si-fi-ca-tion
ver-sion
ver-sion-al
ver-sus
ver-te-bra
ver-te-brae
ver-te-bral
ver-te-bral-ly
ver-te-brate
ver-tex
ver-tex-es
ver-ti-ces
ver-ti-cal
ver-ti-cal-i-ty
ver-ti-cal-ly
ver-ti-go
ver-ti-goes
ver-tig-i-nes
ves-i-cant
ves-i-ca-to-ry
ves-i-ca-to-ries

ves-i-cate
ves-i-cat-ed
ves-i-cat-ing
ves-i-ca-tion
ves-i-cle
ve-sic-u-lar
ves-pers
ves-sel
ves-tal
vest-ed
ves-ti-bule
ves-ti-buled
ves-ti-bul-ing
ves-tib-u-lar
ves-tige
ves-tig-i-al
ves-tig-i-al-ly
vest-ment
vest-pock-et
ves-try
ves-tries
vet
vet-ted
vet-ting
vet-er-an
vet-er-i-nar-i-an
vet-er-i-nary
ve-to
vex
vex-er
vex-ing-ly
vex-a-tion
vex-a-tious
vexed
via
vi-a-ble
vi-a-bil-i-ty
vi-a-bly
vi-a-duct
vi-al
vi-and
vi-brant
vi-bran-cy
vi-brate
vi-brat-ed
vi-brat-ing
vi-bra-tion
vi-bra-to

vi-bra-tos
vi-bra-tor
vi-bra-to-ry
vi-bur-num
vic-ar
vic-ar-ship
vic-ar-age
vi-car-i-ous
vi-car-i-ous-ly
vice ad-mi-ral
vice--con-sul
vice--pres-i-dent
vice-roy
vice-roy-al
vice ver-sa
vi-cin-i-fy
vi-cin-i-ties
vi-cious
vi-cious-ly
vi-cis-si-tude
vic-tim
vic-tim-ize
vic-tim-ized
vic-tim-iz-ing
vic-tim-iz-er
vic-tor
vic-to-ri-ous
vic-to-ri-ous-ly
vic-to-ry
vic-to-ries
vict-ual
vid-eo
vie
vied
vy-ing
vi-er
view-er
view-less
view-point
vig-il
vig-i-lance
vig-i-lant
vig-i-lan-te
vi-gnette
vig-or
vig-or-ous
vig-or-ous-ly
vi-king

vile
vil-i-fy
  vil-i-fied
  vil-i-fy-ing
vil-i-fi-ca-tion
vil-la
vil-lage
vil-lain
  vil-lain-ous
vil-lainy
  vil-lain-ies
vil-lein
vil-lous
vil-lus
  vil-li
vin-ci-ble
  vin-ci-bil-i-ty
vin-di-cate
  vin-di-cat-ed
  vin-di-cat-ing
vin-dic-tive
  vin-dic-tive-ly
  vin-dic-tive-ness
vin-e-gar
vin-e-gary
vine-yard
vi-nous
vin-tage
vint-ner
vi-nyl
vi-ol
vi-o-la
  vi-o-list
vi-o-la-ble
  vi-o-la-bil-i-ty
vi-o-late
  vi-o-lat-ed
  vi-o-lat-ing
  vi-o-la-tor
vi-o-la-tion
vi-o-lence
vi-o-lent
vi-o-let
vi-o-lin
  vi-o-lin-ist
vi-o-lon-cel-lo
  vi-o-lon-cel-list
vi-per

vi-ra-go
vi-ral
vir-eo
  vir-e-os
vir-gin
  vir-gin-al
  vir-gin-i-ty
vir-gule
vir-ile
  vi-ril-i-ty
vi-rol-o-gy
  vi-rol-o-gist
  vir-tu-al
vir-tue
vir-tu-os-i-ty
  vir-tu-os-i-ties
vir-tu-o-so
vir-tu-ous
  vir-tu-ous-ly
vir-u-lence
  vir-u-len-cy
vir-u-lent
vi-rus
  vi-rus-es
vi-sa
vis-age
vis-cera
vis-cer-al
vis-cid
  vis-cid-ly
vis-cos-i-ty
  vis-cos-i-ties
vis-count
  vis-count-cy
  vis-count-ship
vis-count-ess
vis-cous
vis-i-bil-i-ty
  vis-i-bil-i-ties
  vis-i-ble
vi-sion
  vi-sion-ary
  vi-sion-ar-ies
vis-it
vis-i-tant
vis-it-a-tion
vis-it-ing
vis-i-tor

vi-sor
vis-ta
vis-u-al
  vis-u-al-ly
  vis-u-al-ize
  vis-u-al-ized
  vis-u-al-iz-ing
  vis-u-al-i-za-tion
vi-tal
  vi-tal-i-ty
  vi-tal-i-ties
vi-tal-ize
  vi-tal-ized
  vi-tal-iz-ing
  vi-tal-i-za-tion
vi-tals
vi-ta-min
vi-ti-ate
vit-re-ous
  vit-re-os-i-ty
vit-ri-fy
  vit-ri-fied
  vit-ri-fy-ing
  vit-ri-fi-a-ble
  vit-ri-fi-ca-tion
vit-ri-ol
  vit-ri-ol-ic
vi-tu-per-ate
  vi-tu-per-at-ed
  vi-tu-per-at-ing
vi-tu-per-a-tion
vi-va
vi-va-cious
vi-vac-i-ty
  vi-vac-i-ties
viv-id
viv-i-fy
  viv-i-fied
  viv-i-fy-ing
vi-vip-ar-ous
vivi-sec-tion
vix-en
vi-zier
vi-zor
vo-cab-u-lar-y
  vo-cab-u-lar-ies
vo-cal
  vo-cal-ic

vo-cal-ist
vo-cal-ize
vo-cal-ized
vo-cal-iz-ing
vo-cal-i-za-tion
vo-ca-tion
vo-ca-tion-al
vo-cif-er-ous
vod-ka
voice
voiced
voic-ing
voice-less
voice-print
void-able
vol-a-tile
vol-a-til-i-ty
vol-can-ic
vol-can-i-cal-ly
vol-ca-no
vol-ca-noes
vol-ca-nos
vo-li-tion
vol-ley
vol-leys
vol-ley-ball
volt-age
vol-ta-ic
volt-me-ter
vol-u-ble
vol-u-bly
vol-u-bil-i-ty
vol-ume
vo-lu-mi-nous
vo-lu-mi-nous-ly
vol-un-tary
vol-un-tar-i-ly
vol-un-teer
vo-lup-tu-ary
vo-lup-tu-ar-ies
vo-lup-tu-ous
vom-it
voo-doo
vo-ra-cious
vo-rac-i-ty
vor-tex
vor-tex-es
vor-ti-ces

vo-ta-ry
vor-ta-ries
vote
vot-ed
vot-ing
vot-er
vo-tive
vouch-er
vouch-safe
vouch-safed
vouch-saf-ing
vow-el
voy-age
voy-aged
voy-ag-ing
voy-ag-er
vo-ya-geur
vo-yeur
vo-yeur-ism
voy-eur-is-tic
vroom
vug
Vul-can
vul-ca-ni-an
vul-can-ite
vul-ca-ni-zate
vul-ca-ni-za-tion
vul-ca-nize
vulcanized fiver
vul-ca-nol-o-gy
vul-gar
vul-gar-ism
vul-gar-i-ty
vul-gar-i-ties
vul-gar-ize
vul-gar-ized
vul-gar-iz-ing
vul-gate
vul-ner-a-ble
vul-ner-a-bly
vul-pine
vul-ture
vul-va
vul-vae
vul-vas
vul-vi-form
vul-vi-tis

wab-ble
wab-bled
wab-bling
wacky
wack-i-er
wack-i-est
wack-i-ly
wad
wad-ded
wad-ding
wad-dle
wad-dled
wad-dling
wad-dler
wad-dly
wad-dli-er
wad-dli-est
wade
wad-ed
wad-ing
wad-er
wa-fi
wading bird
wading pool
wad-mal
wae-sucks
waf-er
wa-fered
wa-fer-ing
waf-fle
waf-fled
waf-fling
waft
waft-age
waf-ture
wag
wagged
wag-ging
wag-ger
wag-gish
wage
waged
wag-ing
wage earner
wage level
wa-ger
wage scale
wage slave

wage-work-er
wag-gery
  wag-ger-ies
wag-gle
  wag-gled
  wag-gling
wag-on
  wag-on-er
wagon master
wagon train
wag-tail
wa-hi-ne
wa-hoo
waif
wail
  wail-ful
wailing wall
wain-scot
  wain-scot-ing
wain-wright
waist
waist-band
waist-coat
waist-line
wait-er
wait-ing
waiting game
waiting list
waiting room
wait-ress
waive
  waived
  waiv-ing
  waiv-er
wake
  waked
  wok-en
  wak-ing
wake-ful
  wake-ful-ly
wak-en
wake-rife
wake--rob-in
wale
  waled
  wal-ing
walk
walk-a-way

walk-er
walk-ie-talk-ie
walk--in
walking catfish
walking delegate
walking leaf
walking papers
walking stick
walk--on
walk-out
walk-o-ver
walk--through
walk-up
walk-way
wal-al-by
  wal-la-bies
wall
wall-board
wal-let
wall-eye
  wall-eyed
wall-flow-er
wall hanging
wal-lop
wal-low
wall painting
wall-pa-per
wall pellitory
wall plate
wall plug
wall rock
wall rocket
wall rue
wall-to-wall
wal-nut
wal-rus
  wal-rus-es
waltz
wam-ble
wame
wam-pum
wan
  wan-ner
  wan-nest
  wan-ness
wand
wan-der
  wan-der-lust

wane
  waned
  wan-ing
wan-gle
  wan-gled
  wan-gling
  wan-gler
want
want ad
want-ing
wan-ton
wa-pi-ti
  wa-pi-ties
war
  warred
  war-ring
war-ble
  war-bled
  war-bling
war-bler
war-den
  war-den-ship
ward-er
ward-robe
ware-house
war-fare
war-head
war-horse
war-like
war-lock
warm
  warm-er
  warm-est
warm--blood-ed
warm-heart-ed
war-mon-ger
warmth
warn-ing
war-path
war-rant
  war-ran-ty
  war-ran-ties
war-ren
war-ri-or
war-ship
war-time
wary
  war-i-er

war-i-est
war-i-ly
wash-able
wash-ba-sin
wash-board
wash-bowl
wash-cloth
wash-er
wash-ing
wash-out
wash-room
wash-stand
wash-tub
wasn't
wasp
  wasp-ish
  wasp-ish-ly
was-sail
wast-age
waste
  wast-ed
  wast-ing
  waste-ful
  waste-ful-ly
  waste-ful-ness
waste-bas-ket
waste-land
waste-pa-per
wast-er
wast-rel
watch-dog
watch-ful
watch-man
  watch-men
watch-tow-er
watch-word
wa-ter
wat-er-buck
wa-ter-col-or
wa-ter-course
wa-ter-cress
wa-ter-fall
wa-ter-foul
wa-ter-front
wa-ter-less
wa-ter lev-el
wa-ter lily
  wa-ter lil-ies

wa-ter line
wa-ter-llogged
Wa-ter-loo
wa-ter main
wa-ter-man
  wa-ter-men
wa-ter-mark
wa-ter-mel-on
wa-ter moc-ca-sin
wa-ter-proof
wa-ter-re-pel-lent
wa-ter-shed
wa-ter-side
wa-ter ski
  wa-ter-skied
  wa-ter-ski-ing
wa-ter-spout
wa-ter-tight
wa-ter-way
wa-ter-works
wa-tery
watt-age
watt-hour
wat-tle
  wat-tled
  wat-tling
wave
  waved
  wav-ing
wave-length
wave-let
wa-ver
wav-y
  wav-i-er
  wav-i-est
  wav-i-ly
wax
  waxed
  wax-ing
wax-en
wax-wing
wax-work
waxy
  wax-i-er
  wax-i-est
way-far-er
  way-far-ing
way-lay

way-laid
  way-lay-ing
way-side
way-ward
weak-en
weak-kneed
weak-ling
weak-ly
  weak-li-er
  weak-li-est
weak-mind-ed
weak-ness
wealthy
  wealth-i-er
  wealth-i-est
  wealth-i-ly
wean
weap-on
  weap-on-ry
wear
  wear-ing
wea-ri-some
wea-ry
  wea-ri-er
  wea-ri-est
  wea-ried
  wea-ry-ing
  wea-ri-ly
wea-sel
weath-er
weath-er--beat-en
weath-er-cock
weath-er-glass
weath-er-ing
weath-er-man
  weath-er-men
weath-er-proof
weather vane
weave
  weaved
  wov-en
  weav-ing
  weav-er
web
  webbed
  web-bing
web-foot
  web-foot-ed

wed-ding
wedge
  wedged
  wedg-ing
wed-lock
weedy
  weed-i-er
  weed-i-est
week-day
week-end
week-ly
weep-ing
wee-vil
weigh
weight
weighty
  weight-i-er
  weight-i-est
  weight-i-ly
weird
  weird-er
  weird-est
wel-come
  wel-comed
  wel-com-ing
wel-fare
well--be-ing
well-born
well-bred
well--dis-posed
well--done
well--found-ed
well--groomed
well--ground-ed
well--known
well--mean-ing
well--nigh
well--off
well--read
well--spo-ken
well-spring
well--thought--of
well--timed
well--to--do
well--wish-er
well--worn
wel-ter
  wel-ter-weight

were-wolf
  were-wolves
west-bound
west-er-ly
west-ern
  west-ern-er
west-ern-ize
  west-ern-ized
  west-ern-iz-ing
  west-ern-i-za-tion
west-ern-most
west-ward
wet
  wet-ter
  wet-test
wet-back
whale
  whaled
  whal-ing
whale-boat
whale-bone
whal-er
wharf
  wharves
what-ev-er
what-not
what-so-ev-er
wheat
wheat-en
whee-dle
  whee-dled
  whee-dling
  whee-dler
wheel and ax-le
wheel-bar-row
wheel-chair
wheeled
wheel-house
wheel-wright
wheeze
  wheezed
  wheez-ing
wheezy
  wheez-i-er
  wheez-i-est
  wheez-i-ly
whelm
whelp

whence-so-ev-er
where-abouts
where-as
where-by
where-fore
where-in
where-on
where-so-ev-er
where-to
where-up-on
wher-ev-er
where-with
where-with-al
wher-ry
  wher-ries
whet
  whet-ted
  whet-ting
wheth-er
whet-stone
whch-ev-er
whim-per
whim-si-cal
whim-sy
  whim-sies
whine
  whined
  whin-ing
whin-ny
  whin-nied
  whin-nying
  whin-nies
whip
  whipped
  whip-ping
whip-lash
whip-per-snap-per
whip-pet
whip-poor-will
whir
  whirred
  whir-ring
whirl-i-gig
whirl-pool
whirl-wind
whisk-er
whis-key
  whis-ky

whis-keys
whis-kies
whis-per
whist
whis-tle
whis-tled
whis-tling
whis-tler
white
whit-er
whit-est
whit-ish
white--col-lar
white-fish
whit-en
white-wash
white water
whith-er
whit-ing
whit-tle
whit-tled
whit-tling
whit-tler
whiz
whizzed
whiz-zing
whiz-zes
whoa
who-ev-er
whole-heart-ed
whole-sale
whole-saled
whole-sal-ing
whole-sal-er
whole-some
whole-wheat
whol-ly
whom-ev-er
whom-so-ev-er
whoop-ing
whop-per
whop-ping
whorled
whose-so-ev-er
who-so-ev-er
wick-ed
wick-er
wick-er-work

wick-et
wide
wid-er
wid-est
wide--awake
wide--eyed
wid-en
wide-spread
wid-geon
wid-ow
wid-ow-er
wid-ow-hood
width
wield-er
wieldy
wie-ner
wig-gle
wig-gled
wig-gling
wig-gly
wig-gli-er
wig-gler
wig-wag
wig-wagged
wig-wag-ging
wig-wam
wild-cat
wild-cat-ted
wild-cat-ting
wild-cat strike
wil-der-ness
wild-fire
wild-fowl
wild--goose chase
wild-life
wild-wood
wile
wiled
wil-ing
wil-i-ly
wil-i-ness
willed
will-ful
wil-lies
will-ing
will--o'--the--wisp
wil-low
wil-lowy

wil-ly--nil-ly
wim-ble
wim-ple
win
win-ning
wince
winced
winc-ing
wind
wound
wind-ing
wind-bag
wind-break
wind-ed
wind-fall
wind-flow-er
wind-jam-mer
wind-lass
wind-mill
win-dow
wind-pipe
wind-row
wind-shield
wind-storm
wind-up
wind-ward
windy
wind-i-er
wind-i-est
wine
wined
win-ing
win-ery
win-er-ies
wine-skin
winged
wing-span
wing-spread
win-ner
win-ning
win-some
win-ter
win-ter-gree
win-ter-ize
win-ter-ized
win-ter-iz-ing
win-ter-i-za-tion
win-try

wipe
  wiped
  wip-ing
wire-haired
wire-les
wire-tap
wir-ing
wiry
  wir-i-er
  wir-i-est
wis-dom
wise
  wis-er
  wis-est
wise-acre
wise-crack
wish-bone
wish-ful
wishy-washy
wisp
  wispy
wis-ter-ia
wist-ful
witch-craft
witch-ery
  witch-er-ies
witch-ing
with-draw
with-er
  with-ered
  with-er-ing
with-hold
  with-held
  with-hold-ing
with-in
with-out
with-stand
  with-stood
  with-stand-ing
wit-less
wit-ness
wit-ted
wit-ti-cism
wit-ting
  wit-ting-ly
wit-ty
  wit-ti-er
  wit-ti-est

wiz-ard
  wi-zard-ly
  wi-zard-ry
wiz-en
  wiz-ened
wob-ble
woe-be-gone
woe-ful
wolf-hound
wolf-ram
wol-ver-ine
wom-an
  wom-en
  wom-an-ly
  wom-an-hood
womb
wom-bat
wom-en-folk
won-der
won-der-ful
won-der-land
won-der-ment
won-drous
wont-ed
wood-bine
wood-chuck
wood-cock
wood-craft
wood-cut
wood-cut-ter
wood-ed
wood-en
wood-land
wood-man
  wood-men
wood-peck-er
wood-pile
wood-shed
woods-man
  woods-men
woodsy
  woods-i-er
  woods-i-est
wood-wind
wood-work
woody
  wood-i-er
  wood-i-est

woof-er
wool-en
wool-gath-er-ing
wool-ly
  wool-li-er
  wool-li-est
wool-ly-head-ed
woozy
  wooz-i-er
  wooz-i-est
word-book
word-ing
word-less
  word-less-ly
wordy
  word-i-er
  word-i-est
work-a-ble
  work-a-bil-i-ty
  work-a-day
work-bench
work-book
work-day
worked-up
work-er
work-horse
work-house
work-ing
work-ing-man
  work-ing-men
work-man
  work-men
work-man-like
work-man-ship
work-out
work-room
work-shop
work-ta-ble
world-ly
  world-li-er
  world-li-est
world-ly--wise
world-wide
worm--eat-en
worm-wood
wormy
  worm-i-er
  worm-i-est

worn--out	**wrig-gle**	**X chro-mo-some**
wor-ri-some	wrig-gled	**xe-bec**
wor-ry	wrig-gling	**xe-non**
wor-ried	wrig-gly	**xen-o-pho-bia**
wor-ry-ing	**wright**	**X-ray**
wor-ries	**wring**	**x-sec-tion**
wor-ry-wart	wrung	**xy-lem**
wors-en	wring-ing	**xy-lo-phone**
wor-ship	wring-er	**xy-lose**
wor-ship-ful	**wrin-kle**	
wor-sted	wrin-kled	
worth-less	wrin-kling	**yacht**
worth-while	**wrist**	yacht-ing
wor-thy	**wrist-band**	yachts-man
wor-thi-er	**wrist-let**	yachts-men
wor-thi-est	**wrist-lock**	**yak**
wor-thi-ness	**wrist pin**	**yam**
would--be	**wrist shot**	**yank**
wouldn't	**wrist watch**	**Yan-kee**
wound-ed	**wrist wrestling**	**yap**
wraith	**wristy**	yapped
wran-gle	**writ**	yap-ping
wran-gled	**writ-able**	**yard-age**
wran-gling	**write**	**yard-arm**
wran-gler	wrote	**yard-mas-ter**
wrap	writ-ten	**yard-stick**
wrapped	writ-ing	**yarn**
wrap-ping	**write-in**	**yar-row**
wrap-per	**writ-er**	**yawn**
wrath-ful	**writhe**	**year**
wreak	writhed	**year-book**
wreath	writh-ing	**year-ling**
wreathe	**wrong-do-er**	**year-long**
wreathed	wrong-do-ing	**year-ly**
wreath-ing	**wronged**	**yearn**
wreck-age	**wrong-ful**	yearn-ing
wreck-er	**wrong-head-ed**	**year--round**
wrecker's ball	**wrote**	**yeast**
wrecking bar	**wroth**	**yeasty**
wren	**wrought**	yeast-i-er
wrench	**wrought iron**	yeast-i-est
wrench-ing-ly	**wrung**	**yel-low**
wrest	**wry**	yel-low-ish
wrester	wri-er	**yel-low-bird**
wres-tle	wri-est	**yel-low fe-ver**
wres-tled	wry-ly	**yel-low-ham-mer**
wres-tling	**wry-neck**	**yel-low jack-et**
wretch-ed	**wul-fen-ite**	**yelp**

yen
  yenned
  yen-ning
yeo-man
  yeo-men
ye-shi-va
  ye-shi-vas
yes-ter-day
yes-ter-year
ye-ti
yew
yield
yield-ing
yip
  yipped
  yip-ping
yo-del
  yo-deled
  yo-del-ing
  yo-del-er
yo-ga
  yo-gic
yo-gi
  yo-gis
yo-gurt
yoke
  yoked
  yok-ing
yo-kel
yolk
yon-der
yore
young
young-ling
young-ster
your-self
  your-selves
youth-ful
yowl
yt-ter-bi-um
yt-tri-um
yuc-ca
yule-tide
yum-my
  yum-mi-er
  yum-mi-est

za-ny
  za-nies
  za-ni-er
  za-n-est
  za-ni-ly
  za-ni-ness
zeal-ot
zeal-ous
ze-bra
  ze-bras
ze-bu
ze-nith
zeph-yr
zep-pe-lin
ze-ro
  ze-ros
  ze-roes
zest
  zesty
  zest-i-er
  zest-i-est
zig-zag
  zig-zagged
  zig-zag-ging
zinc
zing
zin-nia
zip
  zipped
  zip-ping
zip-per
zip-py
  zip-pi-er
  zip-pi-est
zir-con
zir-con-ni-um
zith-er
zo-di-ac
  zo-di-a-cal
zom-bie
  zom-bi
zon-al
zone
  zoned
  zon-ing
zoo
  zoos
zo-ol-o-gy

zo-o-log-i-cal
zo-o-log-i-cal-ly
zo-ol-o-gist
zuc-chi-ni
zwie-back
zy-gote

explanation

Behavior

appear

two
Ps

absence

Response

Recommend

exaggerate

embarrass

permanent   persevere

existense

Knowledge   stretch

appland
opposed   scary

ocassion

surprise
separate